DATE DUE	
GAYLORD	PRINTED IN U.S.A.

Duras

Alain Vircondelet

Duras

A Biography

Translated by Thomas Buckley

Dalkey Archive Press

First Edition, December 1994

Originally published as *Duras: Biographie* by Éditions François Bourin.
© 1991 by Éditions François Bourin.
Epilogue © 1994 by Alain Vircondelet.

English translation © 1994 by Thomas Buckley.

Note: All translations from Marguerite Duras's works are by the translator. Works that have been published in translation are referred to by their English titles; untranslated works are left in French.

Publication of this book was made possible in part by grants from the French Ministry of Culture, the National Endowment for the Arts, the Illinois Arts Council, and a gift from Jane Ann Coddington.

NATIONAL
ENDOWMENT
FOR THE
ARTS

Library of Congress Cataloging-in-Publication Data
Vircondelet, Alain.
    [Duras. English]
    Duras : biographie / Alain Vircondelet ; translated by Thomas Buckley.
    Includes bibliographical references and index.
    1. Duras, Marguerite—Biography. 2. Women authors, French—20th century—Biography. I. Title.
PQ2607.U8245Z9213   1994   843'.912—dc20   94-8745
[B]
ISBN 1-56478-065-1

Dalkey Archive Press
Illinois State University
Campus Box 4241
Normal, IL 61790-4241

Printed on permanent/durable acid-free paper and bound in the United States of America.

Contents

"She writes, Marguerite Duras, yes, M. D., she writes. She has pencils, pens, and she writes. That's it. That's all there is to it."

—Marguerite Duras, French TV
Channel One, 1988

"I would like to see someone write about me the way I write. Such a book would include everything at once."

—Marguerite Duras,
Le Magazine littéraire, June 1990

"The story of your life, of my life, doesn't exist, or perhaps it's a question of semantics. The novel of my life, our lives, yes, but not the story. When the past is recaptured by the imagination, breath is put back into life."

—Marguerite Duras, *Le Nouvel
Observateur*, 28 September 1984

Preface

This account of Duras's life gradually acquired a life of its own, parallel to that of the writer, unfolding in difficult, patient elaboration.

Like the materials absent from the final version of a work, but nonetheless reflecting its obscure suffering, I lay bare here, just as they now appear, abruptly and at random, the traces of my doubts, my certitudes, and my intuitions. They give sufficient proof of the challenge presented by a biography of Marguerite Duras.

A strange task! How can one grasp Duras, as fickle as the seas and the deserts, always listening for the unpredictable things that are swallowed up in the world without warning, and build his own kind of "disorderly, irreplaceable coherence" that is her very life? In the final analysis, it is as if the order of facts, events, and dates had become hidden from view, giving way to something not yet attainable in a quest full of hesitancy, chaos, and indecision.

In a sense, one could say that the manner in which Duras has led her life is so foreign to that of other people, so abandoned to the fluctuations of time, that it resists any biographical project. There is no reasonably plausible plan for such a life, only mysterious links that it weaves between things and beings, analogies that nonetheless make the story progress.

There are no roads that lead anywhere, none of those free-ways you can settle down on and let your life unfold as in a film, but instead, explosions on these roads and always this image she leaves, that of the little beggar woman of her child-hood, the one from Savannakhet, transformed into herself, who knows sorrow and walks on and on over the land, falls down and picks herself up again, gets lost in sleep and wakes up, and writes, always writes to bear witness to the pain of liv-ing, and to happiness, and to tell of the Passage.

This work really asks questions about the usual biographical techniques, and the appropriateness of applying them. Follow-ing Duras in the adventure of her own life, in order to under-stand more fully the keys to her books, in order to shed more light on our own nights, like the obscure quest led by Pascal, whom she resembles so often, rules out displaying "all those wretched little secrets" so ardently sought after by curious readers. You must keep following her ship as it plunges into the thick darkness, crosses those rough seas of life—her life, but our lives as well for that matter—without the factitious ar-rangements and the chronologies drawn up for the occasion. Each day you must plunge deeper into the infinite strata to which her wandering leads her, across the fault lines of her ter-ritories, into the imaginary, true geography of that "Durasia," as Claude Roy calls it, that she herself hasn't finished ex-ploring, and whose meaning, which we had come to take for granted, is destroyed, recomposed, pulverized, apparently clari-fied, and then obscured, like those Japanese paper flowers that Proust used to dip into the aquarium, and which, upon coming into contact with the water, would spread out, always chang-ing, never predictable.

The biographer is carried along on the same odyssey as the heroine of *The Sailor from Gibraltar*, searching for him on every coast. He must follow in the wake, too quickly engulfed by the sea, of the Nightship upon which Duras embarked so many years ago, and which leads her irresistibly to death in exchange for the enthralling secret of the philosopher's stone.

The Nightship is the dark ink of the written word, the mys-tical night in search of the obstinately silent God, the nights of drunkenness and those of all desires, the comatose nights. An exquisite yet dreadful cruise, setting sail for the abyss, trying desperately, in each port of call, to retain some trace of true life.

Duras's story, her life, is to be found in the writing, her books, the hollows and the pockets, beyond the obscure trapdoors that she has left gaping, not covering them with words, events, in the reflections sent back into the books by the mirrorlike facts.

Do I even dare throw out the term "impossible biography," since Duras's entire body has slipped into the black sea of writing, in her very own chant, that music "thrown," as she says, "across the sea"?

In order to give an exact account of her life, her inner workings, one needs to acquire and rediscover a secret, a kind of alchemy, the nature of her "fluent writing," as she calls it. Seize "the crest of the words," their most fugitive quality, that which, in the course of the sentence, can be expressed, stated, only with great difficulty, and which she is able to catch in flight, like a bird on the high seas. Which then comes rushing forward with the speed of language and in "the black shadow" of memory.

The solution lies in driving out that airiness, tracking it down incessantly, thereby rediscovering the melody of the words, the fluidity of their music, imitating the ebb and flow of the waters, always watching their slow movement, and only then, seizing that being and her work so intimately related, settled permanently on the margins, on the edges of abysses, as the outline of their life comes into sight.

Today Duras is unable to put this childhood chronology in order. O vanity of biographies that claim to restore day after day the slow, furious groping of time, arrange days and nights of tumult and silence, organize events! To those who ask her for dates, frames of reference, she answers: "I tell it like that, to unburden myself . . . I really must give a date . . . I'm incapable of giving one."

This much remains then, the scene of her books, that "trail of images which the sudden surge of memory brings back to the surface, like a groundswell."

It brings to mind the story of Bonnard's painting, which Duras tells in *Practicalities:* the painter, dissatisfied with his painting of a boat on the sea, wanted to touch it up. When the people who owned it agreed to return it to him, he filled the entire canvas with the boat's sail. Now it blocked out everything, the sea, the sky, the wind. Duras believes that books are made in the same way: a sentence, a word, and its meaning is changed. Off it goes in another direction, toward unlimited possibilities. I would like this biography to resemble Bonnard's sail. A date, a fact, an anecdote should draw the story away toward other dates, other anecdotes, toward unexpected choices. Then it would give the truest likeness of Duras's legendary life.

Neuilly, June 1991

Duras

1

"The Memory of Oblivion"

She is born in the dense, suffocating heat of Indochina, on 4 April 1914, in Gia Dinh, a small suburb on the northern edge of Saigon. The story begins there, at the moment when she is torn away from her mother, from that warm bath of grace, and her infant cries pierce the daylight bearing the promise of death. Outside, on the swarming, crowded, indigenous streets, other children are also born, yellow-skinned, poverty-stricken children; no sooner are they born than beggar women begin carrying them on their backs, bundled up in strips of cloth and always the same wailing, the same cries as those uttered by her, the last born of Marie Donnadieu.

Already, in the syllables of her name, something inexpressible speaks: Donnadieu [give to God], as if, fatally, the father's name doomed her to this unknown God, to make her his slave, that anonymous little creature thrown out to graze, separated from her mother, left to her own devices, "as if," she says later, "they were cutting the child loose, abandoning her."

Why did she dwell in the violence of childhood, if not as a way of exorcising her name, Donnadieu? Very early, she felt obscure forces working deep inside of her, wild outbursts taking hold of her, the need for independence separating her from others, from the settlers, from her family. Rebelling against the Law, she sought out the abundance of jungles, the unpredictable course of rivers; she defied their dangers.

Her father, Henri Donnadieu, a mathematician by training, was from the Lot-et-Garonne region in southwestern France; he had two sons from a first marriage. Was it the call of the sea, the colonial propaganda promising fortune, the "mysterious books of Pierre Loti," or simply the desire to start his life over beneath foreign skies that made him decide to leave for Indo-china? He certainly wasn't one of those adventurers eager to get rich, to make money off the natives, but belonged rather to that generation of idealists brought up on the principles of Jules Ferry, for whom going to Indochina meant carrying France beyond her borders, making a gift of her culture, that naïve dream consisting of the belief that savages needed civ-ilization, ought to be under its wing. Appointed professor then superintendent of education for Hanoi, Tonkin, and Cambodia, he belonged to that aristocratic class of white society that acknowledged his learning, and he respected them. At an early age Marguerite Donnadieu knew the comfort of official residences, such as the former palace of the kings of Cambodia in Phnom Penh where the family resided. She lived in the splendid ruins of what was once part of China, in the agony of pagodas and temples, in the odor of monsoons, with leprosy floating everywhere. As sensuous as an animal, she was curious about everything, listening to the rumors from the wings, the harsh words of the working people and the servants. She was open to the influence of everything that surrounded her: the nimbleness of the natives, the nervous swarming of the streets as well as the silent flow of the river.

There, in that romantic, exotic world, in that fusion of contrasts and in the violence of those images, memory did its work. Already, during this period of infancy, everything was settling into her: the crepuscular light falling on the Mekong, the servants' ritual gestures, the late afternoon hu-midity, the weight of underclothes, even the sheerest, against the skin, the lilting of the tall tropical plants in the gardens, and the green, incredibly green sultriness of the jungles.

And also leprosy, the local disease, spreading like the dark-ness, infecting the entire city, the whole territory, a breath of fever, that metaphor vaguely foreshadowing the world to be discovered, to be explored, identical, it too dying, with its malaria that had been secretly revealed to the little girl who carried its sediment within her.

Her mother, Marie Legrand, came from the northern French Pas-de-Calais area, "in the neighborhood of Frévent," from those cloudy, cold, boundless lands; born of a family of poor farmers, the eldest of five children, with the aid of a scholarship she had studied to become an elementary-school teacher. Upon graduating, her first appointment was in Dunkirk, but her wild, untamable nature drew her away to other spheres where she would be able to make use of the brute force possessing her. The vast, windswept expanses of Flanders didn't suit her; so she applied for a position in the colonial school system, and was hired. "Appointed to French Indochina" in 1905, "the early years of the project for the education of indigenous children," as Duras relates in *The North China Lover*, she would come to know other landscapes, the rough roads through the bush, the rivers, the rice plantations, the mountain chains, the paths where the buffalo gallop. Like her future husband, she was motivated by another, more idealistic dream than that of getting rich, as the propaganda posters promised. In the various posts to which she was assigned, she was immediately introduced to the severity of colonial life, the harsh fate of the poor whites, but having kept alive deep inside her that peasant strength inherited from her parents, within a very short time she felt close to the natives, proud to teach French to the little Annamese, holding "class late in the evening for children she knew would be workers when they grew up, 'blue collar,' she said: exploited laborers." Her devotion, her powerful, lively personality, soon made her popular; she was "the queen without a country reigning over the poor," "the vagabond of the rice plantations."

Then she married Henri Donnadieu and they became a model teaching couple, the pride of the settlement. From their union three children were born, Pierre, "Paulo," the little brother, and finally Marguerite.

Her mother's vigorous and impulsive nature, the energy that she displayed like "a madwoman," had a tremendous impact

on Marguerite's childhood. She was an autocratic mother, devoted to her children, interested in nothing but "the adventure
of everyday life," an expert at survival.

The few photographs from that period afford us a closer view of
them, the father with his triangular face and Second Empire-
style beard, burning with an intense, piercing gaze. As for the
mother, sitting on an Asian emperor's throne with a backdrop
of exotic scenery and highly theatrical tapestries and drapes,
she has the usual bearing of women of her generation, a high,
prominent bust, and an obviously corseted waist, tightly fitted
in austere dresses. A long necklace of black onyx stones adorns
her neck and always, a trait common to the whole family, that
fierce, determined look. All around her, the children. Pierre,
the one Duras later calls the older brother, in a sailor's uniform
or in a white, colonial-style suit, with a somewhat stubborn,
intent gaze, a look of boredom; Paulo, "the little brother" even
though he was two years older than Marguerite, with a fragile
profile, "so thin, slant-eyed," giving the ghost of a smile, vul-
nerable, "different." Then Marguerite, wearing a dress of mus-
lin or light batiste, so that the heat wouldn't bother her too
much, with a large bow in her hair, and long curls falling over
her shoulders. Of her, we mainly see those grave, unbearable
eyes. There is something in her gaze that confronts and defies.
She already has in her, like a mark or a sign, that stubborn,
indestructible will.

Today she is the ultimate witness of her earliest childhood. All
she wants to retain are a few images of which she has kept a
trace in her memory, little facts, things she has trouble letting
go of, like moments she wants to recapture. Stories she tells
one after another, in interviews, in articles, in confessions, and
which make people think that "Duras always says the same
thing," that she's really boring everyone with all that, Cochin
China, the muddy yellow river during the rainy season, and the
piercing cries of the beggar women leaning against the walls.
    In that darkroom of memory, she recalls a few images, a few
banal yet fundamental scenes.

She must have had the same look as the expression she reveals in photographs, intent, impenetrable, when in 1917 or 1918, who knows, at the age of three, maybe four at the most, she saw a Vietnamese worker fall from a ladder, and the man's face, impassive, with pink blood running along his mouth. Her nurse said to her: "Move away from there, come here, don't look." She still remembers it: "I knew immediately that I had just discovered something tremendously important."

Also present among these half blotted-out traces of the past are the summer travels to China with parents and servants, the long, exhausting, magic roads leading there, those vague memories of trails lined with funerary stelae, pagodas, beggars, crossed by the saffron flashes of bonzes' tunics, the whole retinue, wandering already.

The exact dates of this time of exile are never quite certain. It was over there, in that hybrid, colonial land, where the settlers' white dwellings huddled together, along with the natives' houses of straw and wood, in that foreign place. Over there, like all conquered, subjugated, exotic lands, bearers of balmy scents and sweet dreams.

In 1918 the father is appointed to a position in Phnom Penh, the capital of Cambodia. They had to go north, following the wide bends in the Mekong, and they took up residence in new, vast, magnificent lodgings, surrounded by immense, luxuriant grounds where she plays, filled with awe.

But the father is soon stricken with the galloping disease of the colonies, that sudden, infectious fever that seems to empty its victims of all their vigor, all their energy. The diagnosis is amoebic dysentery, and the mother catches it at the same time, although her case is not as severe. The father thus asks to be sent home to France. Marie Donnadieu doesn't go with him, as if fastened to this land of Indochina, a prisoner of her mission. She remains alone with the children, and already the saga of the Donnadieus is beginning, in this family community inseparably welded to the mother, which will give rise to hatred and violence, madness and fear, but also love, terrifying, absolute love.

The mother is afraid of the surrounding yard, of the murmuring density of its vegetation, of prowlers, of the native servants whom she never completely trusts; she has the children sleep in her bed, just as later in her Loire Valley retreat, in the old dilapidated Louis XV-era castle she buys, when it freezes at night she has the animals—the sheep, the chicks—sleep with her in her bedroom.

She has the gift of divination, of clairvoyance; she can read signs, coincidences, events; she predicts calamities. On that very night, the day before she received a telegram informing her of her husband's death, she heard a bird trapped in his study, bumping into the walls, making a terrible din.

It is 1918. The father has thus died without having seen his family again; Duras says that she "never knew him." Time has done its work. It has destroyed familiar objects, yellowed photographs, misplaced the few memories. For a long time she kept the mathematics book he had written on exponential functions, but it too disappeared, and she doesn't know why or how. She now believes that it is not completely lost, that she, or someone else may still chance upon it, in the blind parts of an armoire, misplaced, slipped inside, behind drawers, like the linen undergarment she discovered, centuries later, in the depths of a Louis XV-era chest of drawers that she bought with the royalties from *The Sea Wall*, a fine batiste undergarment stained with pink blood, surely menstrual blood, in any case a woman's garment, and the dust, the color of time, deposited there in the silent night of the years.

Time thus pursues its course. The father fades away, rejoins spheres that little Marguerite forgets, making room in her memory for the image of the mother. For Marie Donnadieu, everything begins all over again. She escapes the danger of fatal dysentery and goes on teaching. From 1918 to 1920, she holds a teaching position in a native school, one of the lowest positions in the civil service hierarchy. Life becomes less comfortable; adopting the new lifestyle requires all of the mother's peasant resources and ferocious obstinacy. She secretly bears for her son, the oldest, the violent, ruthlessly proud one, an irresistible love.

Can she really count on this swarthy little girl with such a penetrating gaze, an unpleasant bearing, slightly perverse looks, absolute disobedience, a strange, peculiar personality? And is the younger son any more reliable, the one who spends his time "climbing the giant mango trees," carefree and a bit simpleminded, "mad," "silent"?

Another wilder, more precarious life begins.

The Duras legend has also begun. There is not only this life traveling along as on a freeway, but countries, places that no longer exist, old photographs that "break like glass," visited by silhouettes, foreign scents, enclosed spaces, parks, crossed by the wafting smoke of incense. And then names, rare, hard to remember, unknown, beautiful names: Luang Prabang, Vinh Long, Little Hanoi Lake. In that childhood there are verandas, languid trees, carved stone balusters and faience-tiled terraces, white lacquered chests of drawers and rattan cane chairs, fragile boats on calm waters, the all-white silhouettes of settlers passing by Annamese water carriers, in the sticky heat of white Asia.

She will always remember that light, that unequal world. One evening at her house in Neauphle-le-Château, it must have been in the 1970s, Dionys Mascolo invited her out to the garden to show her "what becomes of the whiteness of white flowers on a cloudless night with a full moon." This moon's milk flooded the shrubs, heaped more snow on the white roses, drove the red roses deeper into their velvet night. And her memory veered off toward those juicy, moon-studded nights, in the wooden fragility of the bungalows "facing the forest of Siam," when she would read, amid the silently murmuring plants and the animals, amid the buzzing insects, and reread the thick prize book with the red cover, *Les Misérables*, always *Les Misérables*, and Cosette out in the night, and Fantine dragging her feet in the snow.

She was already writing, like all children of that age carried away by the strange air of distant countries, dreaming of what she knew only from her mother's stories and from books. She wrote poems about snow, trying to imagine snowflakes falling on the countryside, skimming the surface of other rivers, sprinkling the trees. "And what else?" asks Alain Veinstein, on his *Magnetic Nights* radio program in 1986. "What would you write about at that age?" "About life, the course of daily events." So many things had already happened: the father's illness, his death, the new, poorer life, the mother's cries.

So then what did writing amount to? The mere recollection of all that? The lining up of words, sentences, a source of consolation for the pain that the world had already inflicted upon her?

When the father died, the mother was plunged into despair and remained so for a long time. It was the same madness that always rose to the surface at difficult times, pitching her from one moment to the next into an unknown, inevitable state. But somehow she was able to muster a feral energy that sustained her and eventually saved her. In photographs of that time, she broods over her little ones, her "lambs" as she calls them, giving the impression that she has everything under control. In fact, she takes charge of everything, recovering her strength, sometimes even scaring others; it is this energy, this will, that frightens people.

One day in 1968, when Madeleine Renaud was rehearsing *Whole Days in the Trees*, they ended up talking about the Lady of the Trees. Duras had very little to say about her, since there was no more to know than what she wrote in *The Sea Wall* and in this play, *Whole Days*. But Madeleine Renaud was patient; she knew that she would eventually disclose scraps, morsels of her childhood: "She wanted pictures," says Duras. "I showed her one, from my youth. And I gave her a few bits of information, strictly external aspects of the person. This woman was the daughter of Pas-de-Calais farmers. Schoolmistress for native children. A little chieftain of elementary-school teaching. Jules Ferry was her mentor.

"And aside from that? Her dresses?"

"No dresses. Gunnysacks. No attempt to be stylish or attractive."

When night began to fall, in Phnom Penh as later in Vinh Long, the mother would often take the children for a ride in a carriage. They would pass alongside the Sông Co Chien, a lazy branch of the Mekong, pass the makeshift hospitals where contagious patients were kept in quarantine, the long avenues lined with palm trees, and it was as if the weight of exile were accompanying them, a strange nostalgia, the same one that overwhelmed all Europeans there, a free-floating melancholy anchored in the heaviness of time, a breeding ground for maladies of the soul.

It was the era when French Indochina was called "L'Indo," the era of colonial injustice, of races living side by side without knowing each other, the era of conquests, when civilization was imported, when "boys" waited on the settlers hand and foot, while the other natives simply submitted to their rule, the era of racism and swindling among poor white trash, of shady businessmen, of society women. Next to the big hotels, right behind them, began the footpaths and the bush, and the green immensity of the jungle, the muffled cries of the animals. That is where Marguerite Donnadieu would go now, where she would feel at home in the middle of the jungle, in the hollow of the deltas, in the tumultous course of the *racs*, those little streams that flow into the sea, in the branches of the giant mangoes.

Those were her favorite places for shedding tears "of emotion, of love, of childhood, of exile," abandoned to the raw forces of nature, to her earliest youth.

The little brother would come sleep near her, and it felt as gentle as the golden rising of the dawn. The older brother surprised them once. He struck the little brother. "That's when it began, the fear he would kill him," she says in *The North China Lover*.

Fantasy or primal scene, nobody knows. Life drifts off toward legend. The boarding school friend in Saigon is already aware of this:

"Tell me about your little brother again."

"The same story again. . . ?"

"Yes. It's never the same, though you don't realize it."

Very early in life she knew the violence of clandestine pleasures. The desire to take risks, to climb over the wall.

Perhaps it was because of the mother that she would run away from the house, seeking refuge in wild, foreign places. For the mother spoke of nothing but the father's death, the despair of raising children as a husbandless woman, the fear that she would be unable to give them a proper upbringing and go on living. How far away now were the propaganda posters with French couples relaxing in rocking chairs, "while the smiling natives bustled about, fussing over them," the quivering grace of the banana- and cinnamon-tree leaves rustling in the warm wind, colonial splendor!

So Pierre Loti's books hadn't told it all, the misery, the corruption, even the crimes of the colonial administration. They had captured only the dream, its exotic images, its clichés, its assured riches. At the very bottom of the social ladder, on the same level as customs officials or postmen, Marie Donnadieu was no more respected than her students. She had to submit to all of the humiliations of the administration in every teaching post to which she was appointed. After Phnom Penh, which she left with the children in 1924, she went to Sadec and then to Vinh Long, never far from the Mekong that crossed the towns and the plains. As valiant as a soldier, the little schoolmistress from northern France, occupying the humblest rank of the institution, slaved away in the damp heat, in the miasmas, in the overpowering, suffocating humidity of the luxuriant vegetation. That life would last nearly ten years, in materially miserable conditions, ten years for little Marguerite to return to the untamed impulses of primitive life, to build up her strength in the brutal fervor of her instincts.

The saga of the Donnadieus in white Indochina would be related by Duras several years later in *The Sea Wall*. It unfolds into an epic, resembling the odysseys of Faulkner's or Steinbeck's heroes. The mother becomes mythical. Was she ever that pianist buried in the orchestra pit of a seedy movie theater

in a French colonial outpost, paid by the evening, thus better-
ing her family's daily fare? Indeed she could have been, that
Mother Courage of the colonies; and it is even possible that on
those evenings, huddled against the piano, the two youngest,
"the little brother" and Marguerite, worn out from their escapades, fell asleep in the pit, dark as a tomb, of the Eden Cinema.

Similar to many of the primitive dramas of consciousness
punctuating this "exotic" childhood, tarnishing forever the
wild joy of the escapades in the jungle, when she is eight years
old she meets a beggar, "the madwoman of Vinh Long," who
utters cries in an unknown language, and terrifies her: "If
the woman touches me," she admits, "even lightly with her
hand, I too will slip into a state far worse than death, that of
madness. . . ."
     She sees her again later, in Calcutta on the way back to
France, her or her sister, in any case that same wandering sort,
"on the banks of the rice fields," in the "pestilential forests,"
incarnating all the motifs of her future work, unconsciously
initiating that long meditation on the "inconceivable condition of human existence," on the symbolic journey of Life,
eternal wandering, the absurd, inexplicable curse of living, the
pain of having discovered too early "the abyss inhabited by the
orphans of the world."

Often, while the mother worked, teaching classes in Sadec or
in Vinh Long, Marguerite would cross the boundaries of the
school, the bungalow, and penetrate into the forest. It was
forbidden, and she knew it, but she couldn't resist; she went
beyond the edge of the trees and plunged deep into the
Annamese forest, the Annamese air, undergoing a transformation, becoming, along with the little brother, a foreigner.
     And yet the mother always spoke with enthusiasm of France
and the farmlands back there, in the north. She glorified the
wheat fields, the raw milk, exalting the brutal tenderness of
French soil. Marguerite picked up other echoes. Beyond the
school were the great fruit-bearing mangoes amid the jumble of

their leaves, and she would go mango-picking the way others go off to war or to the hunt.

By what sympathetic magic did she herself become Annamese? Did her eyes become slanted? Did her complexion turn yellow? Did her features undergo a transformation? Already, deep inside, she was half Asian; she liked to disobey, to discover affinities with the things of this land, to enter into complicity with it. She feared nothing, neither sunstrokes nor infectious diseases, as if she were immunized, or rather, protected by this country. Now, as time marks and ravages her face, as she puts it, she looks like an old Annamese woman, bent over as if by the weight of the water buckets carried all her life, forever burdened.

Sometimes when her mother catches her returning from her expeditions, she beats her, screams at her, wails out in grief, and the recurrent theme of her lamentations is France. She expresses the pain of being alone, of not being able to do anything about this child who is too hard, too obstinate, so different from her. And she cries: "You dirty little Annamese."

Smoldering tensions quietly undermined the family. The mother, a Frenchwoman through and through, would have to find a way to instill the rudiments of a Gallic upbringing into her little Annamese pupils but also into her "youngest," as she said, reluctant to call them by their names. Meanwhile, they dreamt of nothing but running through the virgin forest; they liked to flee at naptime, when everything is dozing off and soaking in the moist heat. They spent their time pulling over-ripe fruit from the branches of mangoes, with the "sticky juice trickling down" on them. Still later, Duras remembers, she realized that by stuffing herself with rice, with mangoes, she "is filling her belly with a different race than her mother's." Her childhood feeds on these violations, along with her passages and metamorphoses.

Of that land, so foreign and yet so infinitely familiar, all that remains in her memory is desire. For fruit-picking, chases, always with the little brother, for jungles thick with dangers, for confrontations, for natural forces. She knows all of its delights, the strange, different sensations of complete abandon, and the joy of sleeping in the arms of her little brother. She is no stranger to desire; she became acquainted with it long ago. She must have been four years old; it was in Tonkin, on Hanoi Lake just before they all moved to Phnom Penh. Between the kitchen buildings and the servants' house, a young Vietnamese boy led her over to the lake and asked her to fondle him. "His penis is soft and smooth, and he tells me what to do. I have never forgotten the shape in my hand, the slight warmth." The thought of that moment remains engraved on her. It returns, is transferred over to "the darkroom" of memory, and the water of the lake around her is always present at this first pleasure, this unknown tremor, which she knows is limitless.

The black box of memory houses those signals, those banal scenes torn—why?—from the loosely woven web of time. Would she ever have written without them?

Her entire oeuvre feeds on sources in white Indochina; from that mixed-race food she liked so much, she will draw what henceforth seems inexhaustible, even today, when she tells the present-day story of that unheard-of and yet real love, Yann Andréa. Traces of that time perforate her words, crop up in her books. She relates that one day at Les Roches Noires, the luxurious hotel in Normandy where she spends long months, her nearby friends—whose balconies, like hers, look out over the sea to the infinite horizon—were awakened by the wailing of a siren. Scanning the beach now deserted by the tourist trade, they saw an all-white yacht standing out against the darkness of the Norman coast. White Asia is like the yacht. It passes by, disappears, calls out with its foghorns, goes away and then returns, without a warning, never leaving "the crest of the words."

Her childhood became impregnated with the pestilential odor of cholera. That's all she really likes, "cholera-infested filth," forbidden by the mother, who forces them, the little brother and her, to eat apples, Norman apples. But Marguerite refuses to eat them, claiming that they taste like cotton, that they make her choke, that she prefers bottom fish, "cooked in brine with nuoc-mâm." The gulf between her and the mother grows. She is of another world, obtuse, one of those who swarm along the Mekong, strangers in their own land, exiles on their native soil.

The days of boundless happiness are those she spends in the Annamese world, where she is the kindred spirit, the sister who has chosen her race. She likes to help wash the verandas, pouring buckets of water over them "with the servants' children. . . . And it was a great fraternal celebration." She likes to take her "little brother" into the luxuriant, dangerous forests; the lazarettos where the seriously ill lie dying don't frighten her, for she is of this land, too thick-skinned to be moved by pity.

There is water everywhere. "My native country is a land of water." The water of violent rains, like cruel little blades making the skin ache, water beneath the ferryboats that she takes at night, in the raucous din of the crowd devouring duck soup, the glaucous water of the springs, the torrents, the pools wherein wallow tadpoles, amoebas, millions of living particles, microbes, extravagant flora undulating like jellyfish or kites.

The story of her mother "resembled an American movie." There were good guys and bad guys, exploited misery and gangsters who shamelessly robbed the widow and her orphans. And despite the disappointments and failures, there remained the emblematic, indefatigable figure of the mother, the enormous, immense mother, a fragile silhouette but strong, as tenacious as a rock, taking after those peasants in the north of France who pushed the ploughshare, never showing their emotions, but keeping their hearts full of that obstinateness that bound them to the land.

Since she had the legal right to purchase a parcel of land, the mother applied for one from the Colonial Office of Land Grants. She obtained it in 1924, if we are to believe Duras's 1977 play *The Eden Cinema*, though it may have been two

years later. The parcel they allotted to her was located at Prey
Nop, in the Cambodian province of Kampot near the Siamese
border, on the edge of the China Sea, devastating and unpredictable, rimmed by mangrove forests. She poured twenty
years' savings into it, what she had managed to put by, but very
soon she realized that the land was untillable, covered over
"six months of the year" by the sea, flooded by the tides. Like
a madwoman, she decided, after having lost her first sowing,
to fight against the elements, persisting in her useless toil, re-
planting stubbornly, and the sea always seeped in quietly when
it didn't inundate the entire plot.

Such arbitrary allotments of land parcels were nonetheless
commonplace in Indochina at that time. The entire system
depended on the whims of a corrupt administration, which
distributed lots like lottery tickets, taking bribes, selling barren plots that were subject to passing typhoons, huge floods,
hordes of wild animals, diseases carried by invisible, subterranean germs. There were some poor fools who believed that
evil spirits were trying to devastate their land, spreading fevers,
making it impossible for them to get settled. For once the
property had been purchased, one had to become acclimated
to this part of the bush and recruit workers, figuring out which
ones—the Chinese, the Indians, the Malaysians, the Cambodians, or the Annamese—would be the hardest-working, the
most honest and loyal, dealing more often than not with crafty
village chiefs who unloaded their troublemakers on new settlers who were both naïve and ignorant of the local customs
and way of life.

They were all chasing moonbeams, fantasies hatched in
Europe, dreams of great farms on which Breton cows would
adapt to the humid climate of Cochin China, like René Leroy,
the famous settler who in 1906 was granted some 1500 acres of
swampland on An-hoa Island in the middle of the Mekong and
turned them into productive rice fields.

But they weren't all as lucky as he was. Young settlers lacking the robust health required by such undertakings were sent
back into exile. Some were driven to despair, to suicide, while
others, already in the grip of the fevers and the comatose haze

of malaria, died in the bush, without ever fulfilling their dreams.

Did little Marguerite understand the tragedy of her mother's plight, that furious rage that made her howl in the middle of this watery desert, these humid rice fields? Had she never lived anywhere but there, in the land of passion, intensity, and madness? Of life, of existence, she perceived only the frenzied fits. Other people, the peasants, the land grant officials, took her mother's perseverance for stubbornness. Marguerite confusedly recognized something fatal in this unequal struggle waged by her mother in the harsh, unjust colonial world. She was discovering, gaping before her, "the grandiose, incommensurable absurdity of life."

And yet nothing frightened this immense mother, this ogress, "this uncontested, food- and love-providing queen." Neither the waves, nor the rains, nor fate. She came up with the idea of building dams against that brutal, devastating sea. Two archaic forces thus opposed each other, defied each other. And the implied utopia seemed quite natural to her children. On the plain facing the sea, mangrove logs, hundreds of logs, and the terrible, desperate waiting for the waters to come. And they would come anyway, making a mockery of hope, overthrowing everything in their path. Then the mother would cry, howling over the devastated land, but her lament rang out to no avail.

The children splashed about while the waves covered the planted fields, rotting beneath the overflow, and with their bare feet they would occasionally stumble against the heavy bodies of rats, squirrels, peacocks that were swollen with water, swept away in the disaster along with all the rest.

Nobody could ever win against this fatality. That much was clear when one saw the dead rice paddies, and the water, like life itself, carrying everything away, wearied, creeping toward something, somewhere.

What dark rage dwelled within the mother, causing her to continue the impossible battle of the sea wall? Descended from a race of colonists, she was sure of her rights and prerogatives, but thoroughly honest, she was cheated by the great exotic dream of Asia, caught in its nets, feeling incapable of returning to live in Europe, deeply rooted in this land, having definitively broken with her past. From France, she had kept that tenacity of the soil, which she had inherited from her peasant family, those unpolished manners, that taste for rough-hewn objects, all of which explained her contempt for the civil servants' swindles and corruption. She was thus not above mixing with the Indochinese and accepted their customs, sometimes even drawing inspiration from them in everyday life. She was like her daughter would be later: from nowhere, both rooted and uprooted, an expatriate wherever she went. If on the one hand she refused to let go of her civilizing convictions, if she continued to believe steadfastly that teaching the natives was honest work, pursuing in that way her husband's mission, she was also willing to integrate into her daily life certain local practices and Oriental objects, even having her daughter pose in a sarong or silk slacks. It was as if she were a prisoner of this magical Asia in which she believed, living side by side with sorcerers and spiritualists, curers of unexplainable diseases who physicked with philters and plants.

Marguerite would have no trouble understanding the mother's madness, for at the age of twelve she experienced her own revolt, a terrible force growing within her, then rising to the surface and overwhelming her completely. She discovered hidden deep inside herself the immense fear that submerged everything, just as the tides would pass over the dam, flooding the plain; and she too screamed, cursed nature, "made bloodthirsty speeches that she couldn't stop." She felt her reason waver, and saw herself pursued by a kind of irrational, threatening, omnipresent terror.

Only in 1981 does she attempt to explain the madness that overcame her too, devastated her, and made her curse her mother. The malediction covered the whole family, this country, this life that was making her unhappy. It was in 1925; they were on vacation by the China Sea, in a little resort called Long-haï: "I had my period for the first time, and it went on and on. I kept going swimming, and my period just wouldn't stop." An undercurrent of guilt seeped into her, while the ubiquitous blood stained her, followed her, soiled her, and made her hate this mother who couldn't see anything and couldn't understand what was happening. In that decisive week she began to curse God, to insult him, uttering murderous, blasphemous words each night. No, she wouldn't give herself to this God who made her blood flow; she would never be God's little victim, consenting, offering herself, abandoning herself to him. She would rather kill her mother and her brothers, they who accepted her blood offering. A "bloodthirsty madness" possessed her as she discovered her own violence, the barbarity of her innermost being, and the immeasurable chasms hidden within it.

Everything was transformed by these contradictory moods of violence and hatred, fury and abandon. She felt this ardent force inside of her, this fracture which could precipitate her into "her" madness in a second, making everything vacillate, and this tremendous flexibility that facilitated her integration into this country, into the slow undulations of the Mekong, with its infinite number of islands. And what she would eventually learn was the fervor of the landscape, between the river and the forest, between the odd meanderings of the black sampans, and the virginal lands where tigers and snakes lived.

She was filled with hatred and love, violent, untamed impulses, and infinite tenderness for the little brother, "so thin, with slanted eyes, crazy, silent," and for whom she felt love, yes, "such love for you." With him, she formed the elegiac couple, the innocent couple; she engaged in incest, "a basic assumption," as she will later say, of the life she led there, on that naïve, untouched land.

There was nothing to explain, nothing to say; it was there even before it was there.

At that same age again, about twelve years old, she met the beggar woman once more. She will keep her alive for a long time in her books, to the point of becoming herself the little beggar woman of Savannakhet, wandering like her, rattling off her litany, that chant, punctuated by silences, jolts, repetitions, the lament of existence.

Today she walks through the shopping malls of new towns, on the tiled plazas of Vitry-sur-Seine and Créteil in the Parisian suburbs, surrounded by tower blocks, between the abundant fountains and the neoclassical architecture, and her frail, stooped-over silhouette resembles that of the beggar woman of Cochin China, pursuing her route.

It was on a day like other days, in that contradictory country, where in a "flower scent lurked . . . leprosy," that the beggar woman was roaming around the family bungalow in Cochin China with her little girl in her arms, maybe two years old, maybe six months, "infested with worms." She left her with Marie Donnadieu, who in turn gave her to Marguerite the way one gives a doll as a present. And then she went away again, headed off across the plain, disappearing forever. This story of wandering had to be preserved, her uncertain itinerary followed, in order to inject each book with the miserable epic of that beggar woman, to hear her sing. "Yes, seventeen years old . . . she is pregnant, she's seventeen . . . she is thrown out by her mother, she leaves . . . she asks where to get rid of the baby."

This was an enormous shock to little Marguerite. She will always hear the song of Savannakhet, that plaintive chant, all the distress in the world, and the child who dies abandoned, and the land grant officials, implacable in their white uniforms, impeccable, managing the misery, the hunger.

For hunger could be seen everywhere, in the sickly bodies, in the dropsy-swollen bellies, in the children's empty gazes. Marguerite lived in the company of dead bodies, and often saw corpses left out in the open, waiting to be hastily buried. "So many people died that no one cried anymore," and in that state beyond pain, she was learning about the terror of the world, its very structure, its merciless laws, its cruelty, like those deep holes she had seen in the ditches along Cambodian roads in which criminals were buried up to their necks, left out in the sun, waiting for a slow death.

So she would return to the water-covered expanses, to the wild jungle's edge in order to cleanse herself of that misery, and these childhood games grew to legendary status. Always accompanied by the little brother, she was straight out of a Kipling story, free, infinitely free.

But the tremendous spectacle of primitive nature brought her back to the laws of the world. When "birds lay bleeding from the throat, victims of the tigers," it was murder, and contemplation of the suffering animals reminded her of children's corpses.

How to explain this fascination with the images of childhood? The overwhelming profusion of memories, their shifting movement on the surface of the words which, on each page, and as if in an ever-greater hurry, follow on her heels and assail her?

Already she is writing, garnering images, and later her books will tell of swimming in the lukewarm, leaden waters, with the mangrove branches brushing against them, and running along the wild slopes of the Elephant range, with the lianas falling like leashes.

How will she possibly escape the haunting refrain of the beggar woman who will sing even in Duras's alcoholic coma, running through her writings as well as through her comas?

Is it in memory of the abandoned baby that she has a frantic predilection for children, granting them a certain innocence, an untouched truth? That she associates them with the great movements of the universe, capable of understanding everything, especially silence?

Theirs is the power to save the world, to know how to look at the sea with that fervor and that gravity she detects in their eyes, to go beyond the limits of the horizon.

She loves children because they open trapdoors; their gazes create echoes, reflect back to ancient stories, hidden secrets that words bury and prevent from ever reaching daylight. She loves them because they teach her things, about the world, the velocity of the stars, and the motion of the waves as she watches for them on the beach from her Trouville apartment window at high tide. There is some of that same innocence in her, that same obstinacy, that same ferocity too, that radical understanding of the universe, and the listening to silence, the realm of mysteries and great questions.

Thus she lived in the dazzling beauty of primitive nature, in the exaltation of the forests, at the mercy of the prodigal earth, in the complicity of that race. With her little brother she shared a kind of spiritual union, a sisterhood reflected in primitiveness, in tenderness, and in those bridges that joined them time and again. Today, she talks about him obsessively; she always comes back to him, and says: "the little brother, the dearly beloved brother, my little brother," and her entire childhood springs forth, brutally, like the water in the *racs* that runs along until it gushes violently into the sea.

When she was with him she could forget about everything, the swindling, the corruption, human cruelty, the ugliness of self-interest, and all of the injustice done to her mother.

They nonetheless respected that mother. She was feared and loved at the same time. She was the monster who defied the administrative officials, moved by a strength unknown to women of her condition, endowed with abusive, authoritarian, panic-energy. She went forward, a sort of Louise Michel of the colonies,* a local Saint Joan of the Slaughterhouses, daring to knock on the doors of the administration, confronting it, and the powerful charm she radiated made slaves of her children, such was the frightening, subjugating nature of her personality. She assumed the role of prophet, becoming an object of veneration for the natives, and the children would flee out of the

---

*Louise Michel: French anarchist (1830-1905), participated in the Commune of 1871 and was deported to New Caledonia as a result —TRANS. note

need to escape, a kind of survival instinct. The brother and sister confusedly felt smothered, overwhelmed by that supernatural woman who also braved the sea and the earth; in the density of nature, in the proximity of giant, century-old trees, they
found new sources of life, and other means of nourishment.

But deep inside them remained a bitter taste, the impression
that the jungle paradise was only illusory, that in the vast colonial venture, there was nothing more to do but watch the slow
bleeding of those wild, tender native lands.

The spectacle of their mother, uttering insults and threats,
the weariness which her struggles induced in her, the despon-
dency that could turn suddenly into a fit of madness, the injustice reigning side by side with self-complacency and scandalously acquired fortunes, everything pointed out to those who
had eyes to see the morbid suffering of that country, its agony,
its blood flowing like the latex seeping out of the ancestral
trees, emptying them of their sap, the enslavement of an entire
people, and the compromising of poor whites, themselves exploited and nonetheless submissive, proud of their civilization.
Within Marguerite, a subterranean revolt was coming to life, a
knot in her throat, when she saw children die, babies' intes-
tines burst like bubbles, old people beg, and on the other side
of town, "the useless, orgiastic presence . . . offered to passersby
of the powerful at rest."

This country became the very image of failure, of impotence, of the terrible, solitary human condition. Even the forest, a place of refuge in its boundlessness, made it impossible to
struggle. It inspired a kind of resignation, for man would never
be able to overcome the irresistible force of the elements, and
the desperate fight against the tide seemed absurd and vain.
The flights into the jungle resembled immersions in those
waters as heavy, as dangerous, as those that stubbornly devastated the sea walls; something sovereign and sacred gave the
forest a monstrous, supernatural appearance. A place of refuge
for the natives, for those who were fleeing the colonial order,
the geographic matrix for Marguerite's and the little brother's
true origins, for whom it was a means of fleeing civilization; but

the jungle was nonetheless a place of death and murder, of barbarity and savagery. "The vines and the orchids . . . enclosed the whole forest and made of it a compact mass as inviolable and suffocating as the bottom of the ocean." No matter which way one turned, there was always the same irresistible force of nature, with its same violence, there in the line of mangroves, derisory ramparts against the China Sea, or elsewhere in the grandiose, untrammeled luxuriance of the vegetation. Already, unconsciously, a revelation was being confirmed: "Life was terrible," and nothing could change the relentless struggle, the revolt. One had to live to the rhythm of that cruel sea, its tides, that sap which made the lianas grow longer and longer, compressing them, so that one day they would eventually smother everything. And how could one resist that tragic force? More than anyone, perhaps, she observed the miserable peasants, doomed to immemorial injustice, as if they were engulfed in that lukewarm, pestilential, muddy water. They became an allegory for man, condemned, pathetic, alone.

As if doomed to inertia, to the illusory certitude of its frontiers, to blind, brutal centralization, perpetuating its principles of progress and its slogans of pacification—in a word, sure of its presence, when in fact everything pointed to a rude awakening—the half-imagined Indochina of the good old days, with its generous, pioneer spirit, was dying in those years between 1920 and 1930. The "beautiful colony" as it was then called was rotting from the inside out, consumed by misappropriation and corruption of every sort, by the rigidity of its regulations, by its intolerance, and its refusal to consider the point of view of the colonized. The administration became the shrine of injustice and exclusion, of the most senseless conformity. The hierarchy hardened, and figures as picturesque as Marie Donnadieu were in turn rejected by farcical despots who meted out law and order, showing the deepest scorn for second-class civil servants such as schoolteachers, forest rangers, postmasters.

The problem was that the Lady of the Trees, as Duras later calls her mother, antagonized people with her unceasing energy, her naked vehemence, her denunciation of scandals, and in turn became scandalous with her insane projects, her defiance—a source of laughter at social gatherings—her mixture of deference and rebelliousness. Her capriciousness, always accompanied by her sense of social order, her muddled life, and her angry outbursts stood in too great a contrast to the proprieties of colonial society. Her fits of madness and delirious ravings placed her among the ranks of the strange, morbid souls who, driven to such a fate by years spent in Asia, risked their lives on this land capable of killing them with its fevers, its cholera, and its fatal bacteria.

The mother's continual entreaties to the land grant officials, her incoherent, insane revolt against them while at the same time pleading with them to intervene in her favor, produced diametrically opposed attitudes in the Donnadieu children. The more she appealed to justice, without ever calling it into question, the more letters she wrote to the administration, the more they would flee, refusing even to take meals with her, preferring to stuff themselves on mangoes provided by a different mother, the Annamese jungle. A dialectic of freedom and revolt was developing secretly; they were slowly learning disobedience, absence, and suspicion.

Was it because of all that, "the vines and the orchids," the rice plantations as far as the eye could see, the buffalo crossings, and the hours spent lying in wait for the black panthers at the mouths of the *racs,* that she was already disenfranchised from that colonial society to which she nonetheless belonged, as hostile as the future little Ernesto, the child in *Summer Rain,* when it came to learning things that she didn't know, but completely open to the forces establishing an intuitive complicity with her, an immediate closeness?

Again like Ernesto, she would *know* dupery, hatred, theft "by the force of circumstances"; so she learned denial of this world, the joy of disobedience, the jubilation of living on the outskirts of society, the risks of utopia.

Such were the games that revealed to her the contents of solitude and strengthened the untamed, rebellious character that made her brave the overhead sun and the Annamese forest.

She holds inside of her forever, like the guardian of a sacred trust, strong images that will always obsess her, those of misery, of injustice, of dazzling nature. There is the beggar woman who reappears in her imagination and the peasant who hired himself out each season as a scarecrow, and who, for hours on end in the dirty, muddy waters of the plains, remained motionless; there is the ferocious, cunning work of the crabs gnawing on the mangrove logs, and the unparalleled, spectacular collapse of all the dams on the same night, and the whole cycle set in motion once more, the mother's cries, the furious, sorrowful chant.

She still holds, like the rot suspended in the water, riveted to the roots of the rice sprouts, this fear firmly attached to her family, nourished by an older brother not unlike Harry Powell, the psychopathic criminal who, in Charles Laughton's *The Night of the Hunter*, tracks down children, a brother and a sister, in the American countryside, following them down rivers, ready to kill them in order to find out where they have hidden the ten thousand dollars given to them by their father. This is the Robert Mitchum cult film that Duras admires so much because it is the symbolic equivalent of her childhood terror, what she calls "the fright," which the older brother, like a diabolic incarnation, spread throughout the house. Meanwhile, the mother had given up trying to "prevent anything," letting "happen what must happen."

In Vinh Long, in 1930, just before she left her mother for Saigon, there occurred another event that Duras has carried with her all her life, like the beggar woman with her bundle of crying flesh. As if receiving a blow to the face, she took in the slender figure of the new general administrator's wife, Elizabeth Striedter, whose name she will later forget, and who will reappear as Anne-Marie Stretter, the mythical name of the phantasm, the name that sets her writing in motion.

The Mekong, running through the town, has its source near the China Sea, threading its way north, beyond Cochin China, over the lands of Cambodia, of Siam, and into Laos, where the little beggar woman of Savannahket roams. In Vinh Long, there are mixed neighborhoods, as in Saigon, potpourris that seem to swarm with bustling natives, Chinese, Annamese, Cambodians, Malaysians, vagrants, and servants whom the Laotian "nationals" deem sly, thieving, and lazy.

And other, nearly silent neighborhoods, with residences meant to re-create a French atmosphere, but adapting it to the requirements of the climate, with balconies, verandas, and arcades for protection from the sudden rains, adorned with balusters and cornices. In the gardens where all sorts of exotic plants bloom, bougainvilleas and red jasmine, there are tennis courts hidden from view, their presence revealed only by the muffled sound of the bouncing balls. Immaculately polished, beautifully chassised Léon-Bollée touring cars roll slowly down private lanes, gliding along as if "suspended in an impressive half-silence."

At the time Duras is about fifteen years old. She has lost her slightly plump adolescent figure, her insolent look, and she is less inclined to walk barefoot through the parks, although she has no fear of the prickly plants or the brown scorpions that are found crawling everywhere and often slip unnoticed into beds and books.

She likes to observe colonial society, noticing that it engenders immutable hierarchies: first the natives, generally considered subhuman, then the poor whites, scorned, the merchants and the petty clerks, the military men and the VIPs, and the higher civil servants who belonged to the world of consulates, embassies, and administrators. The lascivious wives of eminent men sometimes daydream like Emma Bovary, all of them in the same melancholy, the same humid, sun-induced torpor, victims of a mortal ennui seemingly heightened by the paleness of their faces.

They dream of a special life, like prostitutes of another world, dancing like them, too, in the same scented vapors of the Manilla or the Long Than bar. Again like them, they display the same sagging shoulders, the same indolent bearing, the same slender grace.

It so happens, in fact, that Elizabeth Striedter passes by in her car, taking her two daughters out for their usual ride: red hair, pale complexion, and in her gaze, the impression that death lies in wait for her; she is consumed by an invincible wave of ennui.

She seems far away, already gone, elsewhere.

Duras, forever roaming, curious about everything, immediately recognizes Elizabeth Striedter. In her diaphanous transparency, she sees in her a resemblance to death, to love also, but isn't it suddenly the same thing? Sometime later, since in that colonial microcosm news traveled very quickly, she learned that she "had no friends," only lovers. And always that same languor in her bearing, the impression of being apart from others, in the damp heat of Vinh Long, in her overpowering boredom, in the sweet, already faded fragrance of flowers blooming on late afternoons.

But this woman whom she would follow around town, fantasizing about her, imagining her as a legendary princess, was an object of reprobation for the entire bourgeoisie. Her mother vociferated against her, judging her literally "out of place," that is, not in conformity with the customs of colonial life, with its moral obligations, which forbade women from resembling those eccentric slum-dwellers who sipped rice beer, or from getting drunk in wainscoted embassy drawing rooms on French champagne which gushed here, not in order to bring back memories of the mother country, but mostly to obliterate those vague yearnings, that desire for nothing, that forced idleness, that longing to die without really dying.

She learned that a lover had just killed himself out of love for her. And suddenly, Elizabeth Striedter became the dispenser of life and death, the sea goddess who gave herself to men and then took herself back, pretended to belong to them but brought death to them. Terror and fascination filled Marguerite, who confusedly saw herself in her, imagining that love always went hand in hand with death like this, that it was a game with no alternative to complete revelation. She had discovered in the future Anne-Marie Stretter the archetypal image in her books, the secret of women, their distant, timeless memory, their millennial weight leading her, a stranger to others, into the realm of the most undecipherable mysteries.

Marguerite watched her, spied on her through the tennis court fence, along the avenues, the tree-lined lanes where she strolled with her daughters, always silent, nearly invisible. In *Les Lieux*, Duras says: "Sometimes I tell myself that I wrote because of her."

What fascinated her was this wandering phantom of a woman and what she incarnated, the adulteress, submitting to the vagaries of her husband's career, his posts in Asian capitals, no longer in charge of herself, prey to the curious eyes of others, men, children, returning in her car to the reserved, preserved, rich white neighborhoods, "the magic brothel where the white race could treat itself, in untroubled peace, to the sacred spectacle of its own presence."

And the image of that apparition will always remain with Duras. It follows her in everything she writes; it is right there, behind her, in *The Vice-Consul, India Song, Son nom de Venise* —everywhere, Anne-Marie Stretter, who sets her writing in motion, rouses out words, urges them to tell, to reveal.

What she also liked about Elizabeth Striedter was her scorn for colonial life, the marginal existence she led, her singular presence at receptions, and suddenly the shift to another life, to the hell of her desires, to the jungle of her sensuality. There was a kind of danger in her, which is why she envied this mother, this woman who defied her class, that white aristocracy which made a show of its own opulence, its superiority.

She too, the schoolteacher's daughter, had found in her escapades at the vaporous hour of the siesta, in the freedom of nature, with her feet in swamps swarming with slimy bottom fish, reasons for fleeing, for transgressing the colonial order, completely open to the ways of the other race, quivering with desire for other people, repulsed by that inequitable order, and the applied, legalized violence contained within it.

And she in turn became a millennial passageway for the centuries and all the forces of the universe.

What she has learned of the world thus far is abandon: things that wear out and are left to stand, as in Calcutta or in Cairo, rubbish cities that can no longer be reconstructed and fall into hopeless, inevitable decay. The China Sea is too powerful; even the mother resigns herself to that fact. The lands behind the sea wall are offered to the whims of passing waters, winds, and storms, while the bungalow remains unfinished, amid general indifference, as crabs nibble away at the piles, devouring the floorboards.

The mother is aware of all that, the absurd meaning of life, yesterday Phnom Penh, today Vinh Long, located on a branch of the Mekong, the Sông Co Chien, then Sadec, near Vinh Long, all these French outposts with their "perpendicular streets and gardens, gates, and then the river, the French quarter, the tennis courts," with their ports, their sawmills, and their soap factories which give off strange, bland odors on windy evenings.

And then she left the plain—the always wet expanses of the rice plantations, the flights to the beginning of the world in the innocent jungle, where all the fragrances of the earth, the air, and the water meet, "united in a primeval melting of differences," the primitive joy of eating mangoes—and went away to the city.

It was Saigon, the colonial capital, right at the beginning of the thirties.

At that time it was called "the Paris of the Far East," frantically trying to imitate Parisian fashions and elegance, and perhaps even attempting to erase its own local color. An artificial, factitious world, drawing together in the famous rue Catinat Saigon's high society, its elegantly dressed women, its businessmen, its colonial administrators, its crooks in tailored suits with pencil mustaches, sipping Martell-Perrier or Corsican mineral water from Orezza or Pardina, at sidewalk cafés in the warm late-afternoon humidity or amid piano bar sobs provoked by exile nostalgia and soul-sickness. At the racetrack, all of the sportsmen show up wearing white colonial outfits prescribed by fashion magazines brought from Paris, with slight alterations on account of the climate. As at the turn of the century, the upper classes still meet at the theater, where they play Strauss, Offenbach, and Franz Lehár as usual, and exquisite operettas like *The Merry Widow*, or light operas like *Madame Butterfly*; they gather around the kiosks, in the parks where philharmonic societies play lively, triumphant airs, in dark movie houses where *The Blue Angel* is a great success, and at the most popular meeting place, the balls, very frequent here, veritable junctions of social life where time glides by in an atmosphere of ennui and unsatisfied desires. Pre–World War I social codes are still in effect, giving the city an immutable, almost cellular way of life. There are indispensable calèche rides, along the avenue of the acacias, around the lakes, like memories of Proust passing the Verdurins in the Bois de Boulogne.

But there was not only this visible part of the town, with its coolies like foreign extras passing each other on the streets, that self-righteous world even if it was mainly composed of the dregs of France who had generally come here to get rich, to plunder this land in the name of so-called civilization. There was also—more bizarrely, and probably closer to that era's usual notions of exoticism—the world of gamblers, casinos, prostitutes, easy nightclub girls, financially ruined women on the arms of late-night restaurateurs who, in back rooms, cleaned out military men and social servants, import–export merchants, and highly prominent citizens.

And all around, the smell of the forest, as if Saigon lived by breathing in the overflowing confusion of mangoes and tamarind trees, giant ferns and badam trees, with their miasma-filled odor, suffocating the city, giving it that appearance of naptime agony, that impression of anemia, the deleterious face of something slowly dying, as if in desperate defiance.

It was here, in the false order of this society ruled by decay and the disorders of the soul, that she received her first intellectual training. More than from books, it came from the discovery of this bastard world, divided between civic morality and the mystery of the rivers and the forests, on hot, sticky afternoons.

In spite of all this, Marguerite was sent to Saigon for the first few years of secondary school. Attending the Lyautey boarding school, a small establishment run by one of her mother's friends who had come to Indochina in 1905 like her, she didn't have the means to go home to her family in Sadec on weekends, like the other girls at her lycée. She thus stayed in the big city, learned other modes of behavior, other ways, and became strengthened, comfortably settled in her certitudes. Walking through the white side of town, she envied the luxury and scorned it at the same time, fascinated by the cleanliness reigning there as much as by the swarming filth of the indigenous neighborhoods, or by those of the "shameless colonials." She must have dreamt of sitting down at the sidewalk tables in front of the great white hotels, on heavily scented magnolia evenings, which gave such places a supernatural quality in her mind. She was helplessly attracted by that charming life which throbbed to the rhythm of rituals invented locally or imported from Europe, and she would have liked to slip into the malodorous alleyways of the poor districts, become saturated with other, stronger, spice-filled odors, and especially the smell of poverty, not to mention that of the other places, in "the teeming brothels along the waterfront."

She had no "moral sense" in the meaning usually given to that term by society, especially colonial society. Too archaic, too untamed, too independent, she would submit to no law, civil or religious, and she always bore her family name like a burden. The pent-up violence in her, that cold anger, rare in a sixteen-year-old, made her favor instead the downtrodden, the poor, and the prostitutes. Brothels held a special fascination for her. Standing in opposition to a bourgeois sense of decency and propriety, to the frustrations engendered by religions, the brothel was the shrine of desire, of imperious desire, "the fatal world, that of the species considered as a fatality . . . the world of the future, luminous and burning, singing and crying, strangely beautiful, but whose cruelty was an indispensable condition of entry."

That is why she imagined brothels as further extensions of the jungle, breeding grounds for new, boundless vegetation, different from that which proliferated in the mountains, places of freedom, of madness, of irrational carnal surrender, and she dreamt of those beings given anonymously. Therein lay her religion, her sense of the sacred, in that brutal mingling of the senses, in those natural reunions.

In Saigon, she would go to the botanical garden on Sundays with her landlady. The spectacle of a boa devouring a live chicken attracted bystanders and others in search of strong sensations and curiosities. The short story drawn from this autobiographical anecdote that Duras published in 1954, "The Boa," is very revealing as to the way in which her imagination was forged, her problematic developed. The sight of that devouring boa would surely have roused her to indignation and disgust if it hadn't been invariably followed by the ritual that her companion, a withered old maid stinking of virginity, forced her to perform upon their return, after tea, and which consisted of admiring her lingerie. Thus, the boa's cruel feast paradoxically gave her the desire to live, to struggle, to be bold and shameless. The wild animal at least devoured the chicken in broad daylight, for all to see, and its silent, untroubled shamelessness made it strong, exemplary, miles away from those who always hid to protect themselves.

In her nearly fervent contemplation of the crime, she swore to herself that she would be like that boa, yes, she would always be on the side of the audacious, the violent.

Fascinated by the spectacle, she thinks of her brother, the younger one: she must have been eight years old in 1922 when he asked her to show him her sex and, in view of her refusal, he told her something that she hadn't understood at the time but that she now understood, observing her boa and the old chaperon: the body was for other people to use, to know, to desire. Generous by nature, it must give itself to others as the object of their contemplation, as an agent of fecundation. That was the meaning of life. This gift, with its implied freedom, entailed the courage to offer it, the strength to accept, to be tossed back and forth, rejected by it, then taken back into its arms.

Can one find the memory of that story in the chaotic march of her life to come? Has Marguerite Donnadieu become Duras, the little beggar woman of Savannakhet, with her face devastated by wrinkles, but beautiful, possessed by the beauty of life, ravished by it, having accepted its sorrows and its wonders?

Just as she like to blend into the thick jungle, thus returning unconsciously to the first days of the world, in the tenderness and cruelty of the beginning, she dreamed of going into those Saigon movie theaters, inaccessible places of the impossible, and losing herself in "the artificial, democratic night . . . the night in which every kind of shame is consoled, and where every form of despair disappears." That plunge into a dark auditorium from which images loomed, as mobile and fluid as life, would have given her the impression of "cleansing herself of the hideous filth of adolescence," another way of wreaking vengeance on misery, on injustice. Standing in front of the kiosks, where newspapers and magazines were suspended like clothes on a line, she lusted after *Hollywood Cinema*, the springboard of dreams, the leaven of desire.

That whole artificial world, those lives arranged for fashionable young ladies, those falsely heroic destinies, carried off to the usual, indispensable, mythical places, Venice, the islands, luxurious vacation resorts, unfurled her imagination and excited it.

The silent, obscure fraternity, completely frozen in the same fascination for movie theaters, gave her the certainty that she would drown there, melting into the vast night of phantasms, abolishing herself one day in the pitch-black, unknown part of herself.

In the same way she would surround Elizabeth Striedter's apparition in a shroud of secrecy, burying her in that night, whence she would make her arise later, in the violence of books, obsessive Elizabeth Striedter transformed into Anne-Marie Stretter, bound forever to the pilings of that strange epic childhood made of exile and immensely strong emotional ties. Not even her mother would know about that intrusion into her life, that image of Woman and Death mixed together, of wandering in colonized towns, places in the middle of nowhere, with no identity, like her.

One day, nearly fifty years later, in 1977, she received a letter from a young woman on behalf of her grandmother, Elizabeth Striedter, finally emerging from fantasy and inviting her to a little party that she was planning to give a few days later in her retirement home.

Duras didn't go, and a month later received another letter, this time from Elizabeth Striedter herself, who wrote: "You are right to remain silent. Out of the young woman I was, your imagination created a fictitious image that retains its charm precisely on account of that mysterious, preservable anonymity. I am so deeply convinced of it myself that I decided not to read your book nor see your movie. The discretion of memories, of impressions that keep their value by remaining in the shadows, aware that their reality has become unreality." A year later a notice appeared in *Le Monde* announcing her death. Thus there would be no more Elizabeth Striedter, but only Anne-Marie Stretter, and Delphine Seyrig's nearly unreal, cat-like haunches swaying down the great stairway in the Rothschild's Bois de Boulogne villa, that absolute, archetypal image from *India Song*.

She would thus pass over from Vinh Long to Saigon, from the strange town buzzing with all sorts of commotion to the uncivilized plain, from the swarming or the posh neighborhoods of the city to the unfinished bungalow on her mother's lands, from Cambodia, from the boardinghouse where she stayed, in "the terrible, corpselike odor" of her landlady, to the unbounded, deserted lands of the sea wall, from the solitude of the city to fabulous, sumptuous reunions with overflowing nature, an immoral place of "carnal exchanges," of "orgiastic, untroubled matings." And the means of crossing between the two opposing worlds was the ferry, which carried her from one bank to the other, symbolically, an anonymous medium without reference, a mode of passage. The ferry went back and forth between one phantasm and another, silently setting up meetings, as it glided over the flat waters of the river, disclosing secrets, revealing her to herself.

It was on the ferry, in fact, that she happened to meet the Chinese man. He was "the one who was crossing the Mekong to Saigon that day." She has just left her mother, in Sadec, where she spent the holidays. She is on her way back to Saigon now, back to the boarding school. She boarded the bus in Sadec, and the ferry will take everything, the bus, the passengers, the automobiles. She is always afraid of the water's secret movement, eddies, currents that could pull her down to the fathomless depths. She has gotten off the bus. Leaning over the handrail, she looks at the river, the countless rivers carved out by the constantly moving streams and islands. She is decked out in a "felt hat the color of rosewood, with a wide black ribbon," sequin-studded gold lamé shoes, and a light silk dress, very tightly belted at the waist.

Near her on the ferry, there is a Morris Léon-Bollée touring car. Sitting inside, a Chinese man wearing a light-colored tussore suit. He looks at her. She already knows exactly what is going to happen, inevitably.

In her 1984 novel *The Lover*, she described the "big funereal car," the exquisite, singular outfit, and that sky so yellow, so mobile, that it resembled a stretching band of water, but what should we conclude from it? How can we distinguish between the true and the plausible, what happened and "what must have happened," that mysterious, shifting borderline on which memories unfurl, limitless, nourished by time, by Duras's capacity for forgetting, and by the breath of imagination? And what if, from clinging, obsessive, adolescent memory, Duras had invented the story of the Lover, reinventing it with each book, nourishing a legend?

So there she is, supposedly, on that morning of their encounter all alone on the ferry, and he, the Chinese man, is watching her. He comes up to her, introduces himself, says that he has just graduated from college in Paris, "that his family's from north China, from Fushun," that he too lives in Sadec, like her, but on the river, "the big house with large balconies and blue ceramic balustrades." His parents belong to "that minority of financiers, originally from China, who own all the property in the colony's working-class districts."

He offers to come pick her up after school and take her back to the boardinghouse. He is immediately mad with desire for her. A strange, clandestine passion rises up in them. She knows that there is no way to resist it, that she has to accept. He comes by on a Thursday afternoon, when there are no classes, and she leaves the boarding school, just as she used to run away from the bungalow and go into the forest. In the huge car she discovers Cholon, the Chinese district, and his windowless, shutterless bachelor flat, whose openings, drawn with blinds, bear the outline of the street and let all the sweet, acrid smells of Cholon seep in.

When she talks about sensual pleasure, she says that it's the sea, raging and calm, that she has just discovered. All of this becomes familiar to her, a new kind of knowledge: the water, the continual movement of the waves, the ease with which they rise and fall, and their complicity with the wind, the sky, the clouds.

She will always preserve the story of the Chinese man in her memory. The Chinese lover, deeply linked to passion, desire, the desire for desire. She kept it intact because she associated it with another story, the discovery of other worlds, the transgression of her white race, that liberty whose contours she could make out within herself, a hollow shell, ready for her to enter. With the Chinese lover, with the same certainty she claimed to possess already at the age of twelve when she announced to her mother: "I will write," she slipped into the undisclosable, hours spent contemplating nudity, amid "the rubbing together of bodies and the friction of the city," so close to forgetting others, the mother, the wall so close to death. And always the sea, "immensity drawing together, moving away, coming back."

In *The Lover*, then again in *The North China Lover*, she tells of that movement. She can only describe it when, in her paragraph fragments, like bridges between images, she uses what she calls "fluent writing." Like a divining rod, the pen seeks out the place of origins, finds multiple waterways irrigating the terrain, the memory, and from there she draws her images. Everything is mixed together; there is no semblance of coherence in those scattered scenes she left buried in her night.

The lover's desire and her own are intertwined with love for the little brother and this hatred for "my mother, my love." Her books, open to limitless interpretations, to the vastness of the seas, are like sketches in which one can find Duras's life. "My life," she says in 1988, "is in the books. Not in order, but what does that matter?"

More than anything else, her clandestine life is what defines her. One of burying, of wells which she likes so much, and wherein she finds secrets, light, or hell, "who cares, as Baudelaire would say, as long as it's something new." The places of her life are "places of distress, of shipwrecks." From the submerged lands of the sea wall to the Rothschild palace of *India Song*, left to be ravaged by time, to be furrowed by the rains, it's always the same world that is crumbling, like the wooden pilings holding up Venice, gnawed away by the glaucous waters of the lagoon, by the moss, the bacteria, marine vermin. Here, in the Chinese district, with the Lover, in this anonymous bachelor flat, while fragrances of brine, nuoc-mâm, cinnamon, and broiled fish are swallowed up, in this place abandoned entirely to the time of passion, in this body tense with desire, something new happens anyway, is discovered, carried out in astonishment of the apparition—love, passion: she doesn't know exactly what yet—in any case of self-abandonment, in this gaping body where they both moan while the Lover penetrates her. We should say drowns, loses himself in her waters, for his pleasure cries out, bursting, like the water, like the sea, proclaims his absolute presence.

To love the Chinese man from Cholon is also to slip into Cholon, the town where whites were forbidden from entering, the "foreign" town, just as the Casbah of Algiers during the same era was a closed, Arabic, impenetrable place for the French. She imagines her life, even very young, in that crossing, in that pleasure of disobedience: the discovery of obliterated places; inside her, always lying in wait, treachery, the violent desire to pass through the mirror, to go beyond the limits.

Cholon is also the city of pleasure, where visiting tourists go at night to immerse themselves in the low life, at their own risk, amid the smell of opium in smoke-filled back rooms, beneath the gaze of passing prostitutes, whereas during the daytime the streets are invaded by a noisy mélange of automobiles, tricycles, bicycles, a cacophonous torrent. The rue des Marins, like the rue Catinat in quiet Saigon, is bursting with boutiques, stalls, variety stores, and trading counters. Nearby, along the canal, junks dump their goods in rice fields and warehouses.

She comes into contact with another world, a different people, little fly-by-night street vendors with their two-bit stalls, the hairdressers, the tooth-drawers, the itinerant chefs with their countertop ovens where they prepare hot noodles. Lighted Chinese lanterns roll out endless, nonchalant, unreal spectacles on the storefronts. She is swallowed up in the Lover's desire just as she penetrates into his world, his odors, his rituals.

She learns everything from this bastard, creole childhood. She is constantly returning to it; she has never written but one single book, that of her childhood amid the scent of the tamarind and cinnamon trees. "The Sea Wall is the true book of memory," she says, "and I wasn't quite thirty when I wrote it." And from those days, worn threadbare by time, there remain strong images, like primal scenes that she reworks and re-embroiders, weaving the great tapestry of life, like one of the Fates.

In that moist heat, where dangers roam ceaselessly, in that fever country, when leprosy was palmed off along with a few piasters, the yellow earth becomes initiatory. In the Saigon boarding school where her mother placed her, there is also the companion she will later call Hélène Lagonelle, the girl her own age who will reveal her to the splendor of women's bodies, the firmness of their breasts and their bellies, that full, smooth quality of their skin, that offering which they always make of it.

It is a land of exile that nonetheless gives rise to extreme agitation, made more acute and violent by the "culminating heat," and that exhausts minds, giving the impression of finality, a land of agony whose ardent tension, electric atmosphere, and sheer lassitude, whose passive, suffocating heat, inexorably reflect death and the end of all passion, beings, and time.

She likes to live that way, in that nearly deleterious state, in despair, as if it were better suited for making things understood, for providing that intelligence as extreme and definitive as it is terrible and painful.

Early in life she becomes accustomed to it, that association between tenderness and harshness, the combining of the two, and their life in apparent unison, in a dangerous, destabilizing proximity. The Lover douses her with "the water in the earthenware jars," and his hand, gentle and sure, brushes across her skin, and ever-present in the novel is the water from those jars flowing over her body. And his hands, the Lover's delicate hands, caressing it. Outside, cruel Saigon, the promiscuity of the poor neighborhoods and the white neighborhoods, colonial dishonor, and the seething mass of natives hurrying around on the innumerable streets. On the one hand the silence of the tennis courts, and on the other the deafening noise of the Cholon district. And at her house, in that Faulknerian family, the older brother's past and present violence, the tension to which he subjected them, "the little ones," the desire for death they resisted, that taste for destruction, the mother's fits of madness, and the odd attraction of the life she now leads.

All of that lies within the realm of fatality. Later, when she is ill, when alcohol submerges her again and pushes her to the very edge of death, Yann Andréa will lavish upon her the same attention, the same love. He will bathe her, run water over her swollen, destroyed body, a far cry from the one she let the

Chinese man caress, and yet love and extraordinary tenderness are still circulating there. Nonetheless, the pain of not
pursuing love into the abyss of carnal pleasure, that love to
which Yann Andréa cannot gain access, and which instills
terror, causes suffering, but remains a form of love, that fragile,
indescribable state, perhaps only comparable to music, to the
miracle of music, welling up astonishingly, prodigiously, as
fragile and short-lived as incense burning at the indecisive
hour when night falls, and spreads in bluish wreaths throughout the rooms of the dormitory at the Lyautey boarding school,
or in the great drawing room of *India Song*.

Duras's places are always permeated with that smell of
churches, Asia, and crematoriums where memory is concentrated, places recalling death and things long gone, with only
remembrances as proof. Places like mausoleums or catafalques,
where victims of love lie in state on beds that might as well be
coffins: Marguerite Donnadieu's body in which the Chinese
lover "is engulfed," Delphine Seyrig's unassailed porcelain
body in *India Song*, Duras's body in the grip of a coma, in a
secret room at the American hospital.

These constant incursions of life into death—the proximity
of death, the desire so strong in her to know its secret through
absolute, radical, impossible love—haunt her life and her
novels. Everywhere, wherever she happens to be, the photographs show it. This presence in her legend, built into book
upon book, and suddenly, in the gaze, an absence, the inevitable call of distant places, the taste for clouds of dust, the look
in her eyes, that of a foreigner, a stowaway, out of place, no
longer there, overwhelming those who meet her and making
them love her, that vast expanse of certitude, "the desire to
die."

This is her way of thinking, of understanding the world,
chaotic and divided up, then suddenly spreading out like the
sea that covers everything as far as the eye can see. From the
time of her childhood in Asia, she would be in possession of
this language of contrasts, abrupt counterpoints, the obverse
and the reverse, life and death permanently telescoping into

each other. Initiation to love in the arms of Hélène Lagonelle, and in those of the Chinese man, in the escapades with the little brother, the discovery of death that she deduces from it, from the pain, from the abandon, and this prescience of something that will never be given again, never, of time fleeing and carrying everything away with it, erasing present joys, counterbalance each other in her autobiographical work and in the interviews she has granted to various journals. There can be no youth without wrinkles, no fervor without doubt, no plenitude without separation.

She prowls around the Buddhist monasteries and, frightened to death in her hiding place, peers at the processions of saffron-colored bonzes chanting litanies in the stridency of their hand-rattles. And she always keeps her ears open to forbidden sounds. Elsewhere, she recalls the pleasantness, so rare, of a day in Sadec, of that vacant, almost gaping state in which her mother, taking advantage of the rare moments of leisure left to her by school, glided into sleep on the veranda terrace, in the soft breeze, swinging gently to and fro in the rocking chair. And it was like a state of grace, an immobilized image frozen in the time of memory, while all around her, as if forgotten for a brief instant, the cries of madness, misery, hunger, the "hooligan" brother. . . .

Time in *The Lover* is lived like a chant sung to the rhythm of the mother's outbursts. The omnipresence of that woman prophet in her words, the adventuress who so seldom looked after her, ardent nucleus of her problematics: what can we make of this mother, of her choices in love, of that affection which she apparently reserved for the rascally, bullying, thieving brother? In her mother's company, Duras learned the fragility of things, the easily accomplished destruction of what was, the splendid state of decomposition and discomfort that would reign everywhere in the aftermath, for as long as she would live, and beyond. She existed at the gates of madness, on the edge of the abyss, like being in the arms of the man from Cholon, or always in borderline situations, on the brink of falling, "on the crest" of the waves, tossed about, ready to vanish.

She wants to fight against that immense, enormous, terrible mother and her "bursts of madness." She wants to write. To that her mother replies that such a notion is "childish." Ever within her is that nostalgia for what is still unlearned and has no social reference, that cruel, tender, seamless childhood life, those primal states in the forest, the Book to come, the novel of origins she wants to write, that beach where she can finally rest, in a discovered golden age. She would be there with the little brother, following lioness tracks into the opulent jungle, as in her earliest youth, or else that little girl still of school age, with gold lamé shoes, tramping through the town and its swarming fury, soon to be reunited with the Lover's warm body. Yes, she would be that free little girl, as in the first days of the world, and she would not be scandalized if they were to devour their bodies, with a violence and a gentleness new to both of them.

Is it this childhood of desire that will give her the claim to prophecy? She speaks and she is an oracle. As a little girl, she already knew everything. It was something irremediable that she couldn't even control. She knew about the void, the improbable return of time, and the flight from everything in the intolerable splendor of worlds, of forests like cathedrals, abandoned palaces carved out of wood, white colonial cities smelling of rot, and inaccessible love. And the fleeting glimpse that gives knowledge of the inconsolable she knows has disappeared forever, causing Lacan to say later: "This woman knows."

Something should also be said about this "family of stone, petrified in a thick mass with no access whatsoever," as she describes them in The Lover. And about the obscure light that reigns in her home, her mother's madness, the older brother's pent-up violence, felt despite his absence, the little brother's wounded innocence, and her, at the confluence of that darkness, those excesses, brutal and tender, rebellious and servile.

They need to be discussed because they shed light on the entire work to come, following on its heels and, in the evening of her life, Duras talks about them constantly, as if she could never fill those bottomless pits.

She mythicizes the little brother; with him she has the most obvious, simplest, most essential relations. She loved him because she believed he was immortal. To the older brother she also gives the stature of a legend: there he is, in the dead center of the family, an arrogant and "brutal" lord, an "assassin without weapons." It is to him that she dedicated her first murderous instincts, concentrating against him that load of hatred and anger of which she is capable, to be vented later in the painful outlet of writing.

Thanks to the Chinese lover she comes to know rejection, the fringes of society, and her classmates' scorn, but her defiance continues. She becomes the talk of the town, in that colonial society with its narrow, racist, moral views. She becomes the bastard, and exile strengthens her determination, increasing constantly the violence pent up within her. Bodily pleasure, that joy of making a gift of oneself, that brutal way of defying loneliness, that refusal to preserve herself, everything impels her to celebrate the birth of that pagan body, offered like those of sacred vestals, in the revolt against all constraining institutions. From now on her goal would be to use up, driven by the urgency of a life she had observed escaping too often and too early, all of the possibilities that remained to be discovered. She definitely would not give this body to that fatal, moralistic God, but instead to the great cosmic Unity, as brutal as it was gentle, to all the suggestions of this primitive desire that spoke in her and that she wanted to express. Thus the body so loved by the Chinese man, the mythical Lover, became the instrument of passage, of transgression, a means of saying no to the mother, to all authority, to all forces of power in one fell swoop.

Water presided once again at these new nuptials, water as a major reference of her world, water which, moving and swirling, makes it possible to seize the world in its boundless immensity, in its endless nuances. And as the ferry glided along, the story of a love affair was being born.

At that time, when the Chinese man appeared, she is beautiful, petite, with the striking, nervous, wild look of an animal.

He says that he "loves the little girl"; she says that it's "only natural." A sensual, untouched force emanates from her, drawing her toward desire. In her eyes, in her entire bearing, there is something determined, impudent, still rebellious, and intelligent. In this risk taken for desire, she recklessly throws away everything that her mother tried to instill in her, the honor of being white, and superior as a result of learning and colonization, the honor of being a virgin. Irresistible passion flows through her as she crosses dangerous lands in the humidity of Saigon afternoons, the very lands she will explore over and over in her work to come, borderlands, lands burning with desire, brushed by death. When she gives herself to the Chinese man, she opens her trapdoors, explores her cellars, and thickens the blackness of her nights, burying unacknowledgeable facts that would always serve to place her in a time frame ruled by danger.

Before the woman of Hiroshima, she says to the Chinese lover: "You're killing me, it feels good." In his arms she discovers red-hot zones, even surprised to love like that, violently, without real love, without the presence of feelings or psychology, to love amid the fragrant, exotic confusion of this country, with all of its elements mixed together, hoisted up to her, like incense on the altar rising to the implored God, like the wafting smoke of the cones of incense that embalm Anne-Marie Stretter's photograph there on the grand piano in the Calcutta drawing room.

To make love with the Chinese man in that unknown room, over and over, to brave customs and the Law, to live in the urgency of danger, means, once and for all, reconciliation with the forces of nature, siding with the boa, the exuberant green of the jungles, finding her place in the world of scandal that she will inhabit from this point on.

It also means mingling with the odors and fragrances of that ill-begotten country, with its noises and the acrid dust stirred up by the rickshaws, swept away by the breath of the jasmines, carried along by the rank odors of the itinerant kitchens where bottom fish and caramelized meats are reheated in the blackish stagnation of sweet and sour sauces.

And in that borderland, to know pleasure, deliverance, an insult to the Law instituted by fathers, to pass over to the other side, to become free, deliberately free.

In pleasure renewed, in cries uttered in a state of fulfillment, she discovers the reality of desire, making up for the mother's screams, drowning them out, putting a gag into the mouth of that desperate pythoness, crying out like one being born, and then coming back into the world, preparing to cry out in agony.

All of that is what led the young Marguerite, albeit confusedly, to meet the Chinese lover during those months in Saigon. A time of apprenticeship and learning, wearing her little pink felt hat, a man's hat, and dancing shoes like a little *Hollywood Cinema* starlet, with the song "Ramona" in her head, sweet and terribly romantic, and beneath the song, even further away, the beggar woman's never-ending lament, her wandering in the land of her ancestors, her misery.

The reign of the older brother is nonetheless present, absolute and evil. He robs his mother and the Chinese in the opium dens. He is all-powerful, borne along by the unhealthy air of the colonies. The little brother and the sister are at his mercy, subjected to his hauteur, his hatred, his fascination with murder. Meanwhile, he spends his time doing nothing, or gambling, a stranger to morals, uncivilized.

His mother knows he is lost, that no parental guidance will ever make him change, that he will remain the same, in that state of barbarity from which no guardian can save him.

Shortly before they return to France, she nonetheless asks that her son be repatriated, for, torn apart by his absence, she "can't live without him, it's impossible."

He will go to France, and it is a relief for the "little ones," whose sense of intimidation she can feel, especially Paulo, too fragile, too "simple," persecuted.

As for the sister, she rediscovers life in the arms of the Chinese lover from Cholon. Her senses tell her that now she is not in her mother's house; she is reminded of it by the strength of being, in being alive which she feels when he is "swallowed up" in her, when all the smells of indigenous Indochina penetrate her in a blur. In the eyes of others at the boarding school—who learn from the women in her mother's neighborhood that she is the "nasty little girl," the one who is sleeping with a Chinese man—she is the shame of the colonial community, the scum of civilization. Marie Donnadieu knows and doesn't want to know at the same time. She has unbending principles, but deep inside her there is an inexpressible admiration for her daughter, for her courageous audacity, her contempt for morality, for what others think.

Between the Chinese man and Marguerite there are none of those romantic plans dear to first loves, no future. Between the two of them there is a devouring, heedless, inadmissible passion. They must plunge to the heart of this frenzy, understanding nothing of it, explaining nothing, allowing the fumes of incense to penetrate their open bodies, merely living it, filling themselves with the pain.

In what obscure, tow-lined place, in what darkroom, will all of those images be hidden, buried beneath a tombstone of oblivion? How can one name that place she will later define, when she is called Duras, as "unbreathable, on death's edge, a place of violence, of pain, of despair, of disgrace," a place of writing, hidden, then acknowledged, taken up again in other stories, embroidered and re-embroidered, hidden once more, before finally revealing itself in broad daylight?

The chance to write springs from that daily violence, the mother's sheer despair, there in "that shared history of ruin and death that characterized the family."

Meanwhile, she desires the Chinese man who makes her heart and body throb. Her face has that smooth beauty of unwrinkled flesh, that impeccable tension of the skin, which gives her every kind of impudence and defiance.

But the knowledge of desire will soon coincide with the passing of time. She sees it pass in her pleasure, in the way she moves about, so mobile, like the undulating surface of water, knotting up inside her, like a knot of death, rejoining the abysses of all that she has hidden inside, which will nourish her from now on.

In the reflections of that undulation there is also, in 1932, the family's last visit to the damlands. She remembers it today, Siam facing them, on the now-abandoned veranda, Siam in its immensity, with its dark forests wherein lie hidden the wild animals that she would approach brazenly, and the sand-speckled sky.

She remembers that moment of silence, that solemn hour when all of the images come together, that eagerness to recover the least detail and take it away, ever further. There must be a warm, dry wind blowing, making the vines on the veranda sway softly, and the silence of that failure and that fervor, the silence of that inner cry expressing the pain of permanent separation, of exile.

And wandering gives the whole family that air of "foreignness" separating them from the colonial world, so active, so productive, so enterprising. Like the brother, she "learned nothing, except to watch the forest, to wait, to cry."

Thus, of that childhood, all that remains are those founding, "essential" images, torn from memory, spoken over and over or perhaps withheld from speech, invented again, and reinvented each time she talks about them. How to resist what she calls "the ritual of evocation," the words that come to mind spontaneously now, which don't really reflect the truth of the moment but, filtered by memory, try to reconstitute the story, giving it coherence amid the inevitable chaos.

Too many failures, inner wounds, and material difficulties had damaged the mother. She had fallen victim to her own energy, her own rage, her own madness. She had had to abandon too much since the days when she was a young schoolteacher, full of illusions; she had been victimized by too many swindlers. She was worn out, even if her madness suddenly restored illusory brute strength in her. She was not leaving Indochina in response to the call of her native land; there or elsewhere, what did it matter, really? She was mainly concerned about her children, wanted Marguerite to "get an education," "go to college." In her daughter she felt that effrontery which perhaps she herself hadn't had the courage to flaunt. She recognized her as her own and then turned away from her, violently. Money had always preoccupied her more than anything else. She had worked and saved a great deal for the older son, who demanded more each day. To go back to France was to keep wandering, to begin life over again, and to find the older son. Theirs was a family of nomads, of bohemians, living precariously, never settled.

Physical pleasure was not the only thing Marguerite sought in her encounters with the Chinese lover. His social position fascinated her; there was something of a challenge in the seduction of this young Chinese man, the son of Cholon bankers, a jubilation in seeing him disobey the laws of his race, marginalizing himself. Sometimes, when her brothers and her mother came to Saigon, she would have the Chinese lover take them to the best restaurants in town. And they would eat the most expensive dishes, ignoring the man, offering him the secret of this "unbearable community" that the four of them constituted, hating each other detestably, yet loving each other with an infinite, ageless love, completely inaccessible to others.

With the mother's approval, she will extort five hundred piasters from the Chinese lover, "the sum required for the move to Paris," she says in *The Lover*.

Perhaps the hardest part was abandoning the lands of the sea wall, knowing that they would never go back to the swamplands of Prey Nop, to that beach they had all thought they could farm. That ruined land was left to the natives, but it still belonged to them, especially to the mother, who had slaved away on it until, threadbare, exhausted, she had no more strength to prevent herself from falling, screaming, into the yawning chasm of irrationality.

2

The Formative Years

Like all of Duras's essences, the sea is a recurring part of her geography, and this time it takes her back to France. The episode of the Chinese lover ends, like consumed passion, tinged with the smell of denial and powerlessness.

She embarks on one of those long shipping line steamers of the Messageries Maritimes. On the pier, just as the tugboats unfasten it from its berth to tow it out to sea, she thinks she sees the funereal car, as black as a casket, the Chinese lover's car with him sitting inside, watching her depart.

The voyage back to the mother country will take a long time, with stopovers along the coasts, in ports bearing magical names that seem to have been invented, Calcutta, Lahore, Colombo, lined with luxurious hotels like the Prince of Wales. The steamer is leading young Marguerite toward her destiny. Something tells her that she must follow it to the very end; the Chinese man's "little girl," "the child," goes off toward other worlds, other, genuine French lands. Will she ever see Indochinese soil again? How will she manage to resuscitate its odors, its noises, make its men and women come to life again? On the sea, in that vast, uncolonizable space, on that perpetually moving expanse, where nobody can move in and impose his proud will, she spends days on end. There are parties organized to kill time, and ports of call with strange names where she catches brief glimpses of more white bungalows and the edges of dense jungles.

At the dinner hour she could meet people like Elizabeth Striedter, different people, but she mostly notices snobs, and among the lower classes, on the deck, miserable little stooped-over settlers. The ship is white; it cuts through the sea. Sometimes she is afraid of it, when she leans over the side and sees the surging mounds of water swallowed up in each other, constantly renewing the rippling surface. The sea beats against the hull, and she fears this no-man's-land, as terror-stricken as the mother seeing the tides loom up on the damlands of Indochina. She leans over the handrail, and the water propels her back to oblivion, as if everything were sinking into the millennial night, crumbling into millions of unknown particles, with no common ties. Meanwhile, on the ship, she's horrified to learn that a young man has jumped overboard. Suicide. Returning to the Great Oneness of the ocean, its chaotic mingling, its eternally renewed turbulence.

She also says that the Chinese lover's body disappeared just like that, gone forever, never to be found again. She peers into the depths, wanting to know what is down there, what they keep hidden beneath the foam. Below the waves, an entire story to be heard, secrets murmured in undulating, soughing tones, a mixture of nothing and everything.

She doesn't exactly know yet. All she knows is that something black is moving forward toward France, her country, she is told, her race, her culture; she doesn't understand. Inside her there is other knowledge, the fragrance of jasmines and rose laurels, and the strange scent of leprosy sticking to her, glaucous rice fields where she used to splash about, children whose distended bellies burst like popping bubbles, and the absolute desire she feels for the Chinese lover, lying deep within her.

But in the shadow of the white boat, there is the Nightship, the black shadow of the images concealed in childhood, life, love, and especially death, and how can they be described? In the trapdoors, the word holes that she glimpses in the vortices made by the waves, in the enormous, gluttonous foam crevice opened by the wake of the ocean liner. She doesn't know where this ship is going yet, but it is moving forward, "on the sea of black ink." She knows that she possesses a particular kind of knowledge in this availability, this porousness that she consolidated within her in those distant, exotic lands so well suited to those who love to peer over the edge. From now on the images from her darkroom, taken along with her in the holds of the Nightship, will begin to drift, like the beggar woman of Vinh Long, across unknown territories, and books will become ports of call where she can stop and try to understand the march of time and her life.

And so she will never again set foot on that land. Colonial France has left her. Deserted are those luxurious white hotels festooned with wood and zinc lace, those melancholy songs played in the piano bars and those sobbing, dolorous tangos; all of that has vanished. And upon the ruins of white Indochina, new wars, more bloody, fratricidal battles, new colonial powers will give those lands back to her once they have been scorched, napalmed, so that she could never again see the dazzling green jungle, the jasmines blooming in a single evening in the splendid white brothel, the home of the upper crust.

All that she will be left with is the darkness, nothing but the darkness falling on the land of her birth, making her into someone born nowhere; only what she has invented out of Vinh Long, out of Cambodia; what she is left with is fragmentary, the fabric of her days and her nights suddenly illuminated, sublimated by the coming of the beggar woman, by the silent passing of red-haired Elizabeth Striedter, by the children's cries and mothers' scolding. Only the legendary story, reconstituted, rewoven a thousand times over, restretched by the grace of memory, the waves rolling in from that swell, and deposited there, in writing, in the uncertain domain of words, in that immense jumble of lands crisscrossed by travelers going from Saigon to Calcutta, from Lahore to Vancouver, more or less at random, for the story is the same everywhere, begun again in each new place. Reinvented.

It's as though she were carrying a load that she must sooner or later bring to light in the great, painful parturition of writing: the hated, unjust, dreaded, and revered mother; the little brother with the Annamese look in his eyes; the older brother, the hoodlum, the "black sheep"; and the slow procession of black sampans gliding along toward an unknown destination, for an unknown reason, on the Mekong.

But her childhood is also her good fortune, the one that authorizes writing to be born, to live, and encourages her to put up with the indescribable suffering of existence only because of it. One night in 1977, while *The Eden Cinema* is being performed at the Théâtre d'Orsay, as if all the phantoms of her childhood were reappearing, she has a strange dream, which she relates in *Green Eyes*. She tells about entering a house with colonnades, and verandas stretching out in front of it. And always the same nostalgic air of the waltzes, the colonial-era tangos, the music of Carlos d'Alessio, and the mother in the background, "already taken by death," claiming that she is the one who is playing. " 'But how is it possible? You were dead.' She said to me: 'I led you to believe that so you would be able to write all these books.' "

The unavoidable mother haunts her dreams and the black oeuvre. She already knows on cool nights in the middle of the sea, on this ship cutting through the dark, that this mother, "flayed alive by the blade of misery," will be her ink, her unlimited source of ink.

There she stands, then, leaning over the rails, leaving behind those lands of exoticism, that trickling stream of otherworldly light, that unique vegetation, those swarming masses of multiplying, unknown lives, and she feels in the gluttonous bubbling of the wake, in the jolts of her Nightship, "the immense, swelling tide of voices calling out." She knows that she knows nothing and everything at the same time, as though everything had been decided beforehand, especially knowledge of things visible and invisible, in their black scintillation, in those holds of the mind where ideas overlap and harry each other. "That is what I want to do: write."

She returns to France; her mother would surely like her to go back to the north, where she herself was born, in those vast grain-producing plains, or else, perhaps to study in order to have a permanent career one day. But Marie Legrand, the assiduous scholarship student, the "stubborn, mad" little peasant woman from Flanders, was dreaming. She had no comprehension of what was now agitating her daughter Marguerite, in her "thin, weak-looking body," and yet what fervor, what a maelstrom of desires, violence, and savagery!

Down there in the churning mass of foam, in those heavy, black seas, there is a kind of metaphor for writing, the call of the abyss, which must be what writing is: to melt into the void, to hear loud, wild, uncertain clamors there, and to be alone, just as now, on this night at sea, belonging to no one and everything at the same time, porous enough for things to go through you, all these indescribable mixtures that make you go crazy, sending you "to the end of the world, to the end of your tether."

Something that cannot yet be said, or written, but felt intuitively, almost at this very instant of life and death, and which yearns for the wide open sea. Just as there used to be wide open spaces in the dense jungles with the little brother of desire, and in the Chinese lover's arms, where she became the whore of Cholon, cut off, rejected by others for that same reason. And there, in the boundless sea, with yet more sea on the horizon, and the night, she feels "the wide open sea of literature," that mysterious place where she suspects he is waiting for her, where other forces are raging, where the meaning of life is given a different slant, where God, the gods, those words that "beckon," are explained in another way, where that which escapes ordinary meaning, visible reality, is finally explained.

It is in the flow of those waters sliced by the ship's hull that she understands the nature of the act of writing, in that abyss untiringly opened up, it too constantly renewed and ready to transport her.

She feels dizzy, but not from the swell that's making the deck pitch about, the moving sky that seems to be stealing away and ignoring the fixed points of the stars, but from the darkness, the invisible forces, the secrets, the depths revealed by this abyss, the brutality with which the waters cover and uncover everything almost at the same time, forcing one to know, to search.

She would be, her intuition tells her, that seeker of meaning, in quest of the absolute, and that is why she would accept
all of the dangers involved, would risk her life in any game, any
amusement that could point her in the right direction, show
her the way to meaning. She vaguely apprehends this, and feels
ready for it.

Has so much time really gone by, do that many years separate
her from then, has time completely erased the difference between the little girl in Saigon hurrying to throw herself into
the clandestine arms of the Chinese lover, and the woman of
yesterday, of today, alcoholic, pathetic, the broken, destroyed,
spent woman who has lost even her voice, thanks to this
damned cannula that has perforated her throat, betraying her
inimitable poetic speech, that music of the soul coming from
far off; between the little girl on the ocean liner beneath the
countless stars, out at sea, and the beggar woman of today,
stooped over, clinging to Yann Andréa, the unique, greatest,
immense, and yet virgin love?

Has that much time passed between the steamship from
the colonies, in those first days of the thirties, and the present?
Sixty-three years separating the two banks, of life, of love, of
struggles, battles of all kinds to come, refused, taken up, em-
braced and hated, this same route again aboard the Nightship
taking her where she has always intended to go?

Everything had already been learned by then, dimly discovered in the darkness of the night. It all began in that uncivilized land where the mother had given birth to them, her
"gnos,"* as she affectionately called them, in that place where
neither art nor the niceties of life were of any importance, only
work, unyielding work, "eating and sleeping." And therein
perhaps lay Marguerite Donnadieu's strength: "that desperate
mother" who had given her an intuitive feeling for misfortune,
and whose sorrow she would carry hereafter, just as the beggar
woman carries her bundle of leprosy, that ghastly baby, the

---

*The Vietnamese word for children—TRANS. note

only protrusion from the gaunt, hunched-over frame resembling her own.

She will transcribe this overwhelming moment in her life in *The Lover* and *The North China Lover*, where the core of writing can be best understood as a transcription of the past. What she questions in the approach taken by Jean-Jacques Annaud in the 1991 film version of *The Lover* is precisely the way in which, according to her, he confused biography with "translation." Between what really happened on the ocean liner and the account she gave of it, a passage is made from life into writing, the whole story unfolding through the secret, obscure workings of literature.

Archetypal scenes reveal the meaning of her life: the young man who committed suicide, the wash of the ship, the sparkling night, and the melodies escaping from music rooms, filling the streets, "popular among young people in those days . . . expressing the wild joy of one's first love and the inordinate pain of losing it." It is as if Duras's life were concentrated there, in that unidentified space, between two lands, a foreign zone, a place of exile.

Of that mythical France the mother had talked about so often, she knew nothing, not even the family home in the southwestern Lot-et-Garonne region, near the little town of Duras, overlooking the Marmande Valley. It was a vast house built of local stone, a kind of small castelet not uncommon in the area, an undulating country of scattered villages, far from the population centers, a desolate, uncivilized country despite the grace of the houses and rolling hills.

Europe has neither the violence nor the sensual brutality of Asia, that mingling of all different scents, misery, and flowers, the pungency of loose earth and the stale smells of spices wafting out of the alleyways of Saigon, amid the reigning climate of agony and terror, invisible perhaps, but already perceptible.

Her mother wanted her to study mathematics in eventual preparation for the "agrégation," the highly competitive national teaching exam. Nothing was too prestigious for her daughter, "the little one"; she would follow in her father's footsteps, carrying his name to spheres where he himself had shone. But that wasn't what Marguerite wanted, as though studying barely interested her, determined instead to discover the world through other means. If only she would do something "worthwhile," cried her mother, "real work" instead of this joke of a writing career that had caught hold of her when she was fifteen and a half and wouldn't feed her, would leave her destitute, prevent her from being taken seriously, exclude her from society. For social recognition was what the mother dreamed of, not having been able to acquire it in spite of so much toil, "assassinated" by society.

Nonetheless, the mother knew that she wouldn't stay in France, that she wouldn't find her place there, that she was inundated by an immense melancholy on what was no longer her land. Possessed by Indochina, she decided to go back there, leaving the beloved son and Marguerite, taking the little brother with her. She will stay there from 1932 to 1949, at which time she will return to France for good. Henceforth she would live, not for herself, destroyed, repudiated—she didn't exist, anyway—but fiercely determined to earn money, some of which she could send to her little Parisians, money orders, more and more of them for the older son, who lived by his wits, temporary jobs, shady schemes, even earning his keep as a gigolo, as Duras implies in *The Lover*.

Scholarship in hand, Marguerite enrolls in college, where she studies from 1933 to 1936, first at law school in Paris, receiving a degree, then at the Catholic Institute of Political Science; she wants to specialize in mathematics, but endowed with a nature whose immense rebelliousness had been fuelled on the damlands, she can't manage to fit into a well-defined slot, or to envision her future in an orderly bourgeois setting. She herself admits having completed a "very vague course of study. Except for math." "And even there it wasn't on account of a definite liking for the subject, but rather a mechanical reflex."

During that period, she still lives near the older brother. His "harmful" presence continues to instill a kind of terror, an abstract fright in her. He hangs around, accompanied by a cortege of lies, theft, indifference, and force. Something obscure, undefinable that sought to dominate, to coerce, a dark, fierce energy, unfailingly wild schemes.

About those years, Duras remains quite chary of information. A time of transition, of settling in a land of exile, of integration from her status of bastard, of foreigner, of one born nowhere. She says back then she wanted to bury it all, forget her childhood, the colonial racket, the black panthers, the crocodiles and the sampans, that whole imaginary world suffused with contrasts and fragrances waiting to be evoked in spite of everything. This lack of identity, this anonymity pleased her nonetheless, increased her freedom. She was not yet aware of the force of that childhood, the little beggar woman's persistent litany, the unforgettable moistness of the climate and of her ardent body in the arms of the Chinese lover. She didn't know yet that the native land would "wreak vengeance," as she would say. The Mekong, the heat culminating at siesta time, the explorations in the dense forests: it would all come back to her, and there she would find the exclusive material for her writing; there she would have to dig, work, lose herself, toiling for years over a book, and then embarking on her later books with an incredible lightness.

Was it already life experience, intuition, imagination that made her indifferent to the urge to settle down, to possess, to occupy a position in society, to be manipulated like a toy?

There still remained within her the image of those boats standing out on the horizon, near the mouth of the river, then slipping out of sight, and plunging into infinity, henceforth invisible—the very representation of life, the notion of leaving without ever being able to come back, the successive ports of call and the necessary separation from one's possessions upon setting out again, the absurd belief in the immortality of things, frustrated and destroyed by time, leaving her further deprived on each occasion, but tenacious, redressing the injury.

In Paris, she is still the little "creole," the one who has lived in colonial Asia, "extradited," she says. She has lost her memory; she adapts. Hidden deep inside her is a compost heap of images that she knows will grow. There is the Prince of Wales Hotel in Colombo, of which she caught a glimpse on the trip back, and the odor of leprosy invariably mixed with the sweet smell of rose laurels. And above all the mother and the older brother, and the little brother, the victim, who she knows will die, "martyred" by the mother's insane, unbearable love for the big brother, yes, by the maternal preference.

In photographs of that period, she is always smiling, but with an enigmatic smile that doesn't believe in the joy or the happiness it is trying to express. She has kept that piercing, "vaguely Oriental gaze," says Claude Roy in *Nous*, "an absent, hypnotizing look, with her eyes always raised toward the invariably taller person facing her," and a special kind of boredom hovering over her, the weight of a certain shame, that which logically accompanies "the necessity of living life."

She is determined to smile, to act out happy, normal, family scenes with her brother, in luxuriant gardens. She looks like a little salesgirl, a little milliner with her light cotton dresses, her belts drawn tight at the waist, and her handbag held primly under her arm. But these are mere illusions: "true life is elsewhere," as the poet said, in that untiring interrogation of the world, in that murmuring of all things that make one dizzy enough to faint and which she has a talent for transcribing.

To that writing haunted by the past she grants the exclusive right to tell her life story. She insists that in reality nothing is falser, more superfluous, more "apparent," than this alignment of facts in which there seems to be a certain coherence. It is more probable that everything proceeds from the chaotic swell of images that remain, with the fragile, discontinuous melody of their music, and the acceptance of oblivion. One must understand that this life can be found only among the traces of reconstituted events, that it doesn't unwind "like a road between two milestones, from beginning to end." Indeed it is not by collecting facts and dates, adjusting them like parts on a machine, that beings reveal themselves more fully, but by observing the traces they have left deep inside themselves, in the most remote zones of what she calls "the inner shadow," where "the archives of the self" are to be found.

Thus later, when she refuses to trouble herself with dates, what does it matter, for in her eyes the restitution of memory is something else entirely: "What is contained in books," she says, "is more authentic than the author who writes them. . . . The stories invented by Shakespeare tell more about Shakespeare than his life does." She is sure that her work is the place to look for her story, her life, and in the hollows and the ditches, in the obscurity behind trapdoors, in words, in the rice fields and the deep fords of Indochina, incessantly washed, agitated, submerged by the China Sea.

She quickly learned of the loneliness in her heart, the obsessive tendency, deplored by her mother, never to be happy about anything, that permanent dissatisfaction, that desire to die so strongly present in her—she didn't really know why—but which made her cry, that melancholy which nonetheless yielded to the joy of laughter and irony, the ability to take pleasure in every act, loving, admiring, learning, drinking, smoking.

Thus the books to come are her sole certitude. The certainty of finding true life there, in those blackened pages, slowly, in the unfathomable necessity of writing, in its painful enjoyment, in what she will call "wonderful sorrow," as dreadfully fragile as true life is, and always bursting at the seams, always on the brink of comprehension.

In Indochina she had never read anything but adventure stories, prize books, all of that morally uplifting literature found in colonial libraries—Pierre Benoit, Pierre Loti, Claude Farrère, Roland Dorgelès—the variety plays in *La Petite illustration théâtrale:* "I would read every issue, that's all there was. Most of it was variety shows," she later tells Gilles Costaz, theater critic for *Le Matin*. In Paris, she could now visit art exhibitions, go to the theater, read novels, discover authors.

If she had laughed at Caillavet's witty retorts when she was an adolescent, the Pitoëffs were the ones who opened her eyes to theater.* With her season ticket at the Théâtre des Mathurins, where the company was permanently established, she didn't miss a single one of their performances. "It was my first drama school," she recalls in the same conversation with Costaz. "There were fifteen people in the audience, but I kept coming back. Eventually the Pitoëffs got to know me and would greet me. I was eighteen. I saw *A Doll's House, The Exchange, The Sea Gull.*"

Already, spontaneously, she is making decisive choices. The Comédie Française is no more to her liking, "because of the diction, the versification," than Jean Giraudoux, revealed to the general public by *Amphitryon 38;* popular French dramatists of that era such as Marcel Achard, Sacha Guitry, and Jacques Deval do not interest her; she feels like a member of the Pitoëff family because they have that romantic, Slavic soul, that *musica* they will draw from the great Russian, Scandinavian, and Anglo-Saxon works. Even more than the surrealist innovations, she reads the classics of the period, Malraux, Mauriac, Carco, Céline. When Hemingway, Faulkner, and Virginia Woolf are translated into French, she will recognize herself in their writing, all of those who hear wild inner voices, muffled cries deep inside them, as if rising, barely audible, from the bottom of a stagnant pool, or issuing faintly from the soul.

Paris in the thirties is both gay and somber, refusing to believe its own presentiment of disaster, becoming heady and boisterous in its creation of rumors. The ceremonies of the Colonial Exhibition are barely over, but some people are doubting France's chances of keeping her empire intact. Gone are the "roaring twenties," and the coming years appear alarming, threatening by comparison. Duras, attentive to the spirit of the times, senses that questioning, that uneasiness. Even if she doesn't share their views on writing, she lives in a city where Roger Martin du Gard, Aragon, Jules Romains, Giraudoux,

---

*Gaston Arman de Caillavet (1869-1915): author of opéra bouffes and light comedies, a friend of Proust's; Georges and Ludmilla Pitoëff: 1930s producer and actress at the Théâtre des Mathurins in Paris.—Trans. note

Nizan, Emmanuel Berl, and André Breton are writing their most powerful works, giving writers a new status, more political, more engaged. It is the era of nascent militancy, a force which draws her fellow students to the Communist Party or to the right-wing Action française.

She nonetheless drags along with her that continual impression of having been abandoned, originally by her mother, that profound loneliness which fed her hatred and her jealousy toward her older brother. She wanted to understand the affection that the mother and the son bore for each other, to know everything about their relationship, how much of it was abuse and how much was love. But therein lay the main thorn in her side, her greatest source of pain. How well she remembers that evening on the veranda, in sight of the sea wall, right before leaving, when her mother said to her: "My little one!" It was surely the first time she spoke to her with such affection and really saw her. And there was love floating all around, all the way to Siam, off in the distance, on the other side, beyond the mountains.

That suffering is so great that she will devote her first three books to it, fascinated by the forces tearing them apart, determined to understand the mechanisms, the functioning of that passion. The terror she associates with that brother will always assail her, in a conversation, on a walk, in a bar, in a garden: an uncontrollable, violent, deadly panic. There are photographs from her private collection that show her with him; his face is terrifying, with his hair plastered straight back, cold, piercing eyes, and the twill suit he is wearing making him look like a gigolo in a movie. As for her, sitting against him, she has those narrow eyes that give her an Annamese look, the look of one who was placed in this family by mistake; and in her, upon her, that odd superfluousness of the body, already abandoned, as if everything had been irretrievably finished long ago.

Even if she claims to have the strength to fight against him, as in the past when she refused to submit, defying him, while her mother beat her for "going with the Chinese man," and he stood at the door, fanning the mother's rage, deriving pleasure from her blows; even if one day he tried to prostitute her to a customer at La Coupole, she knows that between them there is something that has to snap, destroy itself, even if they both live in those places where violence and mourning roam.

Prewar Paris educates her intellectually and makes her grow. She lives, as Dionys Mascolo, the future father of her son, later says, "in absence of law," in defiance of herself, just as she used to walk the streets of Cholon in colonial reprobation. She feels totally free, free to love, to experience, to know everything.

She will love men, students, like the young Jew she remembers, especially his reading from the Bible, the Old Testament, out of which rose the awe-inspiring kings of Israel, of Jerusalem. It is perhaps because of him that her memory still contains traces of the sacred, of all the indecipherable images, the immense territories discovered in the "divine swamp," as they unfurl in the Bible. Perhaps then she also became aware, like Ernesto in *Summer Rain*, of that secret knowledge which no university, no instruction can give her and which she suspects of having many passages, crossings, and enigmas.

She has always loved men, desired them, needed them, coming back to them even in the heyday of the feminist review *Sorcières* and of the women's liberation movement, when she seemed to be surrounded exclusively by women, most of whom didn't like men. In their company she seeks out the secret *musica*, the sacred, hidden stories they keep of things from the past, handed down by their mothers, and makes them violent, wild, gentle, and tender like the Chinese lover when he rinsed her with water from earthenware jars.

It is during those years spent at law school that she will meet Robert Antelme, a student like her, from Sartène in Corsica, three years younger than she. After a childhood of wandering for the most part—on account of his father's occupation, a subprefect assigned to an administrative post in Oloron-Sainte-Marie in the southeast, then in Vienne in the French Alps and in Bayonne on the Spanish border—he had entered law school in Paris after passing the baccalauréat.

Antelme was from a middle-class background, where he had received a Christian upbringing; he and Duras formed an intellectually speculative couple, while remaining present in the world, and possessed of a presentiment concerning great, dark, social upheavals to come.

His youth was all but swallowed up, however, like that of his entire generation, by the specter of war. He performed his military service from 1937 to 1939, only to be mobilized from 1939 to 1940, and later arrested by the Gestapo on a fateful day in June 1944, when he was drawn into the tragic machine that would mark him forever.

In the company of Antelme, Duras would nonetheless live the last bright, happy moments before the skies darkened over Europe, then over Paris. With Antelme a certain peacefulness returned to her, a kind of equilibrium that he carried inside of him, a great mastery of his temperament. Much later, in her hospital bed in Neuilly, she answers Yann Andréa, when he tells her that Antelme called, that he sends his love, and that he would like to " 'see her calm down,' that's the expression he used": "Can you believe it? He always wants to see me calm down, he's been saying that for thirty years. Isn't that just like him?"

In this doomed world, where hatred and violence reign, she can see the signs: she can see the convulsions of the times, the frenzy of lies spreading over them, the first persecution of Jews put into effect, the right to free speech muzzled. Instinctively, she can feel barbarity settling in.

In other words, she had already predicted it in the mental world she had nourished with images of destruction, madness, death, and dissolution. She had already trampled underfoot the spongy, glaucous land of the colonial concession, dragging behind her the whole train of fears and calamities. At the age of eighteen she had already discovered the fixed image, that of "the irremediable separation of people," and the obsessive, unchanging certitude that nothing can modify those "abominable facts," and she thus considered that she had finished learning, growing, that she was all but dead at eighteen with this knowledge that destroyed her expectations. Even her face made her look as grave, as old, as a Buddha. Yes, that's how everything had come to pass; there could have been that photograph of her at eighteen, with the felt hat poised on the side of her head, that smile, facetious and yet off in a distant dream, long gone in some other direction. And at the same time, it was because of that face, ruined for youth, that she had decided to write, to tell about it: the violence of the sea, knocking everything down, destroying the sea walls, inundating the fields, swallowing them up as it went by. To write about what she had had the opportunity to discover, for, she says, "all writing proceeds from the self; outside of that, it doesn't exist."

Having applied for an administrative post in the Ministry of Colonies at the beginning of 1937, thus unconsciously imitating her mother's same actions years before, she is recruited on 9 June in the Intercolonial Information and Documentation Service. An ambiguous individual who participates in the maintenance of the colonial system and at the same time viscerally repudiates it, knows all of its workings, all of its scheming! On 1 September 1938, she is even appointed to the Propaganda Committee for the French banana trade. Her services are appreciated, for she will enjoy two salary increases in less than two years, first in November 1938 and then again in March 1939.

But that still doesn't mean she is a member of the colonial lobby. With Duras, the trapdoors open onto deep, dark passageways; in this career choice, one can also detect defiance and the pain of exile, pleas for parental recognition, equivocal material to be exploited later by the novelist.

3

"The Sources of Pain"

She marries Robert Antelme in 1939, in both a civil and a religious ceremony, as if in that way she might exorcise the imminent threat of war, and retain by this association some of the authenticity that had joined them, the independent lifestyle, united in their adamant refusal of bourgeois marital codes, with their constraints, their impasses, and their pettiness. She wanted their lives to give another meaning to a utopian marriage; perhaps she had in mind the preservation of the solitude that was so important to her as the sole means of gaining access to writing, of preventing the vast, overpowering maelstrom of desire from becoming frozen by habit, by routine, escaping from the idea, absolutely abominable to her, of the Christian couple, with its fidelity, its unconscious betrayals, its repressed desires. What she wanted was to attempt to prolong "the time of love," to resist its fatal erosion, to make herself stronger than that shameful, rampant destruction. Once again, she was choosing the hardest road, the most harrowing trial, cruel, vigilant, and demanding.

With the help of the writer Ramón Fernández, they rented a flat at 5, rue Saint-Benoît, in the sixth arrondissement—a rather large flat with provincial, bourgeois charm, in a small apartment building, not quite within earshot of the busier, picturesque rue Bonaparte, rue Jacob, and the place Saint-Germain-des-Prés. Thus they were living in the heart of the famous bohemian quarter, near the universities, the Seine and its banks, where the Paris sun streams down in the twilight hours, shedding ocher rays on the stone façades and slate or zinc roofs in a way reminiscent of a Vermeer painting or a Baudelaire poem.

She loves this street, "five hundred yards long," with its merchants mainly from the southern French Rouergue region, determined to stay, in that little enclosed society sheltered from the city, beneath the shadow of its massive church. She likes to talk with her neighbors, the Armenian hairdresser, the second-hand dealer at number 3, the old ladies at the hospice. They seem to have been there forever, which reassures her; she appreciates their sedentariness. She thinks of this neighborhood as unassailable, a kind of wall against invaders, speculators, the well-to-do.

Unfortunately she was mistaken: no less than twenty years ago, the street began to undergo a transformation, its restaurants multiplying, with their specialties becoming interchangeable, clothes merchants getting rich off their "fancy rags," and now hotels light up the sidewalks with their arrogant signs. It was not until dawn, perhaps, that Yann Andréa, unable to sleep knowing that Duras was buried in a deep coma in Neuilly, could hear the high-pitched bell of Saint-Germain-des-Prés, the clapping of pigeons' wings passing over the gray zinc roofs and surging into his room. The rest of the time, the street belongs to the dealers, to that disparate, lost, ruined crowd, to those chronically backfiring cars.

How strange, this loss of things, this immersion of sorrow in the city, Broadway on rue Saint-Benoît, just like up on the Normandy coast, in the Hôtel des Roches Noires in Trouville, to the right of the sea; when you look at it from the high windows, all you see is the new industrial town of Antifer, with its oil drums and its wreaths of smoke billowing across the sky, blowing away the smell of the sea.

It disappears slowly, like something gnawing at you, which you accept however reluctantly, as if prompted by an ancient habit of seeing everything fade away and vanish. For the time being, however, she finds this street unusually charming, resembling an island in its own way, flanked a little further on by its river which gives the town that unconsolable grandeur and beauty.

She must have been inwardly, carnally unconsoled for the loss of that land of her childhood, for how else can one understand the little-known book written in joint authorship with Philippe Roques, published in May 1940 by Gallimard, entitled *L'Empire français*, and signed Marguerite Donnadieu, with no bibliography whatsoever, if not as this last desperate appeal to the Father, the last concession to the repudiated name? Indeed, what other interpretation can one give to that hymn to the "motherland," to "la douce France," to the glory of colonial power, to the "infinite goodness and intelligence of France," this homage to Mendel, Bugeaud, Colonel Mangin, Field Marshals Lyautey and Joffre, even Gallieni, if not as the ultimate atonement before burying the Father?

Nonetheless, in the chapter devoted to Indochina she lets her future imagination speak: the Mekong with its nearly three thousand miles in length, encircling French Indochina from upper Laos to the Cambodian border, "the Sovereign of the Waters due to its majestic course and its breadth," the rushes and the mangroves, and Saigon, the port city, and Cholon, the scene of *The Lover*, with its apartment buildings, its restaurants, its silk and jade shops, "the noise of its streets and its late-night parties," and especially the Little and the Great Hanoi Lakes, with their luxurious sunsets and the pagodas along their shores.

But the writer cannot come into her own until she gives up this paternal name, Donnadieu, to whom she turns in her homework assignment on colonization, like a good student having learned well the civics lesson that he used to teach after the mathematics classes. There would be a real writer only when her name was Duras—the Duras who was born and dwelt in exile to denounce, avenge, and spread far and wide the secret of her native land.

At the beginning of the war, she is already taking it upon herself to set down the story of a family that she carries inside her, a first novel with the inevitable attempts at resolving childhood problems, family tensions, and adolescent conflicts. She writes, faithful to the promise she had always made to herself, ever since Indochina, but also, as she acknowledges, out of boredom: "Boredom is the basis for all writing." She calls this novel *La Famille Taneran*. Raymond Queneau, to whom she takes the manuscript, since he is working for the Gallimard publishing house at the time, finds its style admirable, detecting in this first attempt at fiction an atmosphere unique to the young author, a particular tone, a mood alternating, despite its detachment, between the savage violence reigning within the family and submission to the summer heat, the wind, the terraced lands of the Quercy plateau in southwestern France.

Vastly cultured, gifted with protean curiosity, Raymond Queneau bore infinite sympathy for young writers, and possessed a tremendous capacity for listening to them. A contributor to *La Nouvelle Revue française*, the essential guide to literature between the wars, a philosopher, linguist, mathematician, poet, juggler of words and ideas, all at the same time, he takes a keen interest in Duras, who already shows promise in the original way in which she combines the art of dialogue, the power of imagination, and masterful writing, all qualities he looks for.

Approachable as few others in that world, he alone at Gallimard is fully acquainted with emerging literature, unearthing the future author in a manuscript, detecting a new touch, a rich imagination.

In this novel of intersecting passions, already containing her whole story, he can tell how much she has inherited from Mauriac. They describe the same harsh, conflictual situations, on lands both rich and desolate. Spontaneously, he finds that they share this network of brutal, contradictory, suppressed tensions, but he also admires everything that proceeds solely from her, the description of time, its flight, its slipping away, like a heavy, sluggish fluid, the presence of "isolated, familiar" noises haunting the countryside, suspended in the air, fixed in eternity, now rendered almost silent by the mere fact of remaining there, like "the murmur of the sea," untiring and forgotten.

Something profoundly lyrical unfolded there, but this lyricism resembled that of turn-of-the-century writers, while at the same time trying to find its own way, giving rise to a song already made personal by the obsession with signs and by the secret presence of things.

Nonetheless, in spite of the author's obvious stylistic abilities, Gallimard rejected the novel. But since Duras and Antelme were on very friendly terms with two readers at the Plon publishing house, Paul-Vincent Faure-Biguet and Dominique Arban, it occurred to Antelme to take Duras's manuscript to them.

In her memoirs, Dominique Arban relates the anecdote vividly. One can imagine Antelme showing up at her apartment, at eight o'clock in the morning, starting right in with her about Duras's manuscript, as she got out of bed:

"I'm warning you . . . if you don't tell her she's a writer, she'll kill herself."

Seeing Dominique Arban's surprise upon hearing this, Antelme insists: "I have nothing else to say. She'll kill herself."

It's summertime. She reads the novel. Lets herself be taken in by the dramatic play. Recognizing here and there the inevitable influence of Mauriac, of Hemingway, she is nonetheless sure that this is the work of an artist. Enthusiastic, she asks Faure-Biguet to read it, then Bourdel, the director of Plon. The book is accepted. It is published in 1943 under the title *Les Impudents*. "Marguerite Duras" was born.

She was indeed impudent in decreeing that she would no longer be called Donnadieu, after that absent father she had scarcely known but who, by his very name, had left them an unconscious, fatal heritage, while condemning them to exile, leaving them in the hands of that mother entirely devoted to her oldest son, to the point of abandoning them, refusing them the love they were so ardently begging for.

From now on she would be called Duras, Marguerite Duras, of that name she was sure, with the same certainty displayed by her mother when she would prophesy, announcing to them in terrifying, premonitory tirades, future events to come, misfortunes that she claimed would come swooping down upon them.

She was sure that it would become a writer's name, that she would carry it far. Duras, meaning that place of family and childhood, the countryhouse that the father owned, the small, straggling village in the Lot-et-Garonne region in southwestern France, perched on a mountain, and proud, with its dilapidated medieval castle, surrounded by the entire vast Marmande plain leading all the way to the Pyrenees on one side, and on the other, to the sea. Duras: to escape from that God she had always refused to believe in, even as a little girl, in spite of the catechism lessons their mother inflicted on them, while she remained susceptible only to the spirit of that Asian land, to that blend of strange, luxuriant rituals, lavish with fragrances and colors, and to that unceasing freedom to which she had dedicated her life ever since the escapades in the jungle, the same desperate flights that put a wild, untamable look in her eyes, and gave her a taste for defiance.

She would adopt the new name in order to be an outlaw, with no legal identity, a name for which she alone would assume responsibility, modifying it when necessary, completely caught up in the nocturnal adventure of writing, into which she would plunge to the point of destroying herself, diluting herself, slipping into the world's fracture, divorced from all civil status, in unknown spaces, where henceforth she would be quite simply M. D., with no referent whatsoever. M. D., a writer, that's all, with that life unique to writers. "Yes, M. D.," she would write. "That's it. That and nothing else."

This confidence in writing that would come to her is the same as that of those mystics of the Christian faith who, from their earliest maidenhood, frighten others by the tenacity with which they give themselves to God. Is her consciousness of the difficulty of being such that, as of this moment, she envisions herself becoming entirely devoted to the toil of writing? As she says later about Anne-Marie Stretter, she too is "crucified from within by all that is intolerable in the world." She will have to dilute herself in the literary work, melt into the great matrix of the book, furrow it with her own suffering, empty herself into it, presenting it exactly as it comes, brutally, with no concern for herself, without listening even to the contradictory rumors of her psychology, but creating echoes of what she, Duras, sees and reflects, as if reverberating through her memory and the gaps in it. "Only by virtue of my failing to exist does it [the book] exist so fully," she says. From that point on, so much for the little events of her everyday life, acts of much less importance than writing. All that count are these wells of silence, black and deep, into which one must plunge in order to hear the vibrations. Even her reading at that time leads her down into those dark abysses that she will try to illuminate: Kafka, Gide, Stendhal.

The outbreak of the war, the German Occupation, life and its difficulties had not yet bound her to any particular political activity; she was one of those refractory beings, possessed by "a spirit of insubordination, of disagreement," as Dionys Mascolo will explain later.

There was no way for Duras to conceal that subversive force. Her entire being revealed that tension of the soul, that intelligence coupled with instinctive, brute strength which became more frightening, appeared more dangerous with every passing moment.

Her position is terminated by the Vichy government on 30 September 1940. She thus leaves the Ministry of Colonial Affairs and its administrative network. Henceforth her only tie with the land of Indochina would be the writing that brewed within her, soon to produce the epic song, the lyric hymn of *The Sea Wall*.

Her next job is at the Cercle de la Librairie, where she is now in charge of administrative rather than literary matters. Her role in this bureau will nonetheless become more important during the Occupation and at the end of the war. If she saw all writers, all publishers file by at one time or another, if she was thus introduced to the intricacies of the literary establishment, she also discovered the ignominious conditions imposed by the

Nazi occupier, from the very position she now held in the office of paper allocation.

Pétain had in fact established by decree a commission for the monitoring of paper used for publishing. As of 1942, publishing firms were thus limited to restricted publications, preventing the creation of any truly original work, and favoring the choices of the Propagandastaffel, to which all manuscripts were submitted after having been selected by the Cercle de la Librairie, then accepted by the commission. The quantity of paper allocated for publishing was reduced considerably: it went from 36,000 to 240 tons. That was very little, considering that most of the paper was reserved for writers cooperating, if not frankly collaborating, with the enemy, like Drieu la Rochelle and his friends at the *NRF*, and Nazi writers. High-handedness was the general rule, and it wasn't uncommon to run into publishers in the offices of the Propagandastaffel who had come there to compromise themselves in order to obtain permission to publish. "How many genuflections and repudiations in the French literary world of 1941!" exclaimed Jean Zay, Minister of Education under Prime Minister Léon Blum in the late 1930s, detained at the time in a Vichyist prison, before being assassinated by the fascists.

Authors therefore tried their luck at the offices of the Cercle de la Librairie, hoping to influence fate, to soften the intransigence of the law. Claude Roy thus relates in *Nous* the circumstances surrounding the publication of one of his collections of poetry, which his publisher was having trouble getting printed. Going in person to the offices of the Cercle, he pleaded his cause, implored them to allocate the paper needed for his work. He was received by Marguerite Duras. She asked him about the contents of the manuscript. Claude Roy told her that it contained love poems. She responded by saying that she would do her best, that she would somehow intervene in his favor. Claude Roy obtained satisfaction very quickly, for Duras delivered the required paper to him. Such anecdotes reveal Duras in her moments of dazzling generosity, her unexpected encounters, and the dreamlike situations in which love always has its place, along with utopia.

For his part, Robert Antelme, after having been discharged, is employed as a clerk in the Ministry of the Interior, where he will remain from 1940 until 1944.

Duras's duality lies therein, affirming itself even in the mingled currents of that murky era. She is still a bastard, a half-breed, a creole, fascinated by the violence crashing down on the city and on the world.

She hasn't really taken sides yet, she isn't "political" yet, as she will say much later. The Jews she passes on the street, wearing the humiliating yellow star, don't arouse in her the cry of horror, of despair, of loneliness uttered by the Vice-Consul of Lahore and echoing through her future novels. "We lived in that oblivion, that insensitivity, during a whole period of the Occupation," confides Dionys Mascolo. Is that why she has never stopped voicing the suffering, from the revelation of the Holocaust up to her most recent interviews, as if admitting to an immense sense of guilt that she is unable to expel from herself?

Completely under the spell of solipsism, she had not yet come to grips with the barbarity, the children's misery, the enemy's brutality, the soldiers who had also turned day into night and who, unleashed on the streets like wolves, killed with complete impunity.

Worse, it was as if she were magnetized by what was happening in that city, by the particular status imposed on her, by that abnormality. As she says in *L'Eté 80*, the sounds of war resemble the sounds of the sea and the wind, the convoys give forth the same wailing sounds as the waves. How to avoid their atrocious seduction?

The occupiers' impudence fascinated her, she who was not yet a "Jew" but who enjoyed that "relative security enjoyed by those who are not threatened in their innermost being," as Mascolo put it.

Worse yet, she could already understand those "disorders of the soul," as she says in *Hiroshima Mon Amour*, which cause a woman "to be henceforth without a country other than love itself," "dispossessed" of herself to the point of loving the enemy, like Riva of Nevers.

She could have imagined that "foreign" love, because of the sheer boredom of the war, that indifference it creates after a certain length of time, causing one even to get used to it, to the monotony of its violence, its bursts of machine-gun fire, its shelling, its bombings, its nocturnal descents into basements smelling of saltpeter rot. "In that boredom," she says, "women behind shutters watch the enemy walk across the square. Here the adventure is limited to patriotism. The other adventure must be quashed. One looks all the same. No way to keep one's eyes from looking."

Therein lies Duras's impudence, in her admission that the gaze is an ambiguous act, in that desire sneaking slyly in, behind the inevitable patriotic statements, especially attentive to inner resonances, to appeals to other kinds of logic.

During that dark, evil period, major personal events, bringing her back down to the dimensions of the world and the universe, will seed her life and her imagination. In 1942, she loses her first child at birth, through the fault of a doctor who arrives late. The pain is reborn, the feeling of emptiness, of having given death, of having been the bearer of what became death. She becomes the little beggar woman of Savannakhet once again; she put into port there to give birth to the dead child, and she will set out again, strengthened by the pain still lodged within her, the lot she will always identify with women, "well versed in pain," in that sense different from men who derive their suffering, their tormented existence, from wars, cruelty, rituals. Women's pain is everywhere, in their wombs, in their minds, in the unconsolable knowledge of the world they acquired thousands of years ago and which continues to spread biologically.

On that day in May 1942, the light is white; outside she sees a row of acacias with their flowers grouped together in parasols, also white, and she measures the extent of the disaster, her dead child, and the "terrible" void.

She wants to see it, but everyone—the nuns, Antelme—is opposed to the idea. She wants to know at least what is going to happen to it, this body, this corpse, which looks like her, as they tell her. Since she insists, they admit that it will be burned. Her belly is "a worn-out rag . . . a pall." Thirty-four years later, that love is in her, riveted to her, and she tells *Sorcières* magazine about the horrible pain, the awareness of the void.

The life she lives always brings her back to absence, to abandonment, to that cruel, omnipresent company of death, to the necessity of imagining. The turbulence of the month of May, the sap running throughout the town, despite the oppressive German presence, breaks the silence of the room. The course of time, indifferent, has already forgotten the fatal blunder: "Your child is dead," they told her. Other events are in the making. Only traces are left as reminders.

That same spring of 1942, in the heart of the occupied city, she met Dionys Mascolo.

A reader at Gallimard, he was also responsible for obtaining the imprimatur of the Cercle de la Librairie for the manuscripts that his house planned to publish, and he was in charge, under the watchful eye of the Occupation, of distributing paper and making sure the new publication guidelines were followed. Mascolo met Duras on several occasions, and she entrusted him with reading assignments for the exclusive use of the Cercle. A close relationship thus developed.

Mascolo's temperament—of a rather "dry" type, aggressive and nervous at the same time, endowed with the mixture of violence and tenderness which he possesses even to this day— was certainly closer to hers than was Antelme's. Thus Duras fell madly in love with him in no time at all.

With the modesty, discretion, and self-effacement so characteristic of him, Mascolo will later evoke the relations she managed to establish between him and her husband. Was it the need to create the love triangle always inscribed in her novels? She wants a friendship to develop between Antelme and Mascolo so that the absurd partitions between love and friendship will be abolished, intermingling instead in the drama of love that she would direct. She loves Mascolo in

Antelme's love and vice versa, and the two of them love each other in her love, just as the Vice-Consul will love Anne-Marie Stretter "in Michael Richardson's love." She wants to eliminate the deadly, drowsy routine of the couple, which inevitably rediscovers the solitude from which it was trying to escape. She wants the couple to be reinvented, reinvigorated, so that it may then set in motion "that marvelously unwinding spool, the time of love."

She is trying to carry out, as Mascolo says, "the work of friendship" between him and Antelme, and for that reason she encourages them to meet, even leaving them alone so that they will be in each other's company. Their complicity in this triangle will continue beyond Duras's divorce from Antelme in 1946, beyond the separation from Mascolo in 1957, up until the present time, in spite of Antelme's death and her confinement with Yann Andréa.

What Duras brought to this strange relationship—as though she wanted to make a fantasy real, create a utopia—was the entire weight of her femininity: to magnify the feminine element in these two men whom she loved at the same time, to eradicate from within them the brutality reigning in every man, that "sleeping paratrooper" in all men.

She introduced them to the sphere of women, to their gestures, their customs, their forests, into which, according to legend, men's violent acts have driven them—what Mascolo calls "la féminie," a term he invented to designate that particular comprehension of things and of the world that belongs only to women, in the biological essence of their works, of their language. She accepted both of them into her feminine domain, from which every man is ordinarily excluded, as from the understanding of what women communicate, that song within them, issuing like pain "from everywhere, from the bottom of the world." Even before she goes public with her commitment to women, at a time when her talent as a writer is not yet assured, pulled in different directions by influences too numerous, too visible, she already knows that women are "closer than men to all transgressions," that they have in them capacities for access to silence, to madness, to the child's absence of knowledge, to the innocence which no man will ever approach. By setting up this love triangle, she became its playwright, directing its course, giving it new impetus, so that a new idea of love would begin to circulate, a new force would bring renewal.

This way of living, as if animated by her impudence and the defiance that it represented, nourished new kinds of knowledge, shunned ideology, theoretical dogma, created risks. They might easily have foundered in brutal nihilism, for they defined themselves mainly in terms of what they were against. Duras's music, always the same melodious inspiration that she intended to breathe into them, identified them with poetry, dissidence, the fringe.

This subversive tendency will always fuel her aesthetics. It is as if everything were necessarily destined for somewhere else, a place only accessible by crossroads, tiptoeing across precarious, dangerous footbridges, all the better to give itself, penetrating every hole, every hollow.

In this intellectual love triangle, Duras is thus the source, to the extent that she directs the story, sets the tone. Even today Mascolo bears homage to their relationship, develops the same ideas as hers, giving the impression that the symbiosis between them is absolutely total. Through a kind of mimesis, her very language borrows from that music which snaps things up as they are born, unique to Duras, to her mythic heritage, a subterranean channel where desire, death, and "blind lucidity" circulate alongside femininity, fascination with childhood, and a libertarian spirit.

In her life, in her work to come, there is a perpetual back-and-forth motion, the reawakening of past or more recent suffering, in another surge of pain, a whole network of sorrows that comprises the sedimentary depth of her texts.

At the end of 1942 she will learn by telegram that her little brother has died, the little brother "called back to God." The father's fatal name, Donnadieu, was now confirming its prediction. He had died in Saigon, struck down by bronchopneumonia, during the Japanese Occupation, for lack of medication.

The pain of the stillborn child is revived, merging into the little brother's dead body, far away, thousands of miles away, in Indochina once more, to where he had returned. Coming from a great distance, this madness, this terror takes hold of her, this upheaval of her whole being, this evidence of tragedy, whose influence and intensity she is incapable of understanding. The little brother is dead and in the bright reflection of that darkness, the death of her own son is illuminated, and this scandal from God which ravished the light and denied immortality.

She lives in this succession of chaos and hope, this seesaw of opposites, in a sort of mystical turbulence causing day and night to alternate, the cruel state of blackness with the dazzling glare of whiteness, in their blinding superimpositions, like snow.

Even though they never wrote to each other, the little brother seemed immortal, as if he had stayed over there in order to keep intact the part of their childhood that had always remained secret.

In his company, the mother had begun her life over again, founding an educational institution, the New French School. Her past experience lent her a certain authority. With her usual vigor and determination, she saved money for her children in France, wanting to protect her older son's future, trying to ignore his escapades.

The little brother's death suddenly brought Duras back to that dreadful family which she felt to be so distant and so close at the same time, so hateful and so loving. She will talk about it, especially in *The Lover*, in a lyrical, obsessive assumption of the event. She has also spoken about it in interviews, but never with the same intensity, the same force, as in *The Lover*, as if time had ripened the pain. There are buried zones that she deliberately attempts to bring out in that book, and they spring forth, making everything overflow, modesty, words, syntax. She is driven by two-way movements; she conjures up pain and yearns for the abyss, so that she might vanish in the obscurity.

The little brother's death triggers in her something she is un-aware of, stronger than the death of her own son: the idea of God breaking his word, of an ignoble scandal that he had per-petrated upon him, upon the little brother's fragile body, upon his skin as soft and smooth as the water in the earthenware jars upon her skin when the Chinese lover poured it over her.

Never had she imagined that the little brother's body was hers too, and that when he died, she had to die as well. She sings of this death by consumption until she loses herself completely. The world may well go on, but she no longer exists, she is dead: "He drew me to him and I died."

She is surprised, frightened by the frantic tension that takes hold of her, as though, with the little brother dead, she were exposed, gaping at madness, at the natural inclination she had always suspected in her family, especially in her mother. He was a last rampart against all that, destruction, death. She hadn't kept up any particular correspondence with him, but he was the one who had protected her. Without him, she now understood that there were risks, dangers she would have to get used to, the imminence of nothingness, of emptiness.

With him dead, the coast was clear for the older brother, for his "reign," and the war became total, universal. Even in exile, the little brother temporarily saved her from the activities of the older one, the "hooligan"; now she has the feeling that he is on the prowl, that he is creeping all around, into their minds, into their houses, through the streets, down hallways, into their letters, into their mother. That he delights in this power he has over her, over them, in spite of everything.

Images flash through her pain, those never-ending ones of her childhood, images of mourning, of death, and the dark shadow of the older brother, weighing on both of them, ap-parently never noticed by the mother, even though it sowed fear greater than the escapades in the jungle where the black panthers were waiting to take them by surprise and the little crocodiles lay in the tumultuous waters of the *racs*, ready to be provoked.

Those abysses are where her life can be best explained, her work best understood. The facts themselves are not what matter, but the traces left by them, the tracks that sometimes unexpectedly emerge from the chaotic course of time. And all she can tell about it is the grasping, the hesitant quest, and the work takes on the fragile status of a testimony.

Powerful projectors suddenly light up the stage like an arena, disturb the tenuous peace, throw her into the anarchy of pain and despair, ravage her. She has to get used to that; the only advantage of this life is in the echo of things that have disappeared and have been reinvented by oblivion. The rest of the days get bogged down like other people's lives in the yellow mud of time, photographs fade and turn gray, rust and split like glass, but the turbulence of certain images she thought buried is terrible. Thus the Mekong solemn and superb, thus the little brother with the Annamese face, a heart so simple, so fragile that it might burst, thus the mother's cries, thus the dreadfully black whiteness of the snow which covers the concentration camps and whose pale glimmer will soon appear.

It is in 1943, when *Les Impudents* is published, that Duras, Antelme, and Mascolo join the Resistance. Two Durases exist side by side, one riveted to the business of writing she feels so deeply within her, almost fatally, and the other launched on a clandestine adventure, with that savage instinct pushing her into the deadly arena.

She finds that same heedless, impudent instinct, that art of defying with elegance, in the person of François Mitterrand, who in August 1942 organized his own Resistance network in order to locate escaped prisoners, as he says in his little book published after the liberation of Paris, *Prisonniers de guerre devant la politique* [The Political Challenge Facing Prisoners of War], in order to create emergency support channels, regrouping them into combat units "so that they might participate in every form of struggle against the enemy."

Very quickly, the network so prospered that the leaders of the Resistance established close contacts with it. Of course, in 1943 François Mitterrand alias Morland began communicating information of the greatest importance, as pointed out by Pierre Guillain de Bénouville, who notes: "Thanks to the prisoners of war, we were able to gain access to facts, sometimes decisive facts, concerning what was going on behind the borders."

Indeed his network, the National Movement for Prisoners of War and Deportees, had even spread throughout the camps in Germany, whence he received first-rate information.

Mitterrand, a "mysterious but efficient" man, with a "furiously romantic" side, as he was described by Jacques Baumel and Philippe Dechartre in 1943, had a personality that couldn't fail to attract Duras, always fascinated by people with exceptional qualities, sure of their destinies, fierce like her, intransigent, untamed.

She gives a novelist's version of their joining the Resistance network. What she says to the French president in 1986 is neither a realistic nor a straightforward description of it, but an oblique, almost cinematic view, from a parallel angle. Mitterrand meets Antelme, Mascolo, and Duras at their apartment on rue Saint-Benoît. There is a stove in front of the drawing room fireplace, "one of those made from old oil barrels and that burned compressed newspaper briquets." The three men are conversing on one side of the room. "And all of a sudden," Mitterrand starts smoking. Smoke fills the air, and as if informed by a vague recollection, she detects "the smell of English cigarettes," forgotten years ago. "I cried: *But you're smoking an English cigarette!* You said: *Oh! sorry . . . .* You took your pack and the cigarette you were smoking and threw them into the fire. The three of you immediately began talking about something else. That evening I asked Mascolo if it was really what I was thinking, London; he said he didn't know. I never got an explanation about where the English cigarette had come from. But I understood right then that we had joined the Resistance, that the dice had been thrown."

The story unfolds like a movie playing in her memory forty-three years later, going back, finding the same old places, the familiar odors, in that sensual impressionism which guides her back through time, gathering details, reconstituting situations.

But was her impatience great enough to make her take the risk of publishing in 1943 during the German Occupation? Her political determination hadn't become total yet. Unable to imagine the atrocities she will later witness, or Antelme's captivity and the incredible pain it will produce, she hadn't become completely overtaken by the shame with which literature will soon fill her. She agreed to the publication of *Les Impudents* in occupied Paris, but she was not alone: there was Gide, Sartre, and Beauvoir, and even Paulhan, Mauriac, Eluard, and Aragon. For Duras, for whom it was the first real book, there was a necessity, a violent desire for recognition; she had yet to discover the cellars, the wells, and the underground passageways, the shadowy existence of those living secretly, the rage to kill the Germans, to gain ground on them, the immense anger that would take hold of her: she hadn't lived any of that, and nonetheless she could feel writing tremble inside of her, and the obscure, luminous flashes that it would send out.

She was beginning to embark on the same journeys into the unknown as Henri Michaux, who had only recently come to see her in her apartment. Michaux had already written many of his major texts: *Qui je fus* in 1927, *La nuit remue* in 1934, and during that Occupation period, *Exorcismes*. She was totally familiar with his work because she detected in it her own desire to be elsewhere, that same taste for traveling "to the land of magic." She liked listening to him or surprising his sphinxlike silence because she could hear voices from what he called "the other side," far from this "choking, cold-bellied" world!

Perhaps it will seem surprising that Duras, Antelme, and Mascolo were so late in joining the Resistance. Motivated by a taste for individual adventure, they must have thought that this new clandestine life would give them a share of the danger, provide a meaning to this enterprise, bring them closer to others, as if a fraternal awareness were awakening in them. Their entry into the network corresponded to an assumption, a comprehension, of the world both new and irrevocable.

Always at the heart of such paradoxes, and of the dangers that pass through her life, she nonetheless makes her apartment on rue Saint-Benoît a secret rendezvous for members of the Resistance, a hideout for Jews, when directly above them live Ramón Fernández, cultural adviser to Jacques Doriot's fascist Parti populaire français (PPF), and his wife Betty. A shrine of collaboration, their apartment is open to Drieu la Rochelle, a talented writer and active collaborator who also publishes texts by Fernández in the *NRF*, and above all Gerhard Heller, representative of the Propagandastaffel, which at that time wielded complete authority over French literary activities.

In spite of the Occupation and their opposing commitments, Duras was on visiting terms with Fernández, who had found this apartment for her, and if they were not unaware of each other's activities, they were joined together by a kind of tacit, unspoken agreement. Sometimes Duras even accepted invitations from the Fernándezes, and in fact the proximity of risk, the promiscuity of that deadly corrida, increases her pleasure at being there, small, alone, but fierce, strong, self-assured, confident in her authority, among all of these fascists, collaborators, mortal enemies.

Did she feel real fascination for that strange circle? In the company of Mascolo, Antelme, her own friends and family, she found fraternity, almost happiness in the battle they were all waging, but she was intrigued by the others, their neighbors, as if the novelist found material therein for the exercise of her immense curiosity, arriving at a new, extraordinary understanding of people, never to be recaptured in other times, as if the moment were too exceptional to be thrown away.

It was this world of agony and boredom that she liked, and the violence of the feelings emanating from it, the taste for betrayal, as when she would later seek out murderers and condemned men, rapists and outcasts, for interview material.

The more she observed that world, the stronger her desire to plunge, as Drieu la Rochelle would have said, into "the herd sweating fear and hatred," to make common cause with them, to accompany them, to prevent them from going to the slaughterhouse. That herd, composed of Jews and communists, victims and martyrs, was precisely the group Drieu and his friends wanted to flee and disown, feeling the arrogant joy of the chosen, "the happy few." The more deeply she analyzed their reactions, the further her choices would be from those of Drieu, "in the crowd," a part of it, overwhelmed by an immense love that would transcend personal feelings, but a vast, limitless love for men, the anonymous, the nameless, captured, rounded up, as defenseless as children.

A presentiment would also announce to her the abyss opening up before that society of traitors. Fear too, the immense weariness that she detected in them, contrary to their very energy, their clandestine euphoria, another fear, not that of death agonies, of Good Fridays, but the fear aroused by the desire to live. Two worlds faced each other in that little apartment building where Sainte-Beuve had once lived: the entire war was in fact brought together on two floors. Duras's flat was home to the love of humankind and the force of life, while upstairs reigned, as Sartre said, "self-hatred—and its offspring, hatred of others."

This mole's life, these underground networks in which Duras now moved, were well suited to her nature, as unpredictable as it was secretive, fierce, attentive to silences, and to the vague rumors of all that is hidden, concealed. Having only recently changed her name to Duras, "horrified" by her real name, Donnadieu, an "unspeakable" name, inventing another one for herself, thereby appropriating the father's strength, she could now slip into the shadows, anonymous, reduced to nothing more than her small, hurried silhouette, running through the car-deserted, bicycle-filled streets of Paris, a gray Paris of pedestrians in which people spied on one another, suspected each other, and gave of themselves. In her interviews with François Mitterrand forty-three years later, she tells, with stunningly fresh memories, what their lives were like in those days, the traps to avoid, the ruses to watch out for, the fear, the anxiety, "the fear of being shot, each day, each night."

"I don't think people can imagine," she says, "what our lives were like. We couldn't invite friends over, there was no such thing, we had to phone each other and meet outside, in places beyond suspicion; it took hours just to exchange three bits of information."

Is it because of the war and her life of danger that the novel she wrote in 1942-1943 and published in 1944, *La Vie tranquille*, took a harsher, more violent turn than the first one? There was certainly that same family structure, and even the same setting of Périgord in southwestern France, the same dilapidated house, but the novel was more reminiscent of Faulkner's or Steinbeck's primitive, uncouth worlds than of the psychological tensions in Mauriac's novels. It appeared more as if the author had drawn inspiration from the mood of the times, from rising existentialism and particularly from *The Stranger*, published in 1942 by Gallimard.

This time the manuscript was accepted by Gallimard; still faithful to Duras, Queneau saw in it the confirmation of his intuition, the certainty of being in the presence of a female Camus, for with this novel Duras introduced a new tone, as if driven by the urgency of living, by suddenly attainable happiness in the absurd course of time.

Was she Francine this time, the heroine of *La Vie tranquille?* She had undoubtedly slipped into her skin, adopting her hopes, refusing the slow death that the entire family suffered as fate, realizing that her liberated body was suffocating in the closed family circle. And once again, the sea answered her call. By coming into contact with it she discovers how fragile life is; there is this bar with a foamy crest, deadly to cross though not far from the shore, and there is the water carrying it, with the "delicious noise of its heart beating." The sea is both life and death at the same time, pleasure and danger, "we are present in this present," and sometimes it metes out death. It is in this perpetual back-and-forth motion that she discovers her true nature, ever wild, eager, uninhibited. She is in occupied Paris, with Germans passing by her on the street, and every Frenchman suspected of resistance or collaboration. Something ardent within her is trembling, burning to go forward; like her heroine, she wants to say: "I lived . . . off their expectations for so long that I'm the one who finally dug my nails into the leather bottle of dreams, making it burst." Her joining the Resistance might be just that, exhausted patience determined to act.

"Now," she says in the novel, "time is old." Indeed it was, and she had to recover youth, attempt to remove the millstone around the city's neck, recover, through the pleasure it procures, a taste for sun warming one's skin, and the smell of the sea, rediscover joy and enthusiasm. Like Francine, she no longer wanted to be "miserly" with her life.

Even her language had evolved, from one book to the next, and in so little time. The breath that animated her was more nervous, the lyric outpouring less ponderous, one that tried to express sensations rapidly, bringing to words an elliptic liveliness.

She was already a person who refused the fixity of things, of others, their lack of mobility, of ambiguity, for she believed that truth could only be attained in that perpetual movement of life, in those paradoxes that made it elusive, disconcerting. Her publishing work, the first reactions after *Les Impudents* came out, the certainty that a singular new voice had appeared, one that would have to be reckoned with from now on, the very magnetism of her personality—all this soon made her "fashionable." As of 1943, then, she could be seen at social gatherings in the wealthy neighborhoods near the Trocadéro, at the homes of women who were rich or had once been, and who still entertained. She was seen in the company of Drieu la Rochelle, the Fernándezes, and they talked about Balzac, Mallarmé, always about literature. From the balconies where they lunched on fine days, getting some fresh air when it was too smoky indoors, one could see the faint lights of Paris, the trembling, bluish waters of the Seine, yellow headlights sweeping across the empty, alien streets.

It was already like something from *India Song* floating in the air: one of the guests, seated at the grand piano, was surely playing a slow melody irresistibly reminiscent of exile; from the gardens below rose the fragrance of catalpas, and women glided between the furniture, exquisite, delicate, like the forgotten silhouette of Elizabeth Striedter.

Yes, it must have been like that, a place of forgetting. And a place of innocence, of youth preserved, sheltered from short-lived time, from "the complete bringing to light of the crime." The days would soon grow shorter; patches of night would suddenly descend upon them.

She was happy there, too, in those places where she didn't belong, with the violence in her heart, she who was born nowhere, a foreigner like the women receiving her, Betty Fernández, Marie-Claude Carpenter.

Later she regretted not having been able to speak at length with Drieu la Rochelle, who had taken over *NRF* following Jean Paulhan's resignation, and whose anti-Semitic rage and collaboration were beginning to appear fascinating. She would have liked to hunt down in him, to ferret out, using her inimitable sixth sense, the suffering and the madness that undoubtedly kept him in those murky zones.

Of course, death throes were in the air at *NRF*, and all around Drieu lurked the suicide that haunted him. Violent, deadly tensions animated the review; Gallimard had even drawn up an agreement with the Germans, and they were paying a price for permission to continue publishing most of their authors, from Salacrou to Eluard, from Michaux to Camus, from Ponge to Claudel, from Joyce to Queneau, and even Aragon, who was ready to make so many concessions, while they refused to publish Jewish authors, and turned the review over to Drieu. That whole ambiguous, paradoxical context didn't bother Duras, always attracted by opposing impulses, by the peculiar things that thickened the dark night of human souls, making their behavior even more equivocal.

Drieu was thus the ignoble man, "the man with the little fits of anger . . . and attacks of nerves," as Sartre maliciously portrayed him, but sublime too on account of his solitude, his pride, all of which Duras had seen in him at the Fernándezes: "He spoke little in order not to be condescending, with a dubbed voice, as if in a strained, translated language." He seemed cornered, surrounded by fear, as he admitted in his

Secret Journal, and his long silhouette topped off with "an enormous, dented head" (again in Sartre's words) dragging himself around drawing rooms like a broken man, cut loose, caught in a mortal, metaphysically unbearable "ennui."

Came the month of June 1944. She had already undergone the painful experience of the little brother's death, then the permanent fear that she would in turn die, or be killed, but always with the force to resist, in occupied Paris, the rage to take risks anyway, for after all, that too was what writing was about. She needed to put her life on the line, throwing it into the living arena, as in a bullfight, "to introduce the shadow of a bull's horn" into this danger-filled existence, as defined in the writings of her friend and neighbor Michel Leiris. It was no longer merely a question of writing, in that gray, black Paris where, in the evening, the vague silhouettes of the Gestapo glided by, slipping into apartment building courtyards, hammering at doors, and going away with their prey. How could one think about writing in such times? The very act of writing was transformed, turned into an act of solidarity that consisted of outsmarting the enemy, of setting invisible traps for him, of saving anonymous, innocent people. During that time Duras possessed a gratuitous generosity and a spontaneity that brought her closer to others, a freshness of heart that made her willing to take risks, to forget about fear. But there was nonetheless, buried within her, a kind of ancient terror, not for oneself, but abstract, unable to assume a precise shape, like the fate weighing heavily on Antigone, beneath the overwhelming torpor of Thebes.

"No, we couldn't do anything," she said, except fight, forgetting themselves in that fraternal community of the vanquished, the exiled, defying the Occupation forces, turning into moles in order to carry on the struggle, learning new ways of fighting, using, against the familiar sound of boots, the power of the night, the ardent tones of a different song, lashing ever tighter the ropes that bound them to man, with the proof that there really is one, reimposing love.

In the city occupied by the enemy, life follows its course, all but indifferent to the German banners, the "great theatrical swastika flags," as Claude Roy said, hanging from the facades of hotels and ministries.

All of the activity around Saint-Germain-des-Prés, formerly such a lively part of town, became concentrated in the cafés, "the only place where you could eat, drink, entertain, work." Le Flore and Les Deux Magots are always full, and one can meet Beauvoir and Adamov there, Sartre and Mouloudji, the Kabyle who sang of nostalgia, and Audiberti. Some had decided to leave the capital, Sartre and Beauvoir for example, but had come back, drawn by the proximity of the risk in which intellectuals must have lived there. Strange village, Saint-Germain, where collaborators and Resistance fighters carry on like neighbors, as in the offices of Gallimard where Drieu la Rochelle's friends put the finishing touches on the latest issue of NRF, while, around Jean Paulhan's desk (relates Dominique Aury) "there was always a crowd of people, packed like sardines." Eluard and members of the National Committee of Writers go up there, keeping a low profile, hoping not to run into Drieu in the hallways.

Even more intense is the Resistance fighters' underground activity, in stark contrast to the collaborator's arrogance, as they secretly exchange documents, manuscripts, tracts. This mole's life alternates with celebrations of an excessive, almost surreal nature, as if they were meant to defy the Occupation, calm the fear, the anger, and the humiliation, pacify the murderous instincts circulating everywhere. The main guests at the Leirises are painters and writers, and Picasso, Camus, Sartre and Jean-Louis Barrault, Lacan and Bataille, Beauvoir and Braque can be seen enacting plays there, drinking all night, and awaiting, in a frenzied state described in detail by Beauvoir in her *Memoirs*, the first hours of the day, after the curfew has ended.

The story of the Tanerans, that impudent family torn apart by conflicts, was of no concern to her now, for she was completely caught up in this war situation, which opened up to her personal things still buried within her and that now rose up again; this love for men caught indissolubly in the great maelstrom that destroyed, interned, assassinated them. And also the disobedience, the refusal to accept momentarily victorious, triumphant, obscene leaders.

What remained of writing, except for the derisory knowledge that one must remain in that very tension of life? That too was writing, especially that, as if the war and the Occupation had restored the true definition of writing.

But was it the same thing, the same pain, the same disarray, to know that Resistance fighters and Jews had been penned up, and then sent off to internment camps that one knew nothing about, to learn that this man, your very own husband, Robert Antelme, had just been arrested this June 1st, 1944, at the house of his sister, Marie-Louise, who would die a few months later as a result of what happened at Ravensbrück? Was it the same tragedy, the impossibility of imagining absence, of knowing that it was elsewhere, in this absolute suffering, this solitude, at the mercy of the barbarians? Would she make it back unscathed to her point of departure?

So it is the first day of June 1944, at 5, rue Dupin, where Marie-Louise Antelme is doing the honors in the absence of her parents, who have left for Corsica. The tiny street looks out onto the rue de Sèvres and the rue du Cherche-Midi. The apartment is right above the post office. In his conversation with Duras on 26 February 1986, François Mitterrand relates the circumstances of the arrest. "When the Gestapo came in, there was Jean Munier, Robert, Marie-Louise, Paul Philippe and his wife, and I don't know who else. . . . Munier thought quickly enough to charge into the mass of people, catching them off guard, then running down the stairs and coming out on rue Dupin, a free man." François Mitterrand had also been planning to go to the meeting on rue Dupin. As usual, he called Marie-Louise beforehand, and she answered: "Why insist, sir? I'm telling you you've got the wrong number." Alerted that the Gestapo were in the apartment, he very carefully, very calmly phoned Duras, telling her that there was "a fire where she was, that it was spreading very rapidly, and that she must leave rue Saint-Benoît within ten minutes." Since the police had not yet sealed the street off, he was able to make it out of the post office, then out of rue Dupin, hurrying over to rue Saint-Benoît, where he stood in the middle of the street so that he could wave to Duras who was some distance away, pointing out the best escape route. Such an existence, clandestine, on the very edge of danger, is where Duras's real life can be grasped, as she crosses the arena with her usual impudence, and her gut-level feeling of rage.

Meanwhile, up in Normandy, the Allies land in June 1944. Villages, roads, small towns, cities are rescued one after another from the invaders. There may be cause for hope already. On rue Saint-Benoît, no news but this: Antelme is in Fresnes, then in Compiègne, then in Buchenwald. Lost, forgotten, subjected to deportation and internment, hurled toward an unforseeable future, does he remember what he wrote a few months earlier and was just recently published in *Littérature*, the poem entitled "Train" which, like a premonition, sings of the night of wandering, of the days and weeks unwinding without end?

> The night is worn away by the noise of the train,
> The earth moans softly beneath the journey,
> Upon the faces the noise
> Presses the blue pangs of death.
> This murmur
> Is the wind,
> On the roads fleeing the shadow of cathedrals,
> The train turns over and over in the night
> Where the wheat all becomes silent.
> And we are the travelers:
> Beneath the eyelids of the crushed man facing you,
> Beneath the swollen fold of our camaraderies
> And in these crossroads of our stupidities,
> This murmur
> Is the cry of the eradicated neighborhoods
> And the obliterated names.
> The train prays, howling

For those it has abandoned;
The noise in its fury,
Against every house,
Watches over its stray ones.

Now comes silence, darkness, and doubt. "There is no reason for him to come back. It is possible that he will come
back."

In Paris the wildest rumors circulate. The impassive Seine
continues to carry along its dark water; in the streets, on the
bridges, people walk quickly, having heard that towns are falling one by one into the hands of the Allies. What is the fate of
those just recently deported? And if the Germans decided, in
their defeat, to take their victims along with them?

In an attempt to calm the terror, to temper the panic gaining ground, spreading deep inside her, Duras keeps busy, trying
to find out whatever she can. At that time she is thin, pale,
"dry as a bone," she says. A mad, desperate energy possesses
her, but in stages, pain alternates with activism, an anesthetizing force, capable of erasing almost everything from memory,
danger as well as love.

She will go for months without news, not a single bit of
news, of Robert Antelme, her husband, apart from the images
in her nightmares, sometimes like holes, pits making her
stumble and join him in the oblivion of the camps, that enclosed space where life and death overlap in a ritual movement, like another form of the deadly arena in which she seems
always to have lived.

Duras's commitment intensifies, as if redoubled, even galvanized by Antelme's absence. She creates a search agency
within the framework of the magazine *Libres*, the mouthpiece
of the National Movement for Prisoners of War, to which was
soon added "and Deportees": the MNPDGD. The agency's goal
is to shed light on deportation activity, transmit escaped prisoners' testimony, and serve as a link among their families. The
little group on rue Saint-Benoît is excited during this fall of
1944, busy as a beehive, so active that it seems better informed
than the ministerial staffs.

Duras is propelled by a kind of brutal, archaic rage during
that period. She dedicates herself to this cause with such fervor
that she forgets herself, animated by what Mascolo calls "a task
of loving devotion."

In any event, the only choice now is to move forward, no
longer even thinking, but simply attempting to survive, and
to know, to proceed until she is absolutely certain of what
she suspects, in fact confirming what the scattered, multiple
reports of escapees already mention: horror, loss of human
feelings. But she has actually known that for a long time. Since
childhood, she has known about the passing shadow of death.
Living, brutal, primitive.

In *The War*, which she publishes in September 1985, she
relates this horror of the primeval mists of time, still and forever coiled up in her pitch-dark night. She puts potatoes
on the stove, she is in the kitchen, and it is the belly of the
night, the black core of the night; she feels it and cries out—
her writing of the moment is that cry. That is what writing is,
the cry tearing apart the instant, the cry containing the only
possible words.

Still inside her is this continual, heartrending force that
sways to and fro, hurting her, tossing her from one place to
another, and that is where she will seek the terrifying energy
she holds within her, the force that makes her persevere.

She lives in these ruptures of time, in its chaos. She doesn't
know how to do anything else but live like that, resigned about
the course of things, revolted, indifferent and impassioned at
the same time, gentle and violent. Sometimes she receives
more news of the older brother. And yet, since the little
brother's death he has ceased to exist in her mind, as if de-
leted, erased from her life, from her imagination, but he keeps
coming back, elsewhere, metaphorically, like the ongoing war,
capable of the worst: "Maybe he has turned people in, Jews,
you never know." He pays her a visit during the Occupation,
arriving like an urchin to ask for money, and she gives in, not
having strength enough to "kill" him. She leaves him alone
in the house on rue Saint-Benoît, going off in search of news

about Antelme: she knows that he is going through everything, the armoires, the chests of drawers, just in case there might be something he can carry off. She feels as if she had brought a collaborator into her home, one of those ignobly memorable ransackers, with a dirty appearance and a mind to match. And he takes everything he can find, food, money, jewelry. She asks François Mitterrand, the leader of her Resistance network, to lend him his little studio apartment on La Place des Victoires, during Mitterrand's absence. "It was just one room, on the ground floor, very nice," Mitterrand says. "When I returned, there was nothing left inside, it had been cleaned out."

But she doesn't even want to know what he is doing, whether or not he is a collaborator, preferring silence; as far as she is concerned, he has died. All that remain are the lingering traces of his stench, and this hatred transformed into indifference.

There is thus no other alternative but that of action, in the "needless generosity" with which Mascolo credits her, and the barren loneliness of her cry, as if she, the writer, saw no other application but in that heroic adventure. Any other act, any other attempt would be subordinate, derisory, even despicable compared to this absence, this immense collective solitude, this conflagration of the world, these millions of dead lying in the mud of ditches, beneath the indifferent sky. "Literature made me ashamed," she admits in *The War*.

If she has one persistent quality, it is that constant mobility for articulation and bearing witness. Film, the novel, the interview, debate, silence, a cry from the heart—not a single genre, not one condition that fails to institutionalize the moment, to choose the appropriate, the best expression, at the most crucial source of pain, of distress.

She who convinces the man she calls Rabier, the Gestapo agent who arrested Antelme, that she "writes books, nothing else interests her," is in fact frenetically committed. She lives in a state of urgency in which literature no longer has any place. Too many disturbing premonitory symptoms appear, man's liberty is at stake, his responsibility as a man, his dignity.

This period calls into question the basic assumptions of literature, of which she was already suspicious. Sartre, Malraux, and
Camus wanted to bend literature to intellectual commitment,
but henceforth she doesn't know where Antelme is; she wants
to save him, and beyond him, assume her part of the danger,
using ruse and imagination to break hatred, terrorism, the soldiers, and the ignominious enemies.

And yet she takes notes on this period, notes that she will
later adapt to the rhythm of writing, in *The War*. There is
suffering in what she is saying, what she is living, and also an
infinite aptitude for transporting herself to the death camp,
placing herself in the arena, at the heart of risk, with Rabier
the Gestapo agent whom she now tames, committed to her
cause in a double role, that of liaison officer responsible for
extracting information and that of Antelme's wife. She approaches him slowly, with the cruelty she has possessed for a
long time, discovered, learned over there in Asia, as a result of
being in contact with such a hard world. He is quite fascinated
by artists and writers, whereas she is determined to draw information out of him, and to understand the motives behind his
particular commitment, always fascinated by atypical behavior,
by the murderous instincts that penetrate certain beings, turning them away from love.

In that period of the Occupation, those first days of June
1944, she is the tragic heroine, defenseless and yet strong, on
Rabier's "own turf," "death." She tears her man apart, observes
him, finds him cowardly, miserable, and he fascinates her, but
for the moment he is the one who still has the power. It takes
time and patience to learn a detail, a bit of information, and
the contact between them creates a strange intimacy, an ambiguous closeness. She sees him in bars, and since she lives
nearby, they see each other at Le Flore; they form a curious
couple, sitting there in this existentialist stronghold, in this
place where protest was in the air. Little by little, Duras gets
her man, she listens to him, she pretends to be interested in
him, she knows that soon he will be "in her hands," soon "she
will condemn him to death," she will turn him in when it is his
turn to be defeated.

She has this force within her that gives her every kind of courage; she is in close contact with one of these allies of the Germans, "Huns, wolves, criminals, but above all, psychotic criminals." She knows that it would take very little, a slip on her part, a word spoken thoughtlessly, for him to inform on her, have her arrested, but she handles this situation coldly, with a terrible, implacable lucidity, engaged as she is in this struggle as inevitable as fate.

In this execution, in which she does not yet know who is the executioner and who is the victim, she persists "untiringly in her attention" to Rabier.

At night in her apartment in Saint-Germain-des-Prés, she finds herself afraid, shivering with fear, feeling the weight of an immense loneliness, not her own, but that of people in general, of the human condition, of absurd man, the experience of Roquentin in Sartre's *Nausea*. Sometimes she also knows the joy of Sisyphus, that joy which submerges like the sea those bursts of happiness, those supreme movements of rising fervor whose existence she knows of, like the one she will share anyway, in spite of Antelme's absence, that of liberated Paris, the chiming uproar rising from the churches and, like another kind of day, washing the city of all the blackness, the gray shadows of the militia, the SS vehicles like an outrage, in the streets and the windowpanes daubed with dark blue paint as protection against passing aircraft.

She always lives in these extreme situations, in search of extreme moments in which one is cornered, subject to mystical forces. She hates and scorns Rabier, and at the same time she wants to know how he functions, what makes an agent "tick," how he can be so treacherous. She doesn't judge Rabier, she explores his soul, his behavior, trying to grasp all of his motives, and that is when she feels most like a writer. Later she will write Rabier's story, but she knows that she cannot limit herself to stating the facts. His personality has obscure zones, secret, impenetrable cores, and even when she returns to court during the winter of 1944-45 in order to provide further testimony on his behavior—for he had also saved two Jewish women by helping them cross over into the unoccupied zone—

her clouding up of an apparently clear situation will draw hostility on the part of the prosecutor and irritation in the court. That is the unwearying dialectic in which she exists, in hatred and in love, in the keenest sense of justice, in the attraction for the man she calls "Ter of the Militia," that other traitor to the body of desire, and in her cruelty which has him put in prison, in that sympathy, in the most etymological sense of the term, for humankind.

A feverish agitation runs through Paris in this month of August 1944, rife with all sorts of rumors and dangers at the dawn of its liberation. Bookseller Galtier-Boissière tells of the town's euphoria in his *Mon journal pendant l'occupation*, the confusion, the "riotous unrest and the carnivalesque playfulness."

Shells and gunfire strike the walls of public buildings, the Grand Palais burns down, the German retreat takes place amid jeers, barricades go up, and soldiers shoot from the rooftops. Drieu la Rochelle barely survives his first suicide attempt, and Field Marshal Leclerc's tanks roll down rue Saint-Jacques. It is August 25th, the weather is warm, and people are rejoicing in the street, carrying dazed children in their arms, though the Senate is still in the hands of the SS. An indescribable spectacle whose outcome is still up in the air, in which war and peace, the victorious and the presumedly defeated, are rubbing elbows.

Posters are put up on walls, on tree trunks, everywhere making an appeal to women, to Parisian women. "Women," they say, "your courage is magnificent. Women in the thirteenth arrondissement attack a German truck, in the fourteenth a militant of the UFF shoots down a Kraut with a revolver; on boulevard Raspail, another woman is killed while putting up a Front national poster: 'Join in and kill Krauts, keep up the good work on the barricades.—The Union of French Women.'"

It is during these extreme moments that Duras loves Paris too, in this savage, baroque brutality, with the bells of Notre Dame in full peal, echoing the collaborating militia's bursts of gunfire, with the tracer bullets of the anti-aircraft defense

crossing the sky at night, amid the roaring sirens; in the paroxysm of time, when all is ablaze, as if these conflagrations, these
furies, this distress were the only path leading back to daylight
—that is when she feels "called upon."

Something was bringing about a transformation in Duras and
Mascolo, and Antelme's departure was not unrelated to this
development: escape from this paralysis, from this sort of
acceptance which had caused them to tolerate, in spite of
everything, the yellow stars, the raids, the occupying forces'
swaggering airs, moving away from the utopia, the romanticism
that kept them in the solitude of their selves and prevented
them from taking the step, committing themselves further still.
That is when Duras became a communist, "before the end of
the war," as Mascolo notes, in the fall of 1944. Up to that
point, the very notion of a political party had scarcely occurred
to her. Too independent-minded, too irreverent, too funda-
mentally disobedient, she loathed groups, doctrines, dogma.
But becoming a Party member suddenly took on another meaning: it was as if she were attempting to locate Antelme, to be
near him, to follow in his tracks, to fight in the war in order to
save him. Joining it was like another form of the Redemption,
a way out of the impasse to which she had been confined by her
wild, rebellious, instinctive nature. The very word *communism*
implied a continuing presence among people, a way to fight for
them, for the human race, to stop the black gangrene. That was
the urgency in which she lived, the impulse that always made
her feel things more than she conceptualized them, completely
bound to that "material life" in which she lived, screamed,
cried, completing this cycle of life.

When she joined the Party, it was as if euphoria were emanating from her very self; suddenly things took on meaning, no
longer was there this loneliness and, directly facing her, brutal
terror and murder.

At the time, joining the Communist Party had a certain
mystique, and it seemed to be the only possible choice since,
in the words of Edgar Morin, "to accept German hegemony

was no longer to accept reality," but to opt for Nazism.

Duras felt compelled to act as if out of necessity; it was a way of containing barbarity, of "communing with humanity in its trial of life and death." Duras's fascination with extreme situations, tragic conflicts, places where history became more intense and storms were raging, stirred up her own violence, striking a familiar note within her. An entire generation of intellectuals threw themselves into the communist adventure, driven by "the global alternative."

To be in the Communist Party was really to come to grips with humanity, to find her true family, to know the joys of brotherhood. To be, as they said at the time, "on the same side as those who are thrown into locomotive-boilers" meant exposing oneself to risk and heroic danger, giving meaning to one's life, creating the opportunity to make one's contribution to the advent of freedom, bringing utopia into contact with actual reality. It meant risking death for the cause, accepting it as this "old idea of world revolution," as the internationalist myth of universal brotherhood. It meant feeling the same shivers as the heroes of the great Russian novels, taking advantage of that exceptional situation in order to live fully the concept of commitment whose realization had not yet been made possible by history.

Did she really know the extent of what was happening in the camps? The systematic elimination of human beings, the Jewish race, the intelligence applied to killing, to exterminating a people? Could she even imagine the route taken by those trains, leading to Ravensbrück, Dachau, Treblinka, those rails taking them implacably, from all of the train stations in this destroyed Europe, to the gas chambers?

Here would begin the physical pain. This is where Duras becomes a Jew: a Jew as an expression of exclusion, a Jew as an expression of her solidarity, her camp, the little girl from Saigon, already a Jew in the arms of the Chinese lover, already a Jew in the luxuriant jungles, already a Jew because always in exile, wandering, a Jew like the little beggar woman of Savannakhet.

Here would begin the dizzying descent into her true work. The resemblance with Mauriac discernible in *Les Impudents*, the traces still remaining in *La Vie tranquille*, would fade away with this revelation. To be in danger from now on, insecure, living like a nomad, a Jew—that is her, Donnadieu, Duras.

At that precise moment in history there occurs a shift that sends her to the edge, and off into adventure.

Antelme has not yet returned. Will he ever come back? Militant activity leaves her still standing, adding strength to her life force. Very mixed feelings, of vengeance and anger, agitate her and push her on, in her constant search for traces.

She can be seen at the time wearing those little war-era dresses; in the sixth arrondissement, she is constantly engaged in political activity, in the youth of her revolt, with a cold euphoria gripping her heart, her soul. Crossing Paris on the way to her clandestine cell meeting, she resembles Antigone in her feverish excitement, her frenzy, the urgent need to tell, the courage to cry out: Piaf too, who sings her pain, who walks the streets, small and insignificant, but with such a gleam in her eye, such mobility, that she herself seems to elude the gaze of others. Her eyes, too flagrantly true, dangerous, suspect, like a yellow star, betray her, flying in the face of lies.

She enters into the tragedy she doesn't completely understand. Being a woman gives her the glimmer, the pointed violence, the energy that seems implacable. Precisely because she is a woman, she has the courage that dares, defines, is permanently at risk. She lives in daily insecurity. It's somewhat romantic, purely romantic in the sense of Antigone's imprudence, the fierce strength to say no. She is starting to learn. It is Antelme who, in spite of his absence, gives her strength. And the mother, lodged deep inside her, the maternal atavism, her determination, her obstinate madness. She is in the Party, and that is a sea wall against another kind of leprosy, another plague.

Of this enclosure in what Mascolo calls "féminie," of this love triangle, Duras–Antelme–Mascolo, there remains only the rift. That is how writing works, with muffled sounds, on the unpredictable road to elsewhere. "Sources of pain," as she says, flare up, then smolder, never again going out. Never. It is Antelme's pain that she bears, a palpitating force driven straight into her, the pain that he makes her bear, every day, until those November days when the dead prowl, around All Saints' Day, until that year 1990 when he passes away at the Hôpital des Invalides. She has always wept for him, for that return, those illnesses, those days when he was suspended between life and death, when she made Pain appear as a living allegory, that text she had mislain: "I had left it in the armoire in Neauphle, and given it to Xavière Gauthier, for *Sorcières*. Well I'm the one who wrote it, Garance the actress can now perform it. I did it to bear witness to the fundamental horror of our time," and out of love for Antelme.

Those sources of suffering are where Duras's biography must be constructed, in the chaotic motion of her Nightship, the only place where one can possibly join her, in order to understand, and in that way to give the complete meaning of a life, everything hidden within, smoldering, "brewing," as she says.

The reference points go up in flames; all that matters are these embers, these horrible pains, these knots of sorrow glowing red and black, as in Rimbaud's poems. Rimbaud whom her journey resembles, drunken, free, utopian.

But from Antelme, still nothing. The Allies capture German towns, occupy them, the dark empire disintegrates, and from Antelme nothing. Through the search network that she set up in *Libres*, she attempts to find out, to imagine. She discovers the full extent of the war, the horror. Escaped prisoners are starting to talk, she works out hypotheses, maps out routes, someone is missing on rue Saint-Benoît, him, Antelme, on the roads of the debacle, tossed about on railroad cars, Betterfeld, Czechoslovakia, Dachau, finally Buchenwald, perhaps. Alone in the night, on those endless journeys, on those filthy trains, where the sky, the stars, the fresh air still give reasons for hope, when they are glimpsed, reasons to believe that he is actually alive, and that everything will continue, breath, hunger, and above all the desire to "piss" which he insists on so much in *The Human Race*, now the primary function of life, the demonstration that he is still alive, the proof that this body can still function, even as it destroys itself, becoming purple with cold. And then snow falls on the camp. It softens everything, muffling the footsteps of the kapos, the SS, the prisoners. Deadens noises and voices, the sounds of pickaxes and tools coming from the workshops, spreading ballast. Antelme cannot write what he sees. Writing has no place here. In his memoir he notes nonetheless: "There is no horizon for anyone."

In Paris meanwhile, they are starting to find out. Duras knows some things. The horror is so great that she can scarcely believe it. She needs photographs, testimonies, facts related by the very people who can come back and explain. She has nightmares. The only thing that keeps her going is this fierce Communist Party activity, and her underground Resistance work, the anger she carries inside her. Meanwhile, Antelme waits for nightfall so that he can sink into heavy, heavy sleep: sometimes, through the stalag windows, lights flash like beacons from the watchtowers, casting intermittent glimmers on the snow; the tread of dogs, the footsteps of German soldiers, become muffled, thick.

Something is being born in Duras: "It is as if I had slept for thirty years," she says in 1986, "and after thirty years I wake up and the Jews are being killed and my life begins."

She is overtaken by a boundless obstinancy, the will to know, to discover everything there is to know about this dark night of war, and to find Antelme, take him away from this vacuum, bring him back here, with her, with Mascolo whom she also loves. She must restore life to Antelme.

April 1945. She remembers a singular spring in which Europe vacillates in the victory assured at last, in that painful, bitter joy.

Each day new inquiries produce information about escaped concentration camp prisoners. Will Antelme be among those fleeing so pathetically? A trace of him is found on the 4th, then once more on the 12th, and then silence falls again. The new Undersecretary in Charge of Refugees, Prisoners, and Deportees, François Mitterrand, the former Morland of the Resistance network, promises to help Duras and Mascolo in this impossible quest. The Nightship keeps moving forward without a pilot on the rough sea. Sometimes, as if to break up the long wait, the pain, Mascolo plays the piano. As always, when he wants to rediscover harmonies with the world, to put himself in tune with it, with the most secret, most distant forces of the world, he plays. From the apartment in Saint-Germain-des-Prés rise sonatas, melodies like sobs, flowing variations of Bach, or Brahms, like sea currents.

Ever since that terrible month of April 1945 when the horror of the camps was revealed in its entirety, abruptly, when the ultimate savagery of men alighted on the platform of Paris's Gare d'Orsay train station, something has come over everyone. People are no longer really in control of themselves. It is a debacle of pain far, far from the glorious days de Gaulle is nonetheless proclaiming. Duras lives in the state of panic that always gives her the energy to live, this rage, this cruelty to know, to go on to the bitter end. During those moments she wavers between madness and "terrible, good, comforting" hatred. Others tell her that she must stop hurting herself, that she must protect herself. But she is incapable of keeping quiet. Her recollections of that time are still clear in an interview she gave when *The Lover* was published: "I never took care of myself."

The pain of April restores in her the strength to write. Not in order to publish, but rather to bear witness, in the secrecy of her blue notebooks which she will later abandon, like forgotten archives in the house in Neauphle, left to the dampness, the rains, the scorn of time.

In those notebooks she writes of her state of panic, and the broken, compartmentalized being she has become. She writes in the ellipsis of pain, and her words blend in with the strident sound of the constantly ringing telephone from which she cannot detach herself—what if it was Antelme coming back, he has to come back, he has to be among those columns of returning deportees, "coagulated" as she says, frightened, clinging to each other, as if they did not yet want to involve themselves with the others, the living, not yet mix with the crowd as they did in the past, not feel the compassion, the curiosity in their eyes.

Duras's writing has never cried out louder, as if she has found her voice. Her language is this cry bursting through to silence, this open mouth that can no longer stand to express its pain; she has the faith of hatred, for she doesn't believe in the God who has allowed coexistence between defeated classes and victorious classes. She gets down on her knees and prays, crying out this hatred, going mad. She is aware of this capacity she has long possessed to enter into madness, to slip into it, to feel everything waver within her, and to be given back the means of expressing her truest self. Her words are those of the little woman from Vinh Long who followed her, screaming, when she was a little girl.

The fever gets worse each day, and she can't bear it without pills, plenty of pills, lavished on her by good Dr. Génon-Catalot, faithful friend, best-loved physician in the neighborhood, a man of culture and a patient listener; but she is no longer Duras. She is with him, with Antelme, in the trenches of the unknown stalag where he must now be rotting, dead, abandoned. Others, stronger than he, must surely have trampled on him, stepping on his pitiful body spewing forth dirty brown fetid liquids, like those coming out of her too, there in her apartment on rue Saint-Benoît, those foul green-ish waters, the vomit, the diarrhea, the same as the unknown liquids that streamed out of Saigon children's bellies, or burst out of leprous bodies.

She is scarcely thirty years old and already she is the wandering beggar woman of Cochin China, abandoned, dirty, lost, unknown to others, to herself; she has a way of following through, unrestrainedly, uncontrollably, tenacious, in her distress as in her writing.

She is always prowling, like the beggar woman of Savannakhet around the kitchens in the white neighborhoods, around the train station. There is no reason for Antelme not to be there among the deported, in that interminable cortege of survivors, in that procession of specters who are men nonetheless. When there is a larger group, she says, music is played. She shows up, hugging the walls, but unconsolable. The day of celebration is over, the brass band forgotten. There will be no more rejoicing. Only this distress, this self-neglect, this alienation from oneself, this tendency to recognize oneself no longer, but only the will to find him, to thread her way through the crowd, searching, making it past the roadblocks, lying to get through the checkpoints, insisting, imploring the government agents.

She rebels against de Gaulle. "He's a regular army officer," she says in *The War*. "In my circle of friends it takes three months for him to be judged, rejected for good. Women hate him too."

No, the days of shedding tears are not over. On the contrary. It is only now that the plaintive chant begins, the lament of ancient times, the eternal mourning, for those spoil heaps of Jewish ashes, abandoned there, mixed with the soil of Auschwitz, Ravensbrück, Dachau. Those tons of Jewish ashes returned to the earth. This is the wail that comes out of her. There is no other outlet but that of weeping, draining the cup of horror to the dregs, the fields full of dentures, hair, jewelry, gold teeth, "bathed in coolness," stored in trays, like fruit in market stalls, no awakening aside from that, but terrified.

The music she hears now is the continuous lament of women looking for their sons, their brothers, their husbands. But she is excluded even from that. Now it is not even possible to understand, to penetrate the barrier separating her from others. What remains is this absorption of oneself in pain. And Antelme plunging with her into this absence.

He is over there, on another road, but so weak that he can no longer move, no longer advance, only cry.

He arrives in Dachau. His eyes hurt him, long accustomed to darkness, to the shadows of railroad cars. And yet he can see clearly, right there, a short ways ahead, women stooped over, "picking blades of grass, mauve forms against the green background." Vague smiles, perhaps the hope of returning.

In Dachau, at the end of the road, the wandering, the unpredictable journey, in spite of the signs pointing to a debacle,
there is no longer any source of hope whatsoever, as if the self
had been broken. Somewhere within Antelme lies the certitude only of the past, Duras, Mascolo, the very dear friend, of
going home, finally to go home. But what to do with these
people who have "lost touch" and who are men nonetheless,
as are the SS, but who will never succeed in reducing their
prey to subhumans, making them into mutants, representatives
of another genetic species, but implacably men, like them?
Indeed, what to do with them? One can only live hour by hour,
still feeling the warmth of one's urine, the scent of one's own
dejecta, still marveling at the miracle of these waters, foul yet
tender as a bowl of milk, knowing in that way that one will
always be a man.

Meanwhile, times speed up, for they cannot remain caught up
in that lamentation, that fever. In May 1945, Mitterrand is
sent on a mission to Dachau. He walks through the stalags,
becoming aware of the actual horror, and to an even greater
extent, perceiving the vertiginous descent, the abyss. But yet
a further step must be taken into this horror, this hell. With
Father Riquet and Jean Munier, alias Rodin (as Duras tells it),
Mitterrand goes into the encampment where the dead and the
dying are left. And there, amid the stench of decomposition, in
the morgue where a few souls are still gasping, Antelme, Robert, murmuring: "François . . . François," recognized on account
of the gap between his front teeth. Yes, inconceivable, a kind
of miracle, impossible, they quickly roll him up in a blanket,
lean him against a wall, next to the last survivors. Typhus is
spreading invisibly throughout the camp. The dead who have
just stopped breathing are left alongside decomposing corpses,
the dying with their soft, warm breath, their visible bones jut-
ting out, bursting their skin, and still, ever above them, the
clear blue brightness of the sky, the certitude of cruel, indifferent life, never far away; in the neighboring villages, as
Antelme relates in *The Human Race*, peasants work in the
fields; they play the game, pretending not to understand, not

to know. The dense forest surrounding Dachau deadens the sounds, the moans, the cries of the dying; it also muffled the bursts of machine-gun fire, the blows against the staggering bodies, those which the same dying prisoners had to give when they broke road gravel.

That is perhaps at the origin of Duras's fear of the forest. That dark forest where dogs and soldiers prowl, where the frost "makes the animals burst," where "the ponds are frozen clear to the bottom." The forest in *Abahn, Sabana, David* that she described later, in 1970, as if she had never been able to forget the thick ring of trees gagging the Jews, hushing up their desperate cries. Completely different from the jungle of her youth, that world of creeping plants and roots, in the Elephant range, both enchanting and fantastic, that "centuries-old cluster of creeping plants . . . which formed basins suspended between the trees." And in those natural ponds, fish lived, wriggling about, among the birds. And that forest wasn't frightening, it was even protective, guarding wild, intrepid children like her. Tigers, monkeys, panthers never attacked them, their presence was quite natural. . . .

Mitterrand facilitated Antelme's repatriation, had border passes drawn up for Mascolo and his friend Beauchamps. They drove back, crossing roadblocks without stopping, with Beauchamps behind the wheel on what became an epic journey. For they had to save Antelme, and beyond that, regain life, pulling themselves out of that sorrow, slipping perhaps into this miraculous day of blue sky and renewal. When they arrived in Dachau, they discovered the line of bodies, the dead, the sick, the universally shared indifference, dazed in a survival unreal to them, unaware of their condition, as if only half there. Alongside the walls, like neatly stacked cords of wood, in blankets, men and more men, and the extraordinary smell of death, the smell of leprosy, of misery that Duras used to tell them about. And then a kind of moan, a barely discernible breath; it could be something other than a word, a murmur, a breeze, a passing insect, but it was a call, like a sob. Mascolo's discretion, his characteristic, unabated self-effacement, a kind of intellectual modesty, made him relate this moment in *Autour d'un effort de mémoire*. He says almost nothing, which is what makes him strong. He lets words, short, very simple words, speak, and the emotion passes, and his awareness gathers strength. They flee, leaving the camp like escapees, in spite of their passes. Antelme is terrified of being recaptured. He will always remember that. It is inscribed in his mind. He will hardly ever mention it after he returns, burying everything, once he has written it in *The Human Race*.

But for the moment he experiences a kind of drunkenness of speech. Antelme talks, narrates everything he has seen, undergone, and his full memory unwinds like a skein. Mascolo "doesn't have to question him," his words pour out like birth waters, surging, breaking the silence, leaving his listeners agape. Perhaps death prowling at his heels, the awareness of death, this still precarious breath finding—where?—this strength to tell and, in the wheezing car as it goes on and on, through German towns, Stuttgart, Wissembourg, hurrying toward the border, inventing what Duras later calls "fluent" speech. Yes, here Antelme gives birth to Duras, today's Duras, with her tongue full of holes, repetitions, those quivers of the soul, those mysterious tremors, that melodious stream of music and words. There, in the intermittent glimmer of those nights on the road, when other cars' headlights send out their yellowish rays, recalling the floodlights in the camps, speech unfolds and the "unimaginable" comes into view.

There is an instant when the sacred is revealed, tearing open its veil, startling. It is a strange moment, as if caught at the extremity of all times, at the last frontiers of man, at the end of something and the beginning of a force as yet unborn, unknown, for nothing would ever be the same, devoured by this pain, marked by the murder of the Jews, and the day would soon be over, night would follow without anything ever erasing the memory of that, the light which would always refract the inexpressible suffering of the camps.

For there was more to it than merely forgetting, as soon as one was away from it, believing that one was free in order to

attain freedom. Deep inside there would remain that unutterable terror, that supreme human experience, that always open
wound. Marie-Louise Antelme, the little "cutie pie," as her
brother called her, the little sister of exemplary courage, free
after the liberation of the Ravensbrück camp, is flown to Den-
mark for medical treatment. She was, says Monique Antelme,
"in a state of total exhaustion" (in the camp, she would give
away her bread) "and died there shortly afterward." Dominique
Arban, whom Marie-Louise hid in her parents' apartment, is
moved when she speaks of it, still clear in her memory today:
"Big eyes, fat baby cheeks, radiant in spite of her paleness. . . .
This doll had been created for a major tragedy. . . . What crow-
bar tore away her virginity, what hell used her as a plaything?"

That is the tragic world in which Duras hammered out her
writing, in those beds of coals where life is found, blazing, continually assailed by death.

Facing her, a cry, the cry that sweeps through Duras's life like
a wave, the cry at the heart of the work, last resort, last word,
absolute, savage, of this pain of living, of this obscure incom-
prehension of the world, the cry that rends the lands of the
sea wall, when the helpless mother sees the dikes collapse, and
her cry now when she feels Robert Antelme, her husband, himself and yet another, unknown man, this "scrap" dragging himself around the apartment, almost "embarrassed" at so much
sorrow, at being the object of so much compassion. So the cry
remains as a means of abolishing this fury of war, the barbarity
of the camps, the cry as a means of attaining silence, this sort of
sustained vibration like the pealing of a great bell anesthetizing
everything, stopping the work of time which she doesn't want
to see. As for him, he rediscovers things, the swollen flesh of
cherries here in this bowl, wanting to eat some of them, just as
on the journey home he wanted trout: more than anything it
was their litheness that he envied, their agility in slithering
around, wriggling through streams, like these cherries now, full
of the sun, reddened by its light.

Duras's body is tragic, like Phaedra's, a body of pain, furious,
an ancient body, the victim of piercing sorrow, and of its

"intangible," fatal weight! Now she must learn how to live again, in this new birth of Antelme's, in this renewed innocence, and sure of one thing, of her work to come, this writing she carries within her, as if sealed with this sign of pain, this never-muffled echo of barbarity.

Twenty-two years later, Mascolo recalls, or rather makes an effort to remember, and in spite of his lack of details, emotion springs forth, from this very nothingness of speech, in these holes of silence where the horror stagnates yet, where words cannot find their meaning, but abstain, trembling, a mere semblance in the void. Images will remain, Duras "buried in darkness, behind layers of clothing . . . in the most distant, remotest room," and the immense, more present, infinitely more indelible vision of this Ecce Homo, this sculpture of modern times, "man reduced to his irreducible essence," Giacometti's living sculpture. For what Antelme revealed was in fact the most secret fiber of what composes man, the mystery of his suffering, the inexpressible arrangement of that which makes him human. He speaks of life, the force lying beneath the transparent flesh and overcoming everything, and of the tenacious soul thus named on account of the powerlessness of words, functioning in an unexplained, miraculous way.

This is the period in which Duras and her friends began to undergo a "Judaization complex." Well before the famous slogan of May 1968, "We are all German Jews," they were making this identification which, in their eyes, became inevitable. Yes, she, Duras, was a Jew, following the example of all those who were destroyed in the Shoah plan, a Jew like her future character Aurélia Steiner, a Jew like all of those who were gassed— "there are words so difficult to utter"—a Jew so that she could tell about it, the extermination of the Jewish people, thought out, planned, and beyond that, a Jew in telling of exclusion, rejection by others, a Jew for those who are poor, exiled, exploited, mad, those who write, those who are damned.

She had already experienced this as a little girl in colonial Indochina. Secretly Annamese, she felt like a Jew among her own, as if the word, poetically, metaphorically, suddenly took on a universal meaning, multiplying ad infinitum and all the way into the mists of time the Jewish people with their fatal stigmas, their ancient suffering.

In a culinary issue of the review *Sorcières* in 1976, she describes—as usual, tirelessly, Penelope weaving and unweaving her cloth, continually returning to the woof—the essential activity of her days, the wild days spent in "the giant mangoes," with the little brother, and she still says that: "How is she our mother, how is it possible, mother to us, so thin, yellow-skinned, unknown to the sun, us, Jews?"

For her, Jews are thus half-breeds, disobedient subjects, rebels against families. This Jewishness comes from the very distant past, a curse shouldered, re-enacted many, many times, finally becoming a permanent object of scandal, resituating in a different way the status of the writer, thus giving him back his sacred biblical function.

How many days, how many weeks did it take to bring Robert Antelme back to the light of day? What patience, what love did it take to live through, to accept the slow passing of time during which the weaning prescribed by Dr. Génon-Catalot attempted to put flesh back on the bones of a man she compared to a "sliver," all that remained of him, with his heart ready to burst at any moment, "beating in a void"?

She nonetheless wrote, in her school notebooks, of this pain, the same thing she had felt while waiting at the Gare d'Orsay train station, now deported here, with the specter of the Shoah still before her, for Antelme, in his greenish waters, comparable to those muddy torrents of the Mekong, flowing from him, uncontrollable, fetid, in this "shit" which, as she wrote, invaded furiously, ravaging everything in its path, just as the waters of the China Sea used to destroy the dams, and Antelme became the immense, universal Jew, the exemplary suffering of the Jewish man, the living sign of his curse.

And already, unconsciously, Duras was putting her hand into the fluent "stream," her style, as a result of this pain, in the image of her breathing, was discovering the chaotic, irregular comings and goings of this struggle, these onslaughts of death.

Suddenly she finds prophetic accents, something happens within her, giving her this right to affirm, to express with this force and this sense of ellipsis that make a visionary of her. It is not rare to find in her writing, in her interviews, that inevitable expression of mystics, "I see." She says "I see" and her sentences begin to unfold, almost spell-like, Pythian, and yet simple. Now it is Auschwitz that calls to her, giving her through this man, her husband, intelligence, true knowledge. "And I see," she says, "and I hear. . . . I can see that they are killing the Jews, that Jews are being killed, I see that I don't understand and I haven't progressed beyond that point." It is in this interrogation of the world, of herself, of the injustices, the wounds to the body and the soul, that she surprises herself over and over, heeding the call.

In *The War*, which she writes in the clandestine presence of herself, in that stormy, hateful journal, in that raw description of daily events, already she denounces, taking public cognizance of her duty as a writer, but in a heated, passionate tone that neither Sartre nor even Malraux could ever possess. An anti-Gaullist, she denounces the general's aristocratic point of view, his silence about the camps, his haughty notion of the fatherland when his own sons had been sent to their deaths, his decision to hold a national funeral for Roosevelt but nothing for the Jews. And that unleashes in her a sort of rage, a cold, brutal anger, which once more makes her different from others, and this murderous instinct, this obsession with tragic violence takes hold of her. In Paris, the time has in fact arrived for the settling of accounts. The hour when, as in ancient tragedies, it is again time for atonement, for awakening the infernal machine. The purge begins. And like a Cathar with this faith in herself, in her logic, in what she believes to be her purity, with her usual intransigence, Duras begins her own war. On rue Saint-Benoît, there is the specter of the camps, this vengeance to appease, this cry welling up in her, powerfully, telling those who are punishing collaborators, beating up cowardly informers, the denouncers of Jews and so many other Robert Antelmes, "that's not enough yet," and something infernal is set in motion. She wants them to talk, they'll have to talk, acknowledging their shame, their guilt. And already, in the two notebooks left in Neauphle-le-Château that will later become *The War*, she is that being separated from herself, from her own personality, who no longer says "I" but "she." Henceforth she incarnates the justice of this country: "She is little, she desires nothing. She is calm, and she feels a calm anger inside of her. . . . She is justice as there hasn't been for one hundred and fifty years in this land."

After the war, it is still war. There is a shower of blows, fists, truncheons, as blood flows in the back rooms of cafés, elementary schools, neighborhood cells, and she takes part in this popular vengeance; a secret force deep within tells her to continue the struggle. Outside, in the Saint-Germain-des-Prés neighborhood where she lives, there are people who want things to change. The nightclubs, the Tabou, the Saint-Germain, the new fashions, the melancholy songs which recover their taste for life little by little, and Boris Vian blowing his lungs out with his jazz trumpet, and Juliette Gréco (known here as Jujube) who is sulking like a child, languishing like a dark siren, and singing Queneau, as she slips onto the Naugahyde benches at the Deux Magots with the rather silly affectation of a perverse little girl.

The victory celebration goes on night and day in Saint-Germain-des-Prés; euphoria seems to take hold of the neighborhood in "fraternal debauchery," as Simone de Beauvoir said. The cafés are always full, the Royal Saint-Germain, the Café de Flore, the Montana where the contributors to *Les Temps modernes* would come to write, the Pont Royal, Sartre's turf ever since his reputation forced him to take up residence here, fleeing the Flore where his presence was turning into a show, and finally Lipp, in a more aristocratic style. Saint-Germain-des-Prés is no longer, as Roy said, "the village of the 1940s, the market town beneath its square belltower, with its courtyards reverberating from the sounds of craftsmen's tools, a little community of small tradesmen," people Duras loved so well. It has become the center of hybrid, almost surreal activity in which clans, clubs, opposing cliques come together in fraternal outbursts, a kind of effervescent romanticism in which the young meet the veterans, Artaud, Breton, Queneau, Martin du Gard, and a creative fever invades the sidewalk cafés, the workshops, the offices of publishing houses (Seuil, Gallimard) and reviews (*Les Temps modernes, Esprit*).

What about Duras? If she likes to go to the Café Bonaparte rather than the Deux Magots, it is because the atmosphere there is freer, more relaxed, not as fashionable, therefore less conventional. She can also be seen at the Petit Saint-Benoît, a singular restaurant with family menus where all of the artists and the creative people of the neighborhood gather in a fraternal promiscuity that suits her better.

But crueller, more vengeful business beckons to her.

In liberated Paris, "being twenty or twenty-five years old," wrote Simone de Beauvoir, "seemed a great blessing: every door was open." Nervous agitation spreads throughout the city, and Duras and her friends contribute to it, all of them bent on "avenging the innocent," as Paul Eluard clamored in *Les Lettres françaises*. If all of the intellectuals do not agree on the necessity of the purge, those of the Comité national des ecrivains, those of the journal *Combat*, led by Albert Camus, are its fiercest advocates. Their goal is to avenge the victims, refusing to take sides with the Paulhans and the Mauriacs who would rather "forgive and forget."

Untamable Duras determined to forge on, to bring to light the reality of the base, cowardly actions of the dark, leaden days!

This judgment of which she is so certain, the deadly bearing which she gives to her acts, are a necessity, an urgent requirement for her. She feels as if she were responsible for this horror, this pain, responsible for vengeance. And inside her, hatred and implacable cruelty at the same time, the same weapons as her enemies, and distress, love, the tears that well up in her eyes, this overflowing sorrow, secretly aware of Antelme's message, the one he carries inside him: that between the Germans and themselves, there is no difference, they are all part of the human race. And when Antelme related the story of his deportation, when he told them that whatever might happen, whatever they were turned into, the tattered remains of men, mere scraps, he always asserted that they could never "become either beasts or trees, for mankind is unique." The executioner can "kill a man, but he can't change him into something else."

She remembered when, exhausted, she would put a stop to the torture, asking them to stop punishing the collaborator, and she cried. For how to reconcile the feelings inside her, this hatred and this love? As always, living within her was the conflict of that mother, loved and hated at the same time, and how not to understand that she could exist only in this "madness," in this excess of feelings, in this breeding ground of rancor, of passions, of quests for love? "Disgusting," she felt disgusting, as a woman said about her, though not a collaborator, disgusting, that's what she was. But how not to be? There was an ambiguity in her behavior that would always determine her course, her direction in this world.

She was the cruel, implacable righter of wrongs, and cracks were nonetheless appearing. She seemed to be completely devoted to others, and yet, what freedom she expressed! Paradoxically, she could act like a brutal, obedient, militant communist, and at the same time reveal fissures that made her suspect, dangerous there, too. She could just as well say to the "executioner" "More," as find grace, nobility in the "victim," with whom she felt a greater closeness than with her political friends, "a sort of kinship."

In the company of Ter the collaborator, her prey, she feels his taste for life; like her he has that sensual contact with the world, that childlike quality, which still restrains him. And she is fascinated by his desire to live, his love for gambling, for women, for cars. She too is a mixture, both executioner and in love with her victim; she loves everything that expresses the power of life, difference, violence, conquest, youth.

What does it matter if the result is confusion? She has given herself completely to this blind race of the Nightship, obscure, erratic, and unpredictable, accepting its landings, its changes of tack. It is a kind of vertigo similar to that which she felt for the brutal, cynical, "hooligan" brother: she wishes she could exclude him from her childhood, yet he becomes the stuff of her imagination; she turns Ter the collaborator over to the FFI, yet she desires him.

When she relates these events in her notebooks, which she lets other people read much later, it is for herself alone. The reader, the witness-voyeur, is kept out. She leaves them for decades in her house in Neauphle, and they are like coals still smoldering. She even ends up forgetting about them, caught up in other activities, but the stories mislaid at the bottom of their blue armoires are like vigil-keepers. She tells the reader: "Learn how to read: these are sacred texts." Even in the formulation of her thoughts, she affirms the role she assigns henceforth to literature: initiator, bearer of secrets of light to be discovered in darkness. In those notebooks, a religious notion is developed, not one that obeys some catechism, but something related to mysticism, to that tension between mind and body which expresses itself in the narrowest confines of literature, in all its nakedness.

One whole side of her escapes from what she calls, in 1985, "the nauseating proximity of the Communist Party," to which she nonetheless still belongs, but from which she unconsciously "changes course." Writing rebels against dogma; without even realizing it she flees into zones on the border of the spoken word, as if she could exist only there, among those secrets to be buried, in those obscure armoires where desire, sorrow, and pain are filed.

How to admit now to the desire for Ter the collaborator? How to celebrate out loud her desire for vengeance? Discreetly, outside of the city, in that dark, limited space where writing emerges, she crosses over to the forbidden territory, collective expression, dogmatic simplification.

Henceforth writing is the place of transgression, of ambiguous desire, of unlimited possibility, of impropriety, of disobedience of all laws, of the Law. Inside her, something inexpressible remains intact and mistrusts group enlistments, ready-made speeches, schools of thought. As she can feel already, she would like the book to be conceived spontaneously, in her own storm, in those unpredictable movements of the sea, alternating between calm and waves, in that pitching of the soul which constrains it, forcing it to advance.

She will never really recover from that experience undergone by Robert Antelme. Her future energy, her immense expenditure of work, in defiance, are perhaps because of him. Those silences that well up in her work, those gaping holes, those chasms which, suddenly, the words can no longer cross, and which leave the page suspended, dizzy, with its hollows and its pits are perhaps also because of Antelme—because of the camps, the silence of the camps, the cold nights in the surrounding forests, because of his sister Marie-Louise Antelme's frozen feet, her death as a result of Germany, because of Antelme, that memory of the brutality which he will always carry with him, even later, when he so modestly works for Gallimard, translating, adapting, but silent about the hell he went through, trying to calm, to pacify Duras, to temper her unbridled violence.

Between the two of them, there is a knot of passion that nothing is able to undo. To talk about Antelme is always to return to the pain, to what it has been given to her to know, to that never-buried horror. She still remembers when, during the month of the dead, in November 1990, Dionys Mascolo informs her of his death at Les Invalides military hospital. Antelme will always carry that reverberation of pain, that echo of suffering, perhaps the very core of her work, with its obscure, tragic veins.

Antelme has died, he has escaped from the death camps, but he is there, now, buried beneath the soil of Montparnasse cemetery in Paris, and has she ever really stopped loving him?

One has to believe in the admirable presence of Antelme, that man who, for Claude Roy, belongs to a different species, "exceptional"—such is the extent to which those who approached him and loved him have experienced his charm and felt what must perhaps be called his saintliness. Through his silence

upon returning from the camps, he continued to bear witness, to serve as a model, comparable to Prince Myshkin in
Dostoyevski's *Idiot*, a catalyst for others, forcing each of them
to "come to grips with themselves."

His life was one long lesson in militancy, for in the camps,
to be a militant was to "fight rationally against death"; to be a
militant was also to pick "like a dog through the rotten potato
peelings," without this being an act of degradation or "the least
undermining of one's integrity." To be a militant was also to be
a communist, to believe in the Party (which he joined along
with Mascolo in May 1947) that claimed to fight against man's
exploitation by man, and it was, in spite of the emotional lac-
eration of expulsion, to believe still, as Roy said, "in Marx's idea
that inheritance must fall into the hands of the most disinherited"; to be a militant was also to remain a communist in the
most sacred, most authentically prophetic sense of the word.

Finally, to be a militant was to prove that he was acting still,
in spite of this silence to which he had yielded and which had
become the most eloquent, most essential message.

And yet Duras proves able to push her desire to its logical end:
she wants to live with Mascolo from now on, to have his child.
Does she experience a vague feeling of guilt when she announces this to Antelme? In spite of the psychological danger
it could represent in his condition, she confirms her intention
to him. Antelme receives the jolt, and buries his pain, asking
her if they might "get back together" one day. She says no, it is
definite. Such is the intransigence in which she lives, without
compromise, in that fierce freedom whose demands are cruel,
absolute, pitiless.

August 1945. She accompanies Antelme to a convalescent
home for the deported in Savoie. He has not yet recuperated.
He carries inside him a silence, an absence, a kind of impossible fulfillment that prevents him from being with others,
from speaking, and which suddenly cuts him off from all conversation, as his gaze suddenly becomes disengaged, vacillates,
and floats off into the distance.

In the sky above Hiroshima there rises up a mushroom of thick white foam. Shoah, part two.

The horror is written out in full in the newspapers' headlines. They are talking about 200,000 Japanese dead. "On that day," Duras says, "I cried. It was a personal event. There is nothing that violent, that horrible. A paroxysm felt in a collective, immediate way." And the pain settles like deposits in those silent hollows of the memory. But much of this pain will dissolve, evaporating into oblivion, in the repetition of the days and the nights, in the renewal of desire, in the melancholy course of love affairs.

Such fractures are needed in order to become a writer, such tears are necessary in order to move on down the road. For Antelme, to avoid talking about the German night is to tell of the cold, the deceitful winter that stiffens your hands, your bare feet, the hunger, the filth of the blockhouses, of the striped jackets, the loneliness, the oblivion. He writes a book, *The Human Race*, perhaps the only literary masterpiece that the camps have inspired. Bursts of writing in which sacred energy is expended in an attempt to bring back the slightest detail, the most insignificant moment of the day, the emptiness of that life on the edge, a glance toward the sky, the soft, mild warmth of his urine on his hands, the cruelty of the human race, all of mankind, the SS, the kapos, the prisoners, all of them combined in this enclosure where, as in the arena, as in the closed circle of tragedy, only life and death are played out, their desperate struggle to win, life without need, without desire, and death too, in which nothing is deployed, as Maurice Blanchot would say, except "selfishness without the self," and in which the stubborn will to live is but a "neutral, empty need." It's a dreadful manuscript that he gives to Duras and Mascolo for them to publish at the small press they have just founded, naming it La Cité Universelle, with Duras and Antelme as directors. The creation of that firm hadn't required a great capital outlay, for Duras was helped by a small printer, himself director of Nicéa publications, which had published Duras's "dime-store novels" under a pseudonym during the war.

Moreover, the firm's structure was extremely simple since Duras, Antelme, and Mascolo were responsible for both the office and the editorial work. To publish *The Human Race* was also to reveal the rhythm, the cadence, the breath of that pain, the merciless lucidity then animating Duras and Mascolo, as well as Antelme. Antelme's writing is staggering; it intervenes not in the realm of the psychological, the spectacular, but presents precise, breathless images—finally expressing the pathos of that place of immobility, the camp. It depicts the silence of time, reduced to the same few gestures, in spite of the deportations, the roads, the gray journeys, the silence of a life that had no more future, and became encysted there, in that perimeter surrounded by barbed wire, swept by powerful floodlights, at the mercy of the executioners.

4

"A Militant Antimilitant"

Duras, Mascolo, and Antelme continued to meet their friends in that apartment on rue Saint-Benoît, now given over to conversation, the free play of speech, in a quasi-romantic fervor. "Judaized, communized," in Mascolo's words. There was a new-found freedom in them, a kind of impatience, an intellectual effervescence that, still vague, distanced them from the orthodox communism to which they had committed themselves. At the time they were, as Mascolo says, "ahead of the revolution." Duras's fierce, rebellious nature, the sacred vision of the writer growing silently within her, bore a greater resemblance to the adventures of a Mozart or a Rimbaud than to that of a card-carrying militant.

People as far removed from Stalinist thinking as Edgar Morin, then twenty-four years old, an intellectual sniper, as buoyant as a romantic of 1830, and Maurice Blanchot, already secretly engaged in the obscure maze of writing, participated in those informal meetings in that thoroughfare which the apartment on rue Saint-Benoît had become.

Violent, contradictory winds, suspicious words circulated about what was going on in Moscow; there too, the Nightship moved ahead in troubled waters, trying to make its way along an unmarked route not shown on any map.

Of all the meeting places that sprang up after the liberation, or of all those that grew out of their secrecy, the one on rue Saint-Benoît was among the most powerful in stirring the imagination, the richest in ideas, perhaps the freest. A capricious, untrammeled life circulated there, in which Clara Malraux, Merleau-Ponty, Ponge, and André Ulmann mixed with one another fraternally. The spirit of protest reigned there, amid the bitter smell of coffee; all of those who participated in those encounters wanted simply "to be with the people rather than 'to achieve solidarity' with them." It was in those conscience struggles, conflicts between their belonging to the Party and their desire for freedom, that they came into contact with the century's renewal. Duras, as she is described by frequent visitor Claude Roy, with her usual mixture of ferocity and tenderness, nonchalance and sudden, violent explosions, combined the passion of the Portuguese nun with the abrupt, tense fragility of Edith Piaf, her black diamond hardness. Sometimes "sparks of madness" shot out of her, and she would go off to war with "her goatlike brutality."

Inside her, mixed, conflicting forces revealed those deep veins from which she would later draw the living matter of her novels.

And always at the heart of the conversations, the same interrogation: how to remain a communist while accepting the Party's compromises, while legitimizing its faults with silent approval? How to remain faithful to this youth-inspired ideal that led one believe that only the Party could defend the oppressed, and that under its protection, the world could change?

How to avoid doubting this new man the Party had promised and in whom everybody had believed, angelically?

To that, Antelme, who had just returned from the horror, with a peasant intelligence both surly and ironic, replied: "Yes, the Party created a new kind of imbecile."

There was enthusiasm but also a certain gravity; time bore the face of tragedy, heavy with all the days gone by and with the inconceivable. In 1946 Edgar Morin published *L'An zéro de l'Allemagne* at La Cité Universelle, and Mascolo the works of

Saint-Just. Duras, bearing up beneath the weight of the Holocaust, the Hiroshima massacre, was herself beginning a new life, with her eyes wide open, and marked forever by Antelme's blind, silent suffering.

Nonetheless, one must not imagine Duras at that time only as a tragic heroine. A many-faceted being, she can also give a cheerful, happy image of herself, one that the pathos of her existence sometimes allows to show through. It is in this endless volatility that she can best define herself, in this cruel lucidity of the world and of herself, and in this sort of intellectual euphoria, already sure of the fascination she holds for others. Capable of grasping all at once, with a single look, a situation, or a person, she has that supreme intelligence, that capacity to look beyond and to laugh.

She too relearns how to live after the war; sensual, she needs to rediscover the fragrances of nature, diving into the sea again, without the dreadful fear that once clung to her skin, holding up her skirt and feeling the waves break on her body, the wind of the Riviera at Boca di Magre caress her neck. Joined within her are those two forms of violence, struggle and contemplation, the fury of the aftermath and the immobility of the void.

In 1946, just as she had decided, she divorces Robert Antelme. She wants a child from Mascolo, and she will have one a year later, a boy she names Jean. Antelme is still close to them, as if they still needed each other, their gentleness, their secrets, the unconsolable presence of past love. *The Human Race* is finally published in 1947 after the works by Morin and Mascolo. The book makes a powerful impression, as if carried by a strong wind and a repressed frenzy like a pebble thrown into the pond of writing. In it Antelme becomes the chorist of classical tragedy, and mortal wandering sets out, as Duras would say, "on the high seas of literature." It is nonetheless Antelme's real life, and it is the world beyond, the other sea, its unimaginable and its sublime qualities, in a word the force that lifts him high into the loftiest regions of the soul. How can he write another book after *The Human Race?* how can he regain that high level of thought? wouldn't the least of his writings now put "literature to shame?"

In competition with Maurice Blanchot's *La Part du feu, The Human Race* is awarded the Côte d'Amour prize in June 1949 when it is re-edited by Robert Marin. The jury is composed of nine women, including Gala Barbizan, the founder of the future Médicis prize, Odette Joyeux, Dominique Rolin, Claude-Edmonde Magny, Annette Vaillant, and Nicole Védrès. Eventually, the book will be definitely recognized, but amid that silence and that distance characteristic of sacred books, bearers of terrifying, religious truths.

Duras wanted to know everything about life. Curious, breaking the rules, she possessed the most intense thirst for knowledge, for the disclosure of secrets. Having a child was beyond this proof of love, like the fulfillment of a part of her being, a superior form of learning, a gap she wanted to fill and which she thought all women should experience. Her libertarian spirit, in spite of her membership in the Communist Party, made a clean sweep of all prevailing notions; forever a dissident, she was closer to nihilism than to the communist ideology; hostile to all institutions, she nonetheless wanted to accomplish what seemed essential to women, the miracle of creating life. Weighed down by her femininity, she wanted to see revealed once more from inside the mysterious alchemy of life, the secret murmur coming from herself and from elsewhere at the same time.

Her work to come will nourish itself on this learning acquired through experience, molded by this annunciation to be relayed by all of her books. She will recount all the inner movements of life, those unfamiliar passageways where one loses step, fails to understand, sets off again, blindly.

This desire to discover, to penetrate into the furthest recesses of the self, to the point of silence, that blank space, will make her understand very quickly that she will never find it through the Communist Party. Endowed with that impatience, that ardor, that "volatility" noted by Mascolo, she is determined to make her apartment on rue Saint-Benoît the place where the Spirit will circulate, seething with ideas, giving back to intellectuals their tongue and their role of provocateur, springboard of ideas, glorifying suspicion.

While Sartre invited his friends over to his little apartment near rue Saint-Benoît, on the corner of rue Bonaparte, for memorable evening discussions—which, as Beauvoir notes in her *Memoirs*, often degenerated from philosophy or politics into debauchery—Duras's sphere assumed a different style. Almost immediately she suspected Sartre of serving a different revolutionary cause than hers, of being, as Mascolo later says, "an opportunity waster." She contested the role of prophet that he willingly assumed, denying him a certain authenticity. If they in fact ended up signing the same petitions, their commitment was different, Duras's more absolute, more violent, less "reassuring" than Sartre's attitude. That is why they were not members of "the same gang," did not share the same meeting places. Her suspicion of Sartre continued for a very long time, for in 1984, on the *Apostrophes* television program, she denied him the title of writer. That was in fact what separated them, this sacred notion of literature, which Sartre refused. Sartre's ideological aridity couldn't comprehend Duras's sensuality, so volatile, so aleatory. Desire didn't flow through the works of the philosopher, whereas she already felt language shifting, fluctuating, stirring in wavelike movements within her, the same as those she would attribute to the violent, unpredictable assaults of passion.

The communist commitment shared by most of her guests nonetheless gave an intellectual flavor to the meetings on rue Saint-Benoît. According to Claude Roy, the atmosphere there resembled that "in Russian novels during the times of the intelligentsia, with the constant comings and goings of three ideas, five friends, twenty journals, three indignations, two jokes, ten books, and a samovar of boiling water." Duras was the life and soul of the group, with her "abrupt mind," her "baroque, often comical vehemence, an infinite capacity for fury, appetite, warmth, and astonishment."

In the course of those gatherings, which carried on until very late, with the guests occasionally even sleeping over, one might come across, apart from Mascolo, Antelme, and Duras, Edgar Morin, Jean-Toussaint Desanti, Jorge Semprun, Maurice Merleau-Ponty, Clara Malraux, Francis Ponge, Simon Nora, Jean Duvignaud, and sometimes Bataille or Blanchot. Feverish, vehement, subversive activity encouraged by Duras herself made her apartment a suspect, "divisive" place; there reigned a freedom of tone that was completely foreign to the language used in the cell meetings attended by nearly all of them, although they would soon be torn, after the war, between their visceral, almost mystical commitment to communism and the revelation of meanness, pettiness, lies, words trapped in their ideology, like Aragon's, who soon became a target for them. What he had at first thought to be a strength—this double allegiance, as Edgar Morin said, "to the Party on the one hand and the left-wing intelligentsia on the other"—became in actual fact a crime. Those who believed they were "changing cultural politics" were entering into the era of suspicion: "Everything was decided very high up and very far away from us, not even by Casanova, not even by Thorez, but off in the distant frozen north. Cultural politics thus also became a fate to be suffered patiently, obediently."

If there is a constant in her life and work, it is most certainly that of truly revolutionary, subversive, transgressive speech. She is always haunted by a panic-fear of becoming rigid, settled down. Instinctively, she feels closer to writers like Michel Leiris, Elio Vittorini, and Raymond Queneau than to apparatchiks like Aragon, Kanapa, and Casanova. Likewise, Mascolo and Antelme, who had joined the Communist Party in the spring of 1947, also feel this incompatibility, and barely five years after the war, like Duras, they will have to leave the Party. Duras generally adopts the same language as Antelme and Mascolo, preaches a freedom of speech incompatible with the Party's stereotyped dialectic, draws a portrait of the intellectual unworthy of the pious image of the good Stalinist that was conveyed in official circles of the period. On rue Saint-Benoît, the intellectual "cloister," as Mascolo put it, grows larger and a considerable fracture develops with the "Marxist study group" [GEM]. Formed around Mascolo, Morin and Vittorini, the GEM does not hesitate to criticize the Party, threatening to become "fractional." Duras's personality also encouraged this subversion. She was the life and soul of these meetings, a sort of dilettante revolutionary animating the debates, delighted to gather, to introduce, to number among her guests the cutting edge of the era's intellectual avant-garde.

To remain a communist without the Party's backing was, for her, to attempt an impossible reconciliation. A kind of fidelity kept her there, in the bosom of this "family": fidelity to the war, to this struggle they had all waged, the liberals, the Resistance fighters; fidelity to certain ideas then preached by the Party, the fight against capitalist oppression, selfishness, injustice. So many abstractions in which she still believed, with a certain amount of romanticism and naïveté, she who had become the little cell secretary on rue Visconti. But she couldn't deny the existence of practices that would soon victimize her: excessive, abusive control, the muzzling of speech in public, an archaic official policy. She saw the perfidious infiltration of the police while heads were turned and motions were being passed.

An untamed spirit, whose every fiber rebelled against all forms of law, she always showed a spontaneous aversion to the police, agents of every vice, every brand of treachery. The brutal image of the Gestapo remained with her like a permanent obsession. The police, the dogs, the barbed wire, the wall around the camps and the collaborating, condoning forest are the fatal, funereal symbols of the tragedy of the world evoked in her writing.

There must also have been a kind of fidelity to Antelme in her fraternal presence in the Party, on account of the camps and the part played by Russia in the fight against the Germans. But how could she hold back her anger, her buried violence, fed by her hatred for the shackles and the lies, how could she continue to ignore the utopian purity in which she ended up believing, this grave innocence? Little by little the rupture asserted itself. The taste for destruction, for radical solutions led her to leave the Party. She reproaches it above all for this "leveling of intelligence, this horrible shift from the person to the corpse." For what struck her as she read those reports from the Central Committee in her cell meetings on rue Visconti were the same brigading, the same secular catechism, the same morbid, death-bearing religiosity she had denounced in Germans and Catholics. She felt endowed with a renewed youth that intelligence kept permanently replenished through the practice of criticism, through the questioning of dogma, through the perpetual movement of the ideas to which she submitted.

Her individualism bound her to solitary defiance, to less ideological confrontations, and to constant self-interrogation. Because of this, she knew that she was a writer above all. Also a communist, a militant, but not for long. She suspected that writing could not find its source there, in that gagged language, in those leaden models proposed to her, in such a rigid, brutal framework.

No, a writer could never be a communist as defined by Elsa Triolet and Laurent Casanova, who asserted without batting an eye that an "anticommunist" writer could not have any talent. "On the other hand," relates Edgar Morin, "it seemed that the most exquisite talent authenticated every work of Stalinist edification. Genius was beginning to be measured by the extent of the Politburo's approval."

At the prompting of Andrei Zhdanov, the Soviet Politburo member charged with watching over the storehouse of Stalinist orthodoxy, communist intellectuals were subjected to tight surveillance. In Moscow's eyes, there were only two blocs: the United States and the Soviet Union, diametrically opposed, and the struggle had to be waged in the domain of culture as well. All of those who expressed nuances, like Elio Vittorini for example, who had founded the journal *Il Politecnico* in Milan, distancing himself from the central bureau, and who admired Faulkner, Hemingway, and Joyce, were expelled from the Party, called deviationists.

It was precisely for those reasons that Duras liked Vittorini, the Sicilian from Syracuse, the aristocrat of the mind, "one of those peasants whom princes and great men should be proud to resemble," as Claude Roy described him.

Intransigent like her with regard to cultural freedom, he refused to accept the principle of political interference in art, because for him politics was "a question of necessity, therefore of duplicity and the inevitable lies."

The Party's suspicion with regard to Mascolo and, consequently, Duras, had actually begun very early, after Mascolo joined. The positions taken by Vittorini, to whom Mascolo and Morin had willingly lent their aid when they interviewed him in *Les Lettres françaises* on 27 June 1947—scarcely a month after his entry— had caused Casanova to call them "Vittorinians." Indeed, in this long article, Vittorini spoke a new, completely revolutionary language, which the Central Committee immediately found deviationary. "I believe," he said, "that all philosophy must be completed. It never expresses the entire truth of an era. The forces of reason and the forces of poetry are what produce the works that, as a unified whole, express the truth of that era." Mascolo, under the name of Jean Gratien, oriented Vittorini's thinking in an unacceptable direction, as far as the Party was concerned: "So the writer," he said, "and the poet are essential spokesmen for the truth?" "The writer is the one who 'makes people see,' as Eluard says," Vittorini replied.

Finally, the article resituated communism on a revolutionary path, ever open, ever freer: "It is only in revolutionary action that morality really begins to exist," he stated. "Communism has no desire to build a collective soul. It aims to create a society in which false differences are liquidated. And with those false differences liquidated, to open up all of the possibilities for real ones. . . . One turns to communism out of love for man's complete freedom, out of the desire to realize the ideal of a complete man."

Casanova's anger was considerable: "We have no lessons to learn from an Italian," he asserted with a hint of xenophobia. Vittorini's statement (prompted by Mascolo) "So the principle 'the end justifies the means' can in no way be a communist principle?" "No, absolutely not," sounded the death knell of confidence between Mascolo and his friends (Morin, Duras, Antelme) and the Party's central leadership. Categorized as intellectuals unable to adjust to the working class, they were immediately suspected of agitation and of instigating deviation from the Party line. In September 1948, Casanova kept up the attack in a report published in *Les Cahiers du communisme,* making it clear to them that their presence was undesirable. In spite of the usual oratorical precautions, Casanova's report was quite heavy with disguised threats, as the conclusion suggests: "The act of leading communist intellectuals toward definitive adoption of the ideological and political positions of the working class so that they will bind themselves heart and soul to the proletariat is not incommensurate with the Party's current possibilities. The Party will strive patiently to do so, for it needs them sorely."

But if the report ends with feigned good intentions, it opens in a very polemical manner: "The secretary-general of the Party observed that many communist intellectuals had still not entirely come around to the ideological and political positions of the working class. This observation constituted a very serious warning, for the secretary-general of the Party indicated as well that a dialogue must be pursued with the comrades who are in error."

The report, built around four points (the communist intellectual's attitude toward popular culture, the communist intellectual and the leadership of the revolutionary movement, the relationship between politics and ideology, the dangers of the persistent survival of intellectual habits and prejudices), adds up to a lesson in fidelity and allegiance to the Party. Afraid that these intellectuals would thus play into the enemy's hands by engendering a situation of crisis and demoralization, trying to explain the underlying reasons, Casanova in turn employs sarcasm ("Joining with the proletariat implies for intellectuals the occasionally painful task of criticizing previously accepted values"), false compassion ("It can result, temporarily but quite clearly, in uncomfortable personal positions"), and a frontal attack ("Some are led to seek compromises, inventing ideological and political approximations which, they believe, will facilitate the transition").

Henceforth objects of scorn, Mascolo and Duras (although not having taken part directly in the debate) were not exactly expelled or treated like lepers, as they were three years later, but they became insidiously marginalized, spied upon, a different breed of militants.

In Paris, all deviants are immediately carded, followed, driven to despair; "Stalinism of the second glaciation," as Morin called it, was being put in place, culminating in isolation at the beginning of the fifties: "The little world of communist intellectuals closed in on itself, supplied solely by a mystical bridge with Moscow."

Some, like Garaudy, the painter Fougeron, and Aragon, were reduced to obedience, accepting everything: Budapest, Prague, the tributes to Stalin, the epic hymns to the lumpen proletariat, the spellbinding odes to the Great Union. Duras knew that she was alone now, nauseated by so much disillusionment, so much sadness.

She was becoming acutely aware that the Party was destroying the writer, making him, like Aragon, "a garbage can hero." Her viewpoint already assumed that the writer could exist only through provocation of the reader, in that dialectic which sang of desire and passion, of cries uttered and silence, in the multiple counterpoints composing each book. The writer came to life there, in the ceaseless tossing of the ship, always at sea, a drunken boat under "new skies."

Though separated from Duras, Antelme didn't leave rue Saint-Benoît until 1948, when Mascolo moved in permanently, thus giving the lie to the rumors of a dissolute life, deliberately spread by the Party. That same year Antelme met Monique, a young communist who had been a Party member since 1943, with whom he had an affair and whom he would marry in 1953.

At the time he worked at 10, rue Leroux in a Party center, the Federation for the Deported, the Interned, Resistance

Fighters, and Patriots; he worked with Edgar Morin and other fellow travelers. Pinned to the heart of his story there was nonetheless the memory of the camps, as evidenced by the long analysis he made in 1949 in the magazine *Jeunesse de l'église*, published by progressive Christians from 1942 to 1949, and which he entitled "Pauvre, prolétaire, déporté" [Poor, Proletarian, Deported]. The whole dialectic already expressed in *The Human Race* was developed and asserted in that study, extending the trial of deportation to that of the political struggle being pursued, each day, beyond the war. "There is no difference," he stated, "between the 'normal' regime of human exploitation and that of the camps. . . . The camp is merely the open version of the more or less veiled hell in which so many people still live. . . . Consequently, we cannot receive as such any ethic, or any value, that is not concretely universalizable, in other words, that does not first imply that the conditions for the exploitation of man by man must disappear."

But the frank speech favored by Antelme, Mascolo, and Duras with such obstinacy was incompatible with the line dictated by Party breviaries. Too lucid, too independent, only too aware of the force of the lies and the repudiations, unable to keep quiet without repudiating herself, Duras was led to resign in January 1950 from the Party, which officially expelled her on March 8th of the same year based on the reports of Section 722 of the sixth arrondissement on rue du Cherche-Midi, and more particularly on the insistent recommendations of Jacques and Colette Martinet, active, influential militants in the cell. With her, in the same cart, Antelme and Mascolo. . . .

Mascolo was the first to submit his letter of resignation to Lucienne Savarin, the Party Secretary, on 11 January 1950. His letter intended to avoid all polemic; apparently neutral, it appeared all the more scandalous, more "insolent," to use the Party's expression:

My dear Lucienne,

I hereby confirm that, as I told you two weeks ago, and for entirely personal reasons, temporary ones I hope, but which are unfortunately quite imperative, I cannot renew my membership in the Party.

I especially want to tell you, asking you to inform our comrades of this, that *I am in complete agreement with the political line of the Party*; I know that some have claimed the contrary. It is not true. . . .

Once again, my reasons are entirely personal, but absolutely insurmountable at this time.

Therefore, please tell our comrades that in leaving them, I insist on stating that my fidelity to the Party remains unchanged, and that I have the same reasons for being a communist as when I joined. Those who know me well will not doubt the seriousness of my reasons.

Fraternally,
Dionys Mascolo

Duras in turn drove the point home less than a week after Mascolo's resignation. Her letter, in contrast, was scathing and polemical. It alone was enough to reveal her provocative temperament, her violence, her implacable hatred when she feels betrayed, her caustic, sandblasting irony. Certain features of her letter even announced, already, the humor of her future comedies *Le Shaga* and "Yes," *peut-être*:

Dear comrades,

I hereby confirm what I said to Lucienne [Savarin] on 27 December when she came and brought me my '49 stamps: I am not going to renew my membership in the Party.

It is because I no longer considered myself a Party member that I didn't go to last Wednesday's meeting. If I had gone, it would have been as a former Party member, in an attempt to make the group acknowledge the truth about the meeting in question, on Thursday. But I admit I was unable to overcome the feeling of disgust and, I must say, ridicule that I felt at the idea of having to confront once again the sordid, ludicrous machinations of the poor little fanatics belonging to what might just as well have been called "the Martinet faction," since the word faction is being used abusively.

My reasons for leaving the Party are not those of Dionys Mascolo. No one is influencing me. I made this decision on my own and well before Mascolo. I remain a communist, profoundly, organically. I have been a member for six years and I know that I can never be anything but a communist. I would have gladly expressed the reasons I have for leaving the Party if I weren't convinced that certain comrades are determined to distort the most elementary truth by all possible means. Don't worry. If I can't expose these reasons in your presence, I won't expose them to anyone else in the world.

My confidence in the Party remains unchanged. I am even certain that in the course of time the Party will manage to cast the Martinets far from its ranks. I mean those who, through a vicious sentiment disguised as vigilance, can only satisfy and cultivate their bitter remarks and their petty personal hatred. I think the Martinets actually missed their true calling. They shouldn't have joined the Party, but rather the fire brigade (where, besides the prestige of the uniform, they would have had the opportunity of taking some much-needed showers), or the priesthood where they would have treated themselves to the pleasures of the confessional. But I have no doubt that the Party will manage to lead them back to the straight and narrow. So you see the extent of my confidence and the magnitude of my optimism.

Very fraternally yours,
Marguerite Duras

P.S. I am not confusing the Party with the Martinets.

Antelme and his companion Monique were in turn denounced by the section in the course of a cell meeting. During that memorable session, Antelme's expulsion was announced: Monique was asked to stop seeing Antelme if she wished to remain in the Party, which she of course refused to do, so she too was expelled. For good measure, Monique's ex-companion, Bernard, the father of her oldest son, was also required to choose and he in turn was excommunicated.

On 8 March 1950, following an investigation and lengthy deliberation, the Party wrote the same letter to Duras and Mascolo:

The Saint-Germain-des-Prés cell informs you

(1) that after having examined your political attitude in general, which shows profound disagreement with the Party's political line, particularly regarding literature and the arts, as well as the Kostov and Rajk trials,

(2) that after much discussion in the cell during Wednesday's and Monday's meetings, where you were unable to explain yourself since you refused to attend,

(3) that after having read and fully discussed your letters, full of insolence toward the Party and its democratically elected leaders, and presenting no political argument, the majority of the members

present (eleven votes out of nineteen) have decided to exclude you immediately from the ranks of the Party. Seven comrades, while strongly condemning the terms of your letter, wished to hear from you, in spite of your categorical refusal, before making a decision.

Charges:

1. Attempted sabotage of the Party through disorganization of the cell and a permanent attack on the Section Committee by resorting in particular to insult and calumny, and by using pretexts that hide profound disagreement with the Party's political line.

2. Association with Trotskyists such as David Rousset and other enemies of the working class and the Soviet Union (in particular an ex-attaché of the Yugoslavian embassy, currently editor of *Borba*).

3. Frequenting of Saint-Germain-des-Prés nightclubs where political, intellectual, and moral corruption reigns, which is vigorously and legitimately condemned by the laboring masses and the honest intellectuals of the arrondissement. The exclusion proposal was unanimously ratified by the Section Committee of 16 February 1950.

In accordance with Article 35 of Party statutes, you are suspended from the Party, pending the Federal Committee's decision on the proposal made by the cell and the Section Committee.

This article gives you the right to appeal the decision.

The secretary, for the cell,

A. Vanveers

Of the four of them, only Antelme and Monique will appeal. A year later, it turns out, the cell secretary informs them of their reinstatement, which they will refuse.

In a lyric and Pythian mode, like a tragic heroine, or those mythological beings driven by sacred anger to incantation and lamentation, Duras never stops denouncing the Party's blind night, its massacres, its camps, its lies, its wars of conquest, the gags it stuffs in mouths. A leitmotif of her interviews and of some of her books, it is her wound that she is singing there, her anger at having been misled and, since she lives entirely in excess and passion, her language is beyond measure, barbaric and extreme. "It's shit, it's nothing but shit, that's the only word for what you get with those people," she says in 1990. Those people, she adds, are autistic, dead, frozen in their "closed silence." As for her, she never stops living, she moves forward in spite of the rising tide, she makes a blunder, loses ground, and she moves forward again, but farther, she flies into a rage and she cries, she drinks and she follows drunkenness as far as it will lead her, she loves and she delves into the secret core of her love; she could be at sea, but in the desert as well, for it is limitless, changing, rippling in the intensity of contrary winds.

The three of them, Antelme, Mascolo, and Duras, form something perhaps resembling those excommunicated from Port-Royal. A Jansenist-type aristocracy dwells within them, forbidding their pulverization by the petty bourgeois formalism of communism and the Party's attempts to bring them to heel.

When she learns that she has been expelled, that the Saint-Germain cell has "immolated" her, as Morin says, she feels no bitterness, no despair. At the very most, anger, hatred which will thrive, flow out of her and give rise to the great anticommunist vociferation that even today nourishes her dialectic. Undoubtedly, like Morin, also expelled a few months later, she undergoes some periods of disorientation. How could she rejoice at this loss of communist citizenship to which she had adhered, full of hope, a member of a family she naïvely believed to be her own forever after? How to accept this alienation from the others, who were all "snug and warm in the workers' clubs, in the meetings"? How to pretend not to hear the insults ("Duras is another Messalina," remarked Jorge Semprun unkindly, as Mascolo relates), the lies spread, the insincere arguments?

She loses faith in this brotherhood, whose limits were nonetheless visible to her, and then the days pass. Endowed with tremendous vital strength, deadly energy, she is now free, but as Morin continues to proclaim, "a communist always, forever, but free, finally myself, responsible for myself."

Writing also teaches her to overcome the trial, for what she wants most to write about are the traps of the self, the fragility of authoritarian people, the ropes they throw to one another in an attempt to understand the inexpressible secret of things, and the silent story of those who try to understand. If her distress is momentary, it is not the same for Antelme and

Mascolo, especially Antelme, whose wound is immense, irreparable. After *The Human Race*, after expulsion, he is once again "defrocked, rootless, cosmopolitan, rejected."

His fierce intransigence, reminiscent of Pascal abjuring the Jansenists, his refusal to sign the declaration of capitulation, self-criticism, nails him to the cross of martyrdom. The hysteria all around him is total. His disobedience is intolerable; he is one of those witches hunted down in all totalitarian regimes. Pierre Daix, in the homage he pays him after his death in *Le Figaro* of 30 October 1990, recalls that tragic time: "I will never forget," he writes, "Antelme's distraught face the day he came and announced to me that his cell had expelled him. I held out my hand to let him know that nothing would change between us. He hesitated before taking it. 'What's the use, it's all over. . . .' Considering what had brought us together, there were no words appropriate for that moment. He disappeared into the elevator, more stooped over, more massive."

From that day on, he dooms himself to the silence of writing. After the camps, after the dishonor of expulsion, he joins the silence of Blanchot, the secrets of white writing, the space in which everything is made, silent and full of rumors from elsewhere, protected by that very silence.

On the other hand, Duras speaks enough for two. She hurls insults, in a frenzy comparable to that of her mother, howling, like her, in editorials, covering with insults the Party that claims she is a member of the Intelligence Service, on the payroll of the ideological enemy.

The constant return to that time, in her interviews as well as in her articles, the way she has of believing herself to be free of it, nonetheless exposes clearly the raw wound of her failure, perhaps even her pain.

She talks about the dishonor into which the Party throws its expelled members: "You know six hundred people. All of a sudden, you realize that everybody has received the order not to see you anymore, not to shake your hand."

It is that loss which she will keep inside of her, that anger, ineffective for the moment, which she will convert into writing, into rabid anticommunism, later celebrating with unconcealed joy the breaking up of the Party, its historic set-backs. The Party then becomes an object and an instrument of hatred, informing Duras's entire social stance, nourishing the vengeance that propels her message, explaining the course of history, contributing to the meditation to come on "the inconceivable fate of existing."

Many years later, in 1980's *Green Eyes*, the hatred is still not dead, for her there is no possible satisfying of this anger; when she talks about it, her voice takes on an incantatory rhythm, a sudden violence, the words of a prophetess: "I wish they were dead," she clamors. Thus she continually rises up like Don Quixote against the disloyalty, which she still calls "the betrayal of the people." She relates the Michelet fable in which men would persecute women who talked to trees and animals and maintained a magical relationship with nature, making witches of them, and applies it to the communists. They too hunt down the disobedient, the undisciplined, the libertarian. Thus for her, condemnation of the communists is a continual rehabilitation of speech freed of all constraints, and of writing. In her eyes the writer becomes the outlaw, the one crying in the wilderness, endowed with the femininity inherent in the writer's suspect, dual nature, the one who wants to "spoil the purity of the general rule decreeing mental hygiene."

Cramped by this false fraternal community, by this institutional camaraderie, by this sham equality, by this unlimited expanse of lies, she now recognizes herself only in the act of writing. Writing as a solitary act, the only way to knowledge, with no possibility of return, drawn away to impossible, unknown frontiers, not wanting to reveal what one glimpses of the secret of things and of the world, the pain, the mystery of the waters, their high and inaccessible places, of the vast rumbling silence of space.

Writing becomes the most anticommunist act imaginable, because it is deliberately solitary, detached from the entreaties of Party bureaucracy, and she who accepts its challenge ends up being "her own object of madness," without going mad. It is an ardent undertaking resembling passion, errant and individual, sublime and mortal.

5

Entering "the Wonderful Sorrow" of Writing

How powerful must have been the mourning for that childhood, that little brother, that country where the rice fields spread out like dunes in the desert, the mourning for that disappointed love for the mother, for her to chain herself to the writing of *The Sea Wall* in 1949–1950!

There was of course the influence of American writers, those of the "lost generation," and their taste for great, harsh, cruel sagas, that ample writing unfolding in the novel, that epic rhythm she liked so much in the work of Steinbeck, Hemingway, and Dos Passos. But that wasn't enough; there was something else to delve into, not yet literature, but something that concerned her intimately. The family tension she had expressed in her last two novels, *Les Impudents* and *La Vie tranquille*, came into its own once again, even if she borrowed a lot from Mauriac, and from the violence and unkindness of human relations. But here in this novel she built a kind of epic, or to be more precise, her memories emerged, the "iron gray" Indochinese sky rose, and there appeared the massive silhouettes of the buffalo standing motionless in the rice fields.

And then this vengeance also had to be satisfied, raising to the level of myth the mother betrayed, repudiated, scorned by the "colonial swindlers," attempting to convey their putrid odor, that dying, pernicious society that had broken her.

And there was also her story of the little brother, the companion of her childhood games, when she would go out with him at naptime to kill monkeys in the forest and hear the birds squawk as they were being devoured by tigers. Her brother would say: "Listen, listen to the tiger," and his eyes followed the crackling of crushed, devoured animals.

She writes *The Sea Wall* in a state of silence, the better to hear the sounds of childhood, the smells, the murmurs, the heavy flow of the Mekong's waters, and the muddy pools in the rice fields where the peasants waded, always stooped over when she saw them, invisible beneath their large, pointed straw hats.

She is writing the founding book, the one she will rewrite over and over, as if in reality the writer never writes but a single book, obsessively reworking the same motifs, descending further and further, digging subterranean paths to better understand this need to write, this extraordinary immodesty, this unwearying parturition. She writes that book, and it always returns in the work to come, always calling, like the siren of the Nightship signaling its course, crying out in the obscure night of memory.

Her writing becomes lyrical, unfurling its hatred and its passions. When she writes, the war has barely ended. She hears its last echoes, but Antelme slowly comes back to life, with his unrevealed nightmares. She knows fear even better than before, when she lived it on the streets, in her apartment, in her clandestine activities. The book comes into being, and writing performs its magic. The mouth of the Mekong, all of Asia and its inhabitants unfold on the white pages, but she introduces more order, organizing time gone by, because at Gallimard they tell her that a novel must have that form, that time frame, that coherence.

Inside her, a vague stirring yearns to express itself, but she has not yet attained that confidence in incoherence, in wounds left there, and yet with no apparent organization, at the very heart of her story. That is why *The Sea Wall*, in spite of a perfected style like that of a great classical novel, is paradoxically the endless novel, the groundwork for the other novels, the essential pattern that she will lacerate and destroy, a melting pot for the expression of life, all of life, its elemental breath. A novel of origins, for which she feels "fondness," so close to her. But precisely because of that, this reinterpretation of autobiography, of the myths of childhood, of the mother, and of death, is not yet complete in the field of literature, and remains a renewable source, inexhaustible, like the Mekong River or the China Sea, to be rediscovered, sung over and over until *Summer Rain* ("what the children knew . . . was that below their town was the highway, and the trains too. After the trains, there flowed the river. That the trains ran alongside the river, and that the highway ran alongside the trains' route. And that way, if there was a flood, the highway would have made another river"), until *The North China Lover*.

Her key contact at Gallimard, Raymond Queneau, snugly settled in his little garret on rue Sébastien-Bottin, among piles of books and manuscripts, expressed the greatest, most immediate joy upon reading *The Sea Wall*. One had to know Queneau, his enthusiasms and his exactingness, in order to understand precisely what that meant. He who had told Duras straight out "You are a writer" as early as *Les Impudents* saw his conviction confirmed. With *The Sea Wall*, Duras displayed the rich, powerful imagination that gave an idea of what would follow, the mystery that makes the writer go searching elsewhere in her night for the secrets of the soul.

The first week of publication, in September 1950, was particularly successful: five thousand copies sold. As a result, a second printing was ordered. Reviews were unanimously laudatory, expressing astonishment at the author's epic, "virile" inspiration, convinced that she was a French Hemingway, at the luxuriance of the narration, noting with approval this "art nurtured on humanity," this obvious gift for storytelling.

Once it came out, the novel was nominated for the Goncourt prize, but it was not chosen in the final round: the winner was Paul Colin's *Les Jeux sauvages*, also published by

Gallimard. A strange fate for Duras who, thirty years later, would nonetheless receive it in the evening of her life!

The Goncourt failure confirmed Duras in the extreme, revolutionary position she had already adopted. She persuaded herself that she had been eliminated because she was both a woman and a dissident communist, that the macho Académie had sanctioned her for those two transgressions. That kept alive in her a certain resentment, which would nourish a silent revolt against those she put on the same level as policemen, censors, rapists, "the boys." "I'm talking about certain novelists and critics in whom women instill the desire to kill. You see," she says to a *France-Soir* reporter when *Summer Rain* is published in September 1990, "these are men who cannot overcome the weight of past centuries when they were women's 'bosses.' They are no different from those who still beat women." Her speech will never lose its violent character. Something inside her corresponds to the precision of the great moralists, always finding the dark side which she describes with that cold anger characteristic of her.

And she was becoming a legend, already an accomplished writer, adorned with all the mythology of a foreign past, a firm grasp of narration, of construction, a true novelist, feared and respected, already loved. As it turned out, losing this "boys' prize," as she called it, served to irrigate her violence, to make her advance.

She handled the book's success with a great deal of both indifference and vanity. Sure of herself, she gives very little weight to negative reviews, steering her course with scorn, overcoming the momentary suffering of not always being perceived the way she would have preferred. She is a complex, ambiguous mixture like her protagonists, impudent and fragile, violent and taciturn. Deep inside, she yearns for glory and accepts praise willingly; nonetheless, a profound feeling of despair permeates her more each day, as if the entire farcical literary scene didn't concern her.

Writing actually runs after her, without stopping, and won't let go of her. Almost at the rate of a book a year, she will pursue this dark core that contains her secrets, this very simple, very inaccessible thing, this knowledge, this quest that takes her to metaphysics and plunges her into the night so that she can better understand the day. The Nightship is caught in storms, the darkness is total, often there are no stars, and the sky is oppressive. Such a course is mysterious, unfathomable to idea peddlers, storytellers. She is brutal and demanding. Did she too admire, like the character in the new novel she just published in 1952, *The Sailor from Gibraltar*, Fra Angelico's *Annunciation* in the Florence monastery to which the painter retired?

With her, there is always this passion for revelation, secrets, wonders offering themselves to her, an assumption of the truth of things and beings, and she knows herself capable of penetrating these mysteries, if only on account of her status as a woman, capable of carrying this gift of life, she too prepared to receive the Annunciation at any moment.

She finds most of her material in everyday life. Like Proust, she is curious about everything, taking the smallest details and pouring them into the spiritual comprehension of her novel, as a means of nourishing its matrix.

She spends these early days of the 1950s vacationing with Ginetta and Elio Vittorino on the Ligurian coast between Leghorn and La Spezia. She likes this little bit of beach between sea and mountain, beneath the excessive sun; she likes the juice of lemons flowing into her mouth, and plunging into the sea, not even cool enough to refresh her. She also likes the animation of the *trattorie*, the town dances, the aroma of barbecued meat mixed with the sweet smell of rose laurels. She learns how to live again, to feel free, she listens to people, her passion, preferably simple people, farmhands, truck drivers. She has an instinct for listening. Is that why she says jokingly in a 1969 *Vogue* article on Delphine Seyrig that she would like to "run a service station on a busy highway"? It is her aptitude for penetrating all social classes, talking for nights on end with the era's greatest intellectuals or with an escaped criminal, a cleaning woman, a traveling salesman, that reveals the most about her.

She prowls around seaports, she loves clandestine situations, the peculiar ties that develop there, the adventure in the air. *The*

Sailor from Gibraltar is nourished by this Italian experience, this raging heat that glazes the beach with a leaden hue. The burning sun will return again in *The Little Horses of Tarquinia* in 1953. The pressure it exerts on people makes tragic heroes of them, crushed by fate as by the implacable heat of the sand. Heat that paralyzes the vacationers, making them feel asphyxiated.

The combing of every shore in search of the sailor contains a symbolic richness that reveals her fascination with the edge, people who take risks and refuse to accept the ways of the world, social rituals, and routine. The sailor's joy expresses his freedom: he is an outlaw, he pushes the limits ever further, he loves the sea, because it is changeable and never subjugated: "How he honored the world!" exclaims Anna.

With *The Sailor from Gibraltar*, Duras opens up new paths in fiction. She is not afraid to borrow from the most flamboyant adventure stories, slipping in her own reading, from Roussel to Leiris, from Gide to Conrad, with Segalen in between. The novel coasts along every shore from Tangier to Porto-Novo, from Sète to the Caribbean Islands, as if wandering in search of life, with no limits or constraints, a junior version of *Moby-Dick*. But time is present, and threatens. She will always under-estimate its importance. This is the struggle and the lucidity in which Duras must be read and understood.

Like Anna, she is fond of alcohol. She has inside her "a place for that," she says in *The Lover*. She drinks, thoughtlessly, first of all because she likes it, then because she is breaking off with those who are comfortably settled, because alcohol opens up unknown spaces. It plays the role of God, abolishes restraint, makes one freer. She likes alcohol, all sorts of alcohol, whiskey, bitter campari, red wine, even the worst kind. She talks about it with defiance, provocation, abruptly.

There is a pain inside her as in all living beings, what she calls the planets' "silent indifference toward your pain." Alcohol plunges one into the solitude of infinite worlds, the blind murmur of the stars, the humming silence of the inaccessible cosmos whose meaning and chaotic movement are incomprehensible as is the absurd emptiness of the human condition, with its unavoidable existence. Alcohol helps her to forget that solitude, the distress she feels, coiled up, impossible to dislodge.

She started drinking in this middle part of her life, more and more, until she was almost able to snatch death as it passed by. This constant promiscuity with it suits her well, even if she risks destroying herself, even if the stakes are high.

The houses she likes have all known the solitude of alcohol. At Neauphle, which she has owned since 1958, when she was alone with alcohol, she ended up no longer needing anything else; it filled the void, the nothingness, the terrible absence of God. She didn't even go out into the garden anymore, or out by the big pond, preferring the silence of the house and the vibration of alcohol inside her, around her. Three times, she went to the edge: of death, of a ruptured liver, of paralysis, of a coma, of a brain clot, of madness. She went back to it for years, vermouth, apple brandy, she put on weight, swelled up, but she kept drinking, even in the morning, on a empty stomach, she vomited and drank again. People around her were worried, for they could see her skin becoming leaden, then black, the slumping body, the shriveled figure, but to no avail. Because of the American hospital where she stayed, Neuilly is now the place of death for her; it is there, in the little town with a provincial atmosphere, that she really experienced the Passage.

And yet the writing never stops. When she is sleeping, she is still a writer—the night sends her echoes, traces, passages, flashes—and when she drinks, in this alcoholic slumber, she still remains a writer. The dreadful cure of 1982 left her with images, crossings. She makes books, texts out of them, and gives others the desire to write too, Michèle Manceaux, Yann Andréa. She is the first woman writer who really dares to describe her alcoholism. She tells about the madness of drinking because it is part of the pain, her distress as a woman, this need, which she can only fulfill by writing. When she writes, she doesn't drink; it is afterward that the risk arises. What she calls "the dangerous state," those fragile moments on the slippery slope leading back to a relapse: a single piece of rum-flavored candy, a drop of wine, and the desire returns.

Alcohol gives her that lucidity, the taste for risking every-thing—like Anne Desbaresdes in *Moderato Cantabile*, which she published in 1958—the audacity to face stupidity, imbe-ciles, the nerve to talk to a stranger, the strength of scandal which keeps her moving forward.

She also drinks with the men she loves, as if alcohol brought them closer to that dark core she is constantly seeking, or even more, carried them elsewhere, to anonymity, to the very de-struction of identity, toward something that lightens and yet weighs down the body, the perforated body, soaked like a sponge, at the end of its rope, and the Nightship drifts beneath thick, dark skies, rushing toward that which keeps calling: the absolute.

There were frightful days, when she would rave, when madness took hold of her, when she claimed to see what she called "lami," bugs that swarmed under her bed and persecuted her. The days raced by quickly, as in tragedies, and she talked about it even more easily, especially in the 1980s, when she came so close to death, and returned from it with a pirouette, to everyone's astonishment. First there was the delirium be-cause of the alcohol, and then after the cure, the delirium resuming without it, as if irreparable lesions had been produced and had permanently affected her mind. Michèle Manceaux tells about her odyssey in *Brèves*, her walks with her, and re-calls her slippery, surreal words which make them fear the worst: "There is an equator crossing the Ile-de-France region"; she drinks a bottle of Badoit mineral water and says: "This is used Badoit."

With Yann Andréa, she drinks during the night, during the day, they never go out, enclosed in a tragic arena. They are alone in the big, deserted luxury hotel in Les Roches Noires; the sea, when evening falls, when the cars along the road become scarcer, amplifies its roar, its rolling, while they drink in the kitchen. That is how it was at the beginning of the sum-mer in 1980, when the tourist season began, and then after the tourist season until the beginning of autumn 1982, until the October cure, the hardest one, which she almost didn't sur-vive. Alcohol is what sealed their love, the complicity that joins her and Yann Andréa, just as later, when he continued to protect her and she too watched over him and they invaded each other to the point of conceiving of literature only in this mutual, ardent, unalterable presence of theirs.

Alcohol could destroy her, so she converted her passion into writing, she made books out of it, magnified alcohol, amplified the song heard everywhere, from *L'Eté 80* to *Summer Rain*, bringing her back to the secret of music.

A strange story, playing on the same chords of madness and sorrow ever since childhood, getting lost in this archipelago of memory, in this inner geography, and digging ever deeper into what oblivion has left unhidden, like those derelicts lying in the muddy, sticky sand when the tide goes out.

Right after *The Sailor from Gibraltar* in 1953, she publishes *The Little Horses of Tarquinia*. Once again Italy, in the summer, in the oppressive heat that causes fires, makes the air unbreathable, and turns this little village into a cell.

With this new novel, Duras lays the foundation of her aesthetic, from which she won't deviate; everywhere, the unavoidable Durassian atmosphere, the little melody that greets the ears when time stands still, meaningless, flowing imperturbably like the current in a river, or the sand in the desert, pernicious time, revealing in its absurd course the intolerable human condition.

It is always on this side of life that she roams in this waiting game, even though it wears out people, things, love. Trying to understand, she wants to penetrate into secret undertakings, the undermining work of death.

The books she has written, writes, and will write all arrive at the same conclusion of failure: life has no exit, as in Beckett's play where the characters wait for someone, something, in the indifference of unanchored temporality. Love resists least of all, undergoing the slow erosion of time, weakening the couple's desire, making its duration precarious. Outside, the surrounding forests burn, dangerously encircling the little resort: there is always the sea, with its breeze, its soft, warm coat, "the reverse side of the world," with its bushes of seaweed, its schools of little fish. But the sea is also threatening, for beyond the shallows there is the void, the silence where neither fish nor seaweed venture, but where you can feel the presence of "naked, empty," threatening abysses, the very metaphors of death. Death is thus everywhere, in the slow decomposition of the corpse, still unburied and lying in the sun, in the pine forest consuming itself, in the lovers hurting each other. The image of the abyss haunts Duras's imagination, runs through her writing, and the Chinese lover's sex is engulfed in her body, like the alcohol that leads her off into the starless night.

That is why the novel's very strength lies in its compression: everything must constrict the action, giving the impression of suffocation and monotony, translating this life of uneasiness, the impossibility of happiness.

Starting with *The Sea Wall*, her renown as a novelist grows with each book. And yet her talent is not universally recognized: at first there were violent reactions of fascination and rejection, as though what she was saying was unbearable, or so true that her readers must either accept its absolute truth or refuse it in an incomprehensible revolt. In November 1953, every major periodical reviews *The Little Horses*. Jean-Louis Bory of *Samedi Soir* expresses immediate admiration for her work: "Reality becomes a symbol for something else. It takes on meaning," showing that he understands the real dimension of her writing, the emergence of an inner voice, a vehicle for the transmission of secrets, and of the unknown. *France-Observateur* calls it "one of the best novels of the year"; *L'Express*, while criticizing what strikes it as stylistic negligence, places her at the forefront of contemporary literature: she "thought it necessary to have her characters speak pidgin and think nonsense. It's a shame. Especially since she is one of the few novelists trying to convey the tone now prevalent among members of modern society. Thus, even if it is a failure, her book is worth reading." But since she will henceforth be a victim of her reputation, certain journalists set out to destroy her, denying the validity of her conception of fiction, pretending not to understand it in the least. Critics as discriminating as Luc Estang or Kléber Haedens miss her intentions completely; the former, in *La Croix*, states: "After four novels, we must resign ourselves to the fact that Madame Duras wants only to write American French." The latter, in *Paris-Presse*, suggests: "It is friendly advice to tell her that she's making a mistake; she has talent, life, color, and she is worth more than her spineless, blinking characters whose company nobody enjoys." *Le Figaro*, which has always disliked her, writes sarcastically: "It's a novel to read at the end of December in an ice-cold bath." As for *Le Canard enchaîné*, apart from the satirical criticism characteristic of that journal, it reveals a side of Duras that many journalists will in turn take up, namely her virility. The cruelty in her novels, the cynical impudence of her characters, the defiance of laws, have always struck some readers as specifically masculine traits. That is why Duras has so often rocked the boat: failing to write according to supposedly feminine criteria, she causes trouble and anxiety. "This lady plays hardball and possesses a terse vocabulary. Jesus, what virility! But it is only a facade, for when she chats, Marguerite Duras recovers all of her femininity. Yakkety-yak! Bla-bla-bla! And she spouts off! Warbles! And on and on. Talk about a writer's golden tongue! In the case of Marguerite Duras, one thing is certain: her tongue is the most active part of her body!"

This violent misogyny is again voiced in the comments of a journalist writing for *La Gazette de Lausanne*: "Marguerite Duras's talent appears to be essentially virile, and it is hard for us to understand how a woman could have conceived and developed her work in such an intensely cynical and peremptory form."

In any event, as can be seen from these reactions, *The Little Horses* does not leave the reader indifferent. In novel after novel, Duras establishes a tone that henceforth cannot be ignored, for what she relates, in the tone of a recitative, is nothing less than the throbbing pain of suffering, the contradictions of existence.

For his part, Mascolo publishes at Gallimard, in that same year of 1953, *Le Communisme*, a thick volume of more than five hundred pages subtitled *Révolution et communication ou la dialectique des valeurs et des besoins* [Revolution and Communication or the Dialectic of Values and Needs].

It is a scrupulous work attempting to reconcile Marxist demands and the intellectual's independence while resolving, in spite of their expulsion, the fundamental contradiction to which Duras is equally incapable of responding: "There are no communist intellectuals. But neither can there be non-communist intellectuals." The Communist Party press lashes out once more against the man who had been the subject of so many debates and had sown discord among its ranks. Since they cannot run the risk of letting subversive thought seep in again, the Party's prominent voices denounce the work and "the Mascolos."

"A new revisionism intended for intellectuals," reads Jean Kanapa's headline in *L'Humanité* on 23 February 1954; "Arguments like Mascolo's," he writes, "attempt to discredit communist intellectuals, claiming that there is a contradiction between intellectualism and communism. Insofar as calumny does in fact prevent some intellectuals, and honest ones at that, from taking part in the struggle side by side with communists, anyone can see that it must be strongly opposed as a pernicious diversion. [. . .] We believe it is our responsibility to persevere, to be vigilant, and to destroy it." The work attracts considerable attention, giving rise to debates and controversy; Nadeau and Sartre participate in them, intrigued by the questions of an "enfant du siècle," as a Swiss journalist calls Mascolo. What is particularly emphasized in the work is this permanent task of elucidation to which the friends on rue Saint-Benoît have devoted themselves, in a continual, irresistibly subversive questioning and renewal of themselves.

The intellectual effervescence of their environment would always throw them into volatile, unprecedented experiences. Could Duras already imagine that the new technique she was creating in the novel would earn her a major role a few years later in contemporary theater? Narrowing the scope of action more and more, expanding the importance of dialogue, eliminating virtually all descriptive passages, she was thus opening new perspectives in writing, making it play on various registers, poetic, dramatic, novelistic. It is at this time more than any other that the turning point occurs. Later, all she will have to do is watch the unwinding of the path she has opened, listening to passing moments and capturing their echoes, the silent distress of men, as they pass beneath the cruel, indifferent arch of time.

She is intrigued by shipwrecks, and by the mad, drunken boat that loses sight of the coast, then plunges into the night. She loves those perils because they reveal buried, scandalous things, anomalies to those tucked safely away on land.

From now on, writing becomes her "task." She writes with the conscientiousness of a monk, daily, as others "go to the office." But the work is not routine; she explores, opens up new sites, clears the land. She throws herself into it with that fever peculiar to obsessive people; henceforth she knows that she was meant to write, that what she sees or merely glimpses is the very stuff of her work, and that she must not fail this story that has been given to her, that of her life.

But she will have to wait until 1958 and *Moderato Cantabile* to find the true path, the real trace of the secret on previously worked ground. Later, with the Lol Stein cycle, she will be at the bottom of the pit she was searching for and, overjoyed, she will extract marvels from it. She doesn't completely repudiate these first books, but they correspond to a part of her life that she will abandon in 1958, social gatherings, cocktail parties, soirees with millionaires, with the usual Parisian crowd clinging to the writers currently in vogue. She possesses "that vulgarity," she says, that of wasting her time, of letting it slip by without being master of it, like the characters in her novels in a sense, idle and errant. She drinks a lot during this period, letting herself be carried along by literary fashion, writing in the mood of the times, like another Sagan; and if the characters already seem outwardly unique, on account of the sun, drink, awareness of danger, albeit fugitive, the desire to flee, there is still too much psychology, too many conventionally fictional situations. Yes, she says in *Woman to Woman*, she "cranked those books out, she had an almost sickening aptitude for them," she could write one like that in two weeks, just as she used to write little stories at school, with disconcerting speed, and surprising imagination and inventiveness. But she knows she cannot stop there; her characters themselves are leading her elsewhere, toward a truer, more perfect "sincerity"; already waiting, in the expectation of one to come, ready to break out of the narration and wander off toward the improbable lands where the Nightship is headed.

She is secretly, totally consumed by her ardent, absolute, frantic need to write. She writes not for others, but in order to follow, book after book, the traces of her quest, the ever-deeper landmarks of this initial knot lying at the base of her work, in which childhood traumas exist side by side with the native land, and death's reflection on love, on the film of time.

She remembers what *The Little Horse of Tarquinia* taught her: ellipsis, tersely concentrated situations, increasingly consistent rejection of description and psychology. With the four stories of *Whole Days in the Trees*, her next book, published in 1954, for which she will receive the Jean Cocteau Prize, she goes back and prowls around her childhood, shedding light on certain aspects of that earlier life, trying to understand.

In 1950, her mother returned to France, permanently this time. If she had gone back there, to Indochina, as though she could live nowhere else, plunging into ambitious projects, like the girls' school she founded, with the same ferocious energy she had applied to blocking off the China Sea, if she had remained in that voluntary exile which gradually became necessary, it was mainly because of the "little brother," whose grave she wanted to be close to, but also because of the big brother, to whom she still sent money. And then on account of the war, weary of everything, she decided to come back to her native land, to this imitation Louis XV castle paid for with money earned at the school, a tumble-down turn-of-the-century castle, a "mad extravagance" that nobody wanted.

She was tied to Indochina as if by a spell, like those settlers who could no longer leave that land, marked for life by its strangeness and its magic.

In the course of her second stay in Indochina she changed, as if she too had become impregnated with its culture, gradually becoming rooted in its way of life, its customs, its landscape. The presence of natives around her rather than settlers proved her attachment to this land. She was not like those well-to-do, town-dwelling settlers, the haves, holders of privileges and of the best lands, but more like those bush trekkers who ventured into the dense jungles, those missionaries who lived among the Annamese people and their legends, steeped little by little in native rituals and wisdom.

Though she had always maintained faith in colonial values during those years of the last return, from 1932 to 1949, a well-developed sense of civic duty, she nonetheless opened herself up to the influence of Asia, so foreign, and yet less foreign than old Europe where she no longer wanted to live. Chinese Annamite expressions became grafted onto her speech; she could converse in a picturesque lingua franca and slip with a kind of familiarity into the spirit of this land, its religions, its taste for the supernatural which gave her a break from colonial activism and the cultivation of bourgeois respectability on the far-flung shores of the majestic, indolent Mekong.

Her presence thus gave her a particular status among the French of Indochina, a stranger to their norms and principles; she was more of an adventuress, poetic and witchlike, all the stranger for having held out against the onslaught of the China Sea and the spoliation to which she had fallen victim. She brought back to France with her a little Vietnamese girl named Dô, and otherwise lived alone in that great residence, prey to fears, fits of madness, and bursts of energy which gave her the boldness to try anything, imagine anything. In *The Lover*, Duras tells of her last scheme, the purchase of electric incubators in which she tried to raise six hundred chicks but carelessly let them all starve. The large drawing room in which she put them was surreal, first with the chirping creatures and then with the smell of decomposition.

Duras didn't have complete access to that madness, that singular vigor with which her mother was possessed, but she felt within her the same unpredictable, irrational tendency.

Her mother's bohemian life, her preference for the older son in spite of his escapades, even though he had squandered all of her money, dispossessing her, even though he had sold the woods on her property in Amboise, just like that, in a single night's gambling, all this derived from an eccentricity that was both foreign and familiar to her. But ever since the little brother's death, the mother no longer existed for Duras; she too was dead, like her big brother.

She had nonetheless seen her again in 1950, right after her return from Indochina. She introduced her son Jean to her, but there was no longer anything between the two. The mother must have had only one child now, the beloved older son, her exclusive, only love, from which Marguerite was excluded. In one of her rare autobiographical confessions, Duras tells how silence in fact developed between them. This piece is called "Mothers" and it is published in the second volume of the *Collection/Cinéma*, entirely devoted to her: "I tried to convey to her that one's preference for a particular child could be revealed by barely perceptible, minute details, and that even if the mother was in no way responsible for it, this difference in love caused great unhappiness on the part of the less loved children." The lack of understanding was finally complete and irreparable.

And yet the forgotten, rejected, dead mother was still there. She returned in the first story of *Whole Days in the Trees*, as if Duras were fascinated by this woman and her intolerable love for the son; as if killing her off in *The Sea Wall* hadn't succeeded in severing all memories of her, burning all of the tenuous, secret threads binding her in spite of everything to her mother, that object of her love and hatred.

Nonetheless, she undertook the narration of this family conflict again in the title story of *Whole Days*, re-embroidering it, liberating it from the tension of tragic passions. The thieving son is not only the black sheep she condemned, he is also the rebel, the wild man endowed with this energy to say no that she has always admired; in his own way he is the liberator, the one who rid himself of the mother's alienation.

The mother is no longer merely abusive, but a shameless mother, leading a scandalously bohemian life, ignoring others' opinion of her. The two characters in the story become likeable; Duras thinks of them fondly, with amusement, sometimes ironically. She tries to understand what separates her from this spineless brother, searches for attenuating circumstances for his actions, his wrongdoing; she grants him her compassion, renders him the honor of wanting to feel free, "stark naked, grown-up, subject that night to the weariness of all men."

Such is the human complexity she likes to seize, to take by surprise, just as after the liberation she complicated Rabier's trial by giving contradictory evidence, proving beyond all doubt that nothing is simple, everything is ambiguous, dense.

She attempts to unveil that primal image of the mother and son, bringing it into view, reworking it in the books to come, cutting away then adding on again, presenting it on stage, infusing it into actors, extending it beyond all bounds.

During the rehearsals in 1966 for *Whole Days* which she had just adapted for the theater, she writes in *Vogue* about the brilliant Madeleine Renaud, the Lady of the Trees, the mother in *Whole Days*. She relates how the actress seized the role, carrying it even further into a wild clairvoyance, enlightening Duras about zones she hadn't explored in her mother and which the words, her own words, and the voices of others, had brought to light. The original story has been going on for nearly fifty years, and that is still what makes her write *Savannah Bay* and *The Eden Cinema* even later.

It is very simple and very complicated at the same time; there are no words to describe it. When Madeleine Renaud asks her for details, she is not very talkative; the story is fleshed out with a few dry remarks, but between the two there is nothing but dense silence, full of rumors which the books feed upon, even richer in information.

"In her old age," Duras tells her, "she had become bitter, she wanted to ignore the fact that she had trained many other captains who were fighting for their country's freedom, she no longer wanted to remember, she wanted her despair to be perfect."

"What else?"

"She was thin."

"What else?"

"Of her three children, it was the eldest she loved the most, a superb, tender, wayward son."

"Oh, I see. Had she always loved him more than the others?"

"Always."

From that preference she made the frame of her work, in which crimes and sacrifices are constantly being played out, as in the story "The Boa," the second in *Whole Days*, where she tells about her walks in the Saigon botanical garden, accompanied by her landlady. Yes, more than twenty-six years after the event, she thought like the adolescent she was at the time. From seeing the boa ritually devour the chicken at four o'clock in the afternoon, she derived an intense, sensual pleasure, making a pact with nature, its violence, its savagery. She accepted this perpetual motion of life and death, of good and bad, always convinced that one must live on the border between civilization and wilderness.

Her expulsion from the Party strengthened her sovereign, superb anger; but she still hadn't lost the conviction that Marxism-Leninism could be a solution to society's problems. Only Stalinist communism was repugnant to her, with its diktats and its backstabbing.

As a Party militant she nonetheless contributed until 1950 to the Party's attack on "the dirty war" in Indochina. The communist line of that period, amplified by the far-reaching campaigns it conducted against the "atrocities" committed by the expeditionary force—executions of civilians, reprisals, rape, looting, torture—could only be approved by Duras, all the more affected by the conflict since she felt as if a part of herself were linked to this oppressed people with whom she had so many common roots. But her most active militancy in these final months, when she was so preoccupied with the disagreements separating her more each day from the Party, still had to do with writing. By writing *The Sea Wall*, she showed in her own way the corruption, the institutionalized theft, and colonial violence much more effectively than the Party's outbursts in denouncing "the methods of pacification." She felt, and Vittorini had already expressed similar sentiments, that such literature was the best means of exalting conflicts, the most effective way of bringing them to public notice, since its language was mainly characterized by the force to reveal, to attack. *The Sea Wall* alone would most certainly be worth all the press campaigns organized by the Party, in this last part of 1949, more than all their petitions.

She thus asserted the truth of writing, as a means of access to political reality, to awareness, and true commitment.

From 1950 until the disaster of Dien Bien Phu in 1954, she will take little part in the war controversy. Expelled from the Party, consigned to a certain form of political anonymity, without any precise, organized structure, she will be strangely absent from the ongoing debate. Dionys Mascolo says that the two of them remained silent "out of humility and above all out of powerlessness." For want of an audience, doomed to a certain solitude and to the isolation peculiar to intellectuals, who find it difficult to intervene in the public sphere when speaking in their name, Duras and Mascolo were forced to remain observers.

Not until 1955, with the Algerian war, will they find motives for active commitment, for more spectacular defiance, in a heroic romanticism that brings them closer to the condition of Resistance fighters under the Occupation.

The war in Indochina, moreover, must have given rise to mixed feelings in Duras's mind: torn since childhood between her status as a settler and the spontaneous energy that always drew her nearer to the natives, clashing on account of her unconscious emotional cross-breeding, unamenable to the colonial spirit and at the same time brought up (in spite of it all) by her mother in that violently dual, rebellious, and hampered spirit, she couldn't carry out a completely lucid, radical political analysis. On top of the basic position she had taken, there remained the nostalgia for this land of her childhood, like a pain lodged in her, impossible to "liquidate."

Although the meetings on rue Saint-Benoît were literary rather than political in nature, and the personalities who gathered—such as Bataille, Roy, Blanchot, Leiris—were devoted more to writing than to politics, her main concern was always for the humblest, the most deprived, the unwanted, the rejected, admitting all the while her fascination for murderers and prostitutes. All of those who had in fact crossed a boundary, who had been more or less outside of the law.

In "Madame Dodin," the third story in *Whole Days*, she shows affection and complicity toward that concierge, undoubtedly one of those on rue Saint-Benoît, maybe even her own, and toward Georges, the sweeper. There too, it is another kind of alienation that she describes, caused by consumer society, the suffering of these two humiliated individuals, comparable to the rubbish their trade forces them to collect, solitary and repudiated. The text looks for a way out, a remedy for this injustice, rejecting the "Christian" solution offered by communism, the revolution to prepare, pushing toward nihilism. Grim, imminent danger runs through and threatens the narrative in spite of her droll writing; a righter of wrongs, Duras opts for this underground violence; she has chosen her camp.

Much later still, in 1987, in a film about her produced by the French television network TF1, she sets out to show a Paris dawn, when armies of Africans clean the streets, the great boulevards, in the silent crunching of brooms sweeping up the plastic and glass bottles, the tin cans, the papers, the cigarette butts, and the haze of dust that the dawn will never wash away. With a sharp eye, she films that ballet of outsiders, grasping their solitude, a word cried out in dialect, shaming an entire society, giving rise to the song of misery and humiliation. And her camera conveys grave, monotonous accents, like a sonata for cello, repetitive and haunting.

She thus finds a society guilty of betraying its proletariat, and implicitly condemns those who should have been there to defend it, through these pictures, in black and white, with no dialogue, as silent as solitude itself, through the voice of poetry.

She probably had to feel her way forward in the first novels, wandering through the luxuriance of *The Sailor from Gibraltar*, and the story of the family saga told in *The Sea Wall*, establishing the major principles of Durassian aesthetics, which she will never stop exploring thereafter, hovering before the blazing hearth that conceals, her unerring instincts tell her, the Secret and the Sign.

"The Building Site," the last short narrative in *Whole Days*, is in its own way perhaps the most important text she wrote in that decade. Never before had she so completely explored the silent activity of the romantic encounter, the slow, patient passing of time, torn by events, laying bare the waiting, the emergence of passion, never had she compressed the action to such an extent, so that the meeting between two unknown people might attain its fullest, its ultimate expression.

With this story, the search for the obscure, fascinating, secret alchemy that made the future lovers finally meet each other, after a whole series of silent, ritual passes in which unknown, foreign, uncoded rules came into play, Duras opened up a new fictional space to literature. She liked to watch the man in "The Building Site," particularly the way he "darkened," "slowly sinking, a little further each day, into the red forests of illusion," "henceforth seeing everything as a sign." She had discovered a new dimension of time that no longer yielded to the snags of individual events, to the flow of words, to accidental things, but spread out in a vaster, limitless "kind of oceanic duration."

From now on the Durassian novel would take those routes of knowledge, a secret search for love, with the body playing a major part before restoring it to the soul, with everything finding a logical explanation only in the silent flow of signs and this circulation of desire, founding a true metaphysics of love.

This function of silence and desire wandering in the darkness, this refusal of speech in favor of interior analysis, of the unpredictable course of things, were nonetheless in the spirit of the times. The novelists of the "nouveau roman," as it was then called, also asserted themselves by rejecting classical literature, the usual methods of analysis inherited from the nineteenth century, and the excessive use of psychology. A new, bolder, more hermetic approach was being devised in the publishing laboratories of Seuil and Minuit. And yet Duras, mistrustful by nature, apparently didn't want to join them, convinced that for her it would mean risking sterility and losing her unique voice.

The safe distance she established between herself and the writers of the nouveau roman—"businessmen," she called them —clearly shows her aim of originality in the literal sense of the term. Hostile to all recruitment, to all schools, she feels a sort of visceral repulsion for everything related to group principles, group techniques.

Nonetheless, the fact that all of those "toiling in the laboratory" of the nouveau roman are published by Minuit—in other words, the most intellectual publishing house in Paris— causes her to come into contact with them. She of course establishes ties with Robbe-Grillet and Butor, who are closer to her narrative conception than to "bourgeois" literature, but she always stays in the background, as if she wanted to remain absolutely independent in all political, social, emotional, familial, and intellectual circumstances. In this situation, she reveals the indisputable faculty of second sight, foreseeing the events to come, which would show that she had been right to avoid the traps springing up in her path. Thus, sooner than all the writers of the nouveau roman, she apprehends the repetition, sterility, sclerosis. She is the first one of the group to stand aloof, followed, but much later, by Robbe-Grillet, Sarraute, and Sollers, who will wait until the 1980s before returning to a certain traditional form of the novel. Duras's attitude is still the same, however: she draws the very sap of her being from the history of ideas, of human beings. She capitalizes on certain discoveries of the nouveau roman, like the notion of risk governing things and the world, a perspective that opens up unknown trapdoors to words, all the while remaining carefully on the fringe of any movement, even marginal ones.

This certitude she has always had of possessing a part of the Great Secret, of being more on the side of exiles of art than of established writers, academics, and intellectuals, closer to

Pascal, Rimbaud, and Bataille than to Robbe-Grillet and Butor, this very fervent, essential, and sensual relationship with literature, doomed her to feel immediately cut off from the nouveau roman. Only Nathalie Sarraute seemed to find favor in her eyes, and not on account of feminine solidarity, but apparently because she is the novelist of basic reactions, of the most microscopic "tropisms," constantly tracking down "the barely visible" and "the insignificant." Duras will always take great interest in her work, feeling special affection for her, going to see her plays, reading her books, she who rarely reads her contemporaries. Her own literary adventure is subject to too many outrageous modes of behavior, excessively irresponsible attitudes in the sense Rimbaud and the surrealists conceived of this right to scandal, to the unexpected, to the mystique of writing, for her to identify with the members of the new school, who disapproved of such notions as a matter of preordained principle. Something in the realm of the intuitive, the immediate, of passion, maintains an irreducible distance between them, even if she sometimes finds in "the school of the watchful eye," in its way of observing things, another possible direction for writing. When she writes, impulses, flesh and blood, and instincts cross the page. The work is born of that, this cry springing from her, an ancient sound, from these echoes reverberating from all of the cries haunting her, from the maternal imprecations of *The Sea Wall* to the songs droned by the beggar woman, from the child expelled from the mother's womb to the only possible form of speech, a cry she would never utter as distinctly as at the sight of Robert Antelme dying, while she took refuge, horrified, in a closet. This resonant, dark room is where the work is founded and constructed, in a nearly unknown genesis, in the realm of mystery, in undiscernible darkness. How could she then identify with the rules defined by Robbe-Grillet, with his plan to elaborate a pre-established technique? Intuitively, Duras understands these things. In this decade of the fifties, she is mindful of these upheavals, of what is being set up, and at the same time she knows the dangers of such an adventure: the sterility, the diminishing depth of things and people, a stereotyped language, a coldness that is at odds with her rebellious, seething temperament, the sophistication of theory, aesthetic and theoretical rather than metaphysical preoccupations, and also the loss of that sacred quality of literature she seeks, despite being an atheist, sure of finding there new keys to its mysteries.

She knows that those she admires—Diderot, Rousseau, Proust, the great Russians, Cervantes, Bach, Vermeer—did not first concern themselves with technique, didn't attempt to build a theory around their art, but rather plunged into the thick darkness opening up before them, from which they brought back a few traces of another day. Intimately, she understands that this is where her direction lies, this is her path. The wake of the Nightship, constantly cut open and covered up again, must be the sole object of her attention, along with the abysses it lets her glimpse in passing, the attempt to penetrate the unknown. Apart from that, she has the distinct feeling that all is vain speculation, abstract words having nothing to do with her pursuit.

Stubbornly, she insists on being unsophisticated, as during her childhood when she wrote poems "about everyday life" with the same natural instincts she would later transmit to her readers. *The Square,* eventually published in 1955, then appears on the horizon, a narrative to which she now devotes herself following the success of the previous novels, signaling a new era in Duras's work, since each one of her books is a kind of destruction of the one before it, or at the very least a surprise, another way of seeing and telling.

Even before Sarraute writes her famous essay "The Age of Suspicion," Duras tests words in the text, in the living matter of writing, in that verbal flesh and its deepest, least accessible layers, delving into the secret of what they mean, the back room of the memory, the deep pilings of conversations, the engulfed, obscure, secret Venice of words, that apparently silent space between them, but which she alone hears as it whispers, wells up, cries out. All the murmurs of the unspoken word that, with her brutal, savage instinct, she wants finally to grasp, in the music, as they pass by, in flight, she might say.

Perhaps it is Antelme's terrifying experience that opened the way for her once more. After *The Human Race* and the silence to which he has henceforth given himself, there still remain the whole cortege of deported persons, still living, and the gasps of the dying, the cries of the birds hovering in a circle above the camp, the muffled sound of defecation in the open-air shacks; after his own discovery of the horror, the slow processions of prisoners alighting at the Gare d'Orsay station, the white silence of those killed at Hiroshima; thanks to him she discovered the gaping holes of speech, the uselessness of words, of conversation, the futility of books despite their persistent murmur, and surely something truer, newer, therefore more recently born, closer to the beginning: her ambition.

A persistent belief in the prehistory of words and actions moves her forward, a faith in what is no longer even voiced but is nonetheless heard from behind, back there, hidden, speaking and revealing its shadows.

From her room in the American hospital, in 1982, she cries out, she wants to break everything on the nightstand next to her bed, she throws herself on the floor, tearing her clothes, falling asleep there, at the mercy of her opaque night. In her delirious jolts, even in her alcoholic fits, she knows there is something that must be found, something beyond her grasp; she dreads it, she is terrified, she realizes that she may die, that she will certainly come close to it, the night, the cold night, the void of consciousness, she who always devises mental scaffoldings, throbbing to the point of pain, of immense fatigue, she is sure that Neuilly is the place of death, but she nonetheless adavnces into this unknown, this darkness calling out to her.

It is this end of all things, this tunnel where the glib theoreticians of the nouveau roman never enter, that she enters. And from those abysses, she brings back silences, small, seemingly insignificant sentences and cries and murmurs, anonymous, exiled things with no identity, and which, lined up end to end, weave the web of her work, many-layered, neatly sliced, thoroughly explored, wounded, painful.

In *The Square*, Duras tries to listen to the little maid and the salesman, sensitive to their worries and their misfortunes, the infinite loneliness possessing them, inhabiting them, the "silence common to all of the oppressed." The condition of waiting and respite that she had already described in her previous novels returns here with this nakedness, this absence of revolt, only the terrible observation that "we are abandoned." She, the little maid, "says nothing and acts," and he, he "sings every morning while he shaves. . . . What more do you want?"

No violence, no plan, no regrets, only life wearing out, passing by and slipping into the general indifference of others and of the universe. Even if Duras can be linked to Beckett's imaginary world—like him, she portrays individuals thirsting for words, waiting—there is a particular originality, what will henceforth be called the little Durassian melody, tying her work to the delicate phrasing of a sonata, free of all ornament, naked, limpid, like those of Bach, Beethoven, Diabelli.

Is it her femininity that endows her with this exceptional receptivity, this unwearying capacity for listening generously as she will soon do, especially from 1955 to 1958, indifferently going to meet murderers, convicts, movie stars, shopkeepers?

In her interviews she says that she is convinced of the specificity of the feminine capacity for listening, without confining her position to a militant feminist impasse. What a woman can hear and understand of "general phenomena," in other words, the vibrations of the world, the most remote mysteries of the universe, is absolute and complete: she speaks, perceives, receives, while men settle for words and braggadocio, noise and conquests. With *The Square* she initiates a kind of writing born of the previous novels but that, although dependent on them, has widened and given itself to all the forces of life, abandoned itself to the world's need to be listened to, its cries of loneliness, its despair, these "lowest of the low." A very delicate synthesis has developed, making her the defender of a society's oppressed, the ear attentive to their suffering and the abysses of silence in which they bury themselves, the translator of these hidden, gagged desires.

So she lets them speak, and their words occupy the entire narrative space because that is the only way to make up for the suffering, to limit for a while the ravages of despair. They talk, all they do is talk, they are nothing else for the duration of the book, speech running, not even attempting to listen to others, but spreading itself out, because "it feels good."

Does she understand that, with this short narrative, Duras is moving her work toward theater? The boundless quality of writing, this notion she will soon make the principle of her fiction, the breaking up of one genre into many others, to film and almost to poetry, begins here with *The Square*, in this river of speech, where dialogue becomes the expression of sorrow, the best transcription of the painful passing of time, its undetermined, incomprehensible, absurd course. From this point on the novel can be transferred to the stage, watched on a screen, even better, sometimes become music, a flowing of notes, a melody sung over and over, made and unmade.

Later she will become methodical about it, as if writing were becoming the surest means, once rewoven, of comprehending the world. She goes back to the original work and reinvents it, adding windows without which it remained blind, dumb to extensions of the self, to the echoes of words, and to the reverberations of language.

Sooner or later she will have to "break out" of genres, attempt crossing into other spaces waiting to be invented, to displace zones, roam around obscure poles, red-hot, often undetectable cores, assume the solitary journey of Orpheus, not hesitating to go back down in order to begin the work over again, extending it in the direction it wants to take, on that path already mapped out by Proust, but free. After *La Musica*, there will be *La Musica deuxième*, after *India Song*, there will be the movie of *India Song*, after *Abahn, Sabana, David*, there will be *Jaune le soleil*, after *The Lover*, *The North China Lover*, and so forth, until touching the bottom of those unknown seas crossed by the Nightship.

Written jointly with Claude Martin for the stage, *The Square* is produced on 17 September 1956 at the Studio des Champs-

Elysées by Ketty Albertini and R.-J. Chauffard. But her plays
give rise to criticism every bit as impassioned as that provoked
by her novels. Duras remains the epitome of full-blown scandal, delighting or exasperating. Two days later, the press lashes
out against the play. Max Favalelli of *Paris-Press* calls *The
Square* a "psychological striptease"; the feared Jean-Jacques
Gautier of *Le Figaro* becomes virulent: "It's the soul of ordinary
people, seen by the *NRF*," "a poor man's Maeterlinck" or "a
soporific Beckett."* *Le Monde* sarcastically calls it "a sure
means of hastening the downfall of the theater, leading it to its
death throes. . . . Two heroic actors learned by heart the fluid,
delicately invertebrate text, an ordinary, everyday style, ah!
how ordinary it is! My distinguished colleague Maurice
Blanchot finds it abstract, impersonal, and all the more touching. For perhaps *The Square* is in fact a masterpiece. A masterpiece of pretension, fake simplicity, and woolly philosophy."
Guy Verdot of *Franc-Tireur* suspects Jean-Paul Sartre of "lurk-
ing backstage." But other voices are also heard, less sectarian
ones, more attentive to Duras's monotonous music. Thus *Le
Figaro littéraire*'s Jacques Lemarchand, an early admirer, celebrates "the author's extraordinary art of making people speak
the way they would speak if they ever dared to speak," praises
the discretion of the dialogues, "the alternating song, the song
with two voices trying to harmonize"; Gustave Joly of *L'Aurore*
detects in the play a "fleeting harshness" that reminds him of
Genet's *Maids*. At the revival in May 1958, at the Nouveau
Théâtre de Poche, Claude Olivier of *Les Lettres françaises* states
that "such a play is real theater."

Parisian audiences thus discovered a new dramatic author,
but an original, unique one, who made no concessions, listening only to people's silences, "ordinary sorrow" that can be, as
she says, "conveyed in a dialogue."

At other revivals, moreover, in 1960 at Les Mathurins, in
1965 at the Daniel-Sorano, the play will be all but assimilated

---

*In the original: "En attendant dodo," which puns on *En attendant
Godot* (*dodo* is baby-talk for sleep: "beddy-bye")—TRANS. note

by the audience, proving in that way Duras's truly prophetic quality, her advance on time and history. Better still, *The Square* will become a classic, attaining a graceful balance which the transparence of the dialogue and the dramatic unity help reinforce.

From the era of *The Lover*, in 1930, she still remembers the young man who committed suicide in the middle of the night by throwing himself off the boat bringing her back to France, the all-white steamer, one of those surveyors of the sea, an ocean liner, which had stopped in the darkness, tried to find the body, and then had gone on its way again at dawn without ever recovering him. She is like that young man, engulfed in the suicide of writing, with nobody coming to rescue her, remaining at the bottom of the sea, in the darkest terror, in the solitude of the great depths, "that pure, undetectable mass of water, certainly as convincing a proof of life as the very spectacle of death."

For a text by her doesn't have the permanence sought by academicism. Volatile, it "obliques," twists, asks to escape from the words, to exchange itself. She calls that method "digging up the forces of the text," breathing new life into them, powerful, ever deeper energies, like the Secret.

This "forcing" of the text, wringing from it the worst, most entrenched limits, converts her work into hard labor, concentrated, pent-up, ever-present pain. It is on account of this reexamination, this constant recasting, this life reactivated, breathed into her, that she escapes the sterile traps of the nouveau roman. Theory, which she hates, intellectual speculation, analytical or theoretical discourse: these are of no concern to her. She prefers to grapple with human beings, their lives, their deaths, dragging out of them, through that intolerable curiosity possessing her, the same force with which Proust was endowed, mysteries leading back beyond the night.

Should the publication of Maurice Blanchot's *The Space of Literature* during the same year as *The Square* be interpreted as a sign? Must we look for still another in the article Blanchot publishes in *NRF*, revealing that intellectual complicity, that familiarity with her work, which will lead him a few years later to be one of the frequenters of rue Saint-Benoît?

Reading *The Space of Literature* today, it seems that Duras's entire oeuvre was nourished on this book, for Blanchot's brilliant flashes catch up with Duras on her long trek, the endless odyssey she has undertaken. Blanchot recalls Rilke's famous verse, "We, we who risk everything," applies it to the writer, and to his labor, that of an exile, "without the protection of the common day," "cut off from himself, cut off from his birthplace." Her entire demonstration harks back to this "underlying thread of obscurity," this "fundamental level" toward which Duras is slowly advancing and whose traces, whose first rumblings, beginning to be perceived by Blanchot, will later unfold in the Lol Stein cycle.

One and the same viewpoint joins them in the swell of antagonistic movements, in this perpetual back-and-forth motion between light emanating from the work, "shining upon the obscurity," and engulfment in "absolute obscurity," in the Orphic quest, on the edge of the immense, dark abyss, sucked in by it, divided, torn.

Duras reads this book as a fundamental, illuminating, necessary work. The path she has decided to take unveils the whole road to her. It explains to her what she has only formulated in the opacity of her narratives, on the other side of the words, intuitively, in this prescience of things and of the world that she has always had and that will soon cause Lacan to say that *The Ravishing of Lol Stein* reveals a basic understanding of alienation disorders and describes "clinically perfect delirium" better than any psychiatric report.

Like Blanchot, she believes in this midnight throw of the dice constituted by the writer's work and the emergence of writing; she believes in this inevitable night, the construction of this "burrow" which "opens up the night to the other night," all rumors and surprises, danger and unknown occurrences, and makes the writer the anonymous being, "one who has entered into the realm of the indistinct."

Outside, far from the obscure holds of writing, on the fury-filled edge, the colonial empire is cracking apart on all sides. At Dien Bien Phu, the French soldiers are massacred in the muddy basin. That disaster encourages the nationalist revolts in the protectorates; in Algeria, on 1 November 1954, only six months after the defeat in Indochina, the war of liberation begins. It is the revolt of a half-starved army with no real weapons, composed of men who had always been forced to keep quiet and had been reduced to misery, to the status of sub-humans; they too move into the shadows. She is immediately sympathetic to those they call the "fellaghas," who, at night, also hide in burrows and caves, listening to the other night, attentive to "the flowing of the sand of silence," as Blanchot says. For her, fighting in this war shares the same essence as writing, "the essence of danger." Between the scrublands of Kabylia and that which she inhabits when writing, there is a short distance, the same insecurity, the same proximity of death.

With Dionys Mascolo, Robert Antelme, and other friends, she enters into a new secrecy; she will help the rebels because she sees there a reason for finally putting into practice her sense of fraternity, another way to venture into the arena.

6

"The Midnight Game"

More and more, she wants to add her voice to mankind's struggles and conflicts, as if she saw herself as the standard-bearer of its causes and wanted to share them. Her group's virulence, from the year after the uprising until Algerian independence, leads them to the frontiers of the far left, to a singular kind of anarchism in which their speech is radicalized and they come to be considered as potential terrorists, dangerous subversives. In fact they help the Algerian insurgents, becoming French citizens of shame, those who are called "suitcase carriers." They are in their element in this war, for it sharpens their dialectic, allows them to live, to actualize the concepts of insubordination, desertion, subversion: words that well suit Duras, always drawn toward those forbidden zones of disobedience where "the Midnight Game" is played, as Blanchot says, the close match fought to the death between Day and Night.

In an interview granted to *Le Magazine littéraire* in June 1990, Mascolo explains precisely what drew the little group into the struggle: "It was the affirmation of a right, a heretofore unrecognized right: that of disobeying a State that forced one to become an oppressor." The reports coming into Paris, the questions about torture that intellectuals were starting to ask, the reverberations of what Antelme had endured, became in Duras's eyes the source of new, unbearable suffering. All her life she will bear the weight of these sporadic fits of suffering, which carry her away as a storm would; she will always know these moments of emptiness, of intolerable horror, which make her feel as if she were suddenly engulfed in a hostile, brutal sea.

In the fall of 1955, the rue Saint-Benoît group, at the prompting of Robert Antelme, Dionys Mascolo, Louis-René des Forêts, Edgar Morin, and André Mandouze, founds the Committee of Intellectuals against (the prosecution of) the Algerian War.

"It was a time when a groundswell seemed ready to form in the country," recalls Edgar Morin in his *Autocritique*. "We wanted to take a stand against the very principle of colonial war and in favor of the very principle of a people's right to self-determination." Although the Committee is established at the initiative of expelled former members of the Communist Party, many left-wing intellectuals join it. Communists even rally to it, "disappointed by the Party's tactical softness," but also well-known intellectuals such as François Mauriac, André Breton, Jean-Paul Sartre, Jean Cocteau, Jean-Louis Barrault, Abbé Pierre, Jean Cassou, Roger Martin du Gard, Georges Bataille, and Claude Lévi-Strauss, all joined together on the morning of 5 November, in the Salle des Horticulteurs in Paris, to demand "a stop to the repression," the prohibition of all "racial discrimination overseas and in metropolitan France," and "the opening of negotiations."

The founding of the Committee is a bombshell, and above all "a strange novelty," as Cassou said in his inaugural presentation. In its issue of 7 November, *L'Express* also notes "this consensual nature of the Committee," manifest for the first time "since 1935 and the committees for anti-fascist vigilance." The heterogeneousness of the signatories, justified by the ethical tenor of the manifesto, is maintained for more than a year, until some reservations begin to appear on the part of communists and more cautious intellectuals who are frightened by the radicalism of Sartre and associates. Didn't Sartre state on 27 January 1956: "Colonialism is our shame, it is a mockery and a caricature of our laws; it contaminates us with its racism. . . . Our role is to help it die. . . . The only thing that we can do and should attempt . . . is to fight side by side [with the Algerians] to deliver both the Algerians and the French from colonial tyranny." If Duras doesn't appear in the forefront of the Committee's original group, she has a strong underground influence as the unconscious instigator, like an inner voice whispering the words to the others. The main founders are the men who have counted the most in her life; for all practical purposes the three of them live or have lived under the same roof, suffered the same anguish, carried on the same struggles. How can one imagine her being absent from it, she whom Claude Roy describes so well in *Nous* as endowed with "that infinite resource of fury . . . [and] the intrepidness of a lonely little soldier lost in the advance guard or on the right flank?"

Each day she rises up more defiantly against the State, the powers that be, the institutions; never has this notion of the Jew that she formulated after the war, amid the painful return of the survivors from the camps, found its living justification as here. In this conflict, she is "the Jew," as were the rebels themselves in their own way; Jews meaning the banished, the hunted, exiles from this land which was nonetheless theirs, Jews meaning refusal of those cellars where they tortured people, degraded the words *human being*. She in turn was a Jew, an Arab, a fellagha, it was really the same thing.

An intuitive solidarity with the Algerians made her discover situations she might not have known in another time; the struggle she was waging led her to greater sensitivity in detecting racism in people's eyes and driving it out into the open. From this point on, she is very much in demand with newspapers and journals, which ask her to write articles and essays. *France-Observateur* especially will employ her often, immediately recognizing her talent for grasping the unusual aspect of an event, finding hidden majesty even in the slightest news item, sketching in a few lines the portrait of a princess or a murderer with the same natural ease, by virtue of their human qualities. With journalism she inaugurates a style that she will polish until it has a tone all its own, acutely attuned to the times. She goes out of her apartment, sees a young Algerian illegally selling a few flowers, pulling his cart toward the corner of rue Jacob and rue Bonaparte. She observes the following scene: some plainclothes cops knock over the cart, and "the intersection is filled with the first flowers of spring." She captures, as Dos Passos or Hemingway are capable of doing ("at the curb," Dos Passos would say), attitudes, words, silences, "a woman complimenting the policemen: well done, gentlemen! If everyone did as much, we would soon be rid of such rabble"; some other women, without a word, pick up the flowers and pay the little Algerian. It is this new perception of the world that she gives to her readers, redefining journalism, restoring its ethics, by sketching little scenes in the lightning bolt of the moment, the unnoticed faces on the streets, the crowd, her brief glance fastening onto a situation in a second and exploring it, grabbing hold of it and telling it as it is, in that coarseness of already "fluent" writing, a vision she only wishes Eisenstein had been able to grasp, with his blinding flashes and the savage nakedness of his eye.

That is the word she will never stop using, as if it were becoming the echo of her novel writing, working on parallel roads, those of the Night where she navigates and those of this Day whose tragic, unjust obscurity she nonetheless reveals.

On another occasion, again in *France-Observateur* in 1961, she brings a Warsaw ghetto survivor's testimony face-to-face with that of two Algerian workers in Paris. She has them talk about fear, their terrible loneliness, the hatred surrounding them; she manages to extract a confession from them that makes her ashamed of being French: "I don't wear a scarf or a tie anymore. That way I don't get strangled. You have to leave your tie, your watch, your wedding band at home. That's what we all do now."

She conducts her interviews without pity, trying to draw out the raw, most essential message. She questions, and her queries don't have the least familiarity of tone, the least demagoguery. Sharp and even impersonal, they get to the heart of the matter, mercilessly. When she asks questions, her words come through smooth yet fractured, direct but sinuous. She always attempts to extract from others what is also deep inside herself: fear, loneliness, risk, extreme situations, simple happiness, sought after but beyond reach, for which one must nonetheless struggle.

She tirelessly roams through those conflicting inner and outer zones, "the outside" and "the inside" as she says. She tracks down the periphery of silence, the trembling area of desire and those furthermost places where everything is played out, and at the same time, especially in these years leading up to the Lol Stein cycle, she takes a great deal of interest in events in the world, the streets, and in people, the rising murmur of cities, prisons, convents, theaters, stadiums, shops, the old neighborhoods of Paris, Les Halles, Le Marais, Saint-Germain-des-Prés, the unwonted tragedy of miscellaneous news items. She lives in those alternatives, sometimes outside, full of solidarity and generosity, sometimes inside, in the glowing embers at the core of the soul.

She sees her life in the gathering of all these breaths, in this vague participation in everything that surrounds her, in this multitude of spaces and times absorbed and reprocessed through the filter of her imagination. There, in the resuscitation of sounds and gestures, in her extremely keen interest in them, in the profound meaning she assigns to them, that is where she lives out her life, animated by them, thus able to say that "the story of your life, my life, doesn't exist. . . . The novel of my life, our lives, yes, but not the story."

It is exactly as if writing had devoured her, giving her the only possible answer to life's questions, as if the meaning of "general" phenomena, as she says, were there, hidden, behind the strings of words, between the words, in the miracle of their associations, in the very element that remains beyond their reach, anonymously, with no more literary, grammatical memory.

Because of that she likes Bataille, whom she often sees at this time, and writes about, for what he himself writes, fitting into no code or frame of reference, is like something thrown out into an unknown night which will no longer be understandable in terms of any critical analysis whatsoever. In Bataille she discovers the force of this language cut off from its usual, traditional ties but "emancipated, cured of its bad company," drifting off "into its own darkness." For her Bataille is an exemplary writer of modern times because he too abandons intelligence, no longer competent enough to account for meaning, incorporating into it "the qualities of the body" and "its unknowns," and "its wounds." For those reasons, she will later refuse to recognize Sartre as a real writer, but rather as a theoretician, an initiator of ideas, more often than not an ideologue, and precisely for that reason excluded from the rhythm and the echoes of the body, its revelations, and the knowledge of its lands of exile.

Writing about Bataille, she writes about herself at the same time. She has an intuitive understanding of Bataille's quest, for she travels in the same deserts, to the same crossroads. Everything she says about others is a reflection of her choices in life, in writing, such is the extent of her narcissism, drawing the lifeblood of her story from all things.

She has the certitude of her intuitions, of this inner knowledge she captures from fleeting time, she has complete confidence in herself. Aware of the seduction she exercises over others, of this fascination to which her "musica" gives rise, she plays with it. Her powerful ego devastates others and her curiosity about the world is the immense tool of her creation: she draws other people in, she pumps them continually like a vampire and injects their juice, their vital substance, into her books, into that inimitable song of life she composes.

What attracts her is this language of the body whose depths she is trying to penetrate, catching the echoes of its cries, its lapses, its pleasures. It is this inimitable mixture of sensuality and rigor, distance and brutal possession, that separates her from the frozen lands of the nouveau roman. In this period preceding the sixties, she perfects her interviewing technique, for it deepens her quest which will develop so intensely in 1964 with *The Ravishing of Lol Stein*. Since she has an intuitive understanding of their solitude, their despair, she is able to establish authentic links with her interlocutors, those she interviews for major periodicals. In a 1957 conversation with an ex-convict for *France-Observateur*, she reveals once more her fascination with "unrepentant hooligans," those outlaws who are not afraid of words, who take responsibility for their acts, and in whom she knows how to unlock, with a single question, the loneliness, the sexual misery, detonating a revolt, giving rise to distress. She likes those people, exceptional types, heroes of the underworld or of the Resistance, and likes to reveal their paradoxes, their mixed feelings, taking interest for example in the case of a criminal whose affection for a cat that had adopted him in the penitentiary contrasted with his unalter-able, unbroken violence toward society, unappeased by years of prison.

Meanwhile the Algerian war escalates, along with the opposi-tion to it in France; what had begun as a mere fellagha revolt deep in the Aurès Mountains, what was interpreted as one of those sporadic uprisings that colonial France had known dur-ing its history, takes on the appearance of a real war against an enemy who, while invisible on the ground, will sooner or later have to be met at the negotiating table. France itself is divided, torn between its last bursts of colonialism, the desire to quell the revolt through bloodshed, and the pain of seeing its sons go off to the front. The war spreads to the mother country, threatening to turn into a civil war. In these fractures of his-tory, Duras feels all the more comfortable, as if her entire being found its real meaning solely in these times of passion, of tension, when people are revealed to themselves in danger and risk, forced to choose, with no possibility of remaining neutral. She likes these extreme situations in which her commitment is total, tragedy returns to the world stage and, like a robot, she becomes transformed again into the little heroine of *Antigone*, comparable once more to Joan of Arc, that figure for whom she feels great fascination, "sublime" as she says in *Woman to Woman*.

In those moments she is never afraid, as if the high stakes galvanized her. She dares to confront the State, the entire political establishment, invoking forgotten values and ethics.

She offers hospitality to representatives of the FLN, finds

hideouts for them; whenever she can, in meetings, in interviews, she denounces arrogance, torture, colonial bad faith. Her position is radical, violent, blunt.

Along with Simone de Beauvoir, but in a more subversive and provocative vein, she is one of the few creative women who speak out during this war, daring to defy the government, betraying it, making pacts with the enemy. She is the Nightship with all lights out, cutting through the thick, turbulent night.

She also knows that women like her, women who do not want to remain in their roles of submissive females, are still gagged, imprisoned, tortured; she knows that they are called "witches" because they dare to go against the established order, and won't keep quiet. She is on the side of those who are defending them, actively struggling, Gisèle Halimi the radical lawyer, for example, Simone de Beauvoir. . . .

She makes a vast metaphor of the feminine condition out of Michelet's book *The Witch*, an exemplary fable in which the women left alone by their husbands, who have gone off to the Crusades, talk to the birds, the trees, the animals in the forest, inventing new kinds of speech, new relationships, thus creating disorder and confusion.

In 1957, the Committee of Intellectuals that the little group on rue Saint-Benoît had created is dissolved at her own initiative. Certain militant communists hesitating, as Mascolo points out, to "take a position on the principle of peoples' right to self-determination," as a result of the Soviet invasion in Budapest, the Committee preferred to fold. As time goes on, the former group's founders become more and more radical. The differences of opinion at the heart of the Committee had grown rapidly, for there was a spirit of provocation in the air. "The communists and the progressives," confides Edgar Morin, "were pragmatists, tacticians; they felt repugnance for radical language, always too moralistic and idealistic in their view." Internal conflicts had even shaken the founders' confidence in each other. Morin was thus repudiated by Antelme and

Mascolo because of the Messali Hadj Affair: Hadj was the head of the Algerian National Movement (MNA) and an opponent of the FLN, which appeared to be gaining the upper hand. The Sartreans supported by Antelme and Mascolo opposed the defense of Messali Hadj orchestrated by Morin, and "hysterical" sessions ensued, damaging the Committee's credibility and drawing its energy far away from the real struggle. Weakened on all sides, "the Committee sinks. It had rapidly ceased to be a committee of intellectuals, becoming subjected to political taboos. It had lost," in Morin's eyes, "its moral authority. It foundered in the mediocrity of ephemeral motions and communiqués."

As for Duras, she survived all of these storms. She has always possessed enough strength to remain inside and outside at the same time. Capable of fitting into a group while keeping her freedom, her tragic sense of individuality. Capable of crying out with others, but also in the solitude where she perhaps feels more effective.

That is why the extent of her commitment in the world and her attempt to intervene against the intolerable were and are still widely appreciated. Some incredulous observers feel that her political and social stances helped her, at best, to forge her "image," to use events to serve the work better; at worst, to indulge in self-congratulation. Others see in her a woman in the world, subjected to its cruelty, alien to it and yet always present to remind it of its duties. The fact undoubtedly remains that her main commitment belongs to the task of writing. Into that she plunges, into that atrocious, painful "militancy," into her inevitable, barbarous mission.

Also at that time, in 1957, she breaks up with Dionys Mascolo. But this separation is not total, for she needs the men she has loved deeply; like Antelme, Mascolo will never manage to move away from her activities, from the strange complicity that binds them. Thus, the apartment on rue Saint-Benoît is still Mascolo's. Protected from the city and nonetheless in the city, the place that has seen so many encounters, discussions, passions, is also "inhabited" by Mascolo; he will remain there until 1964.

In his continued preoccupation with the intellectual's role in the world, and what constitutes a commitment, Mascolo publishes in December 1957 at Minuit a little hundred-page volume entitled *Lettre polonaise sur la misère intelletuelle en France* [Polish Letter on the Intellectual Misery in France] following a trip to Poland with some other intellectuals.

The vehemence of his argumentation is very close to Duras's, for in those days their lives and ideas were in perfect harmony. If the account begins in the manner of a news report—a visit to Auschwitz, "capital of universal suffering," to the Warsaw ghetto, interviews with Poles—the heart of the book is devoted to a critique of French intellectuals, "reduced to a diaspora."

In an interview for a young people's journal, *La Ciguë,* Mascolo expresses even better the attitude he advocates, because he lays out his reasoning smoothly, subtly. His discussion begins with the Polish experience: the Poles, he says, "underwent Stalinism and from within Stalinism discovered that they were socialists." "As a result," he writes in his *Lettre,* "the definition of the revolutionary movement is renewed, and its practice rejuvenated."

The *Lettre* thus aims to expose the new praxis which in his view defines the intellectual. He still insists on an ideal of revolutionary ethics, "obedience to that which is necessary, and the application of that which is necessary TODAY to the revolutionary aim, the revolutionary aim being equality." He thus arrives at a communist strain of liberalism: "Thanks to the Hungarian and Polish experiences, we can conceive of passing directly from a bourgeois society to a liberal communist society."

The main thing is never to cut oneself off from "revolution-bearing humanity, in reality the working class. Every effort must be made to remain in contact with the people who, in any event, have more genius than all geniuses combined."

This dialectic is also Duras's at the time: how can one reconcile this liberal communism with the erring ways of Stalinism? It is clear that Duras and Mascolo share the same sphere of ideas, the same idealism, the same quest separating them from the inactivity and treachery characteristic of French intellectuals who "do nothing, think nothing. Nothing serious. It's enough to make you cry," as Mascolo says in his *Lettre*.

The Algerian war, the decay of the Fourth Republic as well as what they call "the putsch of '58" by General de Gaulle, and later the revolution of May '68 give them the means to put their dogmas into practice. But two Durases keep watch within her. A veritable statue of Janus, she switches from one to the other with disconcerting mobility. When Mascolo devotes himself entirely to theory, hard-core analysis, with her approval, she escapes into the novel, the song of literature where other desires gush forth, less constraining, more passionate ones, sometimes even leading away from the political approach, making it inappropriate. Like the woman in Nevers with the shaved head, Duras crosses over to forbidden zones where unknown desires intervene, troubling revolutionary, even dissident consciousness, leading it away to unpredictability, to treachery.

A fleeting attempt, together with Leiris, Bataille, Duvignaud, and Morin, to reorganize the dissolved Committee under the name Committee of Revolutionary Intellectuals fell through after a few months. Is this the moment when this public violence and hatred began to crystallize around Duras more than Mascolo or Morin? Up to that point perhaps the public hadn't paid sufficient notice to her capacity for subversion, the danger she represented, the risks incurred by her position. Duras, for her part, didn't spare her readers. Less of a tactician than Beauvoir, more direct, less tamed, less aristocratic, she would frighten people, rocking the boat, and henceforth she will be unable to escape this anger, this suspicion of being a traitor to her country, its morals, its customs, and to the law of the fathers.

Her particularly explicit confessions in interviews to come, such as *Woman to Woman*, shock others; doesn't she in fact claim to be from no country, connected to no land except that of her memory, a foreigner, a foreign Jew, free?

She considers General de Gaulle's coming to power as a coup d'état, having suspected him ever since the Liberation of indifference and scorn for the people, of encouraging a personality cult for his own benefit, condemning him for having scarcely shown any compassion for the exterminated Jewish people. As a result, she joins Mascolo and Jean Schuster in the anti-Gaullist resistance and contributes to the journal founded by the group in 1958, *Le 14 juillet.*

Only through gifts from some friends, and particularly donated art works from Giacometti and the surrealist painter Matta, is the journal able to get off the ground. A journal of avowed resistance to General de Gaulle, it brings together exceptional contributors: Robert Antelme, André Breton, Jean Duvignaud, Louis-René des Forêts, Edgar Morin, Maurice Nadeau, Brice Parain, Benjamin Péret, Jean-François Revel, Elio Vittorini, and others.

"It is not a question of determining what this man [de Gaulle] really thinks of the republic, of liberty, equality, and fraternity," proclaim the editors in their inaugural editorial. "For us, the point is to recognize in this strange power, sooner or later, night falling on the spirit, the death knell of freedom."

All of those who contribute to the first issue, almost assuming the mode of litany or prophecy, cry out in revolt and indignation, promising to avenge, as Mauriac said, the "massacre of the poor" in Algeria, to denounce the burgeoning dictatorship, giving themselves the status of outlaws, "Jews," "fellaghas," willingly excluded from French society which "lies and kills." In his article "Les principes à l'épreuve" [Principles on Trial], Antelme well conveys this feeling of powerlessness and revolt combined: "The party in Algiers," he says, "inspires horror. The Communist Party inspires horror. And what could we say about the unfathomable Marais? This coupling gives rise to a feeling of terror. This specific feeling gives an idea of the extent of the threat. The forces encircling us are neither slight nor innocent. What a multitude, what lucidity, what obstinacy are required to overcome them!"

In this climate of disarray revealed by the review, in what Mascolo thirty years later calls "the spontaneity of intuition," Duras is not the last to express herself. Her words are extreme, radical, and brutal. It is the other side of Duras, always giving way to terrorist, murderous instincts. She becomes the Duras of the Liberation again, the intractable Thérèse of "Albert of the Capitals," the narrative she will later include in *The War*. Her tone, that of a preacher, takes epic turns, resembling in its lyric flights the blazing diatribes of Saint-Just, for whom, moreover, the little group on rue Saint-Benoît has the greatest admiration.

The Soviet invasion of Budapest in 1956 unleashed implacable hatred in her; the article she sends to *Le 14 juillet*, "Budapest Murderers," is inflammatory, incantatory, with an exclamatory, oratorical style. All the figures of rhetoric characteristic of revolutionary discourse are employed: anaphoras, imprecations, ellipses, interjections, a flood of images, and a polemical style, feeding the flow of her anger. As usual, she identifies herself with a little insurgent gagged in the cellars where assassins torture her, just as she was a little Jew from the Warsaw ghetto, starved then shot, just as she is the fellagha that Frenchmen drag across the rocky terrain in the maquis of Kabylia, for everywhere it's the same story repeating itself, the same acts of brutality used to subdue the other person, oneself, in the cellars of Nevers, in the cellars of Warsaw police stations, white villas in Algiers, and elsewhere.

With outstretched arms, she cries out in revolt to all the torturers in the world: "We rose from our ashes a long time ago," she writes. "Give up. You are nothing more than the spokesmen of your own short, henceforth sad, adventure. Your ways are obvious. Your story is closing in upon itself. Look at each other. You're playing at being alive, but your death throes have begun."

Despite the flood of words and the anger riveted to her body, despite this state of insubordination to which she will always refer as the ultimate proof of her humanity, she gives herself over to milder pleasures, moments of peace that only a house can provide. A real house in the country which she buys in that same year of 1958, largely thanks to her royalties, in Neauphle-le-Château. She needs to anchor the Nightship safely away from others, find it a quiet port of call, hidden by walls, in this line of houses bordering hers.

She is faithful to the places she has chosen: rue Saint-Benoît of course, where she can be seen today walking along on Yann Andréa's arm, a fragile, worn-out figure, stooped over like those little old ladies in working-class neighborhoods on their way to the market, with her obviously fine, curly hair, and no concern for elegance, then Trouville, or rather Les Roches Noires, a mythical place par excellence, as if straight out of her own films or *Remembrance of Things Past*.

In Neauphle-le-Château, the houses huddled against each other form a long wall that hugs the road, and on the park side, there is a pond. They are millstone quarry houses, like all of those on this side of the former department of Seine-et-Oise, with little paned windows. She furnished the rooms, but made no effort to complete them, using vestiges from the past with faded odors and colors, cottons, silks, embroideries as old as the century, bouquets of wilted hydrangea, turn-of-the-century furniture, sideboards, cherrywood tables with molded legs, rattan cane furniture, like that which she remembers from the terraces in Vinh Long when, moving back and forth on her rocking chair, her mother would contemplate the sky, the mountains, the Mekong. . . .

There are beds too, in the big rooms, with fabrics, large cashmere shawls thrown carelessly about and mansarded rooms with faintly colored cretonne print bedspreads, and finally, threadbare rugs which must have come from the Orient. On stools lie evergreen plants, dying, never very robust, and on little console tables of painted wood, more wilting bouquets, on the furniture, the tables, the dressers, peculiar objects, things brought back from walks, dried fruit, colocynths, pebbles, against a wall of artificial stone, a Louis XVI-era twisted wood column, strange but almost necessary.

She knows how to talk about houses like nobody else. She likes to tell of the memories buried there, accumulated over centuries, in the obscure mystery of places.

This house is infinitely her own. She is familiar with all of its details, all of its sources. She penetrates its silence, draws out its voices, the stories of those who have lived there, especially the women, all of the women who people her imagination.

Place of women, place of buried desires, laden, surrounded by walls, place of uncertain, chaotic murmurs.

She recognizes in women the capacity to know houses better than anyone. The forbidden, gagged desires one finds hidden therein belong to them, and houses then speak in their silence of walls and stones, in the apparent tranquillity of gardens, in the studious cycles of the grass, in the leaden peace of the pond bordering the park. Yes, they speak of everything women have repressed, denied, the beatings, their loneliness, that which they are closest to, love and death, everything ardent and passionate that doesn't want or even dare to be expressed: between women and houses, there is a living complicity, as when she is all alone in Neauphle, drinking a great deal, alone during the week. And in those days of solitude, she writes, with the help of alcohol, until very late in the night, she listens to the "musica" played by the garden, the trees, the ring of stars.

Around four o'clock she hears the footsteps of children coming home from school, nothing else, not a sound, not a stir, the village seems dead, just the café with its billiard table and jukebox, its neon lights, and some bums, some idlers standing at the bar drinking wine. The rest of the people are cooped up in their houses. Duras too stays in her vast, unreal home, with its dying colonial appearance, the fragility of its furniture, things, and objects, the sort of bric-à-brac in which spiderwebs become ornaments, with languid charm, and where the numerous wildflower bouquets glimmer faintly under turn-of-the-century lamps.

In the very fragility of the place, although thwarted by the naked presence of the stones, there reigns something that reflects Duras's essential being, the absolute writer's dwelling, with its symbolic equivalents, images of time permeating everything, ceaselessly interrogating, echoing back to the very heart of her interrogations.

She is bound to Neauphle-le-Château and Neauphle is threatened when she goes to the hospital in 1982, on the brink of death, abandoned to this pain of existence, the ravages of alcohol on her skin, in her body. The Nightship capsizes, drifts in the dark, starless night; at home her friends are worried; in Neauphle, Michèle Manceaux, who also has a house there, keeps watch. Duras cannot die. When she passes by the house with closed shutters, music plays in her head, "Blue Moon," which Duras sang just a few days ago, with a small, always full wine glass between her ring-laden fingers, the tune from *India Song*.

And Neauphle breathes exile, solitude. Sometimes she abandons her countryside; then the closed shutters are overgrown with creeping ivy and something, perhaps the spirit, is missing. She also says to Michèle Manceaux: "I am crossed by a current. Something is passing through me. . . . I know that deep within me, at the heart of the particular, I can find the universal. It's the same for everyone. All people possess the universal inside themselves. But they don't listen, they don't dare."

In that house she attains "the general," the heart of the secret. Everything there is as if concealed and ready to be said, to her, Our Lady of the Words, Our Lady of Silence, from the confused mumbling made by Silence, in the pleasure of her bareness, in her rapture.

Neauphle is one of the resting places on the Journey. The story moves forward there, then goes elsewhere, comes back, seasons pass, leaves fall from the great trees that fill the park, while the rosebushes are reborn, sprouting new buds. Neauphle is one more proof of the trace, the traces of this night she paces, trying to SEE. In *Practicalities*, she relates this anecdote, which takes on the status of an exemplary fable: the first step of the stairway was becoming too high because the house was sinking into the ground. The mason dug for a long time, going deep in search of the stone-filled bottom, "but it kept going down, way down, toward what? What was it? What was the house built on?"

She is unveiling a metaphor for the quest of writing. It is thought that a book is based on words, but it's not true; words are holes, pits, immense Sargasso Seas in which the Nightship can be engulfed, and true books exist only when they are born of shipwrecks.

Is it from her colonial childhood, her tyrannically provident mother, that she inherited this desire to keep house, to be its guardian, to feel so close to the hearth?

She organizes, plans, so that the house won't founder in disorder and ruin. That is her way of rebuilding the sea wall. Also in *Practicalities*, she mentions the list she composed and pinned up in the cupboards so that nothing would ever be in short supply, from fine salt to adhesive tape; she says she is seeking "autonomy for the boat, the voyage of life, the people I love, and my child."

In this life, which "has no path, no line," as she sketches it in *The Lover*, the genesis of *Moderato Cantabile*, which she will publish the same year she purchases Neauphle, in 1958, is exemplary. She implies that her mother's death was on the periphery of that year, quite probably in 1957. She doesn't want to remember the exact date, nor the place where she is buried. In the interview granted to *Apostrophes*, she claims not to know; in *The Lover*, where she evokes her mother often, she doesn't say anything either, as if in that way she intended to drown the dates in the tides of time, thus making them more mobile, more volatile, subject to the swells of memory, now running aground in the sand, now sinking with the Nightship into traceless oblivion.

But in *Practicalities* she reveals paths that fuel her legend.

She is like Meursault in *The Stranger*. "Mother died" today. She is in Saint-Tropez when she receives the telegram. With a man for whom she feels violent, purely "sexual" passion, as she claims in *Woman to Woman*, she drives during part of the day and the whole night. Like Meursault, she makes love. It takes place in a hotel in Aurillac—as it turns out, not very far from the Loire Valley castle where her mother had finished her life. Between Dô and her brother, the hooligan, the favorite.

She relates all that in *Practicalities*, briefly, almost cynically, as in Camus's narrative, but with a subterranean emotion, something undefinable, coming from far away, from the very heart of desire, unidentified, from a very violent place that frightens and overwhelms her, a marginal place that arouses her suspicion as she crosses into it. She drinks with this man and she makes love to him, and it resembles an act of suicide, a murder, the desire to die, to lose everything.

They take her to her dead mother. She is in the bedroom on the first floor, "the one," she says, "where she had the sheep spend the night around her bed when it froze." There is an atmosphere of abandonment, of completion; a story has in fact just come to an end; it gives her no grief. This death and this new understanding of the world come at the same time, confusedly, and the shift occurs that will make her write more books, without the two events, her mother's death and the passion for this man, having anything to do with each other, as if quite simply a kind of "sincerity" had just seen the light, a feeling that would return her to the childhood of writing.

Thrown out into the jungle of society, the victim of low blows and thieves, henceforth a known writer, but entirely devoted to the mystery of writing and its rituals, even more ardently since the death of her mother, as if that death had delivered her from this tough story, this "family of stone," she agrees to give up her part of the inheritance to the hooligan brother, and accepts her mother's will, unjustly favoring the oldest son. She signs everything she is asked to in order to be done with this family, to settle things once and for all. Who cares what the brother does now, "the hooligan of the family . . . the weaponless murderer?" She will learn later that he is wandering through the provinces, sleeping where he can, selling his mother's souvenirs one by one, the jades, the bronzes, the furniture. In *The Lover* she tells of his downfall without flinching, with that atrocious, splendid coldness in which one nonetheless senses the underlying tears, the love. Everything is said in very simple, very short words, fluent words that "flow like a stream," just as she wants them to unfurl now, in the urgency of the trace merely glimpsed, until the narrative becomes, without her realizing it, a poem, a lyric chant. Later, in the seventies, she will learn of his death in an apartment where he has been found dead, alone. She also adds that according to her mother's wishes, stipulating that only her son be buried near her, they both lie in that Loire Valley cemetery whose very name she has forgotten. "The image is intolerably splendid"; thus she concludes, in this passage in *The Lover*, the story of her brother and her mother. Writing becomes a grave, she can go no further in its oceanic movement, in the ebb and the flow of time, she captures both of them, the mother and the son, beneath the hardened, limited ground of the mausoleum, in a sepulchral photograph doomed to the disaster of time and oblivion.

With *Moderato Cantabile*, Duras makes "a complete break," as she says. Confinement and greater solitude gradually take hold of her, something "stronger" than she draws her into the closed circle of tragedy, which she was already aware of and which now opens up to her. Each book will resemble a Racinian tragedy, another step taken in the dark labyrinth, with that force of destiny which hangs heavily over everything. It's like a new requirement: the words in the books to come, taken from each other over and over, veritable footbridges of the imagination, will target the Great Secret of things, dispensing with landscapes, character sketches, descriptions, going straight to the heart, cutting to the quick. She likes Pascal, Racine, Bach—all artists of the mystical tension residing in books, in music, bound together like a spring and which, in their release, lead into this place that escapes common sense, leaving behind known identity to "get lost in that which exists at the same time" as she, "elsewhere or off to one side, or lost or dead."

She makes her characters disappear like her into the unknown that strikes them down, carries them to the limits of the unbearable, in the unbreathable air of the magnolias, in wine-saturated breath, in that afterworld of desire which can only find its respiration in death. "I wish you were dead," says Chauvin. "I already am," says Anne Desbaresdes.

The heroine's fascination with the murder in the opening pages of *Moderato Cantabile* parallels Duras's for miscellaneous news items, criminal trials, obscure killings perpetrated in the flow of everyday life, that whole other world of darkness whose logic she is unable to penetrate.

In an article for the weekly magazine *France-Observateur* entitled "Horror at Choisy-le-Roi," which she publishes at the same time as *Moderato Cantabile,* she describes a crime of passion that had aroused public interest. How to explain other than by mystery and a "foreign" ritual the murder committed by Simone Deschamps, Dr. Evenou's mistress, the murder of this wife. Duras's analysis stumbles against what she calls "the truth of darkness," and leaves the matter unsolved, ready "to give up in her attempt to interpret this darkness whence they [the Choisy criminals] emerge since daylight does not afford one the possibility of knowing them." That lack of recognition is what she wants to deal with, the impossibility of arriving at a conclusion, of bearing a final, decisive judgment, the irreducible secret of souls and bodies. She is not far from Bataille, whom she often sees during those years, from his certitude that only death lies downstream from passion, death being its natural source, since passion resides solely in the state of release whose plenitude is found only in death.

The romantic passion she is living at that time, the experience of a love affair and not love, as she explains later in the preface to an American edition of *Moderato Cantabile,* the fascination her lover holds for her—she will dedicate the novel to him—the knowledge she draws from him, lead her to believe that thorough exhaustion of desire is what will bring her closest to this carefully watched unknown, and she will arrive at an even better understanding of Anne-Marie Stretter, her languid quest, in the moisture of the colonies, her longing to plunge into the waters of the Mekong or the Ganges, returning to obscurity, to the abyss of the sea.

In a note in the same article she repeats a very interesting anecdote: the story of a sadistic criminal relating his murder in a letter and who, at the precise moment when he is describing the tragedy, suddenly reveals "an extraordinary, unintelligible, yet perfectly penned language of onomatopoeias."

"One seemed to be entering into the truth of darkness."

That is how Duras must be read from now on. When speech gives way to its silences, its fractures, its gaps, its slips, which many find incomprehensible, it enters into that truth, into this blind and yet persistent navigation, as if a secret star were guiding it; it is the realm of the inexplicable, with no further possibility for the writer to attempt explanations, and one must plunge with her into something unknown even to her, and to which she surrenders, dumbfounded, destroyed.

All of the readers who immediately recognized her talent and have continued to follow Duras to this day celebrated *Moderato Cantabile* as a true masterpiece, in which the classical rules of tragedy were maintained, with its unities of tone, place, action, and this profoundly renewed element, which attempted to explain the secret functioning of passion, the ebb and flow of desire, the mysterious echoes of the heart, with a minimum of words, an almost frightening spareness entirely devoted to knowing and which, once the book was finished, left in one's mind traces of fire and glints of solitude, of coldness.

Beginning largely with *Moderato Cantabile*, Duras becomes the object of both a magic, unconditional cult that never abandons her, and of a bias on the part of certain critics. In some, she awakens a fierce misogyny, a sort of hatred that will often pursue her so doggedly that she becomes discouraged, driven to even more extreme solitude and violence. For some, Maurice Nadeau, Claude Mauriac, Gaëtan Picon, she has written "*Madame Bovary* revised by Béla Bartók," and is the hope for the revival of the French novel; for others, from *Les Lettres françaises* to *Rivarol*, with *L'Aurore* in between, united in one and the same attack on modernity, the novel is nothing more than a dry, deadly dull essay, "a hollow nut," a superficial world. "Fools say," as Nathalie Sarraute might remark with a sigh. . . . Duras is ironically dubbed "Durasoir."* She is misunderstood, becoming the subject of ridicule, "known," as she rightly says, "for the wrong reasons."

---

*A play on words combining her name and *rasoir*, a synonym for "a bore."—TRANS. note

The novel nonetheless wins the May prize, and paying no attention to the sarcastic comments, Duras toils on. There is even a change in the nature of her work as it was formerly conceived of. Her entire being enters into the narrative, into this matter whose heart she is scarcely beginning to recognize, so mobile, so fugitive, so precarious when one tries to grasp it, bearing such a distinct resemblance to the mystery of the sea, with its "eternally renewed" surface, its continuously swept floor of sand.

Is it a coincidence after all if *Moderato Cantabile* is published by Minuit, which, along with Seuil, will carry subversion out into the public arena, revealing to the general public the reality of the Algerian war? In 1957, Jérôme Lindon, its director, publishes *Pour Djamila Bouhired* by Georges Arnaud and Jacques Vergès, the lawyer for the young woman suspected of being an FLN militant and a terrorist, arrested and condemned to death, thus drawing the country into a debate about torture with the participation of all those who wielded any moral authority, on the left as well as on the right. *L'Aurore, France-Soir, Le Monde, L'Express,* and the left-wing press combine their voices in demanding that torture be condemned.

Also in 1957, barely a few months after the controversial piece that allowed the young Algerian revolutionary to save her skin, Jérôme Lindon starts up again, revising then publishing Henri Alleg's manuscript *La Question,* a blunt, irrefutable testimony on the reality of the torture undergone by a French communist accused of complicity with the enemy and imprisoned.

The book causes a scandal and is seized, but very late, after more than sixty thousand copies have been sold; intellectuals draw up petition; Malraux, Mauriac, Sartre, and Roger Martin du Gard address a solemn statement to the French president in which they ask him to revoke his decision to ban the book. This "request to the authorities in the name of the Declaration of the Rights of Man and Citizen for the unequivocal condemnation of the use of torture" divides writers, troubles Christian consciences.

It is in this context that the directors of Minuit make the strategic decision to publish Duras concurrently. *Moderato Cantabile* is another literary form of subversion, another denunciation of the violence done to desire, to man's freedom, another way of speaking.

Duras places herself at the cutting edge of the era's struggles, amid the acute, terrible moments of repudiation and infamy. Side by side with Alleg's spare, tragic narrative minutely describing the reality of torture, *Moderato*, just as spare, similarly shows revolt and modernity. Published by Minuit, like Butor who in the previous year of 1957 had received the Renaudot prize for *A Change of Heart*, like all the witnesses to injustice and to the blind war who will expose the torture in Algeria (Djamal Amrani) and in France (*La Gangrène*), desertion (Favrelière's *Le Désert à l'Aube*) and denunciation (Leulette's *Saint Michel et le dragon*), she is confirmed as a writer of marginalization and revolt, of refusal and disobedience, at the heart of struggles and misfortunes, always subverting accepted ideas, reasons of state.

Such is the violence in which, in September, *Le 14 juillet* publishes its second issue according to schedule. Significantly, the leading article in the table of contents is a piece by Maurice Blanchot entitled "Refusal," which could serve as a rallying cry for a global intellectual strategy. A text of vigilance, a bearing of witness, it calls on intellectuals to redefine themselves, to return "to the respect for what they are, which will allow them neither contentment nor indifference." The rhetoric could very well be that of Duras, incantatory, lyrical, and savage, hammering out sentences with the seal of *refusal* repeated no less than twenty times on a single page. Refusal—and the subsequent decision to join the others in "this resolute no": "those who cannot speak," but also those who cry it out and build "the communism of life and of the spirit among friends," in Hölderlin's words.

What *Le 14 juillet* was trying to do was to affirm this fury of speech, leaving "the emotional outburst" in full view, as Mascolo said, for to moderate this frenzy, this anger, amounted to shortchanging the passion for truth, and "gradually led to euphemistic language, then to a murmur, to respectful whispering, and, finally, to silence."

It is in this disrespectful, revolutionary sphere of influence that Duras is always nourished, in these cutting, provocative, epic affirmations. In that year of 1958, the business at hand was the founding of "the Algerian party," the organization of "the only political force capable of opposing effectively the maneuvers of the present regime, the only one capable of getting at the greedy little heart that works to keep it going."

The rights to *The Sea Wall* having been sold to filmmaker René Clément, the movie comes out in France in the spring of 1958, thus enlarging Duras's renown, making her one of the best-known novelists of the era, endeavoring to take from the novel everything it possesses in terms of visual power, dramatic intensity, and conversational verisimilitude. The cast is "dazzling": Silvana Mangano, Anthony Perkins, Richard Conte, Jo Van Fleet, Alida Valli.

Despite the advantages of the production's international resources, René Clément didn't do justice to the story of *The Sea Wall*, which, beyond its epic dimension, its vast landscapes, its perpetually wet rice fields, actually tells yet another closed, tragic story. The film was a flop, as if the story couldn't be produced on a large scale but only through another approach, the opposite of that employed by René Clément, on another, more hermetic, more "extravagant" wavelength.

Although she publishes *Hiroshima Mon Amour* in 1960, she actually finished writing it two years earlier. The work's origin varies, depending on the version offered by Alain Resnais or the one by Duras. She claims that *Hiroshima* was written one year before *Moderato*, but this is contradicted by another statement in *Woman to Woman:* "I wrote *Moderato* during the same year." As for Resnais, he insists in an interview that it was only after having read *Moderato* that he approached Duras about "creating," he says, "a love story. . . . In my mind it was in somewhat the same vein as *Moderato Cantabile*, but would include the anguish of atomic weapons." In any event, it is at the end of March 1958 that Argos Enterprises contacts Duras. This small firm had thus far produced shorts on Watteau, fifteenth-century illuminated manuscripts, Goya, the Mona Lisa, and Beijing, films whose quality made them the beneficiaries of government subsidies. Alain Resnais's *Night and Fog* had also received financing from the Ministry of Veterans and the World War II Study Commission. The script by Jean Cayrol and the music by Hanns Eisler were perfectly suited to Resnais's intentions, and it was an overwhelming success. Argos then made another proposal to Resnais at the beginning of 1958 for a work on the bombing of Hiroshima, this time a full-length film. Resnais, forced to work on a predetermined documentary-type shooting script, was having trouble finding the appropriate tone and making the scenario express the emotion contained in the subject. After three months' effort without making any headway, he suggested a woman's point of view; they considered Sagan, who twice failed to show up at meetings set up with her, then Beauvoir, whose intellectualism put them off, and Resnais, excited by his recent reading of *Moderato Cantabile*, finally proposed Duras. The producers accepted, thinking that her writing would be "more feminine."

From then on, Duras immersed herself completely in the subject, working closely with Resnais whose own research coincided with that of the nouveau roman: manipulation of the discordance between the picture and the soundtrack, fractures in the linear development of the narration, a predilection for silence.

At that time Duras and Resnais "saw each other every day," according to the director. Their meetings were devoted to the amplification of this "purely abstract thing," which Resnais had entrusted to Duras for the clarification of details: "Is it cold in the cellar? Are there any cats?", and so on.

Completed in a short time thanks to Duras's miraculous writing speed, as if the text "came out already finished," born of a "know-how that escapes him," the filmscript was accepted by the Japanese distributor-producer Nagata even though he was more in the habit of lending financial support to commercial projects.

She had first agreed to work on this subject essentially for the money. At that time Duras lived rather modestly, not foreseeing the success of the widely sold editions that now provide her with a steady income. Her contributions to various periodicals stem from the same necessity. Nonetheless she was soon caught up in the subject of *Hiroshima,* which she found intriguing enough to commit herself to it enthusiastically. But whereas the financial backers were hoping at best for a documentary treated in an original way by a novelist who was beginning to be fashionable, she proposed a work having nothing to do with the project, but so amazingly "strange," and with such a magical arrangement, that something fascinating emanated from it. In the movie world, where there is no free lunch and no concessions are made, at a time when the star system was prevalent, the distributors had a stranglehold on everything, and the first "new wave" films had not yet come out, before *The Lovers, Breathless,* or *Le Beau Serge,* she succeeds in modifying the initial project, subordinating it to her own, still developing thematics, the underground story she had already begun narrating a few novels earlier.

In those very long, implacably muted recitatives, she displays the work of time in full, its capacity for burying the memory, for denying it, for exhuming oblivion as the only real presence of what is, for glorifying that very oblivion, thus refusing nostalgia, the past, affirming her attachment to life.

Through the entanglement of themes, love and death, through their very particular rhythm, through the interlacing of stories, through this series of counterpoints like Bach fugues slipping over each other, like successive waves covering the sand, Duras gives language new means of expression, whereas neither Butor, nor Robbe-Grillet, nor even Cayrol had been able to make real, significant changes in it. In their works time doesn't have this mobility or this brilliant moiré that frightens and renders the entire meaning of solitude, making it more consequential, more palpable.

This way she has, now all her own, of interrupting the normal progression of narrative, short-circuiting it with baffling parenthetical sequences and series of coincidences, sets the course of the novel for years to come, based on an attentiveness to time most clearly relayed by Proust and carefully studied by Duras, Beckett, and Bataille.

It is the same situation in Nevers, in the cellar where Riva is hidden, in Hiroshima and elsewhere. Oblivion devours everything. Tragically indifferent time cannot be held back; it flees, always slips away; it escapes and no one can stop it. So writing serves only to gather a few traces of that which changes inexorably, half-erased tracks of what once was, and will never again be restorable to the totality of the "absolute photograph," but only in random images, illegible, unintelligible fragments like mad traces, with no apparent meaning and a jagged texture.

This destruction is an indispensable component in the development of Duras's work, with its autobiographical mirror effects. Everything therein is washed by the waters of rivers and seas. In Nevers as in Hiroshima, in Vinh Long as in Trouville, in those places where she left her mark, water, the periodical flowing of the tide, erases that which was attempting to build itself up, and there is nothing else to do but cry out against this force of oblivion which says that nothing has ever really existed. The proximity of "green river mouths" and of nascent streams or currents lost in the great unknown sea is the very metaphor of her biography.

Oblivion passes by just as the cloth washes the face without rubbing away the wrinkles. She is left with the destroyed face she talks about in *The Lover*, but by whom, by what was it devastated, by what real, unportrayable course of events, consigned only to legend, to the zigzags of new imaginings?

As soon as the proposal was accepted, Resnais's film was shot quickly, with a small budget—twelve million yen, which Argos Enterprises agreed to pay back eighteen months later; seventeen days in Japan, twelve in France, and Resnais finished up the film.

That is how everything always went with Duras, in this urgency of creation, in this kind of fever that makes her fear the words will slip away, going faster than she could. Her script required that urgency, as if otherwise it would never reveal anything more of the secret story unfolding there. It was the same for *India Song*, filmed in record time, and for the writing of *The Lover*, for which a few short weeks sufficed to exhume the traces of her past, the darkroom where the absolute photograph had been taken at a port of call on the continent of time past.

She then enjoys total complicity with Resnais, submitting the pages of her script to him for this first cinematographic experience, for which she is not the least bit prepared, accepting corrections, forwarding to the shooting location the final changes requested by Resnais.

This is new material that the director is working on; nobody is accustomed to this psalmody running like a chant throughout the whole film, its rhythm echoing back to inner, forgotten, unforgettable images.

This capacity for adapting to new registers, while simultaneously bending them to her own desire, to her imagination, as though daring to break the inevitable shackles of the genre, is part of her violent, savage determination. She will do likewise during her own cinematographic experience, or when she tries her hand at feature articles for the newspaper *Libération* during the summer of 1980, renewing and reinventing styles.

Something magic presided over the making of *Hiroshima Mon Amour*. What was supposed to be Resnais's film became that of the scriptwriter. The actress herself, Emmanuèle Riva, seemed to fit in perfectly with this world of the invisible, for her acting was modeled on Duras's incantation, picking up its slightest tremors, penetrating the night in Nevers, that of desire, capable of breaking all laws. Duras's words made Riva disclose the very nature of love, retrieving from the night of memory the impossible lament, that which caused one to forget oblivion itself.

Since the film had been scheduled for the 1959 Cannes festival, the shooting took place in great haste. Nonetheless, it failed to receive the selection committee's endorsement, which went to *The Four Hundred Blows* and *Black Orpheus*, in spite of Malraux's opinion, for he apparently found the film remarkable. Numerous objections were raised: it was argued that the United States would disapprove of the subject, that de Gaulle would be opposed, that its nihilistic viewpoint would upset too many people, and that it was headed for mass rejection. In spite of determined efforts by the little Argos production company, the film was withdrawn from the competition and shown independent of the festival. Its success was nevertheless spectacular. Was it mainly on account of Duras? Resnais's smooth camera work and his new syntax were acclaimed by the entire spectrum of the press; some hailed it as a poem, while others were spellbound. Paul Davay wrote in *Les Beaux-Arts*: "What's the use of taking a poem apart, whether it be by Rimbaud or Resnais?" Bertrand stated in *La Lanterne*: "Alain Resnais has composed an astonishing cinematic poem by speculating on the subtle interferences between words and images." Jacqueline Michel in *Le Parisien*: "All Resnais needs are a few shots to cry out the most violent indictment ever of war." Everyone agreed that he had invented a "cinematic language whose principles had been defined by Eisenstein alone." This chorus of praise kept Duras's script somewhat hidden from view, with some, even among the most enthusiastic, finding it too intellectual, "too literary." Its more numerous detractors saw in it a mannerism and a sophisticated language that only Resnais's masterful work had succeeded in tempering. Riva emerged from this film as a revelation, a great actress with an "astonishing," "entrancing" presence.

And yet, amid the torrent of criticism, positive and negative, the words that return time and again are *magic* and *fascination*, subsequently carried to their highest degree of intensity by Duras alone. Finally, time made the choice. The critic for *Le Métropole* aptly said: "It seems that what will remain after we have forgotten everything else is the poetic tone of the whole work." And Duras was the one who had breathed that tone into it, in her "magic" dialogues, which seemed to snap up spectators, suffocating them, leading them off into unknown, indistinct regions.

The film was marketed with the aid of enormous publicity, which always creates impassioned opposition and frenzied enthusiasm. In forty-nine days, 255,900 viewers had seen it, the record for box office receipts being held by *The Ten Commandments* with 526,000. It was successful on account of its scandalous nature: a point of critical esteem, of curiosity, and undeservedly so judging from the indignation of some spectators who, misled by the billing and the publicity, walked out. Indeed one could read on the billboards: "*Hiroshima Mon Amour*, a love full of gentleness, tenderness, desire!" or even the advertising come-ons created by the Cocinor firm: "*Hiroshima Mon Amour*, a film about love, overwhelming love that defies laws, ignores space and time, Love," "*Hiroshima Mon Amour*, a film about love, mad, earsplitting love that pierces the silence with its cry." At once adulated and reviled, it paralleled the fate of Duras herself, who always carried with her this sweet smell of scandal, arousing hatred and passion. The film received prizes from six organizations: the Society of Film and Television Writers, the International Cinematographic Press Federation, the Union of Cinema Criticism, the Socialist Federation of Film Clubs, the Association of French Film and Television Critics, and the Victoire 59 prize, on the recommendation of the magazines *Le Figaro*, *Cinémonde*, and *Le Film français*.

Such is the extent to which, in the case of *Hiroshima Mon Amour*, the first attempt was a masterstroke. Is that the very reason Duras is always so vehement whenever she recalls this adventure? In 1960 she claims authorship for the entire work, and consequently keeps Alain Resnais somewhat hidden from view, while seeming to apologize for it in the foreword to the definitive edition: "I have attempted to account as faithfully as possible for the work I did for Alain Resnais in *Hiroshima Mon Amour*. It should therefore come as no surprise that Resnais's camerawork is hardly ever evoked here."

The film actually represents a financial failure for her. Considering herself to have been taken advantage of, having signed in complete ignorance a contract depriving her of the smallest percentage whatsoever, she estimates her loss at tens of thousands of francs. "At that time," she says in *Woman to Woman*, "we had so little money that we couldn't afford to go on vacation. . . . Nobody—not even Resnais, I must say—nobody said to me: 'Don't forget to ask for a percentage.' "

This deceit brings her back to the colonial racket, to the swindling of which her mother was a victim, to her status as a woman as a cause for her being cheated, to a keener awareness of money.

Today she notes with a certain cheerful irony that her name is indissolubly linked with *Hiroshima Mon Amour* for, ending up in book form as an offshoot of the tropical vines with which she will subsequently learn to grapple, Duras became an unavoidable landmark on the film's path, to such an extent that Resnais's name is dissociated from it. The text, as she says, "put out to sea," became reunited with its constellation, in the archives of her work wherein lie the palpitating intermittencies of the heart and of the body poured into the eternity of immovable time.

In 1959 she publishes *The Viaducts of Seine-et-Oise*, another story taken from a sensational news item, a sordid murder perpetrated by a peaceful retired couple upon their first cousin who had been disabled since birth. Is it this immense curiosity about the world, her taste for prying, her yearning to know, like Proust, the mechanism within people, their secret, unexpected actions, which she then intends to reconvert into human, metaphysical knowledge, that leads her to borrow from others as well, in the human jungle, the most highly theatrical, imaginative scenes?

What fascinates her once more is the "unexplained" factor, the criminal logic of this couple beyond suspicion, the hidden violence and savagery inhabiting them, the burst of madness that possessed them. She applies her innate sense of dialogue to this quest, and *The Viaducts* illustrates the Durassian style, the tone she will henceforth give to her plays: short lines, like information devoid of all psychology and effusive sentiments, traces of humor, and above all the major presence of fate hovering overhead and incapacitating the actors in the story being played out there, and irreducibly condemning, isolating, striking them down.

A singular voice in the great renewal of the sixties—her novels, carried along in the current created by *Hiroshima Mon Amour* and *Moderato Cantabile* in particular, become best-sellers—in 1960 Duras is chosen as a member of the jury for the Médicis book award. She readily accepted this honor, deciding after her rebuffs by the Goncourt prize committee in 1950 that the Médicis was "the most important French award," as she says in *Practicalities*, when discussing the winner, Gérard Jarlot.

The Médicis's reputation had been established along more intellectual lines than the Goncourt, less commercial, more concerned with research, innovative narrative forms, and writing suspicious of realism. The Médicis aspired to be the most severe, most rigorous of the existing literary prizes, the strictest on the literary quality of the books being considered. She was moreover in the company of jury members who seemed to belong to her literary family more than to that of the Goncourt. Indeed, at that time, in the entourage of Gala Barbizan—patron of the arts, a devoted chess player sitting in her bed drawing religious images with a ballpoint pen, in the shade of the vine arbors of Montmarte—and of Jean-Pierre Giraudoux, the founders of the prize, there were Denise Bourdet, Félicien Marceau, Francine Mallet, Nathalie Sarraute, Alain Robbe-Grillet, Pierre Albérès, and finally Claude Roy, who had recently been chosen to occupy the vacancy left by Dominique Aury. Marguerite Duras succeeded Pierre Gascar, and her presence was judged advantageous by the jury, which recognized exceptional literary qualities in her.

She didn't know yet that she would be incapable of "holding out" in this institution, in what she would later call a "reproduction" of society, "microscopic, but hard as iron," discovering as time went by the gummed-up cogs, the secrets of the inner sanctum. By accepting the position, she thought she could improve the award system, the least unfair of all, she felt, and that she could make changes in the established order. It is even possible that she already suspected the weight of the

establishment, and had decided—in accordance with her usual
ways, her subversive violence, her gut-level insubordination—
to throw things into confusion, sowing dissidence. In any event
she remained in the post for seven years, at the end of which
she resigned in the wake of Claude Roy and simultaneously
with Nathalie Sarraute, who was opposed to Alain Robbe-
Grillet, judging that time and social practices had turned the
prize into "an institution that places more importance on the
award than on the book." She nonetheless prides herself on
having participated in the crowning of Monique Wittig and
Claue Ollier, but her departure was a prelude to the great social
movements of 1968, as if she wanted to move away from this
"new society" before it was too late, refusing to enthrone the
"yes," as she would confide to Jean Schuster in the surrealist
review *L'Archibras* in 1967.

Escaping from what she judges to be literary worldliness, a
high-class farce, she will know from now on that writing finds
its only source far from this world and its intrigues and
struggles for influence. She is secretly obsessed by utopia, and
she dreams of a jury that "would be intended to judge the
judge," "giving out no awards," and would thus "take power
away from the powers that be and redistribute it to the masses,
the readers."

This apology for saying "no" well reflects Duras's mystical
dialectic. This "no" full of meaning for her identity, a constitu-
ent element of her being, gives her all her energy, her untamed
strength, makes her overtake history itself, its fractures, its
street uprisings which will soon set youth ablaze.

A year after *Hiroshima*, Duras's name shines again on La
Croisette boardwalk in Cannes. *Moderato Cantabile*, directed
by Peter Brook, is presented there and is a great success since
Jeanne Moreau is given the award for best actress by the
festival's official jury. That year, 1960, is a good vintage for
cinematography; impossible to choose one over the other, the
Palme d'Or goes neither to Bergman for *Through a Glass Darkly*
nor to Buñuel for *The Young One*; it is given to an outsider,
Fellini, for *La Dolce Vita*. Antonioni also attracts considerable

attention with *L'Avventura*. This is the firmament of film geniuses in which Duras's name circulates, but deep inside she knows that no one else can portray this coherent, singular world she carries. She finds Peter Brook's film "drippy," judging that he "failed to understand the film's subject." Only she can tell the secret of her words, their unfathomable story.

She tells about the nature of love, begun again each time because "time," she says, "undoes all love." It is a form of energy that takes hold of people, anonymous and powerful, and slips from couple to couple, sending those who once possessed it back to the void, to nothingness, to the futility of life, dazzling those who receive it. She knows that nobody can do anything to prevent that, for there is something tragic to be endured, something unknown and irresistible. She sings of that force of love which comes and goes, steals away and gives itself, while no one can subdue it. "Nobody, nobody," she has Maria say in *10:30 on a Summer Night*, published in 1960. It is precisely in this novel, which critics unanimously hail as one of her most perfect works, that she once again takes up the theme of the arena in which she knows her life is unfolding, at once helpless and rebellious.

Maria, her husband Pierre and their daughter Judith, and Claire, a friend of the couple, thus stop along the road to Madrid, overwhelmed by the heat, to spend the night in a hotel overcrowded with tourists. But the little town is seething with excitement, for the Guardia Civil is tracking down a man who has just shot his wife and her lover. Maria can't sleep that night. She is on the balcony, trying to breathe in some of the cool, jasmine-scented night air; in the semidarkness she sees the murderer's silhouette, and on another balcony Pierre and Claire kissing. She decides to help the killer, takes advantage of the patrol's absence to take him a few dozen kilometers away in the countryside, and returns at noon the next day to pick him up, to smuggle him across the border. When all of them come back, they learn that the man has put a bullet in his head. They are back on the road to Madrid. They stop again on account of the heat. Claire says she wants to take a nap as a pretext for renting a room in a motel. Pierre joins her and they make love for the first time in a dazzling renewal of love.

Finally arriving in Madrid, Pierre and Maria have it out. There is no jealousy or malice on Maria's part. She confirms the end of their love, as if it had evaporated during the seven years they had been given to live together; she knows that it is inevitable.

Duras's entire imagination is once more at work: the heat and intensity of passion, the threat of the police, of the storm, and death all around, on the roads, in the fields, alcohol too as a means of surviving in the hell of life, cool Manzanilla intended not to help forget the pain of love but to endure its violence, its implacable law. And time itself, which never stops flowing and flowing, wearing out hearts, minds, ruining faces, aging them, and to accept that, this passage, this necessity: the carelessness with which she runs her hands across her face tells her that she has accepted defeat for good.

Ruined, like Duras's face, with its "destroyed, devastated skin."

Duras's little melody relates the heavy movement of time, its erosion of things, plants, people. It is this ineffable hymn retracing the unknown course of time, its sly, invisible unfolding, the slow repetition of words, sentences, days and nights, and seasons, this courage to go on existing, abandoned to the endless song. "Yes," she says to Madeleine Chapsal, "this time I dared to be lyrical," in the clinical era of the nouveau roman.

Throughout the sixties, she continues to be the chronicler of the lowly, of back-page news items, writing the novel of the everyday events that no one sees, caught up in the constant hum of the Comedy and the City. More than ever, she takes an interest in the fallen, in delinquents and psychopaths, "innocent," doomed criminals, all those who put to shame self-righteous, established society "founded . . . on the certitude of its rights," denounced in the famous dinner in Moderato Cantabile, "the foul tricks of this white colonial breed," repudiated again in 1991 in The North China Lover.

In her interviews on television or in periodicals, in *France-Observateur* and *Vogue*, she tries to get at this flight or this banishment to the margins, seeking in these exiles the very essence of the human condition. Most importantly, she listens without the least demagoguery, without complaisance or pathos; she wants to attempt to penetrate the secret of a Carmelite she interviews in *France-Observateur* and whose mystery she doggedly pursues, stumbling up against the unknowable, failing to achieve her goal.

That meeting leaves her with a strong impression because it reminds her of a conversation with Bataille or with her characters, tempted by movement and caught in this trap of silence, in the sticky, overpowering weight of ferocious time. These experiences always take place on the outskirts, the only place where one can hear, as Rimbaud said, the rolling of the stars, the whirring of the comets.

The most famous of her interviews is undoubtedly the one she calls "Nadine from Orange," published in 1961 in *France-Observateur*. A little girl is kidnapped by a simpleminded, almost retarded man, André Berthaud, then found safe and sound, while her abductor has stabbed himself in the heart with his pocketknife at the police station. Duras thus goes off in search of this mystery, this force of love that bound the two protagonists of the tragedy, pestering Berthaud's wife until she opens the door to her and talks. The interview becomes a kind of tragedy, in its simplicity, its implacability; she presses the wife, who ends up revealing this absolute love that held them together. Using everyday words, she explains this sublimation of desire, its violence transmuted into an unknown hereafter. He "picked flowers for her in the forest, told her stories, children's stories. He liked those stories." She "would kiss him like her father. With her arms around his neck, I'm telling you, all day long."

That is what she gathers in her interviews, far-reaching, simple words that "proper people" aren't used to hearing or saying, words that speak only of the things held within, still cried out by a few rare souls.

This taste for dialogue, for putting into perspective the

secret echoes of human beings, will eventually lead her to privilege playwriting. Although she hadn't given much thought to the theater—hadn't she confided to Geneviève Serreau that she "wasn't the least bit interested in theater?"—it now begins to fascinate her. She understands, and therein lies her greatest discovery, that remaining in a given genre, the novel for example, limits her quest, even prevents her from conveying the bursts and flights of desire, while on the contrary, the multiplication of genres, their interaction, the unimpeded passing from one to another, is perhaps the surest way of tuning in to the secrets her texts try to solve. Today the theater, tomorrow film, later still the visual quest among the unusual raw objets d'art that she sets in gold, everything serves as a means of expression, is handed along from one to another, exchanged in that great mixture of words and silences, in the utopia of writing where she now dwells.

Can it be called intellectual life? It is more like intense emotional activity, a great release of energy completely turned and helped along by absolute narcissism, toward the gold she is seeking, accepting "all the impulses of the self," its avatars and its vexations, its risks and its amazements, eager for the inexpressible to reveal itself, even in the smallest way.

That is how one must understand her resurrections, her escape from elsewhere, in the unreal night of the coma, her lapses and relapses, her losses of breathing, her spells of suffocation, the gasps of a body that was on the brink of giving up so many times and then setting out again, via a different road, on the same quests. It's the same for Rimbaud's adventure, she says: "No single mode of searching was privileged for Rimbaud as a person, as a writer. . . . I can see that the impulses of the self, in Rimbaud, carried him toward an ardent, impartial temper."

Thus from the novel to the theater, from the theater to film, there is no "going astray," but one and the same "shifting" search.

This search is open, and aimed at everything that can provide a clue about the true path to follow. It takes the route of self-listening, of reverberation of things upon oneself, of the noise of the world and the way it reaches her, winding through this taste for human beings, for the mystery that liberates their bodies, for the multiple essences of desire. Deep inside the secret of writing, there is the force of love, for which she risks all. She doesn't necessarily like a man for what he is, for his own identity, but for what he unleashes in her, the echoes of a far-off place, powers of fascination, the risks engendered by such a passion. In 1988 she tells a journalist: "I had to seek out new lovers, new men. . . . I can't explain it. It's impossible. Such a need for men is dangerous. It takes place in the body." She likewise confesses in *The North China Lover:* "The whole body is possessed . . . you can't think of anything else."

She has never hesitated to sink into the dizziness of a new desire, in the kind of urgency that would seize her as when impatient, demanding writing becomes indispensable and, like the Minotaur, asks for its due. Just as books and lovers "saved her," she loves love, "she loves to love."

Henceforth, even names can escape this frantic quest. Is there any reason for revealing that "the man who was a lie" she evokes in *Practicalities* is none other than Gérard Jarlot, the "very shrewd, very funny, very very charming" novelist of the sixties, winner of the Médicis Prize in 1963 for *Un Chat qui aboie?*

What is interesting on the other hand is the way she becomes possessed by him, first feeling irresistibly attracted by his singular capacity for lying about everything, then by his manner of "taking women inside of himself and loving them before even knowing their beauty, their voices," by "his brutality both controlled and savage, frightening and polite."

She loves this man, Jarlot, on account of this immense, destructive desire he arouses in her, this implacability of passion, this irresistible force that sweeps her away, dispossesses her, hurts her, "just when I was dying to experience a new love. On the eighth day, I entered the café as one steps up to the scaffold." She loves him but, being a vampire, she draws from him that which can nourish her writing, enrich it, bring her a little closer to the Secret.

Nothing can change that. "Writing and loving" are Duras's two means of attaining Revelation.

Loving and writing are the same experience, that of "returning to a primitive state," "stripping down," as she says. Everything that keeps her in the world, everything she remembers and has learned, is diluted in the great silence of what she calls "the inner shadow." Something from within succeeds in reaching this cryingly beautiful, unknown part of oneself, this self-essence for which her course is now headed, borne along by her autonomous writing, listening to "the female being" that she is.

One must thus remain silent in order to find the annals of the self, tell all by not telling, as Dominique Aury said about *Moderato Cantabile*, pierce the thick envelope of that inner shadow. A certitude is born inside her: "I am absolutely sure of that," she says. "That," the flowing of oneself into desire for writing and for the body of another, "that," the plunge into darkness, into the memory's forest of mossy pilings, "that," the waiting, the suspense, until forms take shape from the traces left anonymously by the days and the nights, and time immemorial.

Is it by keeping company with Gérard Jarlot, a professional scenario writer, with whom she writes *Une aussi longue absence* in 1961, also as a result of the suggestions he heaped on her during the making of *Hiroshima Mon Amour*, listening to his "criticism, at once demanding, lucid and productive," as she claims in the foreword to the published scenario, that she so suddenly acquired the taste for playwriting?

Is it also this new certainty that made her believe that the written text would find its true secret not only in the very shattering of its written form but also in gestures, in the circulation of words passed on from being to being, from actor to actor, in the picture that theatrical representation can create, on all of the crossroads she now intended to take?

Is it really necessity itself that brought her to it, in that ever-purer expression, in those extremely tenuous ellipses, from which the exterior landscapes, portraits, and psychologisms were automatically excluded, in those dialogues already being performed by virtue of their space-time concentration? Wasn't *The Square*, for example, already a play in its novel form of 1955? Duras launched out into the theatrical adventure as a result of all these factors imposing themselves upon her like so many signs. In any event she must have anticipated it, for she knew that these previously published texts possessed a real dramatic impact; read aloud, they possessed an impressive orality, like her unforgettable voice, in its cadences and its renewals, uttering secrets that were made for revealing.

Her voice today is altered by illness, and in its hissing, its suffering, its cracks, painfully managing to express itself in spite of everything, constrained by the metal cannula she wears like a new means of defiance, which she even thanks for having allowed her occasionally to hear silence better, to refrain from speaking, finally to attain "the silence common to all of the oppressed."

In the sixties, such rich, constructive years for her, rue Saint-Benoît is still the place where the spirit breathes, where plots are hatched against obedience and all the knowledge-guarding institutions, where rebellion stirs. The apartment is inhabited by, charged with, intellectual activity opening out onto the world; Edgar Morin, Georges Bataille, Michel Leiris, and Maurice Blanchot spend time there or drop by as friends or neighbors. The Algerian war rages on. The struggle is now in Paris, in those FLN [pro-independence] and OAS [anti-independence] networks fighting in the shadows. Fascist terror returns. The same shadows that prowled around during the leaden days of the Occupation come back or resurface. Duras easily recognizes —has never ceased to recognize, ever since Rabier and his friends in their black raincoats and felt hats— these young people on the far right who work like moles in basements.

The debate thus intensifies. Ideas become more radical, verbal violence spreads throughout all camps as positions harden. On rue Saint-Benoît, de Gaulle is considered to be a "tyrant, a Saint-Just," as Edgar Morin recalls, and civil war seems inevitable. This is the tragic context in which Le Manifeste des 121 was launched like a bomb in the fall of 1960, first published abroad in *Tempo Presente* and *Neue Rundschau*, then in France in *Vérité-Liberté*, which is then confiscated. Mascolo and Jean Schuster are behind it, soon aided by other intellectuals, communists on the Party's left flank, left-wing extremists and libertarians with no precise political affiliation.

The 6 September issue of *Le Monde*, unable to publish the document, in turn taunts the censors by informing its readers that "one hundred and twenty writers, academics, and artists have signed a petition in favor of the right of insubordination in the Algerian war," and leaking a significant excerpt from it:

We respect and support the refusal to take up arms against the Algerian people.

We respect and support the conduct of French people who feel it is their duty to aid and protect Algerians oppressed in the name of the French people.

The cause of the Algerian people, which is contributing decisively to the ruin of the colonial system, is the cause of all free men.

Prohibited from publishing the declaration, *Le Monde* informs its readers each day of the overt, constantly growing list of names. Seeing the extent of the phenomenon, Prime Minister Michel Debré mobilizes right-wing political and intellectual figures in an effort to contain the scandal. To the declaration of the "121" they oppose the Manifesto of French Intellectuals, gathering over three hundred important personalities of the artistic, literary, and academic world. The group includes Jacques Heurgon, Pierre Chaunu, Henry Bordeaux, Roland Dorgelès, Thierry Maulnier, Louis Pauwels, Michel de Saint-Pierre, Roger Nimier, Michel Déon, Antoine Blondin, Jules Romains, Henri de Monfreid, Gabriel Marcel, Jacques Laurent, André François-Poncet, Pierre Gaxotte, and others. All of them condemn the "121" for treason and subversion, accusing them of belonging to the "fifth column," and of having as their exclusive goal the destruction of "our country . . . and Western Civilization."

Indochina, 1918. On the balustrade, Marguerite Donnadieu between her two brothers. Seated, their parents, surrounded by teachers and students at the school they directed. (*Photo courtesy Jean Mascolo*)

Indochina, 1920. Family portrait. From left to right: the older brother, Marguerite, the mother, and "the little brother." (*Sygma/Jean Mascolo*)

About 1928, Marguerite Donnadieu dressed in Indochinese fashion. (*Sygma/Jean Mascolo*)

With her stuffed animal. Indochina, 1930. (*Sygma/Jean Mascolo*)

Whereas the "121" see in the war the violence of a French "Gestapo" against oppressed masses, the signers of the Manifesto state that "the war in Algeria is a struggle forced upon France by a minority of fanatical, terrorist, racist insurgents." The "121" are called "poisoners of the national conscience," "assassins" who are trying to "mutilate" the territory, thereby causing its inevitable decline.

A patriotic text, the Manifesto allows many of its signers to recover a national virginity at little cost. It is a good opportunity to forge a new voice, in the vein of Paul Déroulède.* And Duras is still on the side of the oppressed, the revolutionaries, suspected of the highest treason, accused along with her co-signers of being an agent of destruction, for according to the claims of Joseph Hours, "if the State mainly represents the power to command, then to challenge that power, defying it directly, is to destroy it."

Destroy. . . . Already the term is certified as belonging to her. Duras will soon make it the key word in her vocabulary, the object of her action.

In Algiers, the putschist generals take over. The time for action has arrived.

Meanwhile, she continues to write. Her writing activity is immense. It unfolds like life itself. It is the only true life she can live, the only one given to her to live. Writing gives itself abundantly, now edging toward the secret core.

Duras's life seems to merge with that destiny, writing, that necessity both existential and essential, that brutality.

All around her a murmur rises composed of hatred, scorn, jeers, and the most fervent admiration. With a rare mania for writing, she plunges into the "toil," observing with satisfaction her novels' potential for being transposed. But she also knows that her writing is not yet ready to be heard by all, even if what she says appears simple to her, relating universal sentiments as well as ordinary events. She writes with complete confidence in herself, in her words: she who will later claim to be a "world

---

*Early twentieth-century French right-wing agitator.—Trans. note.

author" already has this impression of herself in 1960. Never making the least concession to literary fashion, she keeps her course stubbornly, in spite of critics' reservations, theater directors' misgivings, the public's infidelity, sarcasm among screen and stage people, and the still-modest success of some of her works. The 1960 stage version of *The Sea Wall* at the Studio des Champs-Elysées, adapted by Geneviève Serreau and directed by Jean-Marie Serreau, was something of a failure. The financial setbacks are hard to bear, showing a loss of some $4,000, due mainly to audiences' disaffection as a result of the troubles in Algeria. Critics were less harsh, and despite the same remarks concerning the "emaciated style truly characteristic of this era," the impossibility of being touched by this disintegrating world, they leaned toward approval of the play; didn't Bertrand Poirot-Delpech of *Le Monde* mention "exceptional moments" and Jacques Lemarchand "the generosity and intelligence breathed by the work as a whole"?

There was then a kind of curse clinging to her art, a splendid isolation which, using the same obstinacy as the crabs in *The Sea Wall*, felling mangrove trunks, she overcame with an energy recalling her mother's, the colonial violence still in her veins, what she took to be a struggle against life itself. To write was to continue doing that, time and again, pushing back the limits, still standing, alert.

7

"The Toil of Writing"

During those years, the sixties, she publishes books at a frantic rate, nearly twenty titles (counting novels, plays, and film-scripts), as if time were pressing so much that everything had to be said as quickly as possible, responding to the urgency of what she gradually discovers, what she already knows as if through foreknowledge, and which she must say. "A book," she says, "is like entering into the night." She goes in, not knowing where nor how, but she goes in there. Such is the audacity that makes her singular, foreign, suspect in the eyes of others. She goes there because she has nothing else to lose, be it material goods or reputation, and what she goes searching for is infinite.

She discerns more and more efficiently her texts' dramatic potential, slipping from book to stage, being relayed by other, plural voices. She knows that by "taking the book outside," as she says, she can learn more about the unknown matter she digs at and pesters. *The Square* had already been acted out virtually unchanged. A few modifications sufficed for the little servant and the salesman to assume depth on stage, and Claude Martin's staging in 1957 for the Théâtre des Champs-Elysées, Geneviève Serreau's adaptation in 1959 of *The Sea Wall*, even the film René Clément had made from it in 1958, showed clearly that her writing had immense possibilities for presentation, representing an oral and imaginary capacity that could be exploited and amplified by all of the dramatic arts. From now on she will devote herself to this alternating movement.

"True writers have no life whatsoever," she says in a letter to Marie-Pierre Fernandès, the author of *Travailler avec Duras* [Working with Duras], as she describes the staging of *La Musica deuxième* in July 1985. "They cannot communicate the lives they lead." Only later, after things have been seen and lived, can they be restored, in the "infernal memory," as if first extracted, given to the book, then returned to her by the book. She cannot see her own life, and can follow it only in what the book brings back to her. That is why "books are truer" than she is.

Is it because times are moving fast, because the country is heading for chaos, that she exults so in writing? Is that why she gives herself to it like a mythological heroine, accepting this destiny thrust upon her?

Something within her is mutant, ready to explore all possibilities, causing "accidents of love," in order that things will change, habit won't settle in, in order to invent and renew life, urging it on into unknown regions. She wants to question her life, her loves, and above all, the book. "Attempting," as Mascolo says, "to exhaust them, as if she made of them the impossible demand that they attain completion," in recollection of that distant, primal memory she has of eternity.

Now she can go around in circles in her books. She has put into place a sufficient number of motifs, reverberating among one another, so many echoes, already, that there remains nothing for her to do but weave the Work, like one of the Fates, rewriting the books, converting them for the stage, imagining new possibilities, new variations for them. From one book to the next, from one dramatic scene to the next, she draws from writing the song of exile that goes out in all directions, droning it pell-mell: there is the mother, love, the seaside, especially the cries, the waiting, the pain.

In drama she sees the same dark course of the Nightship, that black box from which escape the cries of memory, the same solitude, above all the same fear present, palpable, carnal, the same danger. "Drama is an unveiling of the human being," she tells Sami Frey and Miou-Miou in 1985. Indeed it is the same tragic terror, everywhere; as if at dawn in the faint light of a Marcel Carné film she relates having gone to the slaughterhouses in La Villette to see five thousand gallons of blood poured out on the cobblestones, all of that flesh laid bare, collected, sold, resold.

Whether it be a play or a novel, it is always the same thing. The Nightship is hunting down something that is endless, "bottomless." It is limitless, it could just as well be taken up over and over from book to book, from film to film, from conversation to conversation, from coma to delirium, it would never end. Like the little beggar woman "from the lukewarm waters of the delta," she is everywhere, in Cochin China, in India, in Paris, on the banks of the Seine or of the Ganges, she will never complete her odyssey.

She has not yet taken the step that will lead her to direct her own plays. But the idea may very well have been born at the beginning of the sixties. She is not at all satisfied with what René Clément made of *The Sea Wall*, emphasizing emotion, psychology, almost exoticism. "The story was well told," she would say in 1991, "the events were all there, in order, but the writing was gone."

She knows that in her books, traces undetectable by the usual, "vulgar" means of the camera or the theater, must nonetheless be represented, she would say, revealed in the great parturition of the stage. The invisible shiver that runs through writing, the dizziness born of this gagged cry suddenly exploding, disintegrating into silence once more, is what must be shown. She realizes that no one else can bring this mystery to the strange light of the stage.

During the years between 1958 and 1963 her attraction to Jarlot leads her to work more and more closely with him. She works on scenarios and adaptations with this novelist nine years her junior, a rewriter for *France-Dimanche* newspaper. They combined their respective abilities: he usually imagining the scenarios, she adding her innate, musical sense of dialogue. Thus, not only did he help her in the conception of *Hiroshima Mon Amour*—Resnais insisted on mentioning him in the credits as "literary advisor"—but he also participated in the adaptation of *Moderato Cantabile* produced for the screen by Peter Brook in 1960. Together they wrote *Une aussi longue absence*, which came out in 1961 from Gallimard, Jarlot's publisher, in addition to *Sans Merveille* for television, the story of a pathological liar, which was shown only once, on 14 April 1964; they also adapted for the French stage William Gibson's *The Miracle Worker*, inspired by the life of Helen Keller and her painful acquisition of speech.

Regardless of the extent of Jarlot's contribution to *Une aussi longue absence*, one is struck by the manner in which Duras manages nonetheless to draw back into her inner world, to her own preoccupations, every collective or partial writing endeavor. It is as if writing had come to her independently, remaining at her disposal until she entices it into "the black ink of her sea." Based once again on an everyday event, the scenario drifts off toward Duras's peculiar regions: a woman in Aubervilliers sees a man she thinks is her husband, formerly deported to Buchenwald, and takes him in, but he, now an amnesiac, while agreeing to live with her again, keeps her secret. One day, in a kind of incomprehensible, delirious outburst, he stands with crossed arms in front of a bus, and they send him to Sainte-Anne's mental hospital. From this story, Jarlot and Duras will draw up a scenario that includes all of the themes already present in Duras's past work, as well as several others, as if prophetically, from her works to come. This quest for others, and the magnificent reverberation of oblivion, the fascination for the "idiotic" or "innocent" person, in the manner of Faulkner's protagonists, this reexamining of the theme of the loss of memory that must be assumed in order that life may be lived, the childish joy of the "lunatic"—Duras's entire utopian problematic is there, still accompanied, like a sonata, at once ironic and melancholy, by the heaviness of time, to be recovered, erased, never to be abolished, though one might try.

For a long time she will repeat this refrain, this seduction madness holds for her, set up like great sea walls against banal existence and the erosion of life. In countless interviews of that time, she repeats in every possible way the desire she wants to create, the will to leave, abandoning everything, and beginning again, one day cutting out an opening, a vacancy, providing oneself with a beach, in the refusal to work, becoming a child once more, becoming like the tramp in *Une aussi longue absence*, a man who is so innocent that when he "sees joy, he is joyful. He is like a mirror."

She says that in the manner of the little beggar woman of the Ganges, with a "perforated head," with no memory, having forgotten everything, in the absence of all reference points, new, crossing through times, places, indifferently, here in the humidity of the bush, there in the loam of the Ganges, and stubbornly, like the birds chirping above the river, pursuing her litany.

Today, during happy moments, in the company of Yann Andréa, she can take on that "mad" look, she can walk along the beach, on the boards crunching with sand, entirely free, in this detachment which no longer has any tie with present existence, abandoned to the unknowable, to the games of the sea breeze, to this offshore wind taking away her words, and happiness exists for a moment, a fraction of a second, before she falls back into "the wonderful sorrow of the book," "at the end of the world, at the end of her herself, in continual alienation, in the constant, unaccomplished act of approaching."

Her life is forever played out in this painful alternation between utopia and suffering, broken, resurfacing in broad daylight, broken again, in search of this absolute. "Love is beautiful, it makes you want to cry," she says. "And perhaps even more: madness, the only safeguard against the false and the real, a lie and the truth, stupidity and intelligence: end of judgment."

She often complains about this brain that never stops crying out, always working, hurting, frightening. Then she contemplates the eternity of the sea, its boundlessness merging with the sky, in the twilight of Les Roches Noires; and she wants to vanish, like the "madmen" in *L'Amour*, which she will write in 1971, following, as she says, the music in her head. To hear this cry, this hope: "You are nothing."

The Cannes festival is still interested in her, for *Une aussi longue absence*, filmed by Henri Colpi, a young "period" director, as he is called, is considered to be "France's major asset." Featuring Georges Wilson and Alida Valli, the movie nonetheless meets with a rather lukewarm reception, as if the audience had not yet learned how to listen to Duras's incantatory dialogue: the dead action and the obscure crossroads traveled by the actors themselves lack public appeal, so the film is considered "boring." Henri Chapier judges it harshly: "Marguerite Duras's name is not enough to make us applaud, and if the memory of her collaboration with Alain Resnais created hopes for a beautiful work, the same cannot be said for Colpi." Wilson's "stunning" performance doesn't save the film either, with its "poorly focused images, producing no emotion, continually giving in to intellectual tricks." Chapier concludes with words that make it clear why such an approach is still too bold: "What's the use of wearing out the patience of those who want acting and movement, not a lot of fabricated singsong." Singsong whose beauty the same Chapier will admire at the same festival fifteen years later in *India Song*!

The magazine *Combat* also condemns "the conspiracy of silence that has succeeded in making a literary taboo out of everything that comes anywhere near the 'nouveau roman' and is now attempting to impose its laws on film. To like Marguerite Duras, to be a fan of Alain Resnais, to wish that cinematic orientation would enter into a new phase, does not imply a lack of discrimination."

Only a few publications like *L'Ecole libératrice* grasp Colpi's feat in rendering with "implacable sobriety" the mysterious, subterranean art of the two characters.

Time has always been characterized by that same fatality in her life, that projection of herself beyond the contemporary scene, like Proust discerning the secret of human beings with the acuity of a blind man, while the carefree members of high society danced the polka in drawing rooms or beneath pergolas.

Other people's fleeting lack of understanding leaves her both indifferent and hurt at the same time. The failures serve as a prelude to the triumphs she knows will follow, inevitably.

And so she keeps writing. In 1963 NRF publishes a play that will long go unnoticed, *Les Eaux et forêts*. The relative failure of previous productions hadn't caused her to give up. There was, moreover, keen interest in her work abroad; the theatrical adaptation of *The Sea Wall* had been published in translation in England, in Germany—where Duras would soon be added to the repertoire of several theaters—and in Poland, Yugoslavia, and Hungary.

For nearly two years, the play's status remained unchanged. The young Claire Deluca–René Erouk company decided to perform it. Duras agreed to grant the rights, and thus began the golden age of Durassian theater, undoubtedly the real beginning of her career as a dramatist.

Her life at that time merges with the theater; she knows that there, on a stage, she will give writing another chance, the chance to reveal, to pierce the secret night of the Ship that has carried her away.

She doesn't give up the novel, however, written as a kind of trace to be deposited, in order to reach "the inner shadow" by all possible means. The books follow one after the other, all composed with the same unity, "strange" and singularly classical like *The Afternoon of Mr. Andesmas*, in which the themes she has always privileged return as leitmotifs: waiting, the undoing of consciousness by the implacable progression of the years, the irresistibility of passion and its helplessness against the overpowering force of age, the unwearying cycle of everyday life and the leaden fixity of cruel time. This new work, published in 1962, signals the end of a cycle of novels, still written in a classical mode, with carefully compressed action, setting, and diction, as a means to attain the irreducible precision of the essence, going to the very heart of it. Again she portrays someone who is doomed to waiting, to the wear and tear of the years, neglected by others in spite of his age, his money, subject to the disposition of his daughter and others, reduced to resignation, a victim of passion.

What she builds there is a real tragedy, under the strain of its unities, consigned to the indifference of fate.

Writing comes to her from a mysterious place, for which she is not "responsible"; she doesn't know "how it is done, how it happens," but "that's how writing is," she says to her interviewers in Montreal in 1981.

For example, the house in *The Afternoon of Mr. Andesmas* was not unknown to her; she saw the terrace overhanging Saint-Tropez bay, and this place obsessed her for six months, and then all of a sudden "someone arrives, a very old man, and it was Mr. Andesmas."

The sudden appearance of writing, of the story that she doesn't necessarily control, leads her gradually into a dangerous, forbidden space. She herself is well aware of it, dating from after *Moderato Cantabile* that suicidal departure for zones of the unconscious, though not responding to their call, but becoming engulfed more deeply each day. In this life entirely doomed to another kind of search for gold, there is a feverish vacillation, a slowly opening crack, already suspected in *Moderato Cantabile* and *10:30 on a Summer Night,* now accelerating, risking something like madness, all the more since it is not absolute, all-intrusive, merely prowling around places of asylum, spaces without reference points.

Her confession to Madeleine Chapsal in *Quinze écrivains* that she "is going around in circles in her head" will come as no surprise. The already considerable work traverses the same zones, weaving a kind of phantasmic embroidery onto the same web, on which her fascination never stops working amid the lightning flashes of passionate love affairs, in the suffocating heat of time that pulverizes everything inexorably, people, words, passing melodies.

Letting herself be carried along that way requires a great deal of courage, even madness, a kind of obliviousness, an act of defiance. The world of money and business deals she rejects is perhaps what gives her the means to set other forces in motion. She rehabilitates a certain conception of the writer, that of someone sacred, prophetic, excessive, solitary, damned, unlike those interchangeable, loquacious "storytellers."

In March 1963 she buys a suite in a luxurious apartment building, formerly a luxury hotel, at Les Roches Noires on the outskirts of Trouville, with a view, on one side, of the imposing façade, and on the other, of the ocean's boundless, foreign expanse. She resides there more and more often now, after having first abandoned it in favor of Neauphle-le-Château in the seventies, but since she began living with Yann Andréa, she goes to the country less frequently and stays by the sea for longer periods of time. She loves this place, which she has all but invested with her presence; visitors and sightseers venture as far as the spacious lobby decorated by Mallet-Stevens, not merely to admire the work of the great 1920s architect, but to have another taste of Duras's particular, magical air, the silent music from some of her films made here, a hint of the Prince of Wales, once glimpsed, and filmed by her in *India Song*.

No sooner has one entered there than, by the very fact that most of the residents are absent, silence takes over, striking against the large bay windows that plunge into the sand and then into the sea. Paintings by Gir, a poster artist also from the twenties, form a frieze of dancing women all around the walls; famous people have sat there: Monet, Zola, Proust—whose room looked out over the sea—Reynaldo Hahn, and the queen of Spain, who rented the hotel for her entire retinue. Edward VII conducted some of his love affairs there. Today others live there, coming in the off-season when the beach is deserted, walking along the sandy boardwalk to the casino, returning to their rooms through the lobby, going down long pale pink hallways, while the glass elevator glides up and down. Obaldia, Riva, Terzieff, Duras, Bulle Ogier, and still others have met, continue to meet each other, but in the evening the old hotel is empty, resounding with the echoes of its silence, recalling mythical, uninhabited places, the scene of a crime, a secret passion, or an artwork's point of conception.

In that "apartment suspended above the sea," she writes still, always. Always that same thing, she says in *Green Eyes*, that need anchored in her heart, her gut, her head. The presence of the sea so close, the sand unfolding as far as the eye can see when the tide changes, mixing with the color of the water, making the words flow—all of that provides her with momentum.

That is what she likes most about Trouville. The coming and going of the sea resembles precisely what she is trying to say, that elusive movement of souls and beings, those inexplicable currents flowing through them, which they endure inexorably like the daily motion of the waves, the ebbing tides, the penetrations. There is no more space or time, but only this fleeing swell, beneath the movement of the clouds strangely washed by the water reminiscent of the voluminous depths, the immensity of the abyss.

She can no longer bear to stay away from Trouville, and from its light. She loves to see it falling "straight down from the bright sun," but also the "diffused, white light of an overcast sky and the coallike glimmer of thunderstorms."

She has molded this place to herself; sometimes, through the high windows, one can make out her silhouette, at once massive, stocky, and fragile, bundled up in old sweaters, pushing aside poorly kept, worn curtains. Admirers come by and leave letters for her with the caretaker. She might not read them, called off elsewhere in the movement of writing, in the pain of the love she is living, in her happiness too. And some, if they manage to escape the caretaker's watchful eye, go up to the second floor and leave something in front of her door, an object, a book, a picture; thus with Duras mysterious ties are woven, created solely by the books, the films, out of nothing.

In the off-season, the apartment's lights stay on until very late. Duras is there with Yann Andréa; she says that on those occasions they tell each other "the truth, no matter how terrifying, and we laugh as we did when we used to drink and couldn't talk to each other until the afternoon."

She is a kind of legendary figure in Trouville; people nudge one another as if to say: "Duras, over there, look, it's Duras." Consequently she hardly goes out anymore, staying cooped up in the vast apartment, hearing the sound of the breakers, listening for the high-pitched cries of the sea gulls, the roar of the sirens, and waiting for Yann Andréa to return from his errands, his walks, so that he can drive her along the little road hugging the coast, to Quittebeuf, where they taste the golden late-afternoon light.

Before, in 1980, he used to go away, further and further, carousing through "the big hotels and the hills." When she saw that he wasn't coming back, a pain would rise up in her stronger than anything, uncontrollable, infinite. He would go to see men, she said; he hadn't concealed that from her at all, but there still remained this unalterable love between them.

In Trouville she has learned many, many things from the sea and the landscape, the conversations of people along the waterfront, the rumbling of the waves, the memory-piercing night, furtive silhouettes walking beneath the neon lights of the streetlamps on the boards crunching with sand, the eternity of the sea, and the strange mixture of the river waters and the even deeper seas. She remembers having understood there the powerful meaning of "fluent" writing when one evening, knocking on Yann Andréa's bedroom door, she yells out that one must "write without correcting, throw writing outside . . . remove none of its useless bulk, nothing, leave it all with the rest, alter nothing, neither its speed nor slowness, leave everything just as it appeared."

Les Roches Noires is the shrine of her revelations, for the physical presence of the air and the sea is very strong there, even allowing those who observe them to see the world differently, linking everything with its great mystery, as if filtered through the mind.

She writes a great deal, "texts" as she says, not novels, or at least not what would ordinarily be called novels, considering the fact that their emotional charge, their power of attraction, neither share the status of ordinary narration nor have anything to do with the publishing industry's wheelings and dealings. Instead, she roams around the "memory of oblivion"; she says that memory is primarily what one has forgotten, and what remains is the half-erased, but still present, obsessive imprint. In 1964 she publishes *The Ravishing of Lol Stein*. The shock that that book produces in her, as if it pried open trap-doors sealed shut long ago, holding back violent, fundamental forces, is considerable. From it, other books will be born in the years to come, films as well, all tied to the matrix of the first one, and unfurling stubbornly. What will become known as "The Lol Stein Cluster" or "The Lol Stein Cycle" can be traced back to her childhood in Vinh Long, to the meandering Mekong, and above all approaches the zones of "madness," the absences, the invisible crevices that destroy Lol, reducing her "to ashes." The book will thus become a springboard, reaching all the way to *L'Amour* (1971), *La Femme du Gange* (1973), and *India Song* (1975). Texts and films will spread far and wide the story emanating from Anne-Marie Stretter, the beggar woman, and the Vice-Consul, Michael Richardson. Duras's favorite themes are caught in this web of texts wrought with oblivion and madness, indifference and death, silence and the voices of the world's murmur, the cries of solitude, of all forms of misery, wandering, and passion.

She always returns to this essential function she grants to writing, to words, to their "power of proliferation," as she says in an interview given in Montreal in 1981, to this force in the word, that of containing, all by itself, "a thousand pictures."

What she writes "falls into silence," into those peripheries where new encounters take place, where other dialogues are spoken, where whole, incomplete, and buried words mingle, and the murmur she creates could be silence. Silence spoken, made resonant. Proust also attained those zones when, at night in his cork-lined room, he would reconstitute the sounds from his evening gatherings, the small talk, the society gossip, the confessions he would pick up, after having paid dearly for the privilege of hearing them.

That is what she likes in Pascal, the untamed violence of his prayers, the gasping breath of his intuitions, the cry of his fiery night. For that is the cry she wants to utter, removing the gag from words, customs, reticences, heading straight for the cry, like the Vice-Consul wandering the streets of Lahore one evening, sobbing like a hunted animal, like Michael Lonsdale recording at the Maison de la Radio and filling the corridors with sound so similar to the gangways of the Nightship, the lover's cry when he separated from her, "a long, spoken cry of helplessness, anger, and disgust as if it were vomited . . . a cry coming all the way from ancient China."

The Ravishing of Lol Stein opens up new channels for her quest, taking her further and further down into the holds of the ship. It cuts her off, however, from wider audiences, somewhat disappointed at not recognizing the novelist who wrote *Moderato Cantabile* or *The Sailor from Gibraltar*, whose narrative threads, already slender, nonetheless gave the appearance of a true novel. Showered with praise by some while systematically derided by others, hailed by the greatest minds of the century, Lacan among others, she begins her trek through the wilderness. Duras's personality takes on a prophetic weight that she no longer controls, expressing itself in a kind of logorrhea, a glossolalia against and in spite of herself, without engaging her own responsibility. In a interview given in Montreal, she admits that she doesn't know how it works, how "it" comes to her, "it," that mysterious language, which communicates more than any theory, any known analysis. Sometimes she coquettishly persists in claiming that she doesn't understand psychoanalysis, that her art requires other channels for the same quest, more mystical, more volcanic than the analytic process. When she writes, she surrenders to the flux of her night, which flows through her like "a sieve," abandoning all method, but, like Pascal, at the mercy of trembling, molten fire, using whatever she can gather, lava, fragments, faint murmurs, sonorous echoes.

"A stranger to psychoanalysis," as she claims, she still discloses the passing of tumultous, suffering souls, their nocturnal music, ready to burst.

Duras has readily granted the production rights to *Les Eaux et forêts* to the young actors who requested them. She has high expectations for the play because it reveals her comic temperament, her little-known capacity for humor that recalls Ionesco while remaining enjoyable and jubilatory, making words juggle among themselves, bouncing freely to the point of derision and the absurd. On Radio France-Inter's *Pop Club*, she defines the play in a few words: "It's the story of three people who meet and don't know each other. Three people with no identity, three marginal individuals of the kind often seen hanging around in shopping centers, on street corners. They are not mad, not the kind they lock up, but almost. They enjoy complete freedom, they are anonymous. And they are extremely funny."

Although she is not responsible for the staging, which is entrusted to Yves Brainville, Duras attends numerous rehearsals, contributes illuminating information, and makes written additions to the scenario so that each of the characters will achieve his "explosion," as she calls the supreme madness that takes hold of the text, and which carries it to that high degree of absurdity and buffoonery of Dubillard and Queneau.

She demonstrates that she now knows how to play on all registers, from the romantic to the dramatic, from the serious to the farcical, just as she will soon pick up a camera and rank with the greatest directors, "just like that," because she is Duras. . . .

This doesn't mean, however, that she has abandoned her favorite themes, her tormented conscience, her anguish, her compassion for the deprived, the disinherited. She knows all words are useless: faced with the implacable passing of time, memory flees, as through a torn strainer, and each man is in his cell, thinking he is safe, but at the mercy of the wild wind.

On that May evening in 1965, the critics are enthusiastic. The biggest names in Parisian journalism are gathered at the Théâtre Mouffetard for the dress rehearsal: Guy Dumur, Jean-Jacques Gautier, Bertrand Poirot-Delpech, Jacques Lemarchand, Robert Kanters, Matthieu Galey, and they unanimously hail it as a masterpiece. One name is repeated over and over, that of Claire Deluca, whose talent is "irresistible," "extraordinary," and who seems to combine the "qualities of Flon, Girardot, and Masina." The play is called unique, a work of genius. Audiences are so large that two shows must be held nightly until the lease for the rental of the hall expires at the end of June. Le Studio des Champs-Elysées reserves the play for the fall season, but requests another play for the second feature. That is no problem, for in her notebooks Duras has two more that she gives to Claire Deluca: *La Musica* and *The Afternoon of Mr. Andesmas*, which she has also adapted for the stage. They choose *La Musica*, to be produced in October 1965, along with the extended run of *Les Eaux et forêts* for one hundred and twenty performances. The staging of *La Musica* is done by Alain Astruc and Maurice Jacquemont. Once again, the response is tremendous. The critics, who had already seen *Les Eaux et forêts* the previous summer, come back mainly for *La Musica*. Enthusiastic, they admire the humor of the curtain-raiser and the subtle, poignant gravity of *La Musica*. It is Jules Renard and Chekhov, Monnier and Ionesco, all at the same time; in a single evening Duras is consecrated as a dramatist. It is true that with *La Musica*, she makes real music, the soul-drifting that fits her well, and which she loves to explore, the pains of love when love is gone, confessions, and whatever she is able to gather, scraps, fragments, all those traces of memory, those words amounting to nothing at all, fragile and abandoned, almost killed, perhaps already dead.

She makes that voice heard, especially that one, and even its murmurs when it has subsided, as if after Duras, it were still giving voice to Duras, to the secrets waiting to be revealed.

Discovering her talent for drama, and its repercussions in the world of film, thanks to the magic of *Hiroshima*, she writes *Nuit noire, Calcutta* in 1964, a short for Marin Karmitz, a young Romanian director whose cinematography reflects an awareness of the political struggle, then *Les Rideaux blancs* for Franju in 1965, and most importantly *La Voleuse* in 1966, for Jean Chapot, revealing once more her unusual, foreign voice.

Wherever she places herself and settles down to work, she always gains entry by breaking in, unveiling abysses, nights of the soul so cruel that spectators leave the movie theater at a loss, dazed, or else, as if in an attempt to hide their distress, exasperated.

What she gives to filmmakers are fragments of her world, traces of her imagination. Especially with *La Voleuse*, she takes up the theme of the ordinary event: a child is the object of conflict between his adoptive parents and his natural mother (Romy Schneider) who, six years after having abandoned him, wants to take him back. The dialogue is always a perfect reflection of human truth, throbbing with distress. Duras possesses that art of unraveling the complexity of people, their inability to explain, to understand, to justify. Her voice resides in this state of indecision, of suspension. That is what makes her dangerous, troublesome.

She remains the same, unchanged. Sure of herself, of what she has been saying for a long time, like the beggar woman of Savannakhet, indifferent to criticism, doing as she pleases. She wears her little tight-waisted tweed suits like those that were popular in the fifties, and turtleneck sweaters, or her everlasting houndstooth check skirts and more turtlenecks, with V-neck sweaters on top of them. She already has, as she says, "the Duras look." She discusses this in *Practicalities*: "the M. D. uniform." She finally hit upon this fashion, completely her own, "to stop people from thinking about my height by always wearing the same clothes. So that they notice the sameness of the uniform rather than the reason for it."

That is how she is dressed in 1966 on the set of *La Musica*, in her uniform, directing Delphine Seyrig. The play accurately reflects her conception of the literary work, in the give and take of meanings, ever adding to its significance and depth. She launches into this adventure with Paul Seban, who already has fifty television movies under his belt; more importantly, she has great confidence in him and feels strong affection for him. But whatever complicity reigns between them, Duras knows what she wants to say, and is determined to invest the picture with gazes, interlocking eyes, captured glances, that whole invisible text that communicates more than words. She insists on her passion for directing, that throbbing art which proceeds from no theory, but succeeds in grasping for a moment, in the mobility of a face, the coils of silence when it settles into the heart of the couple. She senses that she will become master of this kind of film, chamber cinema (as in chamber music), taking it from the chamber to the arena, to the closed circle of tragedy. She has intuitive knowledge of actors, chooses her cast with troubling accuracy, predicts their potential, and discovers in their diction the voice that she herself hears in her books—broken, deep, bearing the weight of subliminal conversations, stifled cries, suddenly ready to be expelled, like a liberation. It is the first time Delphine Seyrig acts for Duras. She likes her because she is as elusive as her writings, with her porcelain face, that airy step, never seen before, and especially her voice, with "unrealistic, absolutely unpredictable punctuation, defying all rules," as if, adds Duras, she "had just finished eating a piece of fruit, her mouth still moist with it, and in this sweet, sour, green, summer coolness, the words take shape, along with the sentences, whole conversations, coming to us in a new way."

When she entrusts her with the role of Anne-Marie Stretter in *India Song*, her voice, like a trace or an echo, will lend a renewed intensity of unlimited meaning to the precarious, laconic words. The exact encounter between Duras and her actors gives them a whole mythical power, a legendary status. Such is the case with Madeleine Renaud, Sami Frey, Miou-Miou, Bulle Ogier, Gérard Depardieu, Michael Lonsdale, Jeanne Moreau, Lucia Bosè, Emmanuèle Riva. . . .

Beginning with *La Musica*, witnesses to all her productions tell of the same fascination she exerts while filming: meticulous to excess, imposing an interiorized image of cinema, a spirituality in the art of conducting the film, spontaneously introducing silence. She is always huddled up, as if gathered in upon herself, submitting more ideas, never considering the script and shooting directions final. When she shoots, she is still writing, for a kind of fear takes hold of her, pointing in another direction, upsetting plans, following her visions.

She always dwells in that fear, that fragility of things and people, conscious of the intolerable indifference of time. During the shooting of *La Musica*, a war is raging in Vietnam, in the jungle of her childhood: napalm bombs are destroying the vine-covered basins where fish swim; the pagodas and Buddhist monasteries are in flames, and the flesh of black panthers burns along with that of monkeys. On breaks, she reads newspaper accounts of her native land's agony. Pictures stream through her mind, the swarming streets, visits to the zoo, the humid air, the mixed smells of flowers and spices, and her own form running to meet the Chinese lover, decked out in a man's felt hat and lamé shoes.

But what she is talking about here on the set of *La Musica* is in fact the same thing, this badgered memory, these lost, insular voices stirring in her words. It is something that goes out then draws to a close, approaching death, unable to understand. But at the same time it has to do with another birth; a voice is heard, imprecise at first, then shaking itself off, new, blazing a trail to the lands of origin, uttering its first words, growing.

A "stubborn child": that's how Jean-Louis Barrault describes her after proposing that they work together in 1965, detecting in her this "enormous feeling for humanity," an endless capacity for listening. She asks the Renaud-Barrault theater company to perform *Whole Days in the Trees* (1968), adapted from the story of the same title, published fourteen years earlier, and later *The Eden Cinema* (1977) and *Savannah Bay* (1982). She offers the role of Claire Lannes in *L'Amante Anglaise* (1968) to Madeleine Renaud for the Théâtre National Populaire.

She talks a great deal about Madeleine Renaud, recognizing in her acting all of the reverberations that her texts create like sound waves. In the image of her characters, Madeleine Renaud is like someone skinned alive, penetrated with savage, indecent violence, going to the heart of theatrical darkness, bringing back with her onto the stage, from her mortal journey, glimmers Duras herself had not seen, but which lay deep inside her text. Hearing her utter those words comforts her in the

idea, persistent in her now, of the magic of words, of the unpredictable power they hold and which she sets down there on the
paper, without knowing, innocently.

For the 1982-1983 theater season, she thus gives Madeleine
Renaud the role of Madeleine, an old actress who with the help
of her granddaughter is trying in vain to recover the past, to
give shape to it. "Once upon a time then, in a café, it was in
the afternoon, the café looked out across a square, in the center
of the square, there was a fountain. It was in a land that could
have been southwestern France.

"Or a neighborhood in a European town.

"Or somewhere else.

"In those little county seats in southern China.

"Or in Peking, or Calcutta.

"Versailles.

"Nineteen twenty.

"Or in Vienna.

"Or in Paris.

"Or somewhere else."

Savannah Bay is perhaps the reflective pause in Duras's work,
the expression of what she really wants to say. There is nothing
that can be attempted that is not in vain, doomed to passing
oblivion, in the impossibility of restoring the story of one's life,
bogged down in the silt of time which obscures everything and
makes it impossible to recover memories, mislaid between legend and oblivion.

Savannah Bay thus becomes a kind of metaphor of the
impossible biography; Madeleine's "cracked memory," her
"violent desire to apprehend unknowable events from the
past," end in failure. All that remain are hypothetical con-
structions, traces left in this mud of time, where life passes by
and vanishes. Nothing but vague beliefs, uncertain images at
the mouth of a slow river, swarming with Chinese junks, in
tropical heat, occasional impressions of an illuminated fan of
water shooting forth, only to plunge back into the murky ink
of night.

But the determination is immense, the stake of her writing is
to force that night even if she abolishes herself in the process.

While filming one day in 1975 she sat and listened to the steady rain falling on the garden of the mansion where she was shooting *India Song,* and back came a flood of memories from Indochina. In that summer rain she heard the heavy patter of the monsoon from her childhood, and asked her sound engineer to record it. It is in such unexpected instances that she thinks she holds the real truth, captured in these gaps in time.

Like Lol, Duras persists in beginning the past over again, picking up once more the web of Lol V. Stein and spinning it into another book published in 1966, unwearyingly adding knots to the initial fabric.

With *The Vice-Consul,* the story of the beggar woman is reconstructed, what Duras acknowledges to have been an "enormous traumatism" in her childhood. The wanderer of Savannakhet follows the rivers, the wetlands of that reinvented India, forever singing the lament of despair, the throbbing psalm of sorrow. She roams around outside the embassies and the colonial villas, imposing her madness on those who don't want to hear about leprosy and monsoons. Except for Anne-Marie Stretter, except for Jean-Marc de H., Vice-Consul of Lahore, on the fringes of fashionable society, already on the borders of that madness, both ready to explode, that is, to let out their cry. In *The Vice-Consul* something miraculous occurs, ecscaping words, taking place between them, in the intertwining of gazes, of exchanges, between tango rhythms rising and falling like sobs: "It seems to me," says the Vice-Consul, "that if I tried to tell you what I would like to tell you, everything would crumble into dust . . . the words capable of getting my ideas across, the words . . . to express my thoughts, don't exist."

She always wants to describe this intolerable heaviness of time, this inability of the human condition to flourish, this sticky pitch enveloping it and bogging it down. So if something would just happen, like a cry bursting out, breaking loose, revolt, murder, anger: love!

She still remembers what she saw as a little girl, the ambassador's wife and what people said about her, and one of her lovers who committed suicide. Anne-Marie Stretter is the absolute, ambiguous, dual woman, life and death, fragility and violence, illegibility, limitlessness.

She is the one who made it possible to write, "the very reason for writing," the one who "led me to penetrate the dual meaning of things. From every angle." It is Anne-Marie Stretter who blindly taught Duras this aspect of the world, and Duras long carried her as a mythical figure. Intuitively, the archetypal figure of Anne-Marie Stretter represents the revolt and the savagery of love, the frantic quest for life, true, absolute, exacting life, the claim made on death, because that life is hopelessly inaccessible. She taught her the desire for "the explosion," a term appearing often in her writing, the necessity of losing oneself and becoming deluded in the Great Oneness, far from compromising, disreputable deeds.

She explodes to see Siam again, summoned so many times in her texts; Siam, which enchants her in its luminous, open sonority, the image of life itself. And the Manchuria of *The Lover*, in the great Chinese north.

Despite the allegorical dimension of *The Vice-Consul*, its hermetic appearance, the characters' pain is striking; they are filled with that existential suffering which Duras portrays, like Schubert, through the "musica," the intensity of silence with which she loads the words, like silent bombs. That is the path leading her to politics, and along the same route she perceives the man of Lahore crying out, the beggar woman's rattle, and Anne-Marie Stretter's brazenness. Their scandalous, in a sense illegal behavior, is bothersome, embarrassing, calling everything into question, leading back to the self.

As she says later in connection with *India Song*, this is the cry that no one dares to utter, for it is the confession of our failures, our pain which society hides and ridicules and finds indecent. This cry is a scandal, a traitor to the cause of societies.

It is the cry of "the clown awakening," the one sometimes heard in the ghettos where blacks live, blacks from "glorious

Africa," colonized in Paris, ready to shoulder the broom each morning to sweep up the beer bottles and Coke cans, and for whom she also has this cry of love: "You who have identity, you who are blessed with a name, I love you."

Never has Duras's secret lyricism blazed as in *The Vice-Consul*, in this parturition of pain serving as a backdrop for the low-toned harmonization of uncommon beings whose destiny is errant and endless. She moves ever closer to what she herself comes to call poetry, an imperceptible but persistent listening to this side of words and souls, their obscure, indefinite, trembling margins, and which she is able to render in apparently disorganized, incomplete, almost ungrammatical syntax that, finally, expresses better than anything else the fractures, the holes, the dilutions.

She wants to force words even further, playfully, derisively pressing in on them from all sides, driving them to betray grammar in new ways, to disobey the essential rules within the codes.

Following her first real stage success with *Les Eaux et forêts* and *La Musica*, she gives the young Claire Deluca-René Erouk company two more short texts, *Le Shaga* and *"Yes," peut-être*. They will be performed at the Théâtre Gramont in January 1968. The way the two plays were rehearsed and developed is typical of the kind of work Duras is trying to create. For six months, in fact, these texts, no more than ten minutes long, were written, lengthened, more or less developed in the course of the rehearsals, even drawn out by the actors, continually renewed, the fruit of intensely dynamic activity, a kind of creative effervescence. With them, Duras left the Chekhovian chant of *La Musica* to return to another aspect of her personality, the dimension of laughter, that joy she often expresses in everyday life.

For Duras laughs easily, with a hint of spirited, defiant mockery that "shoots down sneerers," according to Michèle Manceaux, Duras's neighbor in Neauphle who sometimes stays home in the evening and listens to tape recordings of her voice, just because she misses "Margot," whose ample, resonant laughter reflects a simple form of joy.

The same cleansing laughter that she displayed with this unfettered freedom was there, Claude Roy explained, to help bring down "the walls of death," those that bury men in the worst kind of madness, in the fear of that madness, or in war. Duras's revolutionary vein appears, violent, anarchist, totally disobedient, with no concessions to drama or to the demands made by academic critics like Jean-Jacques Gautier or Gilbert Guilleminault. She leads a deliberate revolt and devastating, cleansing laughter sweeps everything away. The texts develop in the course of rehearsals, like mosaics, leading the actors along like "children," until the words collapse irresistibly. "I have prepared . . . outlines. I add to them, erase, redraw as I go," she says. Thus is woven the Durassian creation, in this tentative approach, in the absence of knowledge, in this sudden, improvised discovery.

Since she wants to do everything, staging, going over the text again, even deciding on the costumes, directing the actors. She spends her time at the theater, and the advice she showers upon them enriches the actors and replenishes their roles. And so she tells them, in her stage directions accumulated throughout the rehearsals:

"Your madness has broken out and you use it as a toy of destruction, you change what lies behind other people's ramparts. It reveals itself to be the equivalent of revolutionary dissidence, a far cry from other people's buried madness. . . .

"They are mad, but they don't know it, you are mad too, and you don't know it either. But they remain afraid of madness, while you aren't.

"You are swarming with words, like them, but your condition causes you to see words glide into sentences, and the words slip unnoticed into their sentences."

Feeling her way along during rehearsals, she insistently hammers out her message:

"Shaga is a transgression. They are driving at something.

"I need to hear this liberation, it has to fill the air.

"Act out this availability, this great idleness. They are on the extreme fringes of society.

"You see, Shaga crosses back through time again, like a very ancient language returning.

"The condition shared by all of humanity is madness.

"Each time you slip into amiability, the play stops.

"Keep the freshness, too, the wonder.

"Act out the text in its brutality, as it is, without looking for anything else, without psychology.

"Above all it has to be wild, no niceness, no halftones; what makes it wild is that these are people who have become raw, abrupt, pure again like uncut crystal.

"Shaga's terrifying side must be kept intact, so that it keeps crying out savagely."

That is what she tells Claire Deluca, René Erouk, and Marie-Ange Dutheil as if in a premonition of what would be said a few months later in May 1968.

As is often the case, she feels such things, what she perceives as great outbursts of collective anger and the welling up of violence, like a sorceress. In an interview with *L'Aurore* at the end of December 1967, she confirms prophetically: "I don't think everyone will like it, but the students will undoubtedly be on my side."

She invents Shaga, "a language that doesn't exist," spoken by a slightly crazy woman when she wakes up one morning, according to the story she tells. She also imagines a street scene in New York following a self-imposed A-bomb attack, which becomes *"Yes," peut-être:* "Two women meet; they have lost their memory of the events and of certain words."

But in these happenings at once absurd and brilliant, her defiance of institutions goes too far, destroying habits. Though a few intellectuals like Claude Roy and Nathalie Sarraute recognize the modernity of the two plays—"Theater so innovative that it will necessarily assert itself. The laughter provoked here by ever-present humor is, in my view," says Sarraute, "of a quality unmistakably that of modern theater"—the critical establishment as a whole, led by Jean-Jacques Gautier, denounces them as theater for snobs and idiots, in which "the language spoken is pidgin"; Caviglioli of *Le Canard enchaîné* entitles his article: "While plucking off the petals of la Marguerite Durasoir,* the theater gives birth to horrors," and Guilleminault announces that on the evening of the dress rehearsal, "Fascists and antifascists fraternized in utter boredom."

Sarcasm and insults rain down upon her; each and every critic contributes a witty comment, nonetheless acknowledging the actors' courage and talent in extricating themselves so skillfully from such a shipwreck; Claire Deluca will be the only survivor to escape unscathed, "funny and convincing," capable, according to Georges Lerminier of *Le Parisien libéré*, "of making us guess and understand everything . . . and love almost everything."

Duras hardly suffers from such an attack. She moves forward, always sure of herself, knowing that now they must reckon with her, and that she will never be bound by the dictates of the critical establishment. "That's how she is." She shares this self-confidence with the actors who believe in the ever-penetrating force of *Le Shaga* when they rework it together ten years later, doing various revivals before a much more receptive audience.

In this creative overflowing, she seems to live only for writing, a different task from that of the past, moving toward a source that gives itself freely.

She adopts a radically provocative, utopian political position. Invited all around the world in the context of cultural exchanges between countries—in Cuba, for example, which she visits with other intellectuals—she increases her hostility toward Americans and the French right wing, becomes more attentive to revolutionary movements, to the particular fate of certain marginal experiences, to personalities like Che Guevara and Fidel Castro, and favors the urban guerrilla warfare developing in Latin American countries. She feels resolutely on the side of young people, in the dynamics of their analysis, in their combined savagery and innocence. She remains in contact with them through her son Jean, who rejects all forms of work, moving about in the world freely, certain of

---

*A play on Duras's name that could be translated "Daisy the Deadly Bore"—Trans. note.

what he does not want, strengthened and enriched by his refusal. She perceives such an abundance, such a profusion of life in the students, in this new romanticism that rejects the fangs of a brutal, old, well-ordered, close-minded, self-righteous society.

She exalts other values, the right to laziness, to idleness, to a new fraternal spirit. The humanity she prefers is that which offers itself "without dignity, without honorability, gives in to its desires, sleeps in the afternoon, refrains from eating, goes to the dogs once in a while, displays what the bourgeoisie calls spinelessness." Her home in Neauphle-le-Château and her Paris apartment are glass houses, where women, men, and especially young people, even children circulate, spreading currents of defiance, amid the fusion of ideas.

Also during these years before 1968, she publishes *L'Amante Anglaise*, which she will adapt for the theater, in a sense liberating its narrative form and presenting it on stage after the events of May. Premiering on 16 December 1968, she entrusted it to director Claude Régy, who will often direct her future plays, understanding her silence-laden dialogues. The original cast included Michael Lonsdale, Madeleine Renaud, and Claude Dauphin. Decidedly, as Guilleminault scornfully said about *Le Shaga*, Duras "plays the piece for all it's worth," filling the stage, but making an unusual, dangerous voice heard, one whose frequency has never been picked up in the theater.

It is a risky voice, because it speaks only of what obsesses the author herself: madness, death, the mystery of all human behavior, and the punishing impossibility of judging any act, even murder. She has become accustomed to working on this shifting terrain, never piercing the dark core, and transforming others into strangers who cannot possibly understand. "Yes, at night I feel mad. I hear things . . . I am perhaps very close to madness. Or death," says Claire Lannes, the main character. That is where Duras digs, hammers away, in volcanoes, in those millenary, prehistoric caves, and "for thirty thousand years, I have been crying out to the sea." That is where she tries to reach the black, burning knot buried deep inside those holes "of clay."

And she says that she is touching the peripheries of that secret, for it must remain "inaccessible . . . beneath my skin, as blind as a newborn baby."

To others, the actors for example, she tries to reveal what they too withhold in their innermost being and are unable to bring out. "With her," says Michael Lonsdale, "acting involves the suppression of one's personality, everything remains on the inside. You have to be in love with Duras, become a voice in her own symphony." She cultivates the art of discovering instinctively the actor in tune with her world, her music. Lonsdale, presenting a Duras cycle in Limoges, tells the press: "With Duras, the film is shot miraculously, through a kind of osmosis, without a flow of words, guided along by feelings. One is not really concerned with cinematic form, but with writing. She has in fact no feel for the performance, the images merely reinforce the writing. The cast's job is not to act, but to say the words."

What she detects in Lonsdale, as in Sami Frey or Miou-Miou, first and foremost stage actors, is their ability to avoid all stereotyping, playing instead on several registers, leaving the audience baffled. What she draws out of the players is the virtuosity that she herself reveals in her shifting texts, in her dialogues where dodges, subterfuges, and confessions rub shoulders, in a whisper or a cry—and above all simplicity, which she sees in Delphine Seyrig more than in anyone else, despite the fact that the actress usually appears sophisticated and affected. That is precisely the kind of ambiguity she wants to see her express, knowing intuitively that she will be well suited for the intended script.

With this troupe of actors she always takes with her on her Nightship, these actors who drop everything to work with her, even without pay, because she leads them off on these unique adventures, henceforth impossible on both stage and screen—namely, an encounter with an author who rewrites her play while staging it, showing how writing is done, shamelessly laying bare the words and the creative processes—with these actors, with her authority that none of them would dream of questioning, caught in the magical charm she radiates, she knows she will arrive at the most secret recesses of her intuition.

The rehearsals for *La Musica deuxième* later in 1988 will thus take place in the well-balanced rhythm of a reconstructed, reinvented play. In *Travailler avec Duras*, Marie-Pierre Fernandès tells about the genesis of the new play, its staging, how Duras prowls around the words, replaces one term with another in a way that suddenly changes everything, provoking emotion, making tears come to the eyes, abruptly giving access to silence, to confusion. From the living matter that she directs, she wants to extract whatever is still foreign to the actors, but which they mysteriously hold within themselves, waiting to be discovered by her words. She thus wants to bring out Sami Frey's feminine side, revealing new ways of understanding, "unknowable" passageways. She knows that in these ambiguities of human existence she will surely find the fruit of her quest, so she provokes them, draws them out. Of Mr. Nollet, a character in *La Musica deuxième*, she says: "He leaned over and gave out a howl, just like an animal." That is what she wants to express, the soul in all its savagery, all its nakedness. Thus, as if prompted by Duras, Sami Frey cries out, just as Lonsdale will cry out in *India Song*, and his wound shatters the air.

And so the work is composed of these jolting images and words, of ruptures, holes, puddles of silence, later giving rise, on stage, in the darkened theater, before the undifferentiated members of the audience in the same obscurity, to the unfolding of a tragedy, like a slow march toward death, solitude, and oblivion.

Through this prehistory rediscovered through toil, just as God once molded the clay to create her life, the work remains linked to the sacred, to the idea of God. She kneads this shapeless mass of words, "unintelligible, very obscure, very opaque," and grace is bestowed, while the fissures, the doubts, the discouragement rent by the act of creation remain hidden from view.

8

"Destroy, She Said"

The events of May 1968 find her at the forefront of the riots, with that thirst for a renewed world she had long been working for. May '68 is in a sense "her" revolution, because she felt it coming, intuitively, observing the dilapidation, the decay, and the death throes in all governing institutions. Seeing a rebellious generation of young people brings back the irreverent smile she is wearing that year, tempers her pessimism, gives her new reasons to hope and believe.

The joy of speech recovered and that spontaneous romanticism to which she has often referred unfold exultantly. At the Théâtre de l'Odéon, which Jean-Louis Barrault turns over to the students, she voices the frantic demands of youth, the refusal of established practices, expressed in the naïve simplicity of a cry. For her, '68 is akin to being born: she invents, she imagines, she dwells in the strangely wild innocence of Hölderlins, Dickinsons, "mad people." The insane person becomes a real constant for her, meaning those who don't restrict their language, their lives, their behavior, but, freed of all hindrances, release their imagination, restoring the true nature of words and gestures, the acts of existence. In this student agitation, which gradually spreads to other social classes, winning the approval and sympathy of public opinion, she sees another way of expressing and reinventing politics.

During the first days of the revolution, on May 5th to be exact, along with Mascolo and the group that had created the anti-Gaullist journal *Le 14 juillet*, she is one of the instigators of the call for intellectuals and artists to boycott French radio and television. In mid-May, the same group on rue Saint-Benoît founds the Students' and Writers' Action Committee, which will play an active role in the drawing up of motions, and in the agitation. She is seen again in the troubled times, a firebrand vibrant with the fierce energy that keeps her alive, in her own element on the liberated streets, breaking the law, crossing through restricted zones, inventing the revolution against institutions and the police. She likes this street chaos, this creative effervescence, the same as that unleashed in the uprisings of 1830, 1848, and 1871. Paris is exploding, and new ideas are constantly springing forth, terrorizing government ministries. She feels an all-encompassing love for the crowd, and for others, progressing with them toward "a rigorous freedom."

There also appears an ever more deliberate will to say no, expressed with a silent determination that makes her move forward, with the intransigent lucidity proudly accompanying acts of defiance. A "militant antimilitant," she handles paradox comfortably. In a published credo, she professes the most anarchistic act of faith ever produced by the May revolution: "We are bound by nothing but refusal. On a separate, marginal path from that of mainstream, class-bound society, we lead unclassable, unbreakable lives, and we say no. We take refusal to the point of refusing to become integrated into the political movements that claim to refuse what we refuse. We refuse the programmed refusal characteristic of opposition institutions. We refuse to allow our refusal to be tied up, packaged, and stamped with a label. Or to allow its living springs to dry up, or to let anyone turn back its course." Nobody is surprised at such a manifesto. Duras's work thus far has cried out this same rage; now her flamboyant rhetoric flares up again, betraying the impatience and the spontaneous, wild nihilism that are her identifying characteristics. This allergy to institutions is perhaps a result of her exclusion from the Communist Party, a longstanding wound, even though she denies it. The new place she sings of has no more laws, no more orders, no more militants. Or else, she says, "we refuse, we swallow the poison. We act. We join hands. No solemn speech here, no 'party line.' Here we don't label anyone at the outset. Here the watchword is disorder."

Her determination and her vehemence in denouncing ideologies of all kinds, and those who convey them, lead her to this language of "dream," of unreality. Resolutely modern, she cries: "We are the prehistory of the future!"

Galvanized by all of the previously accomplished work, by the explosion of her texts, she becomes the mouthpiece for a large part of this young generation drunk on freedom, on the idea of "beginning everything over again." Indeed, as she will say later, welcome is the reign of destruction, and in this painful prophecy she can see nothing but joy, that of the builders, the diviners of life: "And may the world destroy itself." She is said to have been the originator of the famous slogan "Beneath the cobblestones, the beach."* In the collective fury reigning in the meetings and general assemblies, it might have been "invented" in a group, but the maritime reference fits her too well for one not to be tempted to attribute it to her. The beach is where "mad people" pace in her novels, and where the children in *L'Eté 80* scatter in spite of their counselor's repeated orders, rediscovering the freedom of wide open spaces, the immensity of the sea before them.

The effervescence of that period and the consequent failure that she attributes for the most part to "the murderous irresponsibility of the proletariat," the return to conservativism, brought back to power in the June elections, lead her to adopt a radical attitude close to that espoused by the surrealists. She feels undeniable sympathy for the extreme left-wing movements then consolidating, for they replace the mystique of consumer society with another philosophy, that of idleness and

*In reference to the freedom to be won through the revolutionary act of constructing barricades, pulling up the paving stones, and pelting the police with them.—TRANS. note.

newfound freedom, a poetic, romantic vision that is vaguely nihilistic and anarchistic, but heavily infused with imagination and creativity. And yet, Duras doesn't join any of them, complying with the refusal of militancy that, ever since her brief membership in the Communist Party, makes her reject all forms of recruitment.

The tenor of all her statements and all the interviews she grants during this period is based on this utopian credo: to live poetically according to the principles laid down by the surrealists, in the dual movement of unrelenting conquest and communal bliss.

The imperative growing out of '68 is first of all to refuse "political ideas," replacing them with "a void, a true void," preferable to the "junk heap, the giant garbage cans of twentieth-century ideology." In politics she sees nothing but lies and deception. In her writing she always refers to the alienation of parties and particularly of the Communist Party, for which she has the harshest words, as if she can't help but condemn it. The proletariat's attitude of refusing the great hope confirms this idea of hers. She sees it as "the refusal of life, of living."

The apartment on rue Saint-Benoît continues to be the clandestine place of civil disobedience, the underground, the counterpower of intelligence. The Council of French Government Ministers dissolves the leftist splinter groups in July 1968. The leaders of the Jeunesse communiste revolutionnaire go into hiding and proclaim the continuation of the struggle. Alain Krivine, founder of the JCR along with Henri Weber, and Daniel Bensaïd, representative of that organization at the time of the Movement of March 22 (the takeover of Nanterre University), are both wanted by the police. Bensaïd and Weber naturally take refuge in Duras's rue Saint-Benoît apartment, writing their testimony on the insurrection, attempting a few quick dashes out into the neighborhood.

Later, in 1977, in the trajectory of this "commitment" unlike any of those made by other intellectuals, especially Sartre and Beauvoir, she will film *Le Camion*. She portrays a truck driver who still believes in the solutions of the Party, alienated forever, of unshakable faith, lost to life, tragically caught in "the night of politics." She sets him in opposition to the woman embodied by herself and another at the same time, but with no identity, as she is in her own mind, "open to the future," moving ahead, surely "mad," inventing for herself the role of mother to all the Jewish children who died at Auschwitz, imagining that she is a Portuguese, North African, or Malian immigrant, "reinventing what she has been taught."

Critics and audiences react with a sneer. She sends them back to their night, their old age, their darkness, their police tactics, their need to identify everything they see. Little by little she becomes more dangerous for this society that proclaims its wealth; despite the first signs of the recession, she increasingly appears to be a traitor to her class, to her country, to her country's ethics. She doesn't care. She makes no concessions, intervenes publicly to denounce the various forms of alienation, of oppression, and secretly pursues her indecisively contoured work, in which the poetic is possibly becoming one of the surest responses to the political.

Her audience is still limited; "people listen to her with varying degrees of interest," as she has the woman in *Le Camion* say, but it is all the same to her. She gradually develops a prejudice against men, whom she judges to be the originators of violence and the thirst for power. In *Woman to Woman*, she says that "a largely unspoken nostalgia lies dormant within all of them. . . . There is a paratrooper in every man . . . the family's paratrooper, there is the woman's paratrooper, the child paratrooper. . . . I believe every man is much closer to a general, to a soldier, than to any woman." That is why she feels closer to the world of women, to women's territory, to their intuitions, their capacity for communicating with the world and the planets, in a kind of silent attentiveness to the universe. At that time she is strongly sympathetic to women's struggles, but also to those men—mostly young, the hippies for example, "idle souls," or else homosexuals, and certain exceptional men— who have managed to preserve their feminine side, and who are thus accessible to silence, to the confused murmur of houses, to the utopia of availability and laziness that she preaches.

In *The North China Lover*, which she publishes in May 1991, she always defines herself in those same inclinations toward idleness, toward availability: "As for her, she remained the little girl in the book, small, thin, daring, whose meaning and identity are hard to grasp . . . inconsolable for the loss of the land where she was born and grew up, . . . in love with weak men. . . ."

It is just such a man she will meet: Y. A.

One day, in 1980, "someone came. He came. He came from a provincial town. He had read my books and he stayed." This man settled into her life, joined her on one desperate day, asked her if he could come, she consented, he showed up, they talked for a long time, and then she told him to take her son's room. That is how it happened. He now seems to be inseparable from her. His name is Yann Andréa. He will write M. D. in 1983. She doesn't conceal his homosexuality; she writes of it, she talks of it on the radio, in her books, in interviews. What she likes about him is the fact that beyond the apparent impossibility there is something unnamed and accessible, which is also the place of love, of passion, without which nothing can ever, will ever, be able to be explained, or even written, and which reveals itself, just like that, brutally, without the two of them seeking this moment, as on this death vigil, in 1982 then in 1988-89 at the American hospital, in this Neuilly of death, she delirious, or in a coma, and he, he alone, at her bedside, waiting tenuously, in evidence of love.

She never stops exploring this other circulation of love among people, analyzing it through her novels and her own life. The "madness" of 1968, its wind of hope and its failure, and the struggle that follows, prompt her to undertake a cycle of novels directly inspired by it. The provocatively titled novel *Destroy, She Said*, published in 1969, symbolically lays out the new steps along her path.

First of all, destroy novelistic matter itself, shatter it so that its uses will be multiple: read, acted, filmed, thrown out—the novel is no longer monolithic; "without identification," it is hurled into the great black, unknown sea. Readers need no hint, no signpost as in Balzacian rhetoric; "there are no more sentences," but words, "words playing all the roles," no more style, but the free interplay of words, doomed to themselves, available, metaphors of the anarchic utopia animating her, the erosion and the destruction of institutions she is hoping for.

With this book, she also begins "the destruction of the writer": something strange and terrifying happens, a kind of dangerous experimentation, as if the Nightship now had no other course but that of absolute wandering, free but ever so risky. She abandons the task she had devoted herself to until *Moderato Cantabile*, perhaps in an effort to prove her continued effectiveness as a writer. With *Destroy* comes this fear in writing, followed by books that are written quickly, in the terror of invisible things, in this strange state of withdrawal, of gaping emptiness. She says in *Woman to Woman*: "I had come to this gap in the chain." From now on the word goes where the night carries it, treading in this darkness, going around in circles like a madman, and she hears its noises, its movements. It is an approach full of madness, an asylumlike structure that makes experience painful, but inevitable. The task she undertakes unfolds in "those still untapped regions" she wants to account for, listening intently.

She is then fifty-five years old. Her last name, Donnadieu, which she has thrown away—the father's name that she hates, the father she repudiates in her work and in her life, but whom she nonetheless loves in a place buried very deep within herself—is now replaced by that of Duras. Whenever her name is mentioned, from now on she is called Duras. The first name is even done away with. Just Duras, as one would say Racine, Pascal, Proust.

She avoids so-called feminine literature. What she explores is the depth of the soul, its sacredness, the lament it utters out of desire when it loves and when it is dying, indiscriminately in man and woman; what she is trying to approach no longer has any sex, any identity, or any frame of reference, but touches the innermost secret of being. For that, she has an autonomous kind of reception, laying claim to a mode of writing that expresses "the wholeness of the individual," abandons traditional syntax, leaves the words there, free of apparent meaning, but ready to be reconstructed, like the painter who, according to Blanchot, "doesn't use colors to reproduce what is, but seeks the point at which his colors create being."

The autism afflicting ideologues and dogma peddlers, with communists foremost among them, forces them to dictate orders, rules of life, and discourses on the method "from without." Within her there is the certainty of no longer having any method; she is at the mercy of the accidents and movements of the characters she brings to life, with their multiple voices crowding around and telling of the voyage she knows to be inevitable, terrifying.

The mood of the times is surely what leads her to this leftist stance, in which the term *communism* is not yet denied, but faithful to its source, its very etymology, giving her another, mobile life, unfurling in the instant, in the refusal of dogmas and leaders.

When she portrays herself in this unclassifiable book, she undertakes what she calls "capital destruction," and first of all that of the couple, the most primitive dogma of organized society, replacing it with the free circulation of desire, wandering from one person to another. At that precise moment she speaks a language that harasses institutions, speaking as a fierce enemy of all powers, the State, the police, the church, the university.

She claims that the revolution, her revolution, the only one possible, takes place in the absence of all waiting, of any future. The Great Evening and the Resurrection are mere traps set by established ideologies, held in place by every variety of conservatism. She makes an appeal to something unknown and spontaneous, capable of bringing into existence another place, another future. Alissa, the heroine of *Destroy, She Said*, is that

messenger, the vehicle for "destruction." Monogamy is considered an absolute form of alienation, a metaphor of the many
kinds of solitary confinement into which people place themselves. Her writing responds to that inner need. It erodes, dis-
penses with all descriptions, everything she now considers as
the mere trappings of fiction, but releases an even freer breath,
recalling the freedom of Alissa, Max, and Stein.

Duras has always thought that about love, the lightning
stroke occurring there, at the unknown moment, outside of
the couple, in another time all its own. She says the couple "is
the brilliant solution for killing time in every society in the
world," because fidelity, established as a principle, leads to "religious prohibition," and by the same token prohibits the
dream of "a new love."

She is in this state of availability, offered up to this "madness," when, one evening, she accepts Yann Andréa, this
young man hardly known to her, and "tells him to come" to
Trouville, where she is alone in a "dark room" at Les Roches.
She deliberately enters the terrifying unknown of desire, knowing better than anyone its dangers, its stakes, knowing that it
will be like "what happens in *The War*," the state bordering on
the abysses where she loses every reference point and plunges
into her story like a stubborn, wild animal.

Is it because of her "profound distaste for the movies made
from her books," as she says, that she spontaneously begins to
attempt once more the film experience she had been dreaming
of since *La Musica*, a portrayal of limits and extremes?

Those books left too many things still adrift, trailing behind
like abandoned ships, floating on "the crest of the words," and
confessions, too many things the book couldn't contain and
which even the theater hadn't been able to retrace.

As Mascolo explains, she therefore had to "suppress this
remaining aspect of writing" which, in the book, "prepares the
message, announces it, and offers it to our ears only after having made it bearable, replacing it with something language-
neutral, or anything else, as long as it is nonlinguistic. This can
only be visual, in order to give the tragic message another

chance to be heard along with what no one should allow to be heard."

Now the problem was to make the book reveal this message that had emerged only with great difficulty from its secret night and to attempt to give it still other meanings, more deeply buried, primitive ones.

Still coiled up inside her was the desire to "break with everything that came before," providing another way of reading, in which the rhetoric of the novel would no longer come into play.

The determination she puts into all things serves as a buttress for this new project. To engage in such filmmaking is to steer away from commercial cinema, going against the grain, moving down unexplored paths. Films of the 1960s are too tied up in money, storytelling, messages, and psychological development to have anything in common with what Duras has in mind. She has the deepest scorn for this "vulgar" cinema of divulgence, this cinema of exposure and the revelation of secrets. For her, cinematography is the attempt to put the book and the film on the same footing, drawing the film toward the inwardness that escapes it, trying to construct images out of invisibility, the most subtly quivering point of contact flowing through people, not afraid to show hesitation, the fragile, precarious part of both the person and the filmmaker.

As usual, she throws herself completely, freely, into this cinematic adventure. She enters this milieu as an outsider, a revolutionary, providing other directors with "a good laugh," amusing the professionals who were taught how to do this, as she says ironically, those who took classes in specialized schools. She moves ahead with silence and darkness as her only frames of reference, massacring the film genre, as in 1981's *The Atlantic Man*, where she denies film even its image-bearing function, leaving the screen blank. She cannot come to terms with commercial cinema, because it will never deal with her chosen subject, the essential quality in words, gazes, gestures, and invisible exchanges. That is why her films are political, because they don't require the enormous sums of money that seem necessary for most movies, because they move as quickly as they possibly can, never wandering off into useless, decorative shots, losing no time in expressing the mysterious human force that always interests her.

She takes up moviemaking the same way she has learned everything, as a rebellious soul who dwells on the outskirts, the margins, among the damned. And what is incredible is that the permanent scandal of her films does nothing to diminish her prestige, which finally leads her to the "sovereign marginality" that makes her continue, obstinately deaf to criticism and mockery. She "hasn't just written nonsense. . . . She has filmed it, too," says humorist Pierre Desproges; but his remark is only a wisecrack. She wants to grind down her books, sending them back out into new galaxies, giving depth to their interior images, going so far as to destroy *India Song*, profaning its cult when she reworks it in another film, *Son nom de Venise dans Calcutta désert* [Her Venetian Name in Desolate Calcutta], a year later in 1976.

Something inside her cannot accept the usual, easy solutions of conventional cinema. She experiences film as a writer, with the economy of words she has used in all of her books; she wants to retranscribe her lightning energy in the movie, tearing holes in it, perforating it with the very density of her vision.

Is it because she is a woman that she encounters so many obstacles and sarcastic remarks in this cinematic adventure, more than in the literary world? That is what she claims. But she knows that as a woman she is extremely fortunate to have the opportunity to make movies. She has always linked her subversive approach and revolutionary activity to the fact that she is a woman; in training her film crews, she always influenced men's misogynist, macho behavior in this profession. Men would avoid dirty jokes, and her deliberate lack of authority would make the technicians more accountable for their work. She manages to give her shoots a community spirit, and everyone involved knows that something new is taking place, for this is a major, irreplaceable, unprecedented experience. The movie is unfolding before their eyes, with all of its hesitations, its changes, and its ruptures in full view, with Duras groping through the darkness with her usual, tentative footsteps.

Those who have worked with her during a shooting are unanimous: it is a unique adventure, made even more so by the crew's small size. All of them, the electricians, the stagehands, the cameramen, the trainees, tell of her "improvised" approach to film and her seemingly disorganized work whose aim is nonetheless precise. Her superiority is that of a writer who breathes meaning into the dialogue she has written, "with such life, such warmth," according to the stagehand in *India Song*.

She goes from book to film with disconcerting ease, guided by an acquired, instinctive force that surprises her more than anyone. The book, moreover, has ceased being a book, "thrown" into other modes of expression, wandering down unknown paths. She doesn't really know what she is doing in the film, but she has no doubts about her shots, her editing, and what the film says. Just as she wrote *Destroy, She Said* in a state of "imbecility," she shoots without knowing, led along obscurely in simultaneous fear and "ease," aware only of this darkness she will dwell in from now on.

With *Destroy*, she claims to rediscover her sources, her true nature. What a strange paradox, a writer condemned to being considered an intellectual by her contemporaries and continually insisting on her lack of knowledge, proclaiming her ignorance!

Just as the book was written in necessary, frightful haste, she shoots the film version in fourteen days in 1969, after a month and a half of rehearsals, in the most precarious conditions possible, with a miserly $44,000 budget, but with a film crew and cast so excited by the new adventure that they are ready to do anything for her. As with the book she had written in the state of emptiness she now preaches far and wide, she insists that she "let herself be carried along" in a state of prodigal innocence and youthful spirits.

She films boldly, regaining lost freedom: "just because you don't know where you're going is no reason for not going there," she tells Jacques Rivette in *Cahiers du Cinéma*. The

point is that in the rising, audible reverberations of the May
'68 movement, the book and movie version of *Destroy* assume
an obvious political dimension. She ran the risk of losing its
rhythm, falling into the trap of didacticism or ideology, even if
it was that of anti-ideology. Nothing of the sort happened,
however. On the contrary, there rose up a new voice, brilliant
and hopeful, proclaiming that "the revolution was still possible, but on a personal level, as an inner struggle," never again
in cells, sects, dogmas, diktats.

She was discovering another path to the tactile instinct that
gave life to *La Musica* and *Moderato Cantabile*, the flowing of
desires she had decided to explore.

In this decade of the 1970s, she spreads the same word everywhere, in movies, in her writings, in interviews: her own life.
What she says in the trailer to the film *Destroy* is her credo, her
profession of faith: "None of us have anything to do with your
State, your society, your schemes. . . ."

"Is it a film that expresses hope?"

"Yes, revolutionary hope."

Does she arrive at this utopian position on account of her
son? As a result of the hippie odyssey? The erosion of the
State's power, the ideal of bourgeois comfort preached by
French president Georges Pompidou? She knows she is "completely immersed in utopia," but she cries it out all the same:
one must create a vacuum, she says, you must take time out for
a much-needed rest, return to ground zero. The same words
punctuate her speech: the seashore, the beach, human absence. She hammers out the same ideas, certain that this void
will give rise to new, different things, closer to the origins, the
mysteries. She lives this adventure from the perspective of
young people, following them in their refusal of exegesis and
scholasticism, and glorifying this empty space, this gestation of
another world.

She says that young people "have a question the size of a
mountain: what? now? what!

"If it continues to grow, it will be a terrifying question. If it
grows, it is the end of the world. Good. Good for them."

She is counting on this refusal of institutions as a way of recovering her freedom, becoming available and giving free rein to her desire.

All of this meets with considerable derision. She doesn't even answer her detractors, those who call her "crazy," nor is she bothered. "I can still say what I want," she proclaims with bravado. Louis Chauvet of *Le Figaro* writes a so-called angry article about *Destroy* and, instead of carrying out a real analysis, makes one long display of sarcasm: "The monotonous, neurotic characters express themselves with sadness, as if they were dying or afraid of waking up the birds. . . . Henri Garcin, Nicole Hiss, Michael Lonsdale, and Catherine Sellers play the quartet in a dazed-loony style well-suited to the script." The right-wing magazines are the most scathing, encouraged by a Chamber of Deputies that supports their position unreservedly. They ridicule Duras, dragging her name through the mud in a way that would leave other writers permanently discouraged. In her case, however, it provides the impetus for further rebellious outbursts, a pretext for her to assume even more shocking stances: "I'm happy to know that the mental hospitals are full. That's proof that the world is unbearable."

She knows that in any event her options are closed now. Her Nightship has led her into waters so strange that any return trip is highly unlikely. It is as if *Destroy, She Said* had "cut her off" from her previous books, drawing her into a new kind of writing, a hybrid form both adventurous and obscure.

Should one establish a link between the fierce radicalism she espouses at this time, and the repudiation of *Suzanna Andler*, a play she had written and published in her 1968 Gallimard volume *Théâtre II*? Completely indifferent to its outcome, she agrees to having the play staged at the Théâtre des Mathurins and performed by Catherine Sellers, Luce Garcia-Ville, and Gilles Segal. Her personality is characterized by repudiations and enthusiasms, sudden loves and renunciations. Too close to the cutting edge, she cannot remain faithful to things and people. Desire surges too strongly within her, and too great is her need to satisfy it.

Not afraid of sabotaging the undertaking to which she has already become committed, she herself speaks out against it, declaring trenchantly: "I can no longer see any merit in *Suzanna Andler*; I wrote the play . . . very quickly, I no longer find it interesting. . . . I never frequented the social circles I depict there, and I tried to describe them but it's clearly inadequate. In fact this kind of character annoys me and I can't understand why I chose her. There are a lot of things I have done, off the top of my head, that I don't like." With a certain amount of bad faith, she claims not to know any Suzanna Andlers, rich women renting villas on the Riviera, even though many of her earlier characters are from the same idle, social-drinking milieu. Caught up in this new revolutionary enthusiasm, she doesn't hesitate to "destroy" her own work. Her remarks are taken up by critics, moreover, and this time they are unanimous, from *Le Monde* to *Le Figaro*, in tearing the play to shreds. They try to outdo each other in attacking her: Jean-Jacques Gautier states that "Marguerite Duras has added three dots to a Henry Bernstein play, and with fewer dramatic events, the action is fifty times slower"; in *France-Soir*, Jean Dutourd asserts that "in the eyes of a critic, Marguerite Duras's last play, *Suzanna Andler*, has at least two advantages: (1) it doesn't last too long for, thank God, Madame Duras is short-winded, and (2) it is so completely and utterly worthless that only a very brief article need be devoted to it." As for Bertrand Poirot-Delpech, usually rather sympathetic to Duras's work, though always ambiguously, he condemns the work, saying that the "subject loses no time in putting the audience to sleep with its lack of truth and interest. So why go to the trouble of producing it?"

A kind of revolutionary enthusiasm has in fact taken hold of Duras now, and she embarks on a utopian crusade that provides "a basis for action." Like a visionary, a discoverer of new lands, she keeps her gaze fastened toward the prow of the ship, leaving behind the tangible signs of its passing.

"The wind makes her lightheaded and dizzy," like the woman in *Le Camion*, which she will soon be filming, free and never again in possession of the least certitude, "inventing her life." She often returns to Neauphle-le-Château, where she devotes herself to "practicalities," doing housework, watching over the farmyard, listening to the cackling of her Cayenne hens, and with the coming of fruit-harvesting season, performing the ritual of preserve-making. She loves this house with its nooks and crannies, and she searches there for traces of her past, of her first story. But the story holds out, oblivion erases everything. Sometimes, through the force of imagination, she sees its inhabitants hiding there in anticipation of the "great events of 1789," and pretends to have heard the rumors from nearby Versailles.

She is reminded of the force and tenacity of life and of passing time by the trees that clothe the vast garden: lilac, larch, maple, elm, fir, and copper beech.

Mesmerized by the endless flow of sand through the hourglass, she "feels as though she doesn't exist." Perhaps that is why she admits to an overpowering love for Diderot, whom she resembles by the effervescence of her ideas and a hyperdeveloped capacity for sensory perception. She is said to bear a certain resemblance to a weathercock, just as he claimed to resemble the one atop his hometown cathedral in Langres, changing direction with every gust of wind whether from a passing storm or an ocean breeze, drunk, in her words, "madly . . . absorbing outside influences."

Her life is thus contained in this perpetual stirring of wind and sea, this "dilapidation of oneself" that leaves her torn open, transparent, mobile, and infinitely available.

She will reveal nothing of this personal life, for she says that she has none, believing that a writer lives off this view offered by the whole world joined together cosmically, painstakingly reconstructing another version of what she has seen, heard, and felt. That path leads her to the mystery of writing, which she perceives in the reconstitution, the rendering of the first gaze.

In the impromptu, wildcat actions of the militant left wing, she sees the means of changing the world, of stopping the exploitation she has always fought against with the passionate determination she applies to everything. During these first days of 1970, she seems ubiquitous, signing petitions, joining commando-type demonstrations like that of 10 January 1970 in which, under the banner of Roland Castro and the militant group Vive la révolution, she occupies the premises of the National Association of French Employers, the sacrosanct CNPF, at 31, avenue Pierre-1er-de-Serbie, to protest against the freezing to death of five Mauritanian and Senegalese immigrants in the corrugated-iron annex to a Franco-African workers' home.

Not alone in this effort, Duras is accompanied by Maurice Clavel, Jean Genet, Pierre Vidal-Naquet, well-known academics, actors, priests, and militants who take over the building for nearly half an hour and wait for the police vans, exulting in this renewed solidarity. Vidal-Naquet and Clavel are injured, while Duras is taken away like the others, and sent to Beaujon women's prison, where she is charged with a misdemeanor. The year 1970 is rich in events that beckon to her, mobilize her, and "politicize" her more than ever; the malaise of French society becomes apparent in spite of President Pompidou's mealy-mouthed speeches: a student immolates himself by fire, fatal accidents occur in the Dunkirk shipyards due to poor working conditions, militant leftists are systematically and brutally arrested following adoption of the riot law in April, and the police capture historic leaders Jean-Pierre Le Dantec, Le Bris, and Alain Geismar. The Gauche prolétarienne movement is dissolved after its commando action against the Fauchon luxury food store, women demonstrate, encouraged by those in New York where huge crowds gather: the Mouvement pour la libération de la femme meets for the first time in October. Meanwhile, the satirical journal *Hara-Kiri Hebdo* is prohibited, and Sartre's *La Cause du Peuple* is seized; vast demonstrations make the streets ring out with the slogans of May '68 denouncing the CRS riot squad: "CRS, SS," thousands of spectators flock to a circus tent to hear anarchist Léo Ferré sing his subversive poems to the glory of "La Cause du peuple," accompanied by the rock group Zoo.

Duras is naturally a member of the Association des amis de la cause du peuple, founded by Simone de Beauvoir, along with the usual group of radicals: Delphine Seyrig, Sami Frey, Cavanna, Jean-Louis Bory, and Jean-Luc Godard.

Such was the strange beginning of the 1970s, trembling with desires, hopes, ideals, swarming with cult books, founding works for modern thought like Alexander S. Neill's *Summerhill*, Deleuze and Guattari's *Anti-Oedipus*, Costa-Gavras's *The Confession*, David Cooper's *Psychiatry and Anti-psychiatry*, so many subversive catalysts engendering still more in the following years, Marcel Ophuls's *The Sorrow and the Pity*, Bertolucci's *Last Tango in Paris*, Kubrick's *Clockwork Orange*, Gisèle Halimi's *La Cause des femmes*, so many fresh minds devoted, as Duras said, to the "destruction" of well-established, worn-out structures: René Dumont, Marco Ferreri, Bertrand Blier, André Glucksmann. . . .

A precursor of many current ideas, as if stimulated by the times, Duras's literary activity is then completely absorbed by the idea of using film as an extension of her books. While writing what will be *Abahn, Sabana, David* in the wake of the film version of *Destroy, She Said*, she is already thinking of the novel's transformation into images, henceforth the "super-exposition" of genres that will reach its culmination in the absolute pleasure of *India Song*, dubbed "text-theater-film." Scandalous Duras, desecrating sacred institutions, provoking audiences, defying the visual forms she liberates by releasing them from the text! To those who say "what's needed here is a picture, not pointless words," to the inquisitors of "show biz," she responds with speech, "generator of meaning and vehicle of desire." With *Abahn, Sabana, David,* she rediscovers her storytelling nature, simply narrating, while "the writing carries the images forward," depicting Gringo, the leader of an unidentified land whose name, Stadt, and climate recall dreaded places. Gringo sends David and Sabana one night to arrest a Jew named Abahn, and the novel describes this night

of waiting until Gringo arrives at dawn. In the frozen darkness of Stadt, David and Sabana carry out a kind of primitive
dialectic, betraying Gringo, refusing to accomplish the mission
he has assigned to them. "No matter what happens now," they
will remain Jews. Duras's obsessions thus persist in the text
fiercely, tenaciously. With each passing day, history proves
her right. French communists' refusal to take spontaneous,
revolutionary action despite the Soviet tank invasion of Prague
in the spring of 1968 provided her with a new opportunity to
scorn them and their attitude in May 1968. Revelation of the
gulags, the writings of Soviet dissidents, everything suggests
that the new text fits in with the political movements of the
times. The incantatory tone and the tension in the dialogue
give it a powerful, poetic quality. The Jew who wanders
throughout her entire work appears here in a formidable way:
symbolizing all forms of persecution, he is nevertheless the
one who "unleashes" things, coming like Christ to awaken
those whom alienation has put to sleep. He is the one who is
"in the way," "déclassé," as Duras will define herself, "the other
person," the harbinger of hope, the "communist who believes
that communism is impossible" and possesses this painful,
tragic certitude.

In a wider sense, he is the writer, the vehicle of disorder, the
disseminator of new ideas. No myth has ever haunted Duras's
imagination like that of the Wandering Jew, who, wherever he
goes, whatever century he lives in, undergoes persecution and
is reborn from his suffering, always incarnating this supreme
life force, this redemption through pain. She admits that she
never got over what was done to the Jews, Auschwitz, the gas
chambers, the endless nights on the train, arrival in the eerie,
floodlit camps, the torture and the starving of children, the
cold, and the surrounding forest that muffles the cries, the revolts, the shootings, and the smell of burning flesh. She bears
the pain of all that, even more than that of her own stillborn
child, more than that of the war and the massacred Resistance
fighters.

She always writes amid the brutally illuminated darkness, evoking the night, silent witness to separating lovers, concentration camps, and Gestapo arrests. She likes to describe tension and passion when they are at the bursting point, for she knows, even better than the various kinds of murder instincts, the ferocious violence, the havoc, and the ravages of love torn asunder. In her nights, the animals are about to die, ready "to burst," and the water in all of the ponds and rivers is "frozen through and through." Gleams of frost, cries of cold and snow break through the dialogue, while dogs howl in the black forest, like threatening shadows in a de Chirico painting.

Then comes the Jew who announces the inevitable destruction without which there can be no reconstruction.

The book is published in 1970 and received coolly by the critical establishment; immediately afterward, she produces a movie version of it. Again operating on a tight budget, shooting in 16-millimeter with both professional (Sami Frey, Catherine Sellers) and amateur actors (Dionys Mascolo) who agree to work for free, she calls it *Jaune le soleil*. It is in black and white, and contains the controlled violence of a Dreyer film, especially in the person of Sami Frey, whose black diamond hardness is accompanied by vacillating tenderness.

In the interview she granted Michelle Porte upon finishing *Le Camion*, she relates that during the shooting, the communists used the filmmakers' union in an attempt to damage her reputation, falsely accusing her, telling Ricardo Aronovitch, "who was in on" the film, that she failed to pay her actors after having received a subsidy of $55,000 from the French government's cinema foundation. For her that typifies the communists' clean form of murder, their enthusiasm for denunciation, and their contemptible schemes.

She bears such hatred for the Party and for the entire communist ideology in those troubled, murky years when the right- and left-wing forces remain locked in confrontation until François Mitterrand takes power in 1981: these are the years of the Pompidou and Giscard d'Estaing presidencies. In the film,

Gringo is transformed into Grinski, offering further proof of her anticommunism. The Party retaliates by calling her a reactionary and capitalist-leaning agent. Her intelligence condemns her irrevocably, for it scares them. For that matter, she is no better loved by the right wing. Her antibourgeois arrogance, her nonconformity, and her nostalgia for a utopian communism, coupled with her reputation as a left-leaning woman who scorns neither luxury nor money, and her landowner tendencies, as if they would help her to avenge her mother and the precariousness of the bungalow in *The Sea Wall*, all of this makes her suspect and ambiguous. Her freedom, more than anything else, is unbearable. She gradually asserts herself as a woman in a class of her own, someone who is violently different.

Profoundly obsessive, wedded to the objects of her hatred as firmly as to those she loves, she softens none of her commitments, subjecting them to no criticism other than that of her certitudes. During this period, the seventies, when her work is fiercely political, she is always ready to express her anger at the Party, never missing an opportunity to denounce it. During one of her later talks with François Mitterrand, in 1986, she steers the conversation onto this subject, and in spite of the French president's reserve, suddenly declares: "I am obsessed by the Party. You don't know them. The only people who know them well are those who have been in very close contact with them, as I have. The only difference is that now they know it's all over. Don't worry, I'll stop talking about them. . . ."

She often speaks about the violence of which she was a victim, perpetrated on her by "them," about the very conditioning that led her to suspect her neighbors, making her afraid to be seen in certain compromising nightclubs or at a cocktail party for fear of being labeled a reactionary.

She never tires of telling what charges were brought against her in the letter informing her of her expulsion: keeping bad company, engaging in moral and intellectual corruption, being too independent-minded, and disobeying orders. She would censor herself, feeling even guiltier on account of her status as a writer, for Sartre had stigmatized members of the writing profession, suspecting them of betraying the proletariat and dubbing them victims of individual alienation.

In *Abahn, Sabana, David*, and in the film version *Jaune le soleil*, she draws parallels between the gulags and the Nazi concentration camps, between the extermination of the Jews and anti-Semitism in Eastern Europe, between the hell of Auschwitz and that of Stadt, both frozen in the ice of hatred.

When the film comes out in 1971, she accepts all of the invitations she receives: aware of the immense revolutionary impact of *Destroy, She Said* and *Jaune le soleil*, she travels readily to universities, municipal youth clubs, film societies—wherever her presence is requested. She is very accessible to her audience, unwavering supporters of her work, curious onlookers and select admirers, fascinated by the magic she is capable of producing in spite of the many difficulties inherent in an establishment whose opposition she meets with unsparing resistance of her own. All of them attend her film showings as if they were going to a place of worship, joining together in the same aesthetic communion. Her public is young, madly in love with her, conquered by her tremendous gifts for seduction and storytelling. The complicity between them is total. These encounters always make her happy, for they plunge her into a living utopia.

Some have asserted that she was engaging in demagoguery, in a concerted strategy, but there is no truth to such claims. Duras's relationship with young people is straightforward. She sees herself as being on the cutting edge of the avant-garde, and possessing a liveliness of thought and judgment, a never-quenched thirst for knowledge, and a curiosity characteristic of the spirit of youth. Still resonating with the life-giving forces of the May '68 movement, she is the object of veritable adulation.

Her speech is militant, but consistent with her position as a "militant antimilitant," it is untrammeled, free of all constraints, hostile to every form of academicism, like her son Jean, whom she loves passionately and still calls Outa, and who in her perspective incarnates total freedom: that arrogance of hope and collective idleness in which bodies and minds work together to upset the smooth running of all institutions and to bring about the downfall of the State. Her indulgence of this son is absolute, similar to her feeling for the teenaged girl in *The Lover*, with her felt hat and lamé shoes and her dress lightly fluttering as she leans over the handrail during the ferry crossing of that branch of the Mekong, the free, impudent, eighteen-year-old girl who resembles her enormously: the two of them are similarly available to fleeing time and the things it carries away.

That is why she lets him live his life according to his likes and dislikes, identifying himself with the music of Jim Morrison, Otis Redding, and Janis Joplin.

During these first years, then, like a scholar who is nevertheless a neophyte, she throws herself into the moviemaking adventure. She drives her little car through the provinces like an itinerant peddler, huddled against the steering wheel, screwing up her eyes to get a clearer view of the road, working to develop a network of sympathies and friendships. She calls it "the new Internationale." Behind her on the backseat lie the steel canisters in which the film reels are preciously housed. She carries with her Sami Frey's intense voice and stature, and beyond him as an actor, the tragic narrative of his childhood which she will tell in Montreal, the story of the little Jewish boy whose mother asks him to go see the neighbor downstairs for a few minutes. He complies, and the police arrive shortly afterward, arresting the mother, who later dies in an Auschwitz gas chamber. Also in order to give Sami Frey the opportunity to act and to be loved, she will tell this story in one of the versions of *Aurélia Steiner*, the night from his childhood with those footsteps and that voice, so somber, so soft, penetrating her own writings at the exact spot where the meaning is most intense, most precise.

In these years following 1968 she keeps alive the spirit of protest, this liberation of the mind, preoccupied by questions that lead her each day further away from conventional society. She influences other people who in turn perceive the world differently, suddenly arriving at a common, instinctive understanding of it. "You know, I remain an outsider," she confides to Colette Godard of *Le Monde* in 1974, "and I'm not alone: there are quite a few of us. We didn't have any choice in the matter; we are simply horrified by what is happening. It isn't an option or an attitude, but rather it has become instinctive behavior."

With other people, her readers as well as those who go to see her films, she is able to create a loving relationship, a kind of family. In order to continue, she needs to love and be loved in this social underground, this utopian society she invents. The actors themselves know that only in this state of love can they find Duras: "You have to become part of her own spiritual, linguistic symphony," says Lonsdale by way of explaining the charm her films have for him.

French academia also begins to show interest in her works during this period. Each year more and more students write masters' theses; then dissertations make their timid appearances on national indexes, while research is already being undertaken in several American universities amidst the feminist surge.

The importance of this is not lost on her, and she grants interviews to foreign journals, which will recognize her well before their French counterparts. "Without foreign support, I would never manage to survive," she says in 1974. Berlin, New York, London, and Toronto form a kind of international union of modernity, of which she unintentionally becomes the Egeria, the rallying point, and the agitator. What she expresses in her books and in her films, the remotest point she is able to reach, is the cry of love and death that lies in every person's heart and calls out unceasingly. It is the same cry that accompanies the music of her language, solemnly meandering, sometimes mysterious and haunting, like the melodies of Carlos d'Alessio.

Her solidarity with the Algerian people and the sympathy she has always shown for their struggle caused her to feel close to misfits, the marginalized, and all of the battles waged by minorities in the seventies following the short-lived blaze of hope in May '68. She signs many petitions and above all actively encourages the feminist movement. It is the time of great MLF demonstrations, resolute marches through Paris in a joyful, colorful atmosphere, the era when she willingly lends her moral and intellectual authority to women's publications: essays, novels, and reviews. She is often seen with militant feminists like Xavière Gauthier, who will become the editor of *Sorcières* and with whom she will write *Woman to Woman* in 1974, an authentic attempt to present in detail the perspective of women, together with their hesitations, spontaneity, and small talk.

But her story merges with that of her work: scraps of her past are woven into one piece, forming a web that is enhanced, enlivened by the winds of events and of history, although never before has she penetrated farther into the world of the uncertain and the unknown. The texts press forward hurriedly, seeming to escape their author's control, roaming in the periphery of Lol Stein, always reworking Duras's main themes: madness, odyssey, death, the massacre of memory and its intermittent resurgences, motifs all comparable to the winding course of the Mekong. Few contemporary writers since Proust have similarly explored this inner geography, searching through this tenebrous backroom where, as Montaigne was already saying in the sixteenth century, "one finds everything, the entire sum of human experience accumulates and piles up," since writing refers only to those self-obtained acquisitions, once perceived and then swallowed up again.

The threads of her experience are so densely interwoven during these years between 1968 and 1980, in which each text is extended on the stage, projected on the screen, and reflects back on itself through other texts, that it is hard to imagine Duras's personal life. She herself confesses to Michelle Porte that she has none, open instead "toward the outside," in the intensity and the desire that form her life, replacing her former passions, her dispersions, her diversions. From Pascal she learned this acceptance of "the internal injunction," this ability to hold at bay the enticements of the superego, thus learning to listen in new ways, tuning in to the distant murmur of "infinite worlds."

L'Amour, published in 1971—and providing material for the filmscript of *La Femme du Gange*, produced and published in 1973, and most probably written during the composition of *India Song*—is a demonstration of this literary stained-glass window whose mountings define their originality and complexity.

This tendency to go beyond the bounds of controlled writing, which she had already analyzed with *Destroy, She Said*, is now confirmed even further. She confided to Germaine Brée that "this text is pure stupidity," and that she "no longer understands what she is writing." Fragments of memory and the residue of oblivion are inscribed there on the page, even imposing themselves for a reason unknown to her, although she is sure of their presence and their necessity. She merely listens to what the words say, as if they were independent of her, borne along by the music in her veins, beating out the rhythms and the rate of respiration that she must follow blindly, for they serve as her model.

Never has a text been as inaccessible and at the same time as simple as *L'Amour*, composed of ordinary language and syntax so eroded that it approaches the laconic with its traces of uncertain, strangely guarded sentences.

She follows the movements of the sea when she writes, just as in loving, in living, she gives in to the desires that come to her, to the cycles of time passing through her. The images evolve with a rolling motion and there is no apparent link between them, recalling her later descriptions, in *Le Camion*, of the Beauce region and of the Party, workers and houses, "unabashedly, freely watching," like "movement of undercurrents," subject only to the arbitrary forces of wind, tides, deep groundswells, and beckoning chasms.

She writes *L'Amour* with memories of Les Roches Noires, and of the old luxury hotel where she stays, going there more often now. She watches from the "belvedere, in this apartment above the sea," which was perhaps a suite at one time, this land "of sand, of wind." And in the landscape of agony crossed by the traveler, the madman, the wandering woman, she also relates the impression of devastation emanating from the hotel, its abandoned, ghostlike appearance, especially in winter, when the few children and residents are gone, and there definitely reigns something dead, faded, and extinct. For the beach fills up with the sea and retires like the breath of a life; the sea gulls' squall, skimming along the sand, and their cries are often deafening, even frightening. At ebb tide the sand is black and strewn with wood, pieces of cork, polished glass fragments, torn nets and dead, eviscerated crabs, emptied of their juicy coral. One feels an immense spirit of mourning here, while off in the distance, in the towns adjoining the big city, the fumes from the Antifer chemical plant give off their nauseating odors, which are wafted all the way to the ocean, becoming mixed with the stink of the estuary. The music in *L'Amour* is drawn from what she sees there, along the boardwalk below her balcony, and in the casino a little further away, near an indestructible Second World War bunker. She can also see the town called S. Thala from this residence, where days, nights, and time itself seem to slow down and stop.

The madman of S. Thala whose dancing follows "the dictation of the music" is her too, when she "closes her eyes . . . [and] sings" in *Le Camion*.

She is completely absorbed by this notion of madness, as if she wanted to strip herself of the intelligence that sows confusion in her head, hurts her and denies her rest. That is why she likes to lose herself through hours of housework in Neauphle, as a way of turning off the flow of thoughts, scrubbing floors, polishing furniture, fading into the undifferentiated mass of the world, with its billions of anonymous, living molecules, like Diderot wanting to slip in among the great vibrant currents of the universe.

The path she follows in those years leads her closer and closer to women and to "the secret life of women" to such an extent that feminist groups, then very active and violent, detecting the apparent sympathy of public opinion, attempt to use her to their advantage by presenting her as one of their leaders. It is true that many of her statements and positions put her in the same camp as those making radical demands: in *Woman to Woman,* she says that the seal closing men off from women "is airtight; we hang around together, pretending, but there are barriers between us," or again, "I think every man is much closer to a general, a soldier, than to any woman."

Her unqualified support for women is in response to their particular way of inhabiting the space of houses, love, children, solitude, and passing time. She admires their capacity for harmony, for being the repository of everything that flows through life, for receiving it and giving it back, for communicating with nature, the seasons, trees, animals, and people. They also possess the ability to remain in each other's company, occupying a place instead of "passing through" it as a man would, making a house into "a cave, a grotto."

In *Nathalie Granger,* shot in 1972 and published in book form in 1973 along with *La Femme du Gange,* she shows the mysterious activities of women, those never shown, their brooding silence while they carry out household tasks. Jeanne Moreau and Lucia Bosè are in the house in Neauphle-le-Château; the voice on the radio announces that two criminals are on the run and hiding nearby in the Dreux forest. The film slowly traces the two women's acts, the long, patient duration of their daily lives, while the camera lingers on their hands, following them into the garden where they gather dead leaves for a fire and then come in for tea. Outside, the air is gray, the pale winter light sending its rays through the various rooms, and what she wants to show is women's bottled-up, repressed violence, their slow, silent journey over the last two thousand years, the clandestine power of witches, who were once killed in public squares, after having been captured while roaming through the woods, like the two escaped killers. Duras says cats are not the only ones with bloodthirsty eyes, "nor the child murderers in the Dreux forest." She invests the image with "deaf and dumb" silence, and every suggestion of revolt, future revolutions, and social upheavals that may be smoldering therein.

She wants to depict this woman's world from which every man seems to be excluded, even the traveling salesman, a stranger to their ways who spends his time making pitches. But she tries to show it from a different angle, a perspective never adopted by any other director, because that would be neither interesting nor gratifying to the public, for the cinema portrays women as objects of desire, sex toys, stars and starlets, just as in painting, before Goya, before Degas, they were seen only in the splendor of their beauty, never in their tubs, fat and ugly, or doing menial, household tasks such as ironing; no artist set out to express this strength "transmitted from the depths of time immemorial."

If *Nathalie Granger* is to be filmed correctly, then, there must be no man present, for in this house of women, men would have interfered with the sliding, slipping movement of those women inside of the house, in the roundness of the garden, in the hollow space of the rooms. They would have blocked off instincts, ruining everything by speaking.

There is of course the salesman who sobs about life, himself, his occupation, his failures, but he is a pitiful character, not a man, although women open their arms to him all the same, just as they open their arms to the mentally ill, to children, and perhaps to murderers.

Something in this house remains silent, buried in time, and its identity is linked to women's secret, prehistoric understanding.

It is the beginning of April 1972. Duras is shooting *Nathalie Granger*. It is obvious that Jeanne Moreau's hands know how to wash dishes, that Duras has not assigned the wrong role to the star of *The Lovers* and *Jules et Jim*; she knows that in her own house in Versailles, Moreau too likes to devote herself to housework, as if attempting to retain part of her violence, channel her ferocity. She had already told Duras this in a 1965 *Vogue* interview that she must have remembered: "If, on account of a war or some such unpredictable event, it were no longer possible for me to be an actress, you see, I could envision myself working in the fields, or preparing meals." Between the two of them there is a sort of complicity, "a feeling of nostalgia . . . that they drag along behind them, of family life led according to its traditional rules." This is the story she wants to tell, along with that of this salesman, an outsider taken in like the pilgrim who accepts the hospitality of a religious community, while he is asked for nothing in return, merely listened to and fed, represented here by Gérard Depardieu, "rejected by men" because he is irresponsible.

And she also wants to tell the story of Nathalie Granger, the little girl who refuses to go to school, like Ernesto, the child in the tale she will write for the Harlin-Quist publishing house, and who resurfaces nearly twenty years later in *Summer Rain*. And the music one hears is the same off-key, discontinuous melody, that of the scales played by the child in *Moderato* and the children in *Nathalie Granger*, but a vehicle of violence nevertheless, with its tortured notes begun over and over again. There is no other story but that, an afternoon at winter's end, a house serving as a passageway for people, animals, lights, sounds, and the camera capturing that life, worried because there is really nothing else but that.

Since this house was built there has never been anyone in it but women, washing, scrubbing, waxing, dressing children, with their inner silence and the "scary" atmosphere that reigns here.

She loves to trace the story of her house, which no man can now inhabit to the same degree as she: not even Mascolo, who lived there for a long time, not even her son Jean, she alone, in the wake of those who toiled there in the eighteenth century while everyone marched on Versailles amid the howling of men. Many generations of women have passed through it, and now the written word is produced in the rooms where she lives. It consists of the mysterious passage from this buried silence to other forms of speech, which she revives in this stream of writing that "tenuously reveals," as Mascolo says, "the inner music."

For the moment, no place can betray better than Neauphle the secrets that plunge her into the autonomous kingdom of writing, in this cruel confrontation she is approaching, in this alternating state of explosion and retention, quivering in anticipation of what awaits her, knowing that everything "remains to be done."

In spite of the silence underlying *Nathalie Granger*, the political and feminist dimensions were perceived more than any others. Duras herself admitted that the film perhaps contained an overly didactic element, which surely explains why her next publication was *La Femme du Gange*, a text better suited to her, at this stage of her journey, because it is "more broken, more shattered."

Nevertheless, the fable of *Nathalie Granger* is what authorized feminists to worship Duras in this unprecedented way and, perhaps out of the need to attenuate somewhat the harshness of her life, she readily accepted being the object of this cult. That is why she is present on Monday, 5 April 1971, for the appeal of the "343," among unknown and famous women like Stéphane Audran, Françoise Arnoul, Simone de Beauvoir, Dominique Desanti, Bona de Mandiargues, Bulle Ogier, Marie-France Pisier, Delphine Seyrig, Agnès Varda, and Marina Vlady—"343 sluts," as the extreme right wing press calls them. Three hundred and forty-three women defying judicial authority, demanding "free access to contraceptive devices and the right to abortions." Duras likes this new struggle, even if the currents lead the Nightship elsewhere in a whirlpool whose motion she prefers to that of society's hubbub, as if something within were driving her ineluctably into the history, the prehistory of her work.

But the act of breaking the law, provoking the powers that be, and male powers at that, reactivates her revolutionary violence. Like Sagan, who admits having signed because, "like many women of her generation, she had been through it," like Jeanne Moreau, who remembers "all the humiliation it involves," like Beauvoir, she says she wants to "abolish hypocrisy." The manifesto caused widespread astonishment. Contradictory, violent debates were held, Catholics mobilized, affirming that abortion "always constitutes the taking of a human life," conservative professors of medicine declared coitus interruptus sufficiently reliable as a substitute for abortion, equating it with contraception. And yet Duras was not among the most actively involved members of the MLF and the free abortion movement. If she lent considerable support to feminism, perhaps encouraged by her friend Delphine Seyrig, whose freedom, she says, "is hampered only by the injustice done to others," and especially to women; if she signed the *Nouvel Observateur*'s April 1971 manifesto of 343 women demanding the abolition of the anti-abortion law, and stating that they had had abortions, she was never the activist that the MLF and related groups would have liked her to be. Too independent, she was able to spot early on the danger of falling into a ghetto in this struggle. She failed to identify with the excesses of militant language, for "every militant proposal is necessarily invalid." Cautious as a result of her communist experience, she feels all schools and all ideological, sexual, and religious groups risk becoming sectarian, autistic, fanatical, and sterile. "What is needed," she says, "is ever greater freedom," swelling with the breath of creation, driven by continually renewed, unknown forces. Ever since her shameful exclusion from the Party, she makes a clean sweep of everything that sets itself up as an institution, from the family (the couple) to literature (the nouveau roman), from religion (churches) to politics.

She nonetheless retains a favorable image with the public, and remains sympathetic to feminist demands, but this is perhaps a result of her affection for certain militant women who urge her to support them. There is Michelle Porte, the author of *Les Lieux de Marguerite Duras*, published in 1977, and the director of *Savannah Bay, c'est toi* in 1984, and Xavière Gauthier, with whom she will compose the famous *Woman to Woman*. This work is an experiment in spontaneous, tape-recorded language, a fashionable genre in those days, whose rhythm, faithful to the natural flow of speech, tends to reconstitute what is said and what is left unsaid, silence and laughter, confessions and hesitations.

She enjoys the company of women more and more, now finding men's speech unbearable, with their authority, their vanity, their pathological habit of talking on and on, and their inability to listen to silence. For her these are infirmities that cut them off from the forces of the universe, the mysterious vibrations of the world, the vacillations contained in people's eyes, this femininity that she believes provides perhaps the only access to metaphysical secrets. If there are men she loves, if she is still able to remain close to some of them, it is because the feminine charge is still intact in them, for they have managed to retain a trace of this androgynous dream-world. That is why she is so fond of Pascal, about whom she would have liked to make a movie, because he doesn't resist the feminine element inside him, showing him the way to the heart of things, opening up to him the field of great, essential questions. Does this mean that in spite of her often reckless, spontaneous affirmations—"man's isolation is perhaps necessary . . . , I have lived with men a great deal, men exclusively, and I've gradually come to realize that I'm changing in this respect . . . and that I find myself more and more with women"—does this mean then that she shows lesbian tendencies during this period, the seventies, in perfect harmony with the literature published by Les Editions des Femmes, from Monique Wittig to Hélène Cixous? It is interesting to observe the exchange of questions and answers on this subject between Gauthier and Duras: her questioner tries constantly to bring her around to homosexuality, to make her express a homosexual preference, but Duras never lets herself be drawn in that direction, rectifying an ambiguous statement as soon as the opportunity arises. Sometimes she even sets herself up as a giver of advice, asserting that "women can't be asked to . . . , to go . . . , to associate only with women, can they? Wider experience is what can get *you* out of this fix!" The two positions, Duras's and that of a hardcore militant whose militancy turns out to contain a great deal of naïveté, actually pass by each other without ever really attaining mutual understanding, as if Duras always perceived a complexity in things and people that only writing could hope to decipher, while protest rhetoric reverts to an excessive, sectarian view of the world.

Duras loves men. She hates their muscle-flexing, their macho violence, but she knows that deep inside she possesses that same deadly force, and that power instinct, even though her every effort is strengthened by the feminine advantage, the capacity for listening to the elements and the secret silence of houses, and for loving children. She is multiple in the sense that, like men, she finds herself enjoying cars, arguing with men, challenging their authority in public debates, seducing like a true Don Juan, handling substantial business and professional chores, and eating with truck drivers in smoke-filled roadside cafés—that is, all of the activities that add to men's strength and virility. Unlike feminists, she tries to unravel the thin, obscure threads underlying masculine thinking, and her open, generous woman's nature is able to seize the "veritable pain that rises up" when she tries to "shed light on it."

That is not the least ambiguous aspect of her personality. Between her and feminists there remains this distance and this impossibility of being totally one with them, this nearly instinctive refusal to fall into the trap of regimentation, the renewed habits of institutionalized couples, and false transgressions.

When she speaks the language of a feminist, she does not seek to exclude others, or to create a sect, even when she is able to regain the spirit of a pamphleteer that animated the tractlike articles of the subversive review *Le 14 juillet*. No, her voice isn't sexist; she struggles for all the exploited: Jews, blacks, women, homosexuals. She speaks about "feminitude" in the same way she would negritude; she rejects all forms of terrorism, so she joins her cries to those of other women, but their voices are not necessarily in harmony.

Since she likes to express her opinion on every subject, politics as well as philosophy, art as well as everyday matters, ever curious, she has shown a great deal of interest in Jeanne Soquet, a painter she helped in her own struggle by writing a preface for her. In *La Création etouffée*, a book by Soquet cowritten with Suzanne Horer, Duras expresses herself with the vehemence of the most rabid feminists, but her statement is primordial, sometimes dealing with other minorities, linking man (i.e., power, the State, God) with every form of violence perpetrated in the world, holding him responsible for every failure: "Man," she says, "must stop being a theoretical imbecile. . . . Man must learn to keep quiet. It must be very painful for him to silence the theorizing voice within him. . . . He silenced women and mad people, but went on speaking his archaic language." For her this still does not mean that women can do without men, as some militant feminists claim, proposing female couples with fatherless children, imagining sapphic Arcadias where silent speech would finally reign, far from "the theoretical hand-rattle" of men. What she wants to tell them in Paris and in the provinces, in Montreal and in New York, is that women must struggle to assert the primitiveness lodged naturally within them, to recover this immemorial strength and to accomplish the most political act imaginable: to invade, with the help of this natural force, "the ancient kingdom of man."

The fact that she no longer wants to live with men during those changing, questioning years, that the life of a couple has become impossible, unliveable for her, still does not imply the desire to lead the life of a homosexual. She has acknowledged the constant presence of a man at her side as a means of palliating a certain isolation, but never as a barrier against solitude, to which writing draws her imperiously. It is as if a lovelife had become fatally unrealizable for her, harassed by the tragic destiny of writing which determines everything, making even a semblance of union out of the question. It is impossible to counter that force, for it is of greater magnitude than one's own, guiding the texts, giving them strength and unity, perfecting her works. "I wrote all my books," she tells Xavière Gauthier, "those you mention, those you find important, without a man, or else with occasional male companions who didn't count, casual affairs that are the exact opposite of monogamy."

She comes to realize that writing, the great black ship that has been carrying her away for such a long time now, through so many books, demands this solitude, requires this sacrifice, which she accepts quite willingly.

And yet she is full of tenderness for women, and it shows in her eyes, the same eyes she turned toward the little brother's body, toward Hélène Lagonelle's breasts when they shared a boardinghouse room in Saigon, toward the green jungle lands, the slow water of the rivers that filled her life, the soft sands on the estuary beaches, the low clouds in the white sky, and the bulging sea when it swells out, filling the lowlands in a few hours. She has the same look in her eyes when she peers into the camera, filming Delphine Seyrig's porcelain body, her pale, fragile breast exposed in the opening of her black gown, somehow picking up its slow rising and falling with each breath, while imperceptible beads of perspiration trickle down, catching up with each other as they go.

That is the gaze Duras focuses on women, on their desire-racked bodies, and it contains the power to elucidate the secrets that are visible only to those who know how to see. Here, on Seyrig's breast, she discerns an "ever so slight mark of hardship . . . a sort of bruise," revealing that she nursed her son. Such is the imperceptible zone in which she works and searches.

As a feminist, Duras is totally independent of the standard-bearers of MLF activism; sometimes she even opposes the movement itself, always remaining on the outside, beyond the boundaries of the Party as well as those of the MLF. The Nightship sails forward in a revolutionary current, reaching "the wild place," "the site of her disorder, her refusal, her dual place always reappearing farther away, wilder, whenever it is besieged by indoctrination."

9

"She Speaks of the Indies"

Indifferent to fads, completely tuned in to the only real story in her work, she pursues the India Song cycle (1973-1976), whose roots she embedded in her early writings, but which she hasn't stopped digging out, "dislodging" as she says, tirelessly working and reworking the narration of this essential scene that runs hauntingly through her memory, until it reaches the ultimate point of fulfillment.

Like the throbbing tune that had already slipped into *The Vice-Consul*, creating silence, the film *India Song* maintains the slow repetition of this phantasm, and heightens the distress of this irremediably foundering, dying world, in the fleeting perfume of the incense whose pungent odor hides all the smells of leprosy.

Duras thus picks up the metaphysical tapestry of her work and, adding a new motif, projects it "into new narrative regions." The texts rise and fall, bringing to mind the eternal ebb and flow of the tides, the infinite motion of brain matter, and the drifting movement of memory, with its ruptures, its holes, and its sudden discoveries.

The places are always the same, from the Vinh Long of her childhood to desolate Calcutta, those of despair, the betrayal of the world, ruins, and death throes. Above the wainscoted walls, beneath the ceilings of colonial residences, fans "turn, but as slowly as a fugitive in a nightmare." Time passes between the sharp blades, an absurd substitute for winds and air currents. Like Racine, she tries to compress the action more and more, giving it the tragic substance that can only be obtained from concentrated time and action. She keeps everything from the founding story, Anne-Marie Stretter and her lovers, and the Vice-Consul, the virginal man, refusing all forms of denatured love, and the beggar woman crying out in her cracked voice in front of the embassy. And the tennis courts and the ball-room, and the moss-covered park, in the moist, suffocating heat of the monsoons, whose luxuriance is frighteningly diffuse, and the smells of rose laurel, like those sweet, violently intoxicating camellia scents in *Moderato*.

She always returns to the distant lands of that exotic child-hood. Again her imagination unwinds its mythical sequence, the residence in France and the palatial Prince of Wales hotel, the gilded drawing rooms, Baudelaire's huge mirrors and his divans deep "as tombs."

Duras's life is there, in that phantasmal geography, an alle-gory for our own pain, in this dwelling and on this land doomed to mourning, in what is the very end of the Western world whose death she never stops singing, like the voice of an ancient coryphaeus presaging evil things to come. "It takes place in 1937," right before the war, during the final bursts of colonialism, in the melancholy litany of tangos and rumbas, but nobody believes in it any longer. Something is dying, crumbling away like the stones of the Rothschild palace where she will film the text in 1975.

She herself says that she wrote *India Song* "like a poem," and the text's ingeniousness in fact resides in the combination of the multiplicity of anonymous exterior voices that tell the story, a sublime choir unwinding in its repetitive, wavelike rhythm, "the legend of Anne-Marie Stretter."

Never has Duras been such a musician, for the interlacing of voices and dialogues creates a kind of "poignant" opera in which the ultimate passion is sung and the narration "slips" into a hypnotic story.

Sometimes there are explosions, those detonations she likes to set off in the hollow of words, in the depths of writing. *India Song*, for example. The path she walks is oblique, whereas Balzac's was straight; passing time is invented at each moment, at different altitudes, so that tiers of duration and silence are organized through transformations. In the space she creates, one instant never follows another, as if attracted by some irresistible development. The movement she chooses, with the text and then with the camera, transforms time into space, anchoring them in a mass of signs where silence is the negative correspondence of these durations, the inner face of music that controls the various elements of the system.

Between Anne-Marie Stretter and the Vice-Consul, what she wants to show is the sort of dynamic inertia that drives the entire, perpetually shifting text.

The film she makes from the book is the high point of the art she has slowly built amid the sarcastic remarks of critics and scholars, both of whom she situates in the same camp.

Duras's greatest model is the labyrinth, with its obscure, deceptive passageways that mislead those who have not already fallen into the traps set by governing bodies, social institutions, and slick hustlers. And like her readers, she can never change course, nor can she escape from her blind alleys. That is why she is so stunned, like those who love her, by its surprises, literally "ravished" by the difficulties with crossroads, switchboxes, bifurcations, intersections, detours, and junctions. Ravished to be in a closed circuit.

India Song is like one long sentence that we know only by its words, some by heart like prayers, and which gradually begins to move, through the magic of those very words, becoming effervescent, taking us to another place, leading us out, away. The beggar woman is rent with leprosy, and her torn rags are those of misery. Like her, Anne-Marie Stretter wears the tatters of the embassy, the last remains of colonization, but her body is also open to everyone, perforated like her head, for she is the whore of Calcutta.

With *India Song*, Duras opens herself to permanent oblivion.

She seems to say: "Set sail, you too, take the leap, don't stay here in the pestilential ruins, in the deadly antique air!"

Does she alone know the unfathomable mystery of *India Song*, where the text finally leads her, carried along by the images toward painting, which she will call "the highest form of expression"—Seyrig's milky breast like a Boucher, the bouquets of roses on a piano like a Chardin, the mirrors and the lights from a Vermeer?

She has always loved the little patch of blue that separates people, loving to explore it and to try to understand it. She manipulates the camera just as she did words, in a prowling voice that hesitates and then suddenly unleashes its truth, brutally, almost provoking, while the lens is focused on this insuperable distance, the centimeter that separates human beings. And she wants to tell of the only thing worth expressing, unbearable pain and suffering. *India Song* is an inspired work, with its polyphony of voices, the lethal slowness that grips its characters, they too silently acting out their own fate, doubly tragic, while all around them, other voices tell their stories.

She "delegated" the offstage roles to Seyrig and Lonsdale, among others. These faceless voices make the spectator an indiscreet witness. All takes places in this tense, restrained atmosphere, this "culmination of passion," a "daily paroxysm."

Everything disintegrates and disappears, dissolving in the heavy waters of the Ganges, even the memory and the body. That is why she loves that country, those fragile lands of her childhood, continually being eaten away by the tides and the crabs; everything crumbles like the people, and the sea becomes a lattice connecting the lands. Even diplomacy, the science of borders, fails in its role, for it is extremely difficult to build dams in these archipelagoes one sees on the map shown near the end of the film, and which could be an atlas, but could also be sinuous, mysterious brain matter.

Such is the road taken by the beggar woman, and by Duras, from the source to the estuary, from the depths of life to death, dissolution, dispersion.

As the whore of Calcutta, isn't Anne-Marie Stretter also the little Saigon "tart" who was the object of everyone's contemptuous stares as she made her way to the closed chamber whose only openings admitted mere slits of light, just as later Yann Andréa will tell her, yelling out his words, that she is "the slut of the Normandy coast?"

It is 1986. After *The Lover*, what others will call raving, her craziness, her peremptory statements, her provocative megalomania, after the oblivion to which "they" abandoned her, she lives with Yann Andréa, there in the Hôtel des Roches Noires, prey to this strange, "boundless" love. And he is like the Vice-Consul who utters his cries in the upper rooms of the hotel, sending their echoes through the empty floors, tapping out her desire on the typewriter while she dictates. She is then possessed by the book, the fatally emerging text, by the incomprehensible, silent generation of the words, amid the explosive outbursts of Yann Andréa, who flees, returns, goes off again to the casinos, the big seaside hotels, comes back late at night, and sees her, still seated at her table, in the alchemy of the book to come, about to be born, a foreigner to all. And he cries out again: "Why the fuck do you sit there writing all day? Everyone's abandoned you. You're crazy; you're the slut of the Normandy coast, an idiot, an embarrassment."

For the moment, she is still an embarrassment. *India Song* is a gem that catches people off-guard, leaving them flabbergasted, in search of a reference point. When this uncatalogued, unclassifiable objet d'art arrives on the scene, critics can't decide whether to call it a masterpiece or a joke, and Cannes festival-goers sneer, while others are captivated, don't know what to say, certain that they have discovered something new, an element from another world that has "slipped" over to this world, as Duras might say.

Carlos d'Alessio's melody is impossible to get out of one's head; her son Jean Mascolo insists that *India Song* will be remembered mainly on account of its soundtrack, for the interminable blues played along with a very slow Beethoven adagio creates a magical effect when the two of them become

entwined, sometimes almost indistinguishable. The music "lac-
erates" the film's duration, tearing apart the "obscure, abominable," concentrated field of vision that the arena affords.

Here Duras uses the same musical orientation as in her
books over the last several years, with her absolute scrambling
and networking effects, as if between the music and the text,
the music and the picture, there were no more airtight separa-
tions, but only this fluid game of life and death.

Duras thus *becomes* the music; the very phrasing of her voice
and her language—"When I write, I hear my voice"—brings
back the most secret undulations of the soul, its darkest falls,
just as foreign variations can be heard in the paintings of the
Italian primitives, in the falls and redemptions of the bodies
on Michelangelo's vaults.

That is why, in her films, she never conceives of music as a
support mechanism, a means of enhancing what the picture,
the text, or the situation says. The music is never melodrama-
tic or event-driven; it is an integral part of the text, an element
of the tantalizing trace, never just background, always embedded in the flesh of the text, blending smoothly in with it.

The seventies unwind amid a climate of effervescence, in the
creative fever that leads her from one book to another, on the
ever greater, blacker sea.

She "dislodges," liberates characters, carrying them away;
she travels as she used to on those great escapades with her
family, across the plains of Asia, along proud rivers. But now
the journey is within, although just as sinuous, and it goes from
Vinh Long to Calcutta, gliding over the lagoon in Venice,
moving down adjacent rivers to the final destination, the Sargasso Sea.

In a 1990 interview for the magazine *Les Inrockuptibles*, she
claims to have no memories of those years, remembering only
the films she made. "Perhaps it is a mediocre period in the history of the human race," she says. Her life is canceled out in
this labor, this certainty that the movie, an extension of the
text, carries its story even further, not the anecdotal version,
but the most pliable, fluid one.

She invigorates her previously published works, blazing new trails that she then proceeds to hide, in order to use them later, making new texts from them. The children's book *Ah! Ernesto*, published by Harlin-Quist, splashed with violent acrylic colors and in tune with the times, goes by almost unnoticed. And yet, in many respects, it contains the gist of the subsequent 1985 film *Les Enfants*, and the 1990 novel *Summer Rain*. The little boy who attends school but then refuses to go because they "teach him things he doesn't know," trying his hand at every role, is already there, he whom some took for a mere tongue-in-cheek character sketch, a Durassian frolic.

What else can be said of her daily, observable, material life? She will talk about it later in *La Vie matérielle* [*Practicalities*], the 1987 book of interviews with Jérôme Beaujour, but she always subordinates it to the works, to the strange destiny of the writing. The text itself is often anterior to her life, to what will happen to her later, like a set of premonitory signs. "What you write is a life that cannot be seen," she says during a *Magnetic Nights* interview on France-Culture radio, "and then there is this other life that can be seen."

Waves of new, peculiar images are then provoking French cinema, like so many challenges. Duras works with untamed zeal, the feverishness of one possessed, "massacring"cinematic rules, imposing another view, pursuing the story of her story. Just as she had castigated writers who were not authors, merely anecdote spinners, circus barkers, recognizing them by their "disincarnated writing," she unequivocally condemns that era's film productions, along with those directors whose main concern is usually with the telling of stories, each one different from the other, while the films she produces every year until 1980 serve as an ample metaphor representing the various periods in her life.

The titles follow one another in rapid succession: before *India Song*, in 1975, there was already *La Femme du Gange* in 1973, then *Baxter, Vera Baxter*, adapted from *Suzanna Andler*, in 1976, *Son nom de Venise dans Calcutta désert*, again in 1976, and *Whole Days in the Trees*, also in 1976, *Le Camion* in 1977,

Le Navire-Night in 1978, *Césarée*, *Les Mains négatives*, *Aurélia Melbourne*, *Aurélia Vancouver*, all in 1979.

The list, an impressive one, reveals the extraordinary energy she possesses, the passion that, hidden beneath the surface, consumes her and invades her life to the point of obsession.

Duras pursues the disappearing images as if they were the clouds of an "approaching monsoon, the floating continent" of her imagination, gliding indifferently toward this impenetrable, relentlessly tormented space. She films *La Femme du Gange* in Les Roches Noires, the middle of nowhere, in twelve days, from 14 to 26 November 1972. This place, which she peoples with her childhood, is the mysterious crucible of a phantasmal universe where everything comes together, the coves of the Mekong and the Ganges, the estuary of the Seine, the bubbling skies, bursting like leprosy, the aggressive smells of iodine and dead fish, sludge and silt, the cries of sea gulls and the impression of a deserted ballroom with plenty of room to accommodate the gliding silhouettes from the Prince of Wales, a hotel as empty as one of those abandoned bunkers on Normandy beaches, doomed to remain suspended in a vacuum, saturated with black and white, in a sterile world, like a cuttlebone.

The power of a phantasm is so great that Duras has imposed her own world on Les Roches Noires. She is like the woman in the filmscript who "in the darkness of her room . . . always stays up, listens, watches, on the lookout for abolished memory."

It is as if her entire personal geography is concentrated here: she has invested the hotel with the phantasmal presences she has been pursuing since *Lol Stein*: the pillars, the smudged mirrors, the sound of the sea which, "reverberating from wall to wall, keeps hollowing out space, whether open or closed." Here in the lobby time is suspended, she says, "it cannot pass."

Sometimes, as if to add comfort to her world, travelers arrive at Les Roches Noires late at night, find their hotel, go through the revolving glass doors, enter the huge lobby, take the elevator that climbs with its pulleys squeaking, and a certain tense, serious look on someone's face recalls the woman of Hiroshima. And indeed, there they are, Emmanuèle Riva, Bulle

Ogier, and Laurent Terzieff, along with Yann Andréa, the specter of *The Atlantic Man*, Duras's cruiser and faithful love.

This world is not dead, but suspended, in "the Open," as she says, quoting Rilke, and standing before it, from where she can see the beach, with its sand wearing away, drowned by the rising tide, only to reappear later, making it impossible to rebuild the old trail that led only to immense space beyond the horizon, the place filled with emptiness, S. Thala.

Writing won't stop tormenting her. It invades her daily life, her relations with family, friends, everyone, and when she needs to temper her frenzy, she goes to Neauphle in search of peace, finding a haven in that house of women where voices from ancient times speak, even though she has lost track of them in the title deeds. *Woman to Woman*, now taking its place in her bibliography, is an example of the absorption of her everyday existence by this phantasmal presence, as if her household activities, in the kitchen or in the garden, were hidden from the haunting power of time, the fullness of this writing flowing in like water, infiltrating, drowning, isolating.

Duras nonetheless breaks out in laughter when the tension becomes too great, threatening the delicate balance maintained by the stillness of the garden and the surrounding trees.

She has a few glasses of wine, and talks about the preserves to be put up, the meal to prepare, while the Neauphle light enters the house, filtering from room to room. But nothing can stop the leprosy "that has spread through her books," stamping its seal upon the entire oeuvre, even the part not yet written.

She is still dealing with leprosy in its entirety when she films *Son nom de Venise dans Calcutta désert* in the deserted parks, the overgrown gardens, and the dilapidated mansion. A strange adventure, designed to "use cinema in ways it has never been used," pursuing it into the "minimal, most barren" space. For she goes back to the soundtrack of *India Song* and returns to the same places, now destroyed, abandoned to the mosses of leprosy, while the images of *India Song* revisit the film.

The slowness with which she films is still not enough to

show the death throes of a white society massacred by its own weapons, for these cracked walls, these wainscoted ballrooms, these reclining stone sculptures, these garden trellises with their broken slats, these high windows with their shattered panes are in fact a metaphorical representation of the dying world, whereas the blues in *India Song*, going round and round like a top, retells the story of the ball, of unconditional lovers, of passion so extreme that nothing can contain it, for the violence of the cry makes everything shatter into pieces.

There lies Duras's place, that of pain and malediction, this "disease of death" that possesses her and reveals the impossibility of God.

The review *Espirit*, in what it calls "an essentially metaphysical mind," traces Duras back to Ecclesiastes, to Pascal. For rarely has a writer asserted her atheism with such vehemence while remaining so close to the preoccupations of the Western world's greatest mystics, and the great prophets of the Old Testament.

Duras has always maintained this link with God, indulging in the ambiguity and the nostalgia that she voices in all her books and interviews. God is everywhere in her texts, in the children, in this fragile, scarcely perceptible unknown, a mysterious presence in her night, in the miracles of love, in the skies above the estuary of the Seine, in the unpredictable movements of the sea, in Yann Andréa's sea-washed gaze, in her walk, with her hand in Yann's. God circulates beneath the little brother's smooth skin just as the water flowed from the earthenware jars, suddenly appearing in the miracle of the book being composed, by some secret alchemy. God is so present in the writing that his name has "become," she says, "a common noun"—"it is everything, it is nothing," but it is an appeal, and remains the object of her quest.

She always appeals to the religious, "this silent impulse, stronger than anyone, and unjustifiable," the incomprehensible staring us in the face, a force that language cannot possibly describe, stumbling miserably, time after time, something unknown that can only be expressed in a stuttering voice, through silence, or words gasped out and, for want of anything better, finding breath enough to say: "The noise, you know? . . . of God? . . . that thing? . . . ."

Throughout her life she has never ceased to proclaim her atheism, asserting it with almost suspect vehemence, but all her words and actions suggest that she understands this void, this absence, this lack. The series of interviews she granted to Xavière Gauthier are thus quite pertinent to this subject. Duras's interviewer seems to take offense at her forays into metaphysics, even expressing her shock when she tries to approach the mystery, giving it a sacred, religious connotation. Her freedom resides here in this attempt to grasp the world and its secrets in their entirety, through all the means at her disposal, without referring to a single school of thought, never hesitating to call herself into question, even renouncing what she has already said. Gauthier has none of that flexibility, that intelligence bent on penetrating the obscure night at all costs.

In the 1990 interview in *Les Inrockuptibles*, she again states: "I don't believe in God, I believe in the kings of Israel, Ecclesiastes, David, and the kings of Jerusalem."

What she considers "the most beautiful sentence in the world" is when Ecclesiastes reveals his identity: "I, son of David, king of Jerusalem, have made pools." In the very mystery of the words uttered, in their decisive tone, she recognizes her own quest, for like Ecclesiastes, when she writes, she too could assert this sacred identity:

"I, Duras, have written these books; I also wrote them in 'the deific field,' the field reserved for God; I have listened to the silence of worlds and the muted cries of births. I have kept my ears open to roots, and to the mouths of rivers; I have drifted with the seas, followed the dense flight of sea birds, peered at the shifting skies high above the tides, and I have brought things back, traces of the Open, cries of silence." For her life and her work, indissolubly mixed, tell of the interminable genesis, the deaths upon deaths that gave rise to the books, the films, and the energies continually renewed in her never-ending quest.

She is aware that writing is the most sacred act there is, the ordering of something enormously "abundant" that is swarming around her, like the waters in Genesis, and when she enters into the book, the feverish state that will give rise to unknown sentiments expressed more precisely than the day before, perhaps she knows that the story leads back, telling of the madwoman, Lol Stein, whose "crippled body" moved one day "in God's belly."

To return to nothing, to everything, to the irremissible silence of the world, to the secret fury of its noises, to this impenetrable mystery, therefore to God, is also to narrow this haunting self, removing the entire weight that writing assumes, that the texts take responsibility for, continually reducing the writer, for to write is to die, the desire to write is the desire to take one's life, perpetrating murder on oneself. "Otherwise, what is writing?"

With Duras, writing leads untiringly back to this interrogation about life, about what it is, and its raison d'être. Duras's physical being, like that of Madeleine Renaud, is slowly shrinking, and the further she advances in time, the less interest she shows in the practicalities of her life, becoming instead a living receptacle of writing, like Edith Piaf in her final years, who was totally consumed by singing, kept alive by the sheer strength of her voice.

What she puts into writing, in the vast workshops that her books are, more and more broken, uncertain in their approach, is something torn from herself, so that, she says, "I will hardly die at all, since the essential part of what defines me will already be gone."

In spite of all it has been subjected to, her body continues to resist fiercely: sometimes, when she speaks, one can hear through the microphone a breath, a faltering respiration, aggravated by her tracheotomy and her emphysema. During the moments of silence that she works in between words, her breathing is perceptible, the syncopated gasp coming from far away, telling of her struggle.

But this difficult, adventurous respiration is also her writing now, her rhythm, her course. Time keeps passing through Duras, always at her heels.

When she talks about her work, she calls it, as she does her life, "a permanent disorder" in which one must "read between the lines." The threads of the tapestry become intertwined, sowing confusion, but in the trap formed by them, there are texts that retell the same sorrow, tormenting the reader. The great haste with which she films, writes, stops her fleeing memories, and opens her eyes to the torment undergone by certain other people, the many movies and the texts that revolve around Lol Stein to the point of driving her mad—all of this is because of the brother, the little brother.

One must think back. It is in Vinh Long, in the 1930s. In the administrator general's yard, where she is not admitted, there are tennis courts. Since the little brother was handsome, and since he played tennis well, "they made an exception for him." She is outside, near the courts, and she can barely see through the mesh of the fence. Excluded, she is looking at Elizabeth Striedter, the woman with the "invisible," almost disincarnate gaze, and that hair whose redness radiated waves of scandal. And then there was the accident, the suicide she learns of, a young man who has killed himself out of love for her, Elizabeth Striedter, the exemplary mother who drove her little girls through the city in a calash, but everyone's whore as well. This fundamental, important scene will haunt Duras's unconscious from that point on. The little brother, in danger inside the administrator general's enclosed park, was perhaps seduced by Anne-Marie Stretter, while she, the little beggar of Vinh Long, wandered around the inaccessible park, betrayed by the little brother, a fascinated rival of the red-haired woman. She puts all of that into her book, in those ostentatious ballroom scenes where Michael Richardson forgets about the young woman he loves, letting himself be carried away by strange Calypso, and where the Vice-Consul, a human wreck, abandoned by everyone, comes looking for her in order to lead her to her death.

"Perhaps she steered me toward writing. Perhaps it was that woman," she says.

But the phantasm at the end of the India Song cycle is not yet elucidated; not until 1980, when she reads Musil's *Man* without Qualities, does she understand the story that secretly tormented her, urging her through all of these texts, as if inevitably. Afterwards, when she understands, when everything becomes clear, she will be able to talk about the incest, the love for her little brother, about what she felt for him, and still feels, forever.

She never stops repeating, and not merely as a means of provocation, that she makes films to "pass the time." Indeed, it's the same time that penetrates her, runs through her, and which she continually draws from, giving it no respite, as if she were digging the dirt from a grave, until she could dig no more.

After the production of Baxter, Véra Baxter, with which she is not satisfied, she returns to family struggles with Whole Days in the Trees, which she had published in 1954, adapted for the theater in 1968, and reworks now in 1976, relentlessly, digging up the sepulchral earth, profaning her story. She films the unfilmable, this web of personalities, these vague, complex fragments, composing them inexplicably. Crouched behind the camera, she shows the terrible, incredible complicity between the older brother and the mother, of which she is the main victim, the one deprived of love, and understanding better than anyone the love that binds the mother to the son. She hates and loves them at the same time, for they too are her life.

She depicts these irrepressible moments of life. The mother sleeps, knowing that the son will always play, for he needs to, but she doesn't care, she loves him all the same. She leaves her jewelry out, aware that he is going to steal it, but she does it on purpose. Once again, she will give him a few moments of pleasure, just like during his childhood when he would slip away and spend "whole days in the trees." That is what Duras films, scarcely anything, nothing visible, the tension between people, the pain, the fear of not being loved enough. Madeleine Renaud and Jean-Pierre Aumont understand these kinds of silence, but what emerges most clearly from her rigorous portrayal of them is Duras's controlled suffering, this now almost joyful comprehension.

10

"The Nobleness of Banality"

From this self-control that writing has magnified, she will draw the female role in *Le Camion*, the most peculiar undertaking she has ever embarked upon. She wants to push cinematic art to its ultimate possibilities, moving in the direction of the unexpected, as she has always done.

Michelle Porte, to whom she grants an interview following the 1977 publication of the filmscript of *Le Camion*, summarizes the film in these words: "In a closed room, a man and a woman—the woman is you—talk for an hour and twenty minutes. The woman tells a story, that of a woman who gets a ride in a truck while hitchhiking, and who talks to the driver for an hour and twenty minutes."

Thus, in what she calls "the darkroom," a man, the truck driver, and a woman, Duras herself, will read what could have been the movie, while other sequences, filmed during vague dawns, show the truck going through the countryside, the Beauce and suburbs, communities whose residents have fled the Yvelines district near Paris.

Beethoven's variations on a Diabelli theme spring from these lands, rolling along with the truck in the junkyards and the dumps, the freeways and the bunkers. She had first thought, she says, of Suzanne Flon or Simone Signoret to play the woman, but since they weren't available, she decided to take on the role herself.

Between her and Depardieu, there is no real dialogue. Too fervent in his political faith, an unquestioning devotee of communism, incapable of questioning himself, he doesn't hear a word this woman says, she who apparently has no identity, "imagining that she is from Portugal, North Africa, or Mali," and who sounds mad to him, for she talks about all sorts of things, anything that pops into her head, in a "disjointed, illogical manner."

She makes speech once again available to the cinematic art, for up to that point it had been a prisoner of the camera; she films these words, and "the pictures that unwind are of the Yvelines."

Such an experience is perfectly consistent with the rest of her work: she perforates the film with her words, her images, leaving it open to everyone, without "telling the story" which, in her view, anesthetizes the audience, to whom she restores the flexibility and the freedom of their imaginations.

She decides that now she will film only with that free use of speech, in what she calls "this overflowing," refusing to use a professional script that has been decisively, confidently predetermined. In *Le Camion,* she continues in this state of vacillation and wandering, like a primitive, prehistoric force springing forth, beyond her control: "All of a sudden, they're talking about the proletariat: well then, all of a sudden they're talking about the proletariat, so be it," she asserts in a provocative tone.

She is really the woman in *Le Camion.* Though the Stalinists would call her alienated, she is the one who talks to everyone and likes to ask people questions about their lives, their apartments, their jobs. In fact she worries about people and, for that very reason, she scares them. She has always been this woman in *Le Camion,* ever since her childhood in Indochina where she was free like the Chinese because, as she says in *The North China Lover,* "they can't catch them and colonize them." Open to every aspect of life and nature, threading her way along the buffalo trails, prowling around "the mess hall dances in the port of Réam," offering herself willingly to the Chinese lover's lust, rich with her mother's secret pride, the pride exposed by the vice principal of the Saigon lycée who, calling her in to see him for having slipped away, suddenly tells her: "Keep doing what you please, listen to no one."

She has always wanted to be an exile, a nonconformist, "boycotted," in fact claiming such a status for herself: "That is the position she wishes to occupy."

She has the same love for "things in general," for the great drifting boat of humanity passing through time. Outside of the "cold room," a room in her Neauphle house, there is the organized world, with its roads, its junctions, its cities, its shopping malls, and its billboards.

She can see this world, she's fond of it, and she films it in its filtered light at the break of dawn, in its nighttime torpor, in its white frost. And then there are the great wheat-growing plains, eaten away by new commuter suburbs, those thick, clayey lands of the Beauce, where the spires of cathedrals nonetheless appear on the horizon.

She invents the film as she goes; the writing is what makes it unwind, what yields its meaning. In order to give a better idea of this simulacrum, she employs the hypothetical conditional perfect: "There would have been a movie. . . . A woman would have been waiting by the side of the road. . . . The truck's cab would have come into view," in this way showing, after the manner of the grammarian Grévisse whom she quotes in the epigraph, that this verb tense used by children at play "in a sense moves the events to the field of fiction," thus destroying Balzac's narrative system.

The "darkroom," the bedroom in Neauphle, is the place where writing is played out, a sort of "mine" in which everything is joined together, "the whole experience of living," and this "unwritten writing is writing itself."

In Neauphle, to which she devotes a book, *Les Lieux de Marguerite Duras* (with Michelle Porte), during that same year, she shows the "darkroom" where an obscure, unknown pressure impels her to write these texts set adrift from their very inception.

Neauphle is heavy with the accumulation of solitude, nights of drunkenness, evenings with friends, and the tangible, nearly unbearable presence of writing, for how can she live without it? The trifling daytime activities, the nights abandoned to silence and to unforeseeable events, the roses from Versailles cut and placed in a vase, the fog dropping down over the park, and photographs of the mother and the little brother pinned onto a frame, cobwebs she no longer removes stuck to the tops of the walls, for why take them away when they would only return over and over?

What she sees are muzzled speeches and political beliefs, every shade of fascism, and rigid parties, with their ability to turn militants into watchdogs.

At that time, she could still call herself a communist, in her fidelity to the first utopians, but she nonetheless breaks away from these labels, referring instead to "political utopia," siding with the inventors, the prophets, the early Fidel Castro, Allende's venture, or Walesa's opposition movement.

Fiercely vocal, her position remains essentially political, but she expresses it by daring to speak freely on every subject, and to be mistaken, to move ahead no matter what, to stay at all costs on the path of truth that has no starting point but keeps going nonetheless.

That is what she calls "the way of cheerful despair." What she or the woman in Le Camion is trying to say is: "Rid yourself of acquired fear," the fear that keeps you from being independent, makes it impossible for you to progress, to see, and that "massacres," as she says, "all spirit of freedom."

But if that revolt takes place in a joyful atmosphere, it will be the most revolutionary step imaginable, for it will frighten the powers that be. She offers this "personal solution" to the truck driver who is too alienated to understand, so that he might stop "the intolerable things in the world."

But to hell with this mindless world; let all the survivors line up with "the last coolie, and we'll start over!"

Henceforth it is as if her very life shed all contingency, other people, obligations, and every form of dependency on society. This narrowing down of material life leads her to spiritual things, to essential acts.

Burdened with secret knowledge, she bears an ever greater resemblance to those storytellers of the Far East, black Africa, or the Maghreb who speak in legends and fables, and seem to be in complicity with sacred, primeval, seismic forces. Rid of politics and the whole party machinery that conditions the militant commitment—in a word, free—she rediscovers the simplicity of primitive speech, the naïveté of the first days, and the ability to listen to silence.

She privileges writing as "the bearer of everything, the derailed vehicle of images, as if it had been fragmented and replaced by its contents, perhaps."

She likes to tell stories, of the past, of the present, letting the words speak, granting them free passage, listening as they slip in everywhere, in places she is unfamiliar with, flowing abundantly.

Meandering along its winding path, the river of oblivion flows impassively, but nonetheless deposits the traces of existence: her publication of *Les Lieux* signals the definite return of childhood, Indochina, the mother, and the legendary epic mythicized by memory. For a long time now, everything has been settled there, waiting, always ready to return to the exact birthplace of that primitive life spent in the water of the *racs* and the thick, moist heat of the jungle.

The primal book, *The Sea Wall*, is tapped like the ocean floor, supplanting every other project, imposing the return to childhood, with its revolts and the mother's sublimated violence.

When, in 1977, she writes *The Eden Cinema*, which she gives to Madeleine Renaud, she thus returns to the days of Indochina, to the mother's madness, her stubbornness, her immense, terrifying love for her own and, beyond all that, the "misery she picked up wherever she went," the little brother with whom she was in such close harmony that they danced "like a single person," the miraculous union that cannot be explained, but only lived, understood in the tension of their bodies, in the widespread amazement that their relationship provoked, and the silence they shared, a sort of tacit recognition that their complicity resembled the mysterious, millennial encounter between the Vice-Consul and Anne-Marie Stretter.

In this new work Duras moves in two different directions, counterbalancing the ever greater, more truthful revelations about her autobiography, with the legend she is building: the nights spent playing the piano for the mother at the Eden Cinema, in the orchestra pit, and the myth of the two soulmates united through dancing.

The novel-writing experience begun in 1943 now shows its existential reality, and while becoming all the more explicit—the mother's peasant origins near Arras, her victimization by swindlers when she purchased land—it rejoins the realm of literature, that stream of symbolic images relayed by the imagination, bearers of a world freed of material constraints and practical considerations.

She returns to this life only to abandon it, stripping it of all chronology, placing it in the time frame of eternity, just as no one will ever know whether the complexities of Proust's childhood found in the first volumes of *Remembrance of Things Past* are in fact real or figments of his imagination.

Is this a turning point? Her writing is clearly more poetic, giving in to this lyric flow, going against all the literary fashions of the time, already becoming the fluent "stream" of language that she will make her rule, subject only to changes of instinct, to the lyricism of desire.

Like Pascal, she moves forward in her "night of fire," in this chasm that is absorbing her, in "this earliest age of human beings, beasts, madmen, and mud."

In 1978, still riding this infernal, inevitable wave of creation, she writes *Le Navire-Night*.

A friend tells her the story of something that happened to him: working at the time as a telephone representative, he dials a number at random one night in June 1973; someone, an unfamiliar voice, answers, and he ends up giving the person his own telephone number. For three years they will thus communicate without ever meeting, three years in the course of which a love, a passion is born. Certain hints reveal that the young woman is ill, and she finally confesses that she is going to marry her doctor. Then she stops calling, perhaps because she has died.

Duras found it tempting—"inevitable," she says—to write this story of night, darkness, and the abyss. Writing reveals the ardor of this passion, its origin drawn from the depths of these telephone waves, its slow maturation in spite of the distance, the unexpected pleasure it produces, amid the tension of language, with one's "eyes closed." To write *Le Navire-Night* is to set off once more for the unknown of life and death, carried away on the great wind of desire, to attain fulfillment.

She needed the film, believing it to be a necessity, a step forward in knowledge, a source shedding even more light on glowing passion. Her diary entry for the first days of August 1978 reads: "A flop."

So why the film? She answers: "How else to pass the time?"

The text of *Le Navire-Night* brings about a change in her life's direction, returning it to literature, to the "toil" of the 1960s, and to the terrible loneliness of being a writer. She presently refutes what *India Song* had led her to believe was an unlimited possibility for extending the written word. It now seems as if the camera were killing the literary qualities of her work, massacring the desire concealed more than ever in writing.

She insists on the primacy of language over visual images, on the secret contained in words and their strange assumption, over "the scarecrow of light."

She tells the story of J. M., "the young man from the Gobelins tapestry works," the same version he gave her, just as it is recorded on tape, and it is hers too: like the characters in the text, she "spends nights" with "the telephone off the hook," referring to her uninterrupted, longstanding relationship with others through books and films.

She too sleeps against the telephone, listening to what is said in mere undertones, amid the silence of the nights and the tumult of dreams.

According to this perspective, "to write is to be no one," to have no identity, no life to describe, no event of one's own, living off the impossible encounter, every type of need, and every form of emptiness.

She always believes that the text should be left completely autonomous, so that it can breathe freely, independently, and that it should able to develop the possibilities offered by the camera, the decor, the actors' voices, and the audience's desire-filled waiting. She thus attempts, that same year, to present Le Navire-Night simultaneously on the stage and the screen. At L'Athénée Théâtre, Michael Lonsdale, Bulle Ogier, and the transvestite Marie-France, under the direction of Claude Régy, pass the text around among each other, none of the roles having been definitively assigned, thus giving the language the force of a groundswell, never to be captured, forever escaping, elusive. "They [the actors] try," says Duras, "to anchor the story in a text, in a film. To confine it to a text. To make it fit into a film."

Then the movie is filmed in a kind of triple echo, reflecting images of a work in preparation, those of the three actors, Bulle Ogier, Dominique Sanda, and Mathieu Carrière, with the offscreen voices of Duras and Benoît Jacquot.

It is in this back-and-forth motion of images, voices, and characters that "the inexpressible part of the text" will be "attained," says Duras. "We turned the camera inside out and we filmed everything that went into it, darkness, air, projectors, roads, faces too."

By doing that she knocks down the walls separating the genres, putting theater and cinema "to the test," determined only to transcribe the dizziness of the abyss, to evoke the black hole, the unknown that she is always tracking down. She says, in an interview for the 29 March 1979 issue of Les Nouvelles littéraires, "As long as people haven't entered into their unknown, they remain strangers to themselves. To know this unknown is impossible. But it is important to be aware that it is present, just as we feel the world around us. Those who can't feel it are handicapped."

She is becoming a legendary image, joining millennial, mysterious gestures with no apparent meaning. Did she invent this? Her critics think so, claiming that she made use of events and the media with perfect cynicism. But her steady, persistent course reveals her fascination for the secret melody of souls, for murmurs uttered in the night, and to this she devotes her life. She is the symbolic literary equivalent of the great mystics pursued by a sign and whose entire beings, outstretched toward God as their sole aim, are engulfed in his obscure knowledge, avid for his light. Henceforth, each act, each encounter, each book is a tangible trace of the Journey, of the Opening before them. That is why political talk and events in themselves no longer concern her; she is the woman who "was crying out thirty thousand years ago." Fascinated by wild, prehistoric forces, she speaks to the cosmos, to the murmur of the stars, more than to the evening news. Her pytoness remarks upset the applecart, and they are greeted with derision, gibes, ostracism. She claims to be indifferent to this, but in private she says that it bothers her.

She is relieved by the critical establishment's frequent weariness and disenchantment with her solitary, narcissistic journey, as if neglect were pushing her further along in this frantic quest, as if there were "thus a price to pay for something in history." "The critic's role is this too: to abandon authors to themselves. That is a very good thing." And with that, she takes a passing shot, in an interview with *Libération* on 4 January 1983, at Pierre-Henri Simon, Bertrand Poirot-Delpech, and Jacqueline Piatier, journalists for *Le Monde*, "for if it had been up to those three, I would never have been published."

In 1979, from the "unused footage for *Le Navire-Night*," she makes the texts and films for *Les Mains négatives* and *Césarée*, two short works relating the same obsession, the same desire to draw people together, reaching across worlds, wars, time itself.

She loves the gestures of the cavemen—unexplained, unexplainable in terms of traditional intelligence and knowledge—when they dyed their hands with blue, red, or black pigment, situating them in her mythical geography on the walls of the Magdalenian caves in "South-Atlantic Europe." She too tries to make negative hands, those printed texts resembling open, ritual acts, primitive acts that express strength in love; like the hands, her writing appeals to love, memory, and time:

"I love you beyond yourself

"I will love whoever hears me crying out

"Saying that I love you

"Thirty thousand years

"I call out

"I call out to someone who will answer me

"I want to love you I love you."

She reexpresses this mad, immoderate obstinacy in *Césarée*, the low lament of a woman who, like the ancient poet, tells the story of Berenice leaving Rome, repudiated for reasons of state by the emperor Titus.

Those are the places where Duras lives her life, in the depths of the ship, with Berenice, deep inside the caves, with the men who preceded history, telescoping epochs, and in that mourning she recovers the accents of the first epics, the rhythm of the first poets, the lyricism of the holy books.

She is Berenice, whom she describes like this: "Very young, eighteen, thirty, two thousand years old." Similarly, she will describe herself in *The Lover*, old at the age of eighteen, "already too late."

Everything leads to apocalypses, crumbling worlds, ruins and devastation. Faces grow old in the space of a night, "bursting ashes" destroy cities and people, and it all resembles the disasters of Herculaneum and Pompeii.

She meets death along the way, for the "quasi-mathematical fixity of this separation between people" is absolute, terrible, making it impossible to live. Her memory still contains the telegram sent from Saigon during the Japanese occupation, announcing the little brother's death, with her in Paris, him in Saigon, not even dying in her arms, so that she might express that love, that which she bore for him, at last managing to emerge from layers of time and the restraints of taboos. In this dead world surrounding her, she seeks light, not always darkness, the wandering ocean liner on which her fate placed her, and she thinks about the perfect roundness of the breasts of her friend Hélène Lagonelle, in that Saigon boarding school, as round as the earth or the earthenware jars with which the

Chinese lover quenched her thirst, as smooth as the little brother's skin, or the old, velvety roses in the garden at Neauphle.

But she still returns to the subject of the Jews, the massacre of the Jews: she has "never gotten over" the Nazis' crime. The variations of *Aurélia Steiner*—*Aurélia Melbourne*, *Aurélia Vancouver*, and *Aurélia Paris*—bear witness to this pain, and to the constant presence of the emotion. She films the first two *Aurélias* in 1979, publishing the trilogy that same year. And in the heart of the text, writing is always considered as a "call" to carry love beyond death.

With the *Aurélias*, she "starts writing again," as if after Anne-Marie Stretter she now had Aurélia to give her the strength, the courage, the defiance to talk about the Jews, to whom she feels attached. "The story of the Jews is my story," she tells her Canadian hosts in April 1981. "Since I lived through that horror, I know it is my own story."

11

"Then Someone Came"

But the 1980s give her life new momentum, a stronger desire to write, freed of writing itself, at the mercy of the great movements of the universe. She believes less and less in the necessity of film, even her own, and in its ability to produce, through the use of images, the very power concealed within words. When Serge July, editor-in-chief of *Libération*, asks her for "an essay dealing not with current political or general affairs, but a sort of parallel chronicle of events she found interesting but which hadn't necessarily been chosen for the usual news," she gladly accepts, seeing in this "parallel" availability the new space for her writing. During this summer of 1980, she lives in Trouville, near the sea, in the continuous movement of the tides, in the wind that sweeps away the pestilential odors of the Antifer chemical plant, off in the distance near Le Havre.

At Les Roches Noires, there is no longer the cushioned silence of *India Song*, the sumptuous agony of the Rothschild palace. The vacation residents have arrived for the season, and although there is no lifeguard on this side of the beach, it is completely covered with summer camp children from Vitry and Sarcelles, Parisian suburbs in the "Communist belt," because they have more room there. In the vast lobby, strangers, mostly tenants, bustle about, busy with leisure-related activities not necessarily shared by Duras. She is like Proust observing the tourists on a mild summer day in Balbec, amid the chiffon charms of budding young ladies.

During this summer of 1980, the weather is variable—long rains sweep the sky, bringing autumn nostalgia to the beach—but from her "belvedere" she wants to see everything, the passersby strolling along in the changing light, "the turbulent water" stirred up to the accompaniment of "motorboat noises," as they coast along near the shore.

She thus writes the chronicle of the summer of 1980. She can feel that this new form of expression allows her a greater participation in the world. She lives confined to that vast apartment, and yet she is "with all of you, with everybody." For she doesn't merely tell how the day progresses; she also reflects on world events, folding them into the commonplace activities on the beach. The news that summer concerns the Shah of Iran's burial, the famine raging in Uganda, hurricane Allen devastating entire islands, and especially the Gdansk shipyards in Poland, where workers are defying the communist regime.

She believes writers have the capacity ("Otherwise what *is* writing—a game?") to weave the history of the world with words, seeing, like true visionaries, the underlying structures that constitute and explain it.

Carrying this even further, she spots a group of young children playing on the beach, detaches them from the landscape, and zooms in on one child who is an outsider, and whom the camp counselor is trying to tame; Duras perceives the trace of a budding love between them. *L'Eté 80* is composed of this latticework of texts, a fleeting chronicle doomed to the disaster of inexorably passing time, telling nonetheless of fragmented, parceled life as it comes and goes, wears out, gives its last gasp, finally dies, and is then reborn elsewhere, here, now everywhere.

Was she returning to the style of her first articles, those in *France-Observateur* or *Vogue*, where she excelled at reporting on miscellaneous news items, and the marginality of certain people who fascinated her? Was she producing these articles because she needed money, as she often claimed?

This way of writing, however, is not new—for it stems from

the same sources that continue to appear, the Ganges and Siam, returns her "to her native land, to this terrifying labor she had abandoned ten years earlier." All of Duras is there, her imagination, her fluid use of symbols, the impressionism again, made even lighter by her "fluent" writing, hurrying along without stopping to analyze its effects, but using its inimitable rhythm to express the variation of time, like Diabelli or Bach, in this surprisingly elaborate innocence, this subtle appearance that seizes "the crest" of the words, in this gaze obscured by thick glasses and which nonetheless can see for great distances. She wants to carry along the whole world, from the microcosm—the sand, the imperceptible movements of the tides—to the macrocosm, the wind, the storms, and that which lies beyond the borders, Poland, Africa, India, Indochina. All that from her windows overlooking the sand-covered boardwalk where everybody passes. So why even bother to go outside? In the apartment she is both inside and outside, like a lighthouse looking out over the boundlessness of things and of the world.

She exists in this perpetual ambivalence that creates the true metaphysical history of the universe. Pascal was no different, alone with his illness, thinking about the world and its daily turmoil, absorbed by the silence of the infinite and yet attentive to the collective and individual evolution of human beings. Nor was Proust, in his cork-lined room, describing the expressible and inexpressible passing of events. Or Saint-Simon, ostensibly cut off from the world in his Versailles attic yet nonetheless observing the rolling and pitching of the world.

In her solitary crossing, she receives letters from people she will never meet and whom she will never answer, but who are like so many signs of light calming the pain, the despair of existence, this tragic burden the world has put on her shoulders. Writing emerges from this density, this strange, uncontrollable matter that follows only her desires.

She reads these letters and hears the voices that write them, crying out their love, this desire to know her more intimately and to fathom her secrets. Some of them are anonymous and don't even arrive throught the mail; she finds them on her doorstep in Paris or in Trouville. Writing to Duras is completely different from writing to another author out of admiration. Her books in fact possess the fascinating capacity to establish another kind of relationship, a more mysterious register in which the forces of desire flow freely. She has attempted to explain this strange bond she inspires. True writers "are sex objects par excellence"; they "provoke sexuality." Something in them holds back fear, madness, pain, and anguish. The work they create brings them close to the abyss, confronts the unknown, dwells on the margins of life, where death looms, removes all certainty, and predisposes one to danger. The very distance between her and others stimulates the desire to penetrate, to force this mystery, to bear witness to it, even precariously. For similar reasons, Proust's body is infinitely sexual, begging to be ravished. The same is true of Duras, whose work has spoken of nothing but these muffled or bursting cries of passion, ready for the strange secrets she receives and which she admits falling in love with time and again.

During this first part of summer 1980, she is alone, without hope, confined to this "foreign land" inhabited by writers, as she says; she also writes letters to perfect strangers, just as she sometimes likes to call people she doesn't know and, in "the chasm of the telephone line," alleviate this suffering by communicating, because "not to love is the worst possible fate." She is sixty-six years old, and is back to drinking heavily, without knowing why; she spends whole nights drinking; in Neauphle, she is nauseated by the smell of the hundreds of roses filling the garden, saturated with the heavy scent, and has only one desire: "To write, always. Always that. All the time." She subjects herself to this tyranny of writing as a way of not dying, of not letting omnivorous time get hold of her. In spite of the wine and the suffering, writing is still a source of support. Because when "I write, I don't die." She is possessed by a tremendous passion for living, a vital energy, and they win out against her pain, "the darkness of time," and "the density and heaviness of the days."

She writes her letters the way women in prehistoric caves

placed their hands on the rock walls, daubing them with color, leaving their imprint like an appeal to the future of the world, a distress signal, an SOS. Her books, her films, and the commuter suburbs that file by in Le Camion, with the dawn's African armada sweeping the streets of Paris, show so many "negative hands" calling out to the world, taking it to witness, leaving their mark.

January 1980. In Practicalities she tells about the disaster of the body. The constant, unrelieved anxiety that accompanies this devastation takes its toll on her mind; she goes on drinking, and faints as a result of the tranquilizers she uses in spite of the alcohol. She is admitted to Saint-Germain-en-Laye hospital; the Nightship drifts in the dark, loses its bearings, spots no more of the "flashes of light" that nonetheless allow her to continue living. A kind of black hole sucks her in, drawing her toward ever lonelier nights, in this inevitable, uncontrollable difficulty of being.

Among the letters sent to her, those "admirable" ones from Yann Andréa stand out, a young student in Caen who, although never having received a reply, meets her there one evening during a showing of India Song. She doesn't want to know him except in the mysterious, spectral tension she maintains with all those who write to her. It is a relationship of desire, that of her own body open to all, like Anne-Marie Stretter, abandoned, everybody's whore, to whom she grants this complicity in making confessions, telling secrets, and uttering cries on paper.

And then Yann Andréa's desire gushes forth confusedly, and she answers him one day, she responds with her loneliness, her cry, "How hard it is . . . to go on living." There is madness in this encounter, something that wants to defy time itself, in the age of difference, the imbalance in their levels of knowledge, and the impossibility of fulfillment.

After a trying winter, she leaves for Trouville. She would like to stay there for a long time, through the fall, to experience the mixture of sky and sea, to hear their murmurs at night when the room she sleeps in is completely penetrated by the elements, and therefore never in total isolation.

And then Yann Andréa called. He asked if he could come join her, and she said yes; he arrived in Trouville. She knows it is "madness," but accepts it. She is aware that something is going to happen, and that it will allow the ship to set out again, and writing to continue in a new vein, defying death, because everything is not used up yet, all has not been said. The living matter within her has not yet yielded each particle to her wringing, gleaning efforts.

This theme of encounter, so romantic, so intensely passionate, calls into question everything she said previously about the impossibility of her continuing to live with men; it quashes all of her decisive statements.

He "quit his job, he left his home. He stayed." Between them there is something inexpressible that ties them together, an irresistible force and a passionate impetus that join them to life in a kind of fusion, sending them back to the shifting land and water formations of the earliest ages, back to the misty legends, and the mythologies in which lovers protect each other from death, living in the silence of their sublime, terrifying love.

The relationship between her and Yann Andréa, one of recognition, is beyond words, even as it expresses the certitude of their love and gratitude for being overwhelmed by it.

With her way of revealing the most intimate secrets in an absolute, affirmative tone, she declares: "At the age of sixty-five I had this experience with Y. A., a homosexual. It is certainly the most unexpected, most terrifying, most important event of this last part of my life, similar to what happens in *The War.*"

From Robert Antelme's visceral act of waiting in the death camps, left to rot between two wooden partitions, like Aurélia Steiner, like one of those children hidden there, "an accident in the generalization of death," to this absolute passion, it is still the same brutal journey, in which dying plays its part, and the precariousness of existence is re-evoked time and again in this uneasiness of life recalling the fragility of sand, constantly subject to the blind forces of the tides.

It is the same story beginning over and over again, the only one she can ever know, as intolerable as it is inevitable, a burning pain, a tragedy. There are always the same violent passions emanating from a kind of absolute, intransigent, mystical experience.

She prophetically said in *Woman to Woman* in 1974: "Women who have committed a creative act of transgression often enjoy . . . the company of male homosexuals." It is thus the feminine side that she likes in Yann Andréa, his difference from other men who, she says, induce "physical fear" in her, whereas Yann Andréa has an intuitive understanding of her work, having "always" known it, as if he were a character who had escaped from her books, one of those people who has passed through the mirrors or remain obsessed by his earliest wounds, and cry out his suffering in the streets of Lahore or Trouville.

And then there is Yann Andréa's voice, the one that speaks from the Nightship, "making things, like desire and feeling."

To keep him near her is to flaunt before everyone the scandal of "this unavowable community," as Blanchot would say, this autonomous couple they form, in which writing nonetheless circulates, so that all of Duras's subsequent books are written in the shadow of Yann Andréa, a mythical figure in her work. To stay with him is to defy others, to begin a new adventure, in perfect harmony with her texts, to bring to light that which nourishes writing, all the buried needs and desires, what, despite the body's refusal, amounts to love.

In her life she has always been close to feminine men, the only ones capable of approaching the uncertain zones where she roams, of possessing that knowledge of desire, of the trembling and agony of roses in the evening, of the vague, fleeting lights of Normandy skies, of that far-off place. She says she has always been "against them," men, against their way of speaking with authority, wanting to come out on top, never listening, forever in this intolerable activity of life which makes it imopossible for them to feel and see. That is the law she has refused, that servitude in which they put her, destroying her, and preventing her from creating. She likes Bruno Nuytten,

Sami Frey, Michael Lonsdale, and Gérard Depardieu for those reasons: they accept the "feminitude" inside them, developing it, making it vibrate, and it is in this play of virile violence and feminine listening that she loves men, in this fragile form of near androgyny, in this freely assumed confusion.

She puts up with Yann Andréa's archaic nature, his bursts of anger and his cries, his furious typing of the book in progress while she dictates, his screaming in the Trouville apartment, like that of the Vice-Consul, cries of impossible love and of the inability to love, to attain this carnal abyss, even as they plunge inside each other when "the sea is calm" and "they are looking at it," when they "enter" a tiny chapel to rest, and the smell of burning candles.

The fascination she always exerts literally "enchants" Yann Andréa. It is like a ravishing, a spell, a fated encounter. As if to keep this love from escaping, she imprisons it in writing, giving it a symbolic, mythological value. Since she claims that "her life doesn't exist," she invents it in this staging of love, in this theatrical creation of herself and Yann Andréa as a legendary couple who would fail to survive each other's death.

She always deplores whatever flees and is stolen by time, for she would like to preserve it, snatch it away at all costs: "You are amazed by the splendor of bodies, the fairness of skin; you say: It will grow, it will disappear, one wants to keep that beauty." What she has tried to accomplish is that precise, transgressive act, to retain the fervor of days, the roundness of bodies, the pulp of flesh, the mobility of the light when, like a Vermeer, it sprinkles gold dust on the estuary of the Seine.

Drinking, writing, loving are so many strategies for thwarting the march of time as it despoils people of the beauty of daylight.

Her life with Yann Andréa is devoted to this ardent quest for primal fusion, creating an insular kind of love, with both of them caught in the developing work, henceforth theirs, made in the passion of this story which holds them in its grasp and then strikes them down.

Better still, the love she bears for Yann Andréa sends her back to the nostalgia for wholeness she has always sought, the utopia perhaps now attained; in love with love, her feeling for Yann Andréa also allows him to approach the periphery of that same sentiment, and therefore death, for "through my apparent preference for you I love nothing but love itself, undemolished by the choice of our story."

To love Yann Andréa is to carry even further this act of defiance, "the source of everything, of all writing, . . . everything that can oppose death." The hell of living as a couple, this terrible complementarity, this ultimate attempt at union are what foment the writing, give birth to it, and make "the text move forward." But where is it going, in what direction, toward what mysterious destination?

She knows that between men and women there is something irreconcilable, a kind of war, even though desire crosses the distance, as if trying to reknit the initial tear, and she also knows that the "hatred of the female body" which she detects in Yann Andréa is yet another avatar of the brutal, archaic separation.

When she opens her door to him in Trouville during that summer of 1980, all it takes is a smile, a kiss, and they know about the fear and the madness, the emotion, the death, and the certitude of a love whose violence "only she comprehends." Nothing more is required, only this presence, like someone she has always known, returning from the mists of time, sitting down and saying nothing else, what's the use, since everything has already been said. They shut themselves up in the Trouville apartment, and they drink. Red wine, medium Bordeaux, black coffee. Duras takes tranquilizers, negates herself in the chasm of writing that calls out to her, demanding its daily allowance. Three hours of work and the rest of the time spent drinking, vaguely aware of what she has written, wondering if it is even worth anything. As Yann Andréa relates, she puts on weight, no longer changes her clothes, bound to the book, to wine, to love. Confusedly, she sometimes hears the sound of the sea, especially at night, but she doesn't go to the window, drinking even when everything is sleeping.

Their story begins in that cruel, tragic passion, in that other palpitating love.

The Nightship cries out in the darkness, and yet she is no longer alone. "With you I did set out, I go where you go." The starkness of the confession overwhelms and demonstrates the truth of this love.

Because of the delirium the alcohol provokes, they occasionally disturb the other apartment dwellers in Les Roches Noires, who are torn between the vague pride of being their neighbors and the painful spectacle in which they sometimes indulge. Certain eccentricities and the unusual couple they form cause a scandal and unspoken reprobation. They don't care, however, devoted as they are to this parturition of the book and what it makes them say, like an indispensable stopping place on their journey.

Nonetheless, the work never stops unfolding, making the most diverse, most contradictory queries with, always at the heart of her problematics, love, that constant questioning of her survival.

Right before *L'Eté*, in April of 1980, she publishes *The Man Sitting in the Corridor*, the reworked version of a short text written at the time of *Hiroshima Mon Amour*, which she brings back from oblivion, giving it new life, a new meaning, faithful to what she believes about writing: that it has this unlimited capacity to explode, to transform itself, to open onto itself like a dizzying abyss that draws one into its vortex.

The little book creates confusion among her admirers and the critical establishment, accustomed to a more allusive form of expression, a more radical ellipsis in meaning. For *The Man Sitting in the Corridor*, with its erotic violence and bold obscenity, surprises, terrifies, or annoys on account of what some believe is nothing more than a stereotypical erotic narrative, with its inevitable motifs of fellatio, rape, onanism, and sadism. But that would be to forget the important place passionate, scandalous love occupies in Duras's entire work. That would be to neglect that which characterizes her entire quest, "this slow trek toward infinity" which she pursues there, in the violence of this wild, hurried romantic relationship in which the woman, a purely passive object, is penetrated by the man's sex. "Force of the earliest times, indifference of the stones and the lichens." Duras's obsession with this enigma of love leads her to describe this fundamental, archetypal scene from the point of view of an outside observer, forever curious, never siding with this barbaric, murderous passion, but rather confronting it, in a sense.

The same obsession pursues her two years later in *The Malady of Death*, counterpart to this text, which she writes and carries inside her from 1980 to 1982, and which still reveals her cry, her need for reconciliation and love, while "in the night" bodies and sexes "search for a place to put themselves" in this desire to find their niche, to slip into the infinity of things, to finally break "the impassible boundary between her and you."

The malady of death is the impossibility for man really to love woman, this "stranger" who makes him impotent, and makes love an inaccessible, irreparable place of union: "She asks you to tell her clearly: I don't love. You tell her. She says: Never? You say: never."

So what can one say about love, how can it be fulfilled other than in murder and suicide, in the ignorance of the other, in their violence, with its "invincible force of unequaled weakness," in "the unleashing of blind, fatal passions"?

How can one escape this malady of death, these fatal miasmas it develops, what can be done in this relationship with Yann Andréa, in spite of its strangeness, how can they escape the failure of total union, and return to the matrix, to the alluvial water, the water "of the vast, deep, river mouths"?

The love she perceives between herself and Yann Andréa, a sentiment she is sure of, a kind of faith, perhaps opens the way to "pure loving" precisely becaue it is singular, springing from the invisible unknown, the impossible, a "sudden rupture in the logic of the universe." Only in the apparent error of this feeling, in its strangeness, in this "displaced" condition is there a final chance of finding love.

She thinks such thoughts with her usual intensity, as if she were gifted with superior, divine perception. During that terrible month of October 1982, when she agrees to undergo treatment for her alcoholism, throughout her comatose period, she "knows" that Yann Andréa, as he watches over her, desires her; in this absent, then fallen state in which "she could no longer even hold a spoon," she "knows" "that Y. A.'s love was true love."

That unexplored place of encounter is where love is born, amid risk, amid danger, through a plunge into obscurity.

It is perhaps there too that she can accede to the sacred, situating this love story in a religious context, assigning to it the godlike meaning she has always given to these different, out-of-the-ordinary moments.

God can be found in that fragile instant when the sun sets over the sea in Trouville, in those late nights when Y. A. comes back from his wanderings and she waits for him, watches over him, fixes him "cheese, yogurt, butter." God is also found when the book becomes laden with meaning, and Y. A. types as she dictates, when he anticipates her thirst for wine on the way to the hospital, when he watches her sleep, in that fragile, destructible peace.

Again in June 1980 when *Les Cahiers du Cinéma* gives her a free hand in a special issue, she orients her writing in another direction, placing her entire self in the book's deepest recesses, hovering around film without abandoning the elements that created her and have always haunted her. The book takes a new path, adapting to different moments, impressions, obsessions. She tries to infuse it with the very rhythm of her life, saying moreover that she "doesn't exist," although subject to the play of mental images and photographs of her childhood, of her madness.

With *L'Eté 80*, to which she gives the status of a book, "resisting the temptation to leave the texts scattered around in separate issues of newspapers doomed to being thrown away," she decides the future of another book, another manner of writing in which her life and all her baggage would be included, no longer avoiding autobiography. Imperceptibly, she removes the veil from certain moments of her life that had been muddled by legend, furnishing details about her own tastes, peeves, and anxieties. She entrusts Yann Andréa with the preparation of *Outside*, the pieces she had once written "during empty, hollow moments," when she was "in the grip of outside occurrences," articles first published in *Vogue* or *France-Observateur*, linked to immediate events in art or politics, and to which she would give a second existence. These chronicles in *Outside*, initially written as a means of keeping the pot boiling, take on another dimension on account of the particular topics selected and the way they are arranged. Included there a posteriori are the founding themes of her life and work, in the extraordinary unity of her writing surpassing itself, confronting and revealing Duras's secret world, her fascination with murder, the fringe, artists, prisoners, stars and whores, nuns and rapists.

At the beginning of this decade it seems that her readers are getting to know her better; apparently signing "the autobiographical pact," she projects a more tangible version of herself, as if she thus intended, in this fleeting side of things to which she now commits herself, to convey the magic, eternal weight of the book, to influence immovable time.

Another revelation furnished by the "tangle" of her scattered texts now bound together in a collection is mentioned by Y. A.: the evidence of her music, which after all is the absolute necessity of writing, the permanance of her song as it flows all the way down into these apparently disparate fragments and declares her a writer, in the most complete, most ancient meaning of the word, in her sublime, quintessential vocation, at the lofty summits of spirituality.

She reveals a great deal of herself now, devoted to this other form of writing, a fluent "stream" of words, catching the spirit of the time, and giving an account of its effects on her, traveling, and stirring up emotions and questions in her wake. Placing herself before her readers, she creates magic among them, shocking them, arousing in them the desire to write. Invited to

Montreal in April 1981—at which time she was galvanized by the presidential victory of François Mitterrand, in whose electoral battle she committed herself totally as an active member of his support committee—she leaves an indelible mark on the memory of her Canadian hosts, who showed their esteem for her in a work published in 1984: *Marguerite Duras à Montréal*. By her side stands Yann Andréa, a still fragile, unobtrusive yet constant presence, whose profile is a cross between Peter Handke and a Chekhov hero, whom she sometimes asks for confirmation of what she says, relaying statements back to him, weaving between the two of them, in a back-and-forth movement, the thread of this already born, yet unborn love.

For the moment she keeps this presence secret, failing to identify him, giving him a mythical force that brings him into her legend. "Then someone came," she says. "He came. He came from a town in the provinces. He had read my books, and he stayed. He quit his job."

She magnifies their meeting, investing it with the theme of the fatal, inevitable encounter. Y. A., as she still calls him in 1987, enters into the mythology of absolute lovers. She makes him a fictional character, like an exile, the little brother, an angel, or the man from Lahore.

In Montreal she reiterates what she wants to attain through writing, since that is the only thing that allows her to exist, and she reaffirms that everything, including the written word, is created in this uncertainty, in this absence of a plan. The book is thus born of its own mystery, which she merely catches in flight, on the wing, gathering whatever falls in front of her, for "in front" is where everything is played out. She insists on the improvised, unexpected aspect of things, this permanent questioning which maintains her in a state of perpetual development, this risk that she always takes and accepts, as when, like Verlaine to Rimbaud, she says to Y. A., the young man from Caen, "Come, I'm calling you, I'm waiting for you."

"That's how writing is," like loving, not knowing ahead of time, dwelling in a state that eludes all logic, all coherence.

This open acceptance, this humanity are surely necessary steps on the path to truth, the unnameable.

That is why she knows Y. A.'s presence is absolute and inaccessible to others, because she experiences it in the unbridled power of transgression, "in a sort of dimension that need not be expressed."

She doesn't attempt to reach an intellectual understanding of this love, its scope, its fabulous secret. She merely knows that it is of the same nature as the text, without any critical possibility, without commentary, there before it is even there, as she would say, always foreseen, not necessarily to show the way, but rather to obscure it, to add more mystery to it, so that one can penetrate this "total darkness" and get "as close as possible" to the sacred.

When she returns to Paris, François Mitterrand has been elected president of France, the first left-wing president of the Fifth French Republic. That is why she says she is above all a "Mitterrandian," fascinated by the man who was once her Resistance companion and who, when he went to Dachau to witness the liberation of the camp, heard, like a miraculous sign from among the other inanimate bodies thrown into a field to die, the exhausted voice of her own husband, Robert Antelme.

In the euphoria of the victory, she appears nearly everywhere, jubilant and happy, with Jack Lang, Michel Rocard, at the presidential palace when Mitterrand is inaugurated, coming to him very naturally to kiss him and speak to him briefly, with her mind certainly full of images remaining from the past, the "memory of oblivion": of her, petrified before her husband's panting, unrecognizable body, near Mitterrand in the stairway, and then fleeing, hiding in the darkness of a closet.

She likes Mitterrand because she credits him with an ethical stance, a certain spirituality, a feeling for the earth, and because he loves writers, those who attempt uncompromisingly to penetrate their own mystery.

In her eyes, in this legend of Antelme's return, he is also the agent of destiny, the sign of his recognition. "You traveled," she tells him during one of her famous interviews with him in 1986, "thousands of kilometers, and you recognized him among thousands of men." This miraculous coincidence is one of the proofs of the secret life she believes in and feels within her.

Each new trial brings her closer to others through this instinctive comprehension of people, while at the same time estranging her through the singularity displayed in her work.

In a 1987 radio interview with Alain Veinstein, she states that "there is no book outside of oneself," setting herself against masculine literature into which female writers most often slip: "talkative, culture-ridden, essay-prone literature." Literature that "stems from pride, from ownership, lacking specificity" because it refuses its ultimate expression, which is poetry. That is why she likes Emily Dickinson, whom she often talks about at the time, and even contemplates translating her. The two of them have certain traits in common: their navigation on uncharted seas, their lack of a name and a country, completely absorbed by their close attention to secret things, in the terrible tension of themselves, forever moving toward the only possible form of expression, that which best restores the uncovered secret, the poem. Like Dickinson, she is in the darkroom, the reverberator of elements that she simply puts into words, with her strange, laconic, intuitive, musical gift, alternating between the abstract and the concrete. Again like her, she knows that the water in the pond and the rosebushes at Neauphle can talk, for they have an "inaudible" but certain life. She "feels," as young Emily says, "respect for these silent creatures whose uncertainty and outbursts may surpass my own."

Her reading always revolves around these secret subjects whose burning cores lie beyond boundaries that lead their authors and texts into hallucinated, threatening zones: Dickinson, Pascal, Rousseau, James, and Musil who, with *The Man without Qualities*, provided the impetus for her to open up the story of her childhood, the singular love affair with the little brother which she ends up analyzing in work after work, suspecting the fatal, overwhelming influence it wields. This is the autobiographical revelation in which she writes *Agatha* in 1981, out of this existential necessity, as if in order to unburden herself, opening everyone's eyes to this stupefying story of

absolute, eternal happiness. "We are in the domain of incestu-
ous love," she says in Montreal, "in other words, the essential."

Duras's life gradually perforates her work, giving it new perspectives, opening forgotten, shaded areas, revealing buried
images. It is laden with the places she loves, those of her childhood, the Dordogne region in southwestern France, the exotic
lands, and especially the archetypal seaside villa, the vacation
villa, and confessions of desire for another person, the brother,
the "clandestine," undying other.

Never had the work come so close to the obscure depths of
Duras's accursed life. Now she realizes that she will never love
anyone as much as the little brother, "little Paulo," who is
present in her dreams, in her comas, for whom she shed so
many tears, even banging her head against the walls when she
learned of his death.

And since it will never be fulfilled, she will give vent to this
"never-ending love" through the "intercession" of others, thus
experiencing "the love she cannot have."

She immediately turns it into a film, which is released on
7 October 1981, featuring Bulle Ogier and Yann Andréa.
Nonetheless, she is convinced that the picture will add nothing to the text, certain that the words themselves are the bearers of the main images, the most penetrating, the greatest,
clearest reflections of the signs and traces of this love. But to
give the role to Yann Andréa is also to "delegate" to him this
image of the little brother, for the very nonfulfillment of their
love enables her to approach this ultimate story.

To love Yann Andréa is to go on loving the little brother,
retaining his trace through the strangeness of this sentiment
and its difficult culmination, experiencing the ordinary cycle
of desire and pleasure, then desire again, knowing the absence
of comfortable certitudes, close to pain and joy at the same
time.

Y. A. also consummates love, as she says, "with others,"
men, "handsome men" whom he chases "from hill to hill."

But between them exists something inexplicable and elusive, which is in fact love, since it keeps both of them in this
place where, always brushing against death, there is a love that

"can never be realized" but is nonetheless realized before their meeting.

She is always waiting, watching, ready to let writing harness everything that murmurs inside her, in "the dangerous state" in which she dwells, ever since her first books, now growing as if the times were becoming more hostile, more intense. Weighing heavily upon her is the threat of alcohol, against which she can offer no resistance, as if it were invading her entire being, breaking through the dams, allowing death to come through the very gaps she opened. She drinks heavily, as does Yann Andréa who, in *M. D.*, published a year later, brings their story up to date, the most implacable confession imaginable, whose dry, almost detached sentences reveal how they were slowly drawn into the abyss. He tells of stalking death, agony-filled gestures, the gradual process of destruction, the incipient disabling of the mind and the miserable physical decay, the trembling, the groping, the transformation of Les Roches Noires into a dark, funereal arena where death bustles about, while the beach goes on bathing in the sea beneath the golden Normandy light, indifferent to it all.

Y. A. decides that they should leave Trouville and go back to Neauphle, where the fall has spared a few remaining roses, but she can no longer see anything; "the feeling that the end is near hovers constantly over Neauphle," confides Michèle Manceaux, a faithful friend. It's as though Duras were abandoned, to herself, to the very impotence of her situation; she is up to five liters of wine per day, says Manceaux. "She couldn't stop shaking, she couldn't walk without using the furniture to prop herself up. The danger was aggravated by senility, embolism, and rupture of the liver." She has always lived like that, as if her desperate state were but another trial in this life she has given to writing. For loving and drinking are a means of knowing, of arriving at a better understanding of this dizzying black hole she is in fact slipping into at this very moment.

And yet she still writes when wine, like a terrible destiny, leaves her a bit of time, an hour, maybe two, and when it gives none, she turns her dazed, absent eyes toward the windows, looking out into the park, at something no doubt invisible, for she can no longer see the dying rosebushes, the foliage gorged with the summer's light. Such is the state in which she writes *The Malady of Death*, which she wants to finish nonetheless; with the sudden brutality of writing that now demands to be heard, despite the wine, miraculously appeased, as if alcohol were leaving this moment for her to finish the story, the book, she recovers her violence, her lucidity, and she dictates as Yann Andréa sets down the words, slipping naturally into that fluidity, that life current suddenly passing through her, carrying her far away.

Finally, she decides to get treatment for her alcoholism. She knows that it will be terrifying, and that she could die from it. Here begins the real story of M. D., Yann Andréa's narrative, in this wild rage to save her, in this implacable acknowledgement of the pain and the waiting that keeps him torn between rue Saint-Benoît and the American hospital where she now lies in room 2327.

It seems that from this point on there is no longer anyone but the two of them; Antelme, Mascolo, and her son Jean leave messages, but the story being played out is theirs alone, a tale of love in which death demands its share in the most absolute, barbaric fashion. To make Duras laugh, and she does, Michèle Manceaux called them "The Thénardiers." So here now lie the Thénardiers, the "hobos" as Duras said, in the chic, padded silence of the American hospital, in the scandal-free, meticulously clean town of Neuilly, whose light falling on the avenue in this month of October nonetheless brings to mind that of the Nightship, silent, leaden, sometimes streaked with yellow rays.

She says, adds Michèle Manceaux, that the hallways in the American hospital resemble an ocean liner's gangways, and that if she were making a film about a boat, she would use these corridors. Everything is a blur; she is on this ship of her life that carries her ruthlessly, forever on the swell of a dangerous, inevitable sea. But the vessel reveals its secrets to her, and she was on board when she understood that the hospital's passageways are gangways, just as she knew that the Paris rain on the

Bois de Boulogne could be the monsoon rain over the distant Ganges. For there lies the essential, in the filming of the rain to reveal the secret of the lands of exile, without having to go there in order to create the illusion of reality. As for her, she resists. The days go by, and the idea of death, of knowing that she is now almost dead, the deliberate awareness that she could die, fades, but she raves, and then sleeps for hours.

Days, weeks pass, with relapses, new anxiety, fears that she will lose her memory, remaining permanently damaged. In the words of Michèle Manceaux, she is "a little bundle."

There is really only one thing she holds on to through the impenetrable darkness, through sleepless hospital nights, as Y. A. notes: "Between you and the rest: writing."

"Alone, before God, following an obvious, tirelessly repeated order, you write."

She worries about her rings, which she has entrusted to the hospital staff, her emerald rings that she is so attached to, asking whether they might not have been stolen. She feels surrounded by enemies, she needs to get away; in her delirium, she is afraid of the "lami," the little imaginary creatures who are knitting underneath her bed, she thinks she sees agents of the Gestapo. She cries out, according to the story told by Y. A., the sole witness: "Why me?"

And then it is the end of November, and she returns to Paris, a fragile little body with the threat of wine still hanging over her head, in the dangerous state that will never end.

Yann Andréa takes her out for walks in the city. The fall slowly comes to an end, shedding its golden light over the Place des Vosges and the banks of the Seine where they walk. She remembers Neuilly, talks about it regularly, and wants to remember everything that happened there. The galley proofs of The Malady of Death arrive—an "intangible" book, one that is impossible to strike off the map.

She returns to life with the furious energy that resuscitates her each time. She listens to music, Y. A.'s favorite music, Beethoven's Diabelli Variations, that other stream of writing she has always been fond of, the only means of intercepting desires, movements of the soul in flight. She recovers her sensitivity to smells, to the fragrances of spices, especially tea, which she drinks "more for its bitterness . . . than for its flavor."

It is exactly as if she were a lay mystic who, not yet called by her God, had returned to the profane world, to the pain of life, to its loneliness, its brutality, accepting in spite of everything its challenge along with its desire.

The autobiographical process accelerates, as if the eighties had opened the crevice through which life can now pour, bringing to light the founding childhood events carried along for so many years in the dark night of the fictional world. In September 1982, shortly before receiving treatment, she also publishes *Savannah Bay*. Before leaving for the hospital she wants to finish *The Malady of Death* and see to the final preparations so that the play can be staged. She is anxious to know whether Madeleine Renaud and Bulle Ogier are free, since they are the actors she had in mind while writing it.

The magical land of Siam returns in the play where waiting is so intense, that which precedes death, and where the old woman, in order to pass the time that separates her from it, and in spite of "the decaying of memory," tries to reconstruct the story of her past, to find a ray of light in the "inaccessible, unfathomable" place where the Nightship rolls in vain.

She still wants to preserve this personal narrative in the archives of writing, thus acknowledging this human existence whose pulse she took so early, in order to measure its loneliness, whose pain was like a heavy weight.

Since Y. A.'s arrival in her life she has produced a whole series of books, mostly thin volumes though extremely dense with violence, in which she tries to express all of the fascination she feels for this man, who is making her understand that perhaps heterosexuality is not "the sole criterion of passion and desire." In his company she discovers new mechanisms for gaining access to love, living with him in the complete absence of sexuality, but acutely aware of the blazing continent, the tempting abyss, and the miraculous moments when the storm dies down, and all is quiet.

Each book is therefore a further attempt to prevent this difficulty from "causing more pain," so that it might be subdued, and lived out in the very plenitude of love.

She thus filmed *The Atlantic Man* in the lobby of Les Roches Noires in 1981, defying cinema, since it begins on a darkened screen, while a voice directs the man, "played" by Y. A., describing how he slowly evolves, telling what happened here only recently: his leaving and Duras's terror all mixed together, then tragic isolation once more, solitude like that resulting from the loss of the little brother. For Yann Andréa goes away, often threatens to leave, fleeing as if he himself couldn't stand the tension of this exasperated love, the burden of her presence, so strong, so obsessive, this crushing weight of a Grandmother, a Seer, one of the Damned.

Nineteen eighty-two finds her once more in Italy, where she films *Dialogue de Rome*, whose premiere in France is 4 May 1983. She offers a Fellini-style meditation on the city, composed of a dialogue between offstage voices, and accompanied by silent pictures of Rome and vicinity. Not once is the Piazza Navona described for its own sake, like a tourist sight, nor the stelae crowned with busts of emperors, for the voices relate the story of a dead love, perhaps that of the two people talking. It is Duras and Yann Andréa, and they also evoke Titus and Berenice, who was forced into exile by order of the Senate. Through this interlacing of themes, through the Beethoven sonata that slips in insidiously, through the emergence of memories, the film gradually becomes a veritable poem, as if the shifting play of her camera would help her attain the mysterious undulations of things and creatures, the extreme fluidity of time.

By staging *Savannah Bay* herself she delves further into her origins, a subject that only she can understand. For a long time she entrusted her plays to others but, never satisfied, she prefers to breathe her own rhythm and music into it. Claude Régy, who was the inevitable director of her plays and who many believed to be the only person capable of expressing Duras's silence and her throbbing passion, didn't succeed in revealing them completely. Too intellectual, freezing his actors in an immobile stance which in turn made Duras "a bore," he wasn't always able to render the spontaneity of her language, the extreme simplicity of her stories, and the "fluent" emotion that runs through them. Consequently, stating that no one else dares to go to the heart of her text's meaning, she recovers the legendary energy, the strength that allows her to reach the exact point of her own truth.

She now applies to the theater what she had previously said about the cinema: "Scarcely anything is ever played in the theater," she says in Savannah Bay, and she confirms this in an interview with Le Matin: "It is said: It isn't played. Racine is not played, not playable. Language provides the only access to it. While the language is taking place, what is there to be played?"

Thus she exhausts the possibilities of language and her unsuspected scenic and dramatic abilities which she brings out on the stage. Words are omnipresent, refusing to let dramatic effects subject them or hide them. She directs in a climate of uncertainty, as when she writes, and admits that she doesn't know where she is going, where her hand will lead her, onto what unknown continent.

As with her first attempts at theater, Le Shaga and "Yes," peut-être, she refuses to give the actors a finished script; the writing continues to evolve during rehearsals, and to attend them is to observe creation in progress, to understand what writing is made of, in that continually renewed, imprecise, tentative back-and-forth motion, returning again and again to the tapestry of words, finally arriving at the burning heart of the story she wants to reach at all costs, but whose staging remains obscure, unplayable.

The same can be said of Racine, for whom language is the self-sufficient expression of drama. An entire play emerges from the conflicting alexandrines, and it uses them to capture the current, the melodious song that must be tamed and delivered to the audience.

One of the major scenic elements in Savannah Bay is the refrain by Edith Piaf, who "vocalizes against death," using her rasping, mournful voice to keep alive memories of Madeleine, mixed together "in permanent disorder."

It is still the same quest for the absolute minimum, the essential.

During those years, 1982 and 1983, she faithfully follows the progress of the socialist government. What she credits it with more than anything else is its attentiveness to the world, its total political commitment to what she calls "the blunt facts: hunger, misery, working conditions"—everything that the right, deprived of its intelligence, fails to see, as if she recognized in the left this visionary tendency, this talent for listening to people, for making them more human, perhaps. She feels "pride" for François Mitterrand, she says, for his stubbornness, for his fidelity to the values of his youth, for his controlled passion, his intelligence, his inability to conceive of "France as private property."

Meanwhile she continues to suffer from life's pain. Antelme is suddenly afflicted with a brain disease that leaves him hemiplegic. In 1983 he is taken to La Salpêtrière hospital and then to Les Invalides veterans' hospital a mere year after retiring from Gallimard where, for nearly thirty years, he had been one of those most actively, most attentively, involved in the prestigious Pléiade series, always sensitive to great writers and texts, giving freely of his time to authors, reading manuscripts, a devoted servant to the literary cause.

Crippled by the disease, he still has "his intelligence, but his memory is partially destroyed," according to his friend François Mitterrand. "The first time I went to see him," adds the French president, "he smiled when he saw me. At the time of my visit, he wasn't able to speak yet . . . a few small words . . . So I spoke to him, about everything, about nothing—you know the little game one plays in such cases, carrying on as if the situation were completely normal. He listened, and you could see by the way his mouth moved that it even amused him. But was he there? Could he locate the events I was evoking in place, in time? I don't think so."

This new "source of pain" revives Duras's suffering, perhaps bringing her closer to Antelme, propelling her further into the realm of the invisible. Death is always prowling around her, haunting her memory and its places, restoring her terrifying vitality, that untamable, continually renewed energy.

12

In the Heart of Durasia

As if bound by the "autobiographical pact" she seems to have signed with *L'Eté 80*, in this self-affirmation, and in her relationship with Yann Andréa, she begins writing *The Lover*, which will be published in July 1984.

She returns to the themes that continue to pursue her, the spicey aromas, the swarming din of the Saigon streets, the terrible family that revealed to her the archaic forces within her and passed on to her its savagery and its murderous instincts. The entire text revolves around the affair she carried on for more than a year with the young Chinese man who, like Monsieur Jo in *The Sea Wall*, came to pick her up in a sports car and gave her a diamond.

Like a stretto, a musical passage in which all of a symphony's themes come together, she mixes into the narrative memories of that sentimental education and the one her mother gave her, as well as everything that followed: the buried secrets, the wells in her memory whose waters will nonetheless spring forth, nourishing her work for dozens of years, shaping it, making it tremble like the quaking earth, straightening the fractures—in other words, the books.

She intones an obsessive plainsong to describe the tragic knot tying her to the primitive knowledge she has always possessed, even during childhood, and "since nobody can make us change memories," she writes *The Lover*, a new version, new light thrown on the complete body of her earlier work.

The book's success is immediate, as if the public, frustrated for so long, would finally know, penetrate the author's intimacy, satisfy its curiosity.

But Duras's successes are always based on the "public's failure to understand," as she says of *Hiroshima Mon Amour*. Indeed nothing is more consistent with Durassian aesthetics than *The Lover*; nothing is less chronological, further from the vulgarity of biography, the visible thread of events.

The book offers an illusory truth characterized by incoherence, that of real life, with vaguely established connections crackling and throwing lightning bolts into the language, finally obscuring completely what seemed clear. Duras resolutely breaks the pact; "the story of my life doesn't exist"; that life is in this sensual, fragmentary approach to things, in this fluid, detached apprehension of people.

"To write about love is to confront the chaos of language: that panic-stricken region where language is both too much and too little," writes Roland Barthes in his *Fragments of a Lover's Discourse*.

Duras feels her way through that region of the unutterable, which she considers to be the only region of her life, mixing together imaginary and real time, phantasms and old photographs, going from I to she, the little girl, she, the young lady, the child.

Her life returns from that perforated, gaping region into which she delves in unutterable emptiness, trying to give a shape to her existence. What she says in *The Lover* is what she sees in life, the free play of "more or less profound correspondences between time periods," and she is determined to let these forces act, without intervening. "The challenge of writing," she says in *Le Nouvel observateur*, referring to *The Lover*, "is to go back each day to the gradually developing book, to come to terms with the Book."

Henceforth her narrative technique is a far cry from current trends; she becomes a sort of phantom conducting its own search for the fugitive phantoms of the past, giving her narrative "the foglike density" seen by Michel Foucault in Lonsdale's rendition of Duras. She writes, as he says, this time in *Les Cahiers Renaud-Barrault*, "in the dimension of memory, a memory completely purified of all recollections, now merely a kind of fog, perpetually reflecting memory, a memory superimposed on another memory, with each new memory erasing every recollection, in a perpetual renewal."

Misunderstanding nonetheless prevails, and the book's title suggests indiscretion, lurid confessions, continues to arouse passions and desires, and becomes popular, attracting "audiences it wasn't intended for" (Pierre Nora). Duras triumphs, for she demonstrates the diverse readability of texts, the multiple levels of understanding that texts must possess in order to attain universality. She appears on the *Apostrophes* television show on 28 September 1984, at the height of a media blitz. She had always refused to take part in this kind of program which, she claimed, cheapened literature, thus siding with Julien Green, René Char, and Henri Michaux. But in one of her frequent reversals, she agrees to participate, provided the program is devoted entirely to her, magnifying, glorifying her appearance. She sports the "Duras look," a turtleneck, a black sweater-vest, rings on her fingers, and bracelets on her wrists. Her face resembles that of Rembrandt's mother, with its fine latticework of wrinkles, both devastating and beautiful. She seems self-assured, punctuating the silence with her measured remarks. Her attitude confounds the host, who believes what she said previously, on different occasions, believes her legend, *The Eden Cinema*—but in her inimitable, somewhat sly tone of voice, smiling, she says that the story is elsewhere, spanning other times, other currents.

She speaks openly of alcoholism, with painful authenticity, of literature, of its secret goal, of other writers, and of their positions (Sartre, she repeats, is not a writer), of everything that feeds the stream of language and cannot be determined ahead of time, but must be tamed, explored, exhumed, offering itself tentatively, all of the materials she has worked with, still works with, and above all, of what she herself is and cannot escape.

The book goes through several printings; its success is so

great that Minuit can hardly satisfy the demand for restocking. Now a candidate for the Goncourt prize, thirty-four years after *The Sea Wall*, thirty-four years and some fifty works later, whether they be novels, plays, or films, she seems to stand a good chance of receiving it, but nobody in the literary establishment really believes it, convinced that the Academy, some of whose choices have already been questioned, won't crown such a prestigious writer, going against the very spirit of the award, which is intended for younger authors.

After three rounds of deliberations she receives six votes out of ten, which shows that she is not chosen unanimously. The Academy crowns an entire oeuvre rather than a book, revealing to the general public a literary figure who for too many years had been rejected and repudiated.

She who had denounced the intrigues and the awards systems ever since her resignation from the Medicis committee now accepts the honor. Some of her admirers would have preferred that she refuse, as Sartre did the Nobel Prize, carrying to its logical conclusion the spirit of scandal that defines her, but she doesn't comply. Perhaps exhausted by so many years of labor, by the immense efforts she has always made so that her work would be recognized by the general public, and perhaps secretly flattered at being finally considered an institution, she assumes the contradiction. She is no dupe, however, and in an interview six years later with *Les Inrockuptibles* she declares, in her usual abrupt manner, "Two hundred and fifty-thousand copies of the book had been sold when I received that boys' prize. There were some committee members who were crying out of despair that evening. All because a woman had won the Goncourt, I suppose."

The book's sales figures catapult her to number one on the best-seller lists for several weeks, pulverizing all previous records: over a million copies, without counting book club editions and translations. In spite of a few discordant voices—from those who find the language too loose, the subject too diffuse, and the syntax faulty—most French critics applaud the book. Claude Roy, Denis Roche, François Nourissier, Pierre Assouline, and Hervé Lemasson speak of the work's enchantment, the delight it produces, the musical score that unfolds and glides from theme to theme, framing her whole story, attempting to immobilize it in a photo album, but to no avail, as if the images were slipping out of the trap, the grave, moving away, into the forever uncompleted space of writing. Americans, perhaps, recognizing in Duras's language the rhythms of their own literature, in particular a narrative technique similar to Hemingway's, awarded her the coveted Ritz Paris Hemingway prize two seasons later, in 1986. She accepts it all the more gratefully since she identifies to a certan extent with the lost generation of the twenties, and she takes advantage of the opportunity to thank American universities for having been the first to study her fiction, to invite her to speak, and to accord her a position of major importance in French literature.

Movie directors are still interested in her work, for, laden with images, it lends itself well to cinematic adaptation. Jean-Jacques Annaud, who directed *La Guerre du Feu* and *The Bear*, buys the film rights and, after numerous trials and tribulations, it is shot in Vietnam, coming to the screen in Paris at the beginning of 1992.

But does the success of *The Lover* give Duras a permanent place in the highly coveted group of best-selling writers? Her subsequent books don't meet with the same acclaim, thus disproving the assertion that she had intentionally sought out an audience, and showing that her writing made no attempt at pandering or commercial manipulation.

Many of her first-time readers, those for example who buy the Goncourt selection as a matter of course, were disappointed. The complexity of her networks, her apparently detached way of saying things, the sometimes excessive brutality or the brilliance of her telescopic style discouraged them to the point of closing the novel without finishing it, while Duras returned to the status of an exile temporarily brought back to the human community by a single book.

Fortified nonetheless by her success, she continues her journey to the center of her mythical past, taking with her on this obscure adventure the notebooks left in the blue armoires at

Neauphle-le-Château. She rereads them, without remembering having written in them, and she knows that therein lies, as if trapped, the terrible moments of the Nazi terror, the camps, the deportation and the return of Robert Antelme. And now she wants to return that time to literature, giving it the sacred intensity in which she, Duras, becomes the very allegory of pain, and Antelme that of rebirth, of the strength of life against all odds. For since 1983, he is again ill and in the hospital; but all she can do for him now is to bring that narrative, *The War*, to the surface of language, trying to find words for it in order to understand it better, to "know," as she often says, "bearing witness to the fundamental horror of our time," even if in the eyes of many of her readers this testimony contains something indecent, which she willingly accepts.

Again repudiating autobiography, or giving it a very personal meaning, she tangles the threads of reality: Robert Antleme becomes Robert L., a name that she insists on using until her conversation with François Mitterrand on this subject, on 26 February 1986. In *The War* she says that "he wrote a book about what he thinks he went through in Germany," thus weakening the link between fiction and real life, reducing the factual and universal scope of *The Human Race*. In this conflictual relationship with her ex-husband, it is exactly as though her writing could only take place through the concealment of others, as if the savagery of her language depended on this abolition of historical truth—indeed, as though she had to commit that murder, observe that silence, in order for the text to weigh anchor, freed of all known references, tossed about by the winds of her imagination, fleeing to the kingdom of myth.

In *The War*, Duras imposes a sad rhythm that propels her to the bottom of the abyss in which her works always dwell; what she calls "the uniformity of pain, the repetition of the days, the poverty of language" is described in tragic tones, like one of Racine's recitatives. New readers discover her militancy, the "criminal instinct" she is endowed with, the dynamic, permanent core of her art.

Critics mistake for theatrics—how can one leave such expressionist manuscripts in "a regularly flooded house," they ask—what is in fact the very secret of Durassian writing, the tapestry she began weaving long ago, the currents of desire she jotted down so quickly amid the brutal flow of words, still too ephemeral to be literature, like notes taken while on vacation, only to be rediscovered and molded into the texts of *Savannah Bay* and *The Eden Cinema*.

If she tells about her desire for Ter the Gestapo agent, it is not out of a predilection for scandal, as she is accused of, but because literature itself is a scandal. There is thus something indispensable about such truth, such desire "capable of anything," even loving a traitor at the height of the purge, for this feeling dominates her, and she can no more resist it than she can the urge to kill and torture Germans and collaborators, since the object of writing dwells in that inevitability, her destination.

Her life has always taken place in these temporal juxtapositions, passing through pockets of oblivion and resisting memory, going against the factual order of time: "I have no story, I have no life," she keeps proclaiming. The only brutalizing force she sees is the present, in which she burns, where the fragments of life shatter like meteorites, before becoming reburied, then springing forth anew amid the greatest chaos imaginable. She doesn't believe in well-oiled biographies, as if they could ever describe the inner reality of true life, the obscure play of desires, wonders, and terrors: "They set off at the beginning of a life and, following the rails of events, wars, changes of address, marriages, they come down to the present," she says, deploring such logic.

The only unity she can claim in her life is "this awareness of death that resembles me, or the love for this man or my child." Beyond that, there are only unfulfilled needs, absences, cavities that in her view "house a life's founding secrets, and that explode from time to time upon the unrelenting insistence of writing."

Amid the frantic activity of this work, seemingly impossible to capture as it turns around like a hand-rattle, digs furiously, drills so deep that Duras loses her own identity, drowning in the impossibility of knowing, destroying herself, what can really be said about this life? What happens to this memory once it has departed or become fluid, vacant, ungraspable, impossible to organize? Could it be a mere odyssey aboard the ship rolling above unfathomable depths, an odyssey on a black sea, letting its "keel burst" once and for all, as on Rimbaud's boat, and yearning to go to sea the way one goes to meet death?

Could it be that there is nothing left in its hold but vague images and fragrances, those of smoked fish sold in back alleys, sweet and sour nuoc-mâm sauce, the slime flooding over the sea walls, its surface laden with dead, water-swollen crabs that have drowned in the rice pools, and the stink of the tide mixed with the stagnant waters of the estuary in the chemical-filled air of the Antifer plant, the monumental petroleum complex near Le Havre, where billowing clouds of nauseating smoke pay tribute to industrialized society, the neon lights, the nuclear reactors, the steelworks, everything without which life would be this void Duras yearns for, as free, as pure as the clear sky in a Boudin painting, rinsed by the ocean air?

In *Summer Rain*, she has Ernesto say: "All the lives were the same, except for the children's. We didn't know anything about the children."

Duras's life is in this trajectory, as if she believed in a return to childhood, always subject to "obscure, unstated modifications."

She has that habit of continually going back to her past work, injecting it with new blood, giving it a new, different configuration, for the true story of her life will emerge from this unwearying task of unraveling and rethreading. Thus she decides to stage a second version of *La Musica* at the Théâtre Renaud-Barrault du Rond-Point in February-March 1985, with Sami Frey and Miou-Miou replacing Claire Deluca and René Erouk, the original cast members in 1965. She directs the play, faithfully carrying out her meticulous task, based on intuitions, listening, and the patience to let the text act, letting it speak, modifying or increasing the volume of silence, making it resound even more than the little melody of pauses and confessions, and all the remnants of the soul gathered together in the main lobby of the provincial hotel serving as a meeting place for the man and the woman who once formed a couple.

The reviews are mixed, as if Duras's acclaim in the media produced an unconscious backlash of disparagement and sarcasm. The author's freedom, exercised over so many years at the cost of great loneliness, deprived of public recognition, her habit of moving ahead in her work and her life without worrying about others, exhibiting what they see as unforgivable narcissism, and her social conduct as a whole hardly instill indulgence and love in critics. The old "enemies" of the past who spared her no sarcasm, temporarily reduced to silence by the extent of her success, start in again, returning to their intrigues and their unjust remarks. Jean-Jacques Gautier especially speaks of the "evil genius" that supposedly led her to produce *La Musica*. "It seems as if she were trying to do a poor imitation of Claude Régy," he says, going on to deplore the lack of inspiration compared with the first *La Musica*.

It is the period when, as if intoxicated by the impact of *The Lover*, she is certain that "a current is passing through her." For, as she confides to Michèle Manceaux, she has always known millennial secrets that are filtered down to her via mysterious genetic channels, magnetic bursts that she cannot contain. Her fate resembles that of those naïve little Catholic saints who were similarly visited by voices uttering uncontrollable, brutally affirmative certitudes. The journal she kept during the summer of 1980 gave her the desire to express herself in this fluent voice, seizing the echoes, the sudden impulses, and the fragments of passing time.

She has an opinion on every subject, writing pieces for *Libération*, for *L'Autre journal*, and granting long radio interviews. In July 1985, she thus publishes an explosive, prophetic article on Christine Villemin, accused of having killed her own son, Gregory. Fascinated by murder, as her entire work demonstrates, she insists on testing her intuition by conducting an investigation at the scene of the tragedy, penetrating "the materiality of the matter," the dense Vosges region in northeastern France, approaching the house, a new dwelling with no garden, surrounded by fir trees and dark, blue-green rivers.

Serge July, editor-in-chief of the newspaper, aware of the danger of such an article in the middle of a preliminary investigation, warns his readers in an insert meant to resituate Duras's text in a writer's perspective that "imagining reality in the search for a truth that is certainly not *the* truth is a truth nonetheless, that of the written text." But for Duras, that writer's truth is the truth of prophetic utterances during biblical times, and she is sure of what she "sees," in a kind of lucidity escaping mere facts, invisible to the journalist and which she reveals, strengthened by the "genius" she claims to possess, her means of access to a superior reality.

Yes, Christine Villemin, "sublime, naturally sublime Christine V.," the "woman of the barren hills," is a tragic heroine, and the murder she is alleged to have committed thus represents vengeance for the murder committed against her, against all women, isolated at "the bottom of the earth," amid the "darkness" so that "they will remain as they used to be," in the millennial night of bondage to men.

The article causes a scandal even though it comes out in the summer, when everyone is on vacation. Duras is denied the right to express herself, to influence a court of law, substituting her judgment for theirs, setting herself up as a pythoness, going to extremes, and taking advantage of her fame.

She pays no mind to the scandal, ignores the gibes, the sarcasm, the insults, confident that she "possesses the universal within herself."

As if success had freed her of fear, she wants to talk "about everything, about things in general," while carrying on her own writing task—"everything, including myself." She carefully chooses those who interview her, or the newspapers that publish her articles, becoming a public witness of the times, opening up singular channels, always making unexpected, inappropriate comments. Political events always draw a reaction from her: the independence movement in New Caledonia,

French hostages in Lebanon, Gorbachev and perestroika, Greenpeace and the Rainbow Warrior affair. . . .

As she says on a television program, one of a series broadcast from 26 June to 17 July 1988, "There's no difference between what I say in interviews and what I write in general." In her media appearances she exhibits a degree of extravagance and passion that situates her at the epicenter of literature. Her writings of this period, whether in book or article form, reflect her haste, her primitive savagery, her rage for knowledge and for life. She remains faithful to writing through her shortcuts, her confrontational way of thinking, and her uncontrolled rhetoric.

Her five interviews with the French president, from February to May 1986 and published in *L'Autre journal*, serve as perfect illustrations. Free from all self-censorship or that of others, comforted by her longstanding friendship with François Mitterrand, she discusses the most diverse problems with him, from Parisian parking problems to the Third World, from the Resistance to the spirit of the earth, from Le Pen—the extreme right-wing politician, whom she finds repugnant, "the garbage can of France"—to Isak Dinesen, whom she calls "the Gothic princess" of Kenya. Truth, confidence, and simplicity flow from her words. Wherever she is, she is forever in this state of abrupt, absolute naïveté, carrying her analyses onto new, uncharted ground.

Her last cinematic experience takes place with two co-authors, her own son Jean Mascolo and Jean-Marc Turine. The film, entitled *Les Enfants*, comes out on 29 May 1985, but it is clouded over with obscure production problems: "Here I am, as if I had fallen out of a garbage can," she says. It develops the embryo of a narrative published in the form of a children's book, *Ah! Ernesto*, and it in turn serves as the basis for *Summer Rain*, appearing in 1990.

Production conditions leave her so bitter that she returns to the solitude of book writing, to responsibility for the fluid persona whose rhythms and murmurs she perceives clearly. For her, "cinema is rotten to the core," she states in July 1985 in *Les Cahiers du cinéma*.

Her work continues along the same path of exchanges and bridges from one text to another, one genre to another. She had been told the story of Ernesto, the little boy who "doesn't want to go to school because they teach me things I don't know." Ernesto is from a poor family, and didn't even want to learn how to read, or anything else, for that matter.

And she makes a film about him, thanks to the French Ministry of Culture, using golden-voiced actresses and actors Tatiana Moukhine, Daniel Gélin, André Dussolier, Pierre Arditi, Axel Bogouslavski, Martine Chevallier, and her faithful cameraman Bruno Nuytten.

Like a farcical version of a Ionesco or a Beckett play, it expresses once more the leitmotif of her entire philosophy: feeling precedes knowledge. In a comical mode, she insists on the anteriority of emotional experience with respect to mental processes, leading her characters into poetry, the absurd, irrationality.

The cadence of her life is patterned after the very rhythm of her books, the "gulag" in which she forces herself to write, to "obliterate, to replace," to take up again the more and more tenuous, frayed thread of her work.

With *The Slut of the Normandy Coast*, published in December 1986, followed by *Blue Eyes, Black Hair* in February 1987, she reaches the apogee of this new genre she now aspires to, in which life and legend are mixed, fiction and reality are entwined. As she explains in *Emily L.*, published the same year: "I don't think it is our story that I am writing. Four years later, it can no longer be the same one. . . . No. . . . What I am writing now is something different into which it fits, losing its identity, perhaps something far greater."

What she is trying to write, to insert into the story told there, is Yann Andréa, to whom the book is dedicated; she wants to "find that man," and inscribe his secret in her text. The genesis of *Blue Eyes* is painful, taking place amid Yann Andréa's cries and howls, amid the suffering that accompanies love, and "hatred of the female body."

She summarizes the book in a few words: "I am eighteen years old, I love a man who hates my desire, my body." She dictates the text to him; he can't stand it, so "he yells at her." Such is the savagery in which the text is produced, a climate that allows it to penetrate the indescribable core of the relations binding them together, the impossible yet palpable, tangible, truly existing love.

She delves into the mystery of homosexuality, which she claims is common to all men, that "illegal" challenge. In the pages of *The Slut of the Normandy Coast* and *Blue Eyes, Black Hair*, she shows this love's oscillation between life and writing, between the unbearable pain and the happiness it procures. That is how she writes, in an "indecent, scandalous" manner.

The boundary between her personal life and what she reveals of it in the book is so hard to define that they finally become indistinguishible, blending together in the writing, the only true center of Duras's vitality. She infuses the book with her suffering "during the terrible summer of 1986," that of her own body, denied by the man she loves, "an impossible story" but also a "possible story" because it is based on actual experiences rerouted for the purpose while remaining in the domain of love.

This unimaginable quality is what she wants to transcribe, her experience with this man who would go off "in every direction, . . . looking for handsome men, big barmen from foreign lands, Argentina or Cuba," returning at night, "happy," to sit with her contemplating the sea.

"Legend or true story," she never stops playing hide and seek with the two terms, adding book after book to the elaboration of this other, more authentic, more sincere self, trying to expose in broad daylight this "absolute photograph" she has been seeking for so long and that would avoid conventional postures, recapturing the entire person.

She now spends more time in Trouville, abandoning Neauphle and Paris, as if the closeness of the sea provided her with new resources, leaving her even more "open to the notion of God." She likes the mild summer days, the yellow light that casts its glow upon the beach, the sand, and the rocks at Les Roches Noires, and the miraculous, throbbing moments stolen from death, too valuable to be wasted. She also loves Yann Andréa's reappearances, their complicity, the walks they often take around Honfleur and Quillebeuf, along the road bordering the estuary, with its marshy fields and its half-timbered mansions lying in isolated, deep green prairies.

Only with great difficulty does she recover from the health problems she had in 1985, having "lost her reason" as a result of the emphysema that prevented the irrigation of her brain, bringing back her usual delirium filled with returning Nazis, the enemies who have always obsessed her, thieves coming to steal her rings, vicious animals invading her room, her space, and finally, the Jews.

In Trouville she rediscovers the rhythm of her writing, and the familiar changeable sea brings to her mind the inflections of the soul, while the boundless expanse of sand when the tide goes out reminds her of the renewed power of words, and of their grave.

13

"The Splendor of Age"

What she wants is "to have a book under way," filling up time, opening out onto the unknown, for life would be empty without writing. She lives constantly in this rush, this unrelenting insistence that weaves the book into a net bursting with the day, its light, love, and children.

With Jérôme Beaujour, a friend of her son, she compiles and publishes in 1987 a book entitled *Practicalities*, consisting of miscellaneous comments and variations on familiar subjects, inescapable questions about her self. As the project takes shape, she abandons the questions and themes chosen by her interlocutor, imposing her own interrogation. Refuting all peremptory, definitive logic, she remains faithful to her usual position: "I went off on my own," she says, "finding the real answers to unasked questions."

She embroiders the affirmations made in *Le Camion*, talks about whatever she wants, the things she cares most about, writers, writing, the Book, Trouville and rue Saint-Benoît, herself and Vinh Long, Hanoi and Yann Andréa, how she composes her texts, from which the words pour out, "going public."

Various unexpected aspects of her personality emerge, her qualities and accomplishments, her obsessions, her fears, her apprehensions. The text represents the assumption of a truth humbly expressed in everyday words, spontaneously, liberated from any concern about their meaning. She divulges little secrets, recipes for life, fugitive thoughts unimpeded by ideological constraints.

The images she projects of herself often contradict those she has already disclosed in her novels. The reader catches her at ordinary, familiar moments, talking about household tasks; as elsewhere, in *The War*, in the Lol Stein or the Yann Andréa cycle, something confines her to the fatal shores of tragedy and death. Her friends are surprised at this mixture of qualities. Michèle Manceaux thus relates how, paying her an unexpected visit one day in Paris, she finds her sewing a sweater vest that she planned to wear as a member of the presidential party on a trip to the United States. In her suitcase are her clothes, rolled up as her mother used to do; she had echoed the millenary gestures of ancestral women, peasant know-how.

After the book's publication, she often tells how it came about, describing the dizzying state in which it was written. She always talks about this abandonment of outside life, and her total participation in the text, to the point of servitude and suffering. Thus she writes *Emily L.* in an emotional trance, as if after Lol Stein, Emily had become "her sister, her next of kin," resembling her in every way.

Yann Andréa has left again, "gone forever," as usual; she hardly eats or sleeps now, even telling Jean-Luc Godard that she thinks she is going to die, and she writes the elliptical story of Captain de Quillebeuf and his wife, joining it to her life with Y. A. *Emily L.* is the book that takes shape before one's very eyes, like the flowering of Proust's work, or the little paper dahlias he admired as a child when, spread out in aquariums, they would turn into vast, floating, surrealistic flowers.

The book unfolds as one reads, it, without her knowing where she is going, interrupting the solitude of each summer day to give the pages she has written to her Minuit editor's daughter, Irène Lindon, who types them and returns them to her the next day.

She brings face to face this perfect pair of drunks and the impossible twosome composed of herself and Yann Andréa, and gradually, as if the story forced her to do so, she begins the search for this English couple's secret as a way of seeking out her own: "Then I have to operate on the book. Open it, cut into it, folding in a third story, that of Emily L. That's the only way I can make the book a living thing, keep it alive."

Then one night she discovers that Emily L.'s secret is that she writes, carrying along with her the "strength of pain" attached to writing, the secret that was destroyed by the Captain when he burned the absolute poem, killing it, so to speak.

Through the Quillebeuf couple, she tries to understand this "young man she loves," this love he bears for her and whose true nature she cannot perceive, for it is an "elusive," unavowable, "gradually unfolding" story.

The autobiographical facts emerge: "What we prefer is to write books about each other," culminating here in the first-person narrative constantly running up against the story of Emily L., until the two of them are indistinguishable. Meanwhile, the days grow mild with the beginning of summer, as the orchards in the Norman woodland become heavy with sap, but there remains the threat of Korean tourist groups with their terrifying, anonymous faces, and she wakes up in the middle of the night, trembling, to go knock on Y. A.'s bedroom door.

The book was not well received—quite the contrary—and Duras talks about an "assassination," which caused her pain comparable to that resulting from the death of her first child. Still dwelling within her is this idea that her books and she herself can never emerge in broad daylight, doomed to remain underground, "hidden behind walls."

She becomes ill again. For the last few years she has been living off her ups and downs, as if each book were one more sacrifice in a long string of wounds painfully inflicted upon her.

The French television channel TF1 devotes a four-hour series to her that is filmed in February-March 1988, receiving mixed reviews. She appears as she really is, with slow passages and moments of silence unedited, leaving intact confessions uttered in a whisper, perceptible only to those who have long known her work. Luce Perrot, the journalist who was to question her, is gradually reduced to the role of silent witness as Duras surreptitiously occupies the space of the interview, like the waters of the Seine imperceptibly entering the sea.

She reads a great deal, effectively using her voice as the vehicle for the secrets continually brought back from her dark night. "A certain breed of critics," as she calls them, threatening and hostile to her for so many years, sneers and depicts it as a parody. It seems that she is no longer taken seriously, having been discredited by public appearances in which she expressed unpopular, controversial ideas. She describes herself as a Reaganite, announces that she likes the popular game shows on French channel 5, as well as television movies, entering into discussions with soccer star Michel Platini, talking at length about pop singer Johnny Hallyday, analyzing events according to unorthodox, makeshift logic. . . .

Many feel that she is a mere caricature of herself, claiming that she is cheating, but "that cheating," she says, "is the sincerest expression of myself."

The height of satire is reached when Patrick Rambaud, a former *Actuel* magazine reporter, writes a pastiche of *Emily L.* for Balland in the spring of 1988, calling it *Virginie Q.* and signing it Marguerite Duraille,* complete with a cover imitating Minuit's, abundant verbal mannerisms and stereotypical exoticism, and so on.

All of this is followed by sarcastic articles in the major dailies on "Madame Marguerite, . . . the burst windbag" (*Le Figaro magazine*), "Marguerite Du Rable," "Miss Dourasse" (*L'Evénement du jeudi*), "Queen Margot," "La Maguy de Saint-Germain" (*Le Monde*). . . .

Duras's very personality "exasperates," as Patrick Rambaud announces to L'Agence France Presse: "She is incapable of minding her own business, always sticking her nose into everything. There is an urgent need to make fun of her. Like Roland Barthes, hers is the art of enshrining trite comments in golden shells. It's baroque." Equating her with the seventeenth-century précieuse Mlle de Scudéry, few people see that her

---

*Duras + déraille = Duras, the raving lunatic.—TRANS. note

absolute, scandalous shamelessness is part of an attempt to understand the world and herself, part of the tragic force encircling and isolating her, the "unflagging hope" that never leaves her alone.

Then illness unleashes its forces on her again, taking her far away this time, from October 1988 to June 1989, so far that everyone expects her to die. She enters a deep, five-month-long coma, with her blood pressure dangerously low. In newspaper offices her obituary is ready, along with other eulogies, awaiting announcement of her death. She is in that silent, padded, comatose state where "echoes of war and colonial occupation" are heard nonetheless, and scenes of rape and agony keep her awake, though lost in a dream.

She is caught in the moment of Passage inside the narrow tunnel of death. In her hospital room, she is silent, deaf to the sounds made by others, worn out by the life she has led, the alcoholism, tobacco, emphysema, and her characteristic self-neglect, refusing to coddle herself, always living on the edge, burning up with passion in impossible situations.

Since she often thrashes around in her bed, the nurses have tied her down, but the mind goes on, rushing forward, plunging into wild, brutal, life-stirring activities. The medical staff says her case is hopeless, but with noble perseverance they apply "relentless therapeutics." And the miracle happens.

She finally wakes up one day. None of the doctors could have predicted that moment when the patient would emerge from her dark night, and find the way back to life, to daylight, to resume her Journey.

With her usual enthusiasm, she searches for signs to mythify this return, so that her life will continue to display this epical, legendary quality. In Beijing, students revolt against a closed-minded system, burning their rulers in effigy, occupying the city, defying the tanks. In her eyes, this is a wonderful moment to be reborn.

The ordeal has left her physically broken, weak, shriveled up, indelibly marked by age. Her throat, pierced by a cannula, is awkwardly hidden by a scarf, but she is indifferent to its ungainliness.

During her convalescence she can often be seen walking around on Yann Andréa's arm, in the suburbs of Malakoff or Vitry-sur-Seine, mingling with the ethnic mosaic of the inhabitants in whose company she finds happiness and joy. Her face is appallingly heavy with illness, but aside from the fatigue it remains the same as when she was eighteen years old, "wide open, extenuated, ringed in advance by time and events." It is thought unlikely that she will survive without serious side effects from the coma, preventing her from writing again. But her secret energy burns from within, breathing life into her, opening her up to the brutality of the written word wildly springing forth. She grants interviews to nearly everyone, but a few months later, as if to rid herself of the ordeal, banishing death, she relates in detail the nature of the deep coma, tying in her explanations with the larger questions of being, the cosmos, and the flight of the soul, eternity, and the mysterious trajectory of life.

Her rebirth is a surprise that has a quieting effect on some hostile critics and revives others. In his *Carnets*, published in January 1989, Philippe Sollers declares: "Duras, the poor thing. She claims to have dreamt of North Africans beating up a Fascist on a train. Her mother used to beat her. She tells about an election night when some fellow came up and started masturbating against her. . . . The president, she adds, finds her irresistible. Well-integrated theatrics. Disintegrating theatrics." Hatred is combined with gratuitous insolence when young Jérôme Leroy, whose first novel, *L'Orange de Malte*, also appears in 1989, portrays himself as the heir to Roger Nimier, a justification for sharpening his claws on Duras: "On his way out, he ran into Marguerite Duras. . . . She was pushing a shopping cart, probably coming back from Monoprix discount store. Everyone lives in the setting they deserve. . . . It is easy," he continues, "to make fun of a great writer when you are a little jerk who is incapable of writing a novel. But in fact he was not convinced that Marguerite Duras was a great writer."

Before her deep coma, before she crosses the "forbidden line" where the soul rediscovers windlike mobility, the lightness of the first days of the world, she begins writing *Summer Rain*, based on dialogues from *Les Enfants*, filmed five years earlier. To return to them is to talk again of the mad love she has always felt for the needy, the "overflowing children" of the suburbs, the have-nots, victims of great injustice and of the unending tyranny of man over man, of millionaires like Bouygues the construction magnate, in what has become her obsession, the innocence and the unknowing nature of children.

She loves these poor people, dispossessed and splendid, who live in this new suburban environment where some are "black, slightly black, very black, and others white, not quite white, or almost white," in this "well-developed mixture" that makes her want to write, and to remain faithful to the utopian Marxism she still professes. After her illness she will go to Vitry fifteen times or more with Yann Andréa, disappearing among the modern buildings, in this heterogeneous space, this "scattered New York City," but always sorrowful, vigilant. As she walks she hears what must be Ernesto's voice, for she rejoins him in his thirst for knowledge and the inner life that animates him, the boy who refuses to learn, isn't interested in knowing how to read and yet understands the great mysteries of the world like Ecclesiastes. Like the kings of Israel, he is in possession of these absolute certitudes originating in the depths of the world, "that silent region that confers its own kind of intelligence."

She emerges from the coma and has Ernesto convey her own revelation:

"I have seen everything that is done under the sun. . . .

"I have seen.

"I have seen that all is vanity and a striving after wind.

"I have seen that what is crooked cannot be made straight.

"I have seen that what is lacking cannot be numbered."

Summer Rain shows how far the subject has carried her since the little children's book published in 1971. Nearly twenty years later, she grafts new material onto this story, now layered with pain, suffering, fear of death, the loneliness of hospital rooms, deserted, aseptic gangways where patients hang on for dear life, taking a few careful steps. The more attentive she is to Ernesto, the more of a religious meaning she gives to her story, as if the two of them combined, the burned woman who has seen so many ordeals, and the immensely learned twelve-year-old child, were joined together in "the field that belongs to God" to keep the already burned Book from falling into the hands of greedy "monsters." This is the text of her origins, the one she has always been looking for, lost in the cruel wake of the Nightship.

There will be other books after *Summer Rain*, but this one is written in a kind of newfound clarity, the freshness of life reconquered through so much love.

She shares Jeanne's love for her brother Ernesto. She is both Jeanne and Ernesto, just as she and the little brother were one and the same person: "She had waited for him to awaken. That was the night they made love. Motionlessly; without a single kiss; in complete silence."

Jeanne asks Ernesto to sing "A la claire fontaine": "I have loved you for a long time, I will never forget you." No, she would never forget the softness of the brother's arms when he used to help her cross the turbulent current in the *racs*, or the broken voices of the deportees, they too singing "A la claire fontaine" as they lay huddled in tarp-covered trucks, for they were forbidden by the Germans from singing "La Marseillaise." She could never forget Antelme's story, Antelme whom she loves in the secret depths of being, incomparable Antelme, whose humanity was denied him by the S.S.—"Alle Scheisse," "You are all shit"—while he stubbornly asserted his place in the human race, thwarting the diabolical plan for biological muta-tion that would allow them to negate his existence. Incompa-rable Antelme, humming "A la claire fontaine" on lonely prison camp roads, recalling the words from his childhood, "on the highest branch sang a nightingale, sing nightingale, sing if your heart is happy."

Summer Rain is that blessing from childhood, that manna, that wind falling and vaporizing the air, restoring a taste for "the adoration of life," in the knowledge of that tragic life—

"one of these days everyone would be separated from everyone else, forever. . . . that was life, that's right, only life, nothing else"—but at the same time in the clear-sighted apprenticeship of its true meaning, this knowledge decanted from the sorrows of society, from ruses and appearances, the secrets revealed amid the light of the burned Book and brought to life in "dazzling glare."

As usual, the publication of her book causes a stir. Critics cry out with joy or insults, admiring or deploring her efforts, but from now on the public sees her differently, with a benevolence she hasn't been accustomed to. They approve of her courage to speak out, "telling it like it is." She again claims to be indifferent to what others think of her work. "The ringed media monster," as Jacques-Pierre Amette calls her in *Le Point*, doesn't listen, but simply works, "manages"; she is "imperial, grandiloquent, cunning, petty, blind, inspired too, and ardent," "immersed," continues Amette, "in this immense sea that engulfs her books."

There remains the wonder of the Book, the Work, the only road leading anywhere, "the future in motion, at once visible, unpredictable, and undefinable." This is the mystery belonging only to children, to the obscure functioning and intimate knowledge of the womb's darkness, the dark, silent biological trajectories, like the planets rolling quietly around the earth, according to laws never to be explained by anyone.

In the soft Norman light where she now spends long months, she is always listening to "this hard-earned springtime" appearing after so much violence. Remaining attentive to the blending of water and sand, to the foghorns calling out on the horizon, crossing the wide expanse of the sea, she is calmer and yet at work, "alert to the book," no matter what happens to the rest of the world. Pain resists, like a pocket of sorrow refusing to disappear, remembering when Antelme dies on 26 October 1990, at seventy-three, the husband held in such high esteem, too high perhaps, he who was her moral reference, the author of the absolute Book, *The Human Race*.

But as if writing were her only proof of life, she plunges into another text, conceived, she says, in pure happiness, the same sort of joy and grace that keeps her alive. Yann Andréa, when asked about her by neighbors he meets in the vast lobby or on the sidewalk in front of Les Roches Noires as he returns from errands, explains that she is surprisingly well, writing incessantly about the lover, still and always about the lover. Indeed she is hardly ever seen outside, completely tied as she is to the risk of this essential writing, "in the very place," she says, "where I share nothing. Where I cannot share. I can't take on anything but myself for fear of missing the incoming tide."

And yet it is the end of the summer and she remains indoors, enjoying neither the gentle Normandy sun, nor the sea breeze, off in "the steady monsoon rain," forever "in the flood expanses of the rice paddies," moving along the trails that lead to the sea wall, in Prey Nop.

She again writes the story of the lover, over and over, for only by returning to it incessantly can she explain the birth of the book, the absolute secrets of writing.

The confinement continues, but now it is imposed by the madly loved native land, the key to everything, "war, hunger, the dead, books, politics, communism," in a word, life.

Is it only because director Jean-Jacques Annaud is working over there on the very ground of her childhood that she feels thus called to tell once more about her magical Asia? Can we read Annaud's failure in the cinematic cues inserted into *The North China Lover* before the movie even came out, in an effort to reconstruct the elusive thread of her life?

The book she is writing, and which she will end up calling *The North China Lover*, takes her once again to the Mekong, "leading her toward the river," "the village of junks" exploding with cries and song, laments and peals of laughter.

The splendor of this book, this night-crossing of the dense forest, consists in reinventing and bringing to the surface of language, exposing to the light of day, buried yet untouched traces of the memory in search of another memory, "a memory upon memory," as Claude Mauriac had already said in 1975. It is as if all the fractures, every chaotic moment of her life, were joined together in the book, in a moving stream of "juxtaposed conversations." Each day that she lives requires her to lift up, to excavate ever deeper, more rapidly shifting, more fluid "layers" lying "ready" to be raised to the status of books. Thus she sees the book being born in these images kept intact, protected against time, but which, one day, inevitably demand their assumption, their accession to the Book, in her eyes the only repository of life.

Her life can now be put into the nutshell of this "indecisive country of childhood," this far-off fantasy land, this "sort of distant China," where the mother sits enthroned like a queen, at the heart of this "kingdom" of "tropical Flanders," abandoned to the fate of this "family of convicts." The lover returns, like the older brother Pierre, already ruined at nineteen, consumed by opium and viciousness, and Paulo, the little brother, "my fiancé . . . my child," revered "as if he were sacred." Everything now points to the fact that the book, still prowling around this childhood, unleashes painful, haunting confessions held back for too many years. The secret of her life, shouted out for the whole world to hear in *The North China Lover*, centers on the "little brother, different" from others, loved in the body's pitch blackness, in the irresistible suffering of desire. The fundamental, primal scene finally emerges. It is the end of the book, nearly the moment of departure. She has left the Chinese man whom she will never see again. Going home, entering the decaying house devastated by bankers, she becomes slowly infused with the agony of this family. She entices Paulo into the bathroom. She undresses, lies down with him, and tells him what to do. "When he cried out, she covered his face with her body so that the mother wouldn't hear the tragic cry of his pleasure.

"That was the one and only time they ever made love to each other."

Duras's miracle consists in rendering the freshness of this childhood in spite of its violent chaos. Not a single aspect of her reconstruction proceeds from typical novelistic skill in a narrative that flows smoothly as it unwinds, leaving everything intact.

The smells, the fragrances bring back memories, as the book (the novel?) steeps in the bland waters of the Mekong, the sweet, spicy odors of the floating markets, in the cluster of junks.

The film bug keeps gnawing at her with the same tenacity, even after her return from the journey "beyond death." She remains faithful to her instinctive method, the technical fluency and innocence that she inaugurated with *Destroy, She Said*. The forthcoming appearance of *The Lover*, directed by Jean-Jacques Annaud, produced by Claude Berri, and feverishly awaited by the press, leaves her indifferent and mockingly skeptical of his ability to create a successful rendition of the work. She denounces the excessive cost of the production, the expectations of commercial cinema, and its constraints: "I think the actress who was chosen is too pretty. In my book, I noted: 'If the little girl is too pretty she won't look at anything, she will let other people look at her.' It's not Annaud I am worried about, it's the inherent limits of film," she says in an interview with *Le Monde* on 13 June 1991.

And yet she gave away the film rights to *The Lover* as casually as those to *The Sea Wall*, *Moderato*, and *The Sailor from Gibraltar*, as if the work, once written, no longer belonged to her, but had gone off someplace where other people, her readers, led it, or perhaps returned to the secret darkness from which she, Duras, had rescued it.

That is why in *The North China Lover* she makes the traditional stakes of her writing intermingle, "theater, text, film," in other words, utterance, music, and memory. Unwinding in the text are the images of the movie to be made from *The Lover*, what can only be seen through her eyes, "the villages of junks. Night . . . the rattle of the old tramways . . . the scene out on the street and then a view from inside the room."

These traces, these echoes having nothing to do with the action are what she lingers over, unlike commercial filmmakers. She always dwells in the violence of destruction, and of youth: "What I would really like," she declares, "are 'accidental' films. Three or four of us would just go out in the street, calling the people in at the last minute, and then we would film. What's needed is a kind of cinema commando."

Judging from her press interviews for *The North China Lover*, she seems to be endowed with her eternal energy, and strengthened by her lifelong devotion to her work. She talks about her texts as if they were a colony of images surrounding her: "That's what narcissism is," she says.

The disagreement between her and Annaud is precisely over the question of her life. The bridges she has built between her real life and her imagined life have given rise to a legend in which she now situates herself, and on which she lives. Each piece of writing is a "translation" of her life, never to be taken literally.

Her life runs up against the phantasmic screen she has allowed to slip between herself and her works, to the point of forgetting everyday life, relayed by the specters of her childhood and native land.

The North China Lover is very well received, a far cry from the remake that critics feared. The narrative is something new, telling a different, smoother version of her elemental life story. In *Le Figaro magazine*, François Nourissier thus opportunely redefines a "true writer" as one who "goes back over old themes, hammering out the words, plunging into several enormously haunting memories"; he who had previously admired *The Lover* now celebrates this "long poem of desire and despair," reducing the entire oeuvre to a single register, that of song.

In the interviews she grants, as if she wanted to avoid all confusion between Annaud's much-awaited film and her own book, she adopts the provocative tone that age has done nothing to weaken, in spite of her serene "splendor." "If I granted the rights," she says, "it was for the money."

Fearing that *The Lover* would be misinterpreted, she inserted cues into *The North China Lover* in the event that another film would be made. She feels dispossessed of her own story, since Annaud works in great secrecy. Notwithstanding the producer's claims to the contrary, she maintains that not one picture, not one interview, not a single press conference, nor even photographs of the actors were made available to her. As a matter of fact, the filming took place on a closed set. Everything, especially the size of the budget, contradicts her conception of cinematic art as being open, poor, spontaneous, exposed to outside influences. The eternal debate between Duras and the adapters of her novels!

The new book is one of the best-selling works of the season, and she shows obvious delight in promoting it, remaining attentive to articles that appear, hostile toward those whose criticism she judges unfounded, always revealing the highest degree of understanding when she agrees to talk about it. Her interview with Bernard Rapp on the *Caractères* television program is exceptional in this respect, rivaling her famous appearance on *Apostrophes*. But this time, a different kind of charm overtakes her, as if, henceforth detached from everything but still possessing that consummate art of rhetoric, she had merely to utter certain words, or to let silence speak in order for the magic to operate. The gasping respiration caused by the prosthesis stuck in her throat leaves the way open for unknown breaths, exposes the physiological alternation of life itself. And in the paroxysm of that utterance, she reaffirms everything that possesses her and has possessed her, everything that sums up in a few minutes an entire life's work: passion, the mother, Indochina, the little brother, the Jews.

The camera shows her residence in Neauphle where the interview takes place at the very beginning of the summer. The house is covered with ivy and Virginia creeper full of the season's first sap. A close-up shamelessly reveals Duras's face furrowed by networks of wrinkles running in every direction. But her eyes are full of vivaciousness and the confidence of miraculous, newfound youth.

The summer of 1991 follows others she has spent in Paris, in Neauphle-le-Château, in Trouville, alone or with friends, in love or hopelessly distraught, but always in the exhiliration of the Book to come, another text that will better express the Journey.

In Trouville, where she will surely go, she will taste the

solitude of the old hotel and the briny air. Since she doesn't venture out so much anymore, apart from the ritual of her afternoon walk with Yann Andréa, she will still look out at the sea, her favorite companion, noticing the movement of the tides, the slowly rising water, and the gray light scarcely distinguishable from the groundswells. In the distance, on her left, there are still the hideous-looking Deauville marinas, and on her right, even further away, but easily identifiable by the factories' tall smokestacks, is the Antifer plant, Le Havre's industrial zone, with its huge tanks bearing the names of Esso and BP oil compainies, visible on a clear day.

But what she will watch most intently is the sea, that force drawing her into its grasp, infinity off on the horizon, the whys and the wherefores that she merely feels and moves closer to each day, this intuition from God that she carries within her, in spite of herself, and which can only be expressed with great difficulty.

Her life goes on, obscure and limpid at the same time, in its tragic murmur and its joyful music, perforated with pain, recalling paintings by Nicolas de Staël in which the colors are muffled and drawn into hazy vortices, riddled like her throat, with its cannula scarcely hidden by her eternal chiffon scarf, night blue or leopard-patterned.

There seems to be no end to this story of a life, subject to the hazards, but also to the fatality of time, for the trapdoors of her writing call for new images, withhold sustenance for new books, project eternity, and irrigate unborn memories.

Meanwhile, she wanders through the labyrinth of the written word, through the muted, violent matter that she brings to others in each work, like the beggar woman from her childhood, indifferent to her own life, but bearing all the world's misery, crossing the lands of Laos, Cambodia, radiant Siam, and Burma.

The only thing that really interests her, since she no longer has even the power to refuse it, is to follow, like the madwoman of Savannakhet, "the roads, the rails, the boats," everything that moves one forward, toward discovery and knowledge.

She dwells in that loss of self, always alone, crying out in the wilderness, "waiting for love," like another Emily L., seeking desperately to understand the nature of loneliness, and, like Pascal, to grasp the inexpressible murmurs of "infinite spaces." As always, "since her life began."

Epilogue

The years from 1992 to 1994 go by in the serene, peaceful
climate that writing creates for her; as always, vigilance with
time is a major preoccupation. In spite of her age and her renown, she is the object of scornful, violent remarks that little
affect her, although she wonders what causes such hatred.
Those who have heaped continual sarcasm on her, like Angelo
Rinaldi, critic for *L'Express*, Frédéric Pagès of *Le Canard
enchaîné*, or the author of a mediocre biography published in
February 1994, Frédérique Lebelley ("90 percent false," Duras
herself points out), refuse to hear what she keeps uttering in a
secret voice, not wanting to admit that, in the literary waste-
land that France has become, she is the greatest living author.
Outrageous, excessive polemics arise over her, and she follows
them attentively, but sometimes, weary of so much commotion, she prefers the isolation of writing, the only real engine
of her life. Her days are spent between Les Roches Noires,
where she performs her usual ritual, taking walks, going for
drives along the oceanfront or in the country with Yann
Andréa, and rue Saint-Benoît. She likes her room there, where
she makes phone calls, writes, sleeps, seeks help from the
breathing device lying on a table nearby: this is her "jungle,"
she says. The walls have retained vestiges of years past, pinned-
up photographs, prints, and letters. The floor is strewn with
piles of books and papers, while her desk and other furniture

are covered with manuscripts and writings she composes in response to requests from friends. Near her bed, there is an enlarged photograph of the Chinese lover, whose eyes withhold a solemn beauty, that of youth frozen in its tracks, almost suspended. No resemblance to the lover in Jean-Jacques Annaud's film, with his Hollywood-style good looks. She says that she talks to him whenever she passes by the portrait, and that she has never left him.

As she advances into the secret of time, sounding it out through her books and her very existence, she herself seems to have entered the Duras legend. Her own words, "if it is written, it must be true," slip naturally into the story told in her works, "the place that cannot be described." In spite of the cannula piercing her throat like a stigma, the now familiar sound of the little valve throbbing when she speaks, in spite of her gasping, she has kept the youthfulness that buoys her: she greets her visitors in a playful tone, a Poulbot cap on her head, a bandanna around her neck, eyes wide open, in tune with the most current evens, and still true to communism, as though such faith were a source of renewal, a fountain of strength. These days she is more willing to talk to others. She grants long television interviews that resemble pieces out of a Duras anthology, and they are appreciated by a wide audience, not merely her faithful "happy few" from the *Vice-Consul* years. Her voice is so distinctive in conservative France that it is a gust of fresh air, a new rhythm of breathing. The era of French Prime Minister Edouard Balladur appears obscenely demagogic and dull to her. What she expects of political figures is poetic perception and inspiration capable of stirring the people, putting the nation back on its feet. That is why she is sympathetic to men like Bernard Tapie, whose political persecution she sees precisely as a criterion of truth. Increasingly, however, she gives herself over to writing, eventually assuming it as an identity, with an impudence that disturbs professional writers of literature and criticism, whose attachment to the "prison house" of the written word, and to "the wonderful sorrow," is less intense.

In 1993 she publishes *Ecrire*, and it too is a triumph: it sells more than two hundred thousand copies in a few months, for a collection of apparently heterogeneous texts, "the bottom of the barrel," according to some critics, but a reaffirmation of the writing adventure, a story shrouded in darkness. For this book she gives in to the pressure of the bookstore near her apartment, Le Divan, when its owner asks her to do a public signing, a ritual she hadn't performed for twenty years. It is a great success: a thousand books are sold in two hours, a line extends onto rue Bonaparte, and she could go on selling all night, but the air becomes unbreathable for her and she returns to her "jungle."

Yann Andréa is still with her. When asked, she repeats that he "is good to her, he takes care of her, always reminds her to take her medication," but one senses an absence, a frustration in her. A pain wells up, and suddenly she has lost her strength, she is tired, old, while at the same time she has strangely regained a childlike quality.

Using her personal language, she reaffirms her "theory" of writing in *Ecrire*. One must use the word carefully, always in quotes, for no part of her wants to theorize, preferring instead to accept the fatality of the written word and the sacred, liturgical mystery that makes her a mystic in spite of herself—a convinced atheist, as she continually asserts in order to avoid any misunderstanding. And yet she never stops talking about God, the Bible, Ecclesiastes. *Ecrire* thus tells the story of that adventure. Its tone reflects the simplicity of the obvious, a transparent quality free of all alexandrine subtlety, all affectation.

It follows the strange progression of the act of writing, a mystery she herself is not totally capable of elucidating. When talking with friends in her apartment, she often mentions the "foreign" road of writing—referring to the absence of an outline—along which she allows herself be guided by the words, for they alone create meaning and coherence. "I think that's what I generally find wrong with books, the fact that they have no freedom of movement. It shows in the writing: it is manufactured, organized, regulated, made to conform, it seems. . . . The writer thus becomes his own cop." Unwearyingly, the book delves further and further into the night. The word resurfaces time and again, almost obsessively, and soon it is inseparable from silence, the main explanation for everything. She says she wants to recapture that era, that of silence. The works written nowadays, she feels, are "day books, travel stories, simple pastimes. But not books that become ingrained in the mind and convey the black mourning of an entire life."

She is thus governed by no plan as she heads into unknown matter, giving free rein to herself in a "condemnation" that she accepts. This letting go, this restoration of the self as the centerpiece of writing, brings upon her the scorn of certain critics and many contemporary writers. She claims not to care: such people are the authors of "charming books that lead nowhere, are incapable of penetrating the darkness, can never capture silence. In other words, they produce 'authorless' texts."

She never loses the prophetic violence that makes her sound more and more like an oracle, which is unbearable to the mediocre, "small-minded literary world," as the Goncourt brothers called it in the nineteenth century. But the story of the fly in Ecrire is what reveals the scope of her entire oeuvre. The observation and the subject explored, seemingly trivial, take on a metaphysical, hermeneutical importance that in turn reveals Duras's sole preoccupation, her interrogation of death, the threshold. Whether it be man or fly, it is always the same distress. There is in fact no difference between the death throes of a human being and a fly's writhing as it buzzes desperately against a windowpane, sensing the approach of death. Her text unfolds, taking such a violent turn that the reader feels a lump in his throat: "I can still see that fly on the white wall, dying. First in the sunlight, and then in the dark, refracted light of the tiled floor. One can also stop writing and forget about the fly, or just watch it. To see how it too struggled in a terrible, programmed struggle, caught in an unknown sky of nothingness." She is sure of the appropriateness of the text, that what it says is perfectly tuned, for she knows that she touches on the most essential things by telling about the death of the fly. Michelle Porte, who was present at the time, couldn't stop laughing about it later after she had read the book. Duras won't forgive her for this laughter. She quarrels with her, refuses to talk to her again. There is this intransigence within her, and it never softens, even for the most minor, socially unimportant things.

Her work continues in various forms; cinema still fascinates her. In 1994 she wants to do a filmed portrait of Bulle Ogier, her favorite actress, in an attempt to grasp the most minute movements of her respiration. The long-announced book, *Le Monde extérieur*, is finally published by P.O.L. It resumes the exercise at which she excels, her "fluent" view of the world, of the emptiness and the plenitude of life, the "medley" which, beneath banal appearances, suddenly expresses an acuity, an art of naked observation, of cleanly drawn sketches that make these texts veritable moral treatises, after the manner of Saint-Simon.

Throughout the world, "Duras weeks" are organized, furnishing proof of the author's widespread influence. In London, in Caracas, as far away as the Andes, graduate students and professors meet to discuss the meaning of her art, trying to discover its secrets. The first international colloquium took place at Cerisy-la-Salle, shrine of French culture, and perhaps its resting place. Scholars of all stripes spent seven days delving into these works, unlike any other literary productions. In France, however, such expressions of interest and sympathy are not unanimously appreciated; some people even find them annoying. Many disapprove of Duras's consecration; she fails to measure up to Angelo Rinaldi's discriminating taste, and in *L'Express* he refers to the "destruction of the critical sense among our contemporaries," dismissing her writing as singsong and incantation. In her short biography, Frédérique Lebelley is unable to conceal her hatred for her subject, stating abruptly: "The life of a star is a continual struggle against her own weight. For a long time she finds sufficient resources to keep from finding herself unbearable. But the fight is hopeless: sooner or later, the forces of gravity win out. And the star caves in on herself."

Nonetheless, critics have no praise for what might be considered an iconoclastic approach. Frédérique Lebelley is drawn into the very violence for which Duras is known ("Madame Duras," as Angelo Rinaldi scornfully calls her). What numerous members of the French intelligentsia would prefer is to muzzle Duras, to keep her quiet. Her freedom, too scandalous, is a nuisance, for it makes others' mediocre behavior stand out, along with their pettiness and their impotence.

But against all odds, Duras continues to make the front page. Newspapers sell on account of her interviews, and publishers get rich from her works. She is familiar with that universality, she endures it as a form of "banality": "I am banality," she says. "The triumph of banality. Like the old lady in *Le Camion*."

From her "jungle," having lived eighty years in spite of alcoholism, a coma, respiratory difficulties, she is more concerned with this urgency of writing that keeps calling out to her than with her renown. She is curious about everything, but especially about the "unknown" of the written word: "the unknown inside of oneself, in one's head, one's body." She remains devoted to writing, which "arrives like the wind. . . . It is naked, mere ink, writing, and it passes by like nothing else in life, nothing except life itself."

Bibliography

[Two modifications have been made to Vircondelet's original bibliography: books that have been translated into English are noted in brackets, and the first section has been updated to include Duras's most recent publications. — Publisher's Note.]

1. Works by Marguerite Duras

Les Impudents. Novel. Plon, 1943.

La Vie tranquille. Novel. Gallimard, 1944.

La Barrage contre le Pacifique. Novel. Gallimard, 1950. [*The Sea Wall*. Trans. Herma Briffault. New York: Pelligrini & Cudahy, 1953.]

Le Marin de Gibraltar. Novel. Gallimard, 1952. [*The Sailor from Gibraltar*. Trans. Barbara Bray. New York: Grove, 1967.]

Les Petits chevaux de Tarquinia. Novel. Gallimard, 1953. [*The Little Horses of Tarquinia*. Trans. Peter DuBerg. London: Calder, 1960.]

Des Journées entières dans les arbres. Stories. Gallimard, 1954. [*Whole Days in the Trees*. Trans. Anita Barrows. New York: Riverrun, 1984.]

Le Square. Novel. Gallimard, 1955. [*The Square*. Trans. Sonia Pitt-Rivers and Irina Morduch. In *Four Novels*. New York: Grove, 1965.]

Moderato cantabile. Novel. Minuit, 1958. [*Moderato Cantabile*. Trans. Richard Seaver. In *Four Novels*.]

Les Viaducs de Seine-et-Oise. Play. Gallimard, 1959. [*The Viaducts of Seine-et-Oise.* Trans. Barbara Bray and Sonia Orwell. In *Three Plays.* London: Calder & Boyars, 1967.]

Dix heures et demie du soir en été. Novel. Gallimard, 1960. [*10:30 on a Summer Night.* Trans. Anne Borchardt. In *Four Novels.*]

Hiroshima mon amour. Screenplay. Gallimard, 1960. [*Hiroshima Mon Amour.* Trans. Richard Seaver. New York: Grove, 1961.]

Une aussi longue absence. Screenplay (with Gérard Jarlot). Gallimard, 1961. [*Une Aussi Longue Absence.* Trans. Barbara Wright. In *Hiroshima Mon Amour and Une Aussi Longue Absence.* London: Calder & Boyars, 1966.]

L'après-midi de Monsieur Andesmas. Novel. Gallimard, 1962. [*The Afternoon of Mr. Andesmas.* Trans. Anne Borchardt. In *Four Novels.*]

Le ravissement de Lol V. Stein. Novel. Gallimard, 1964. [*The Ravishing of Lol Stein.* Trans. Richard Seaver. New York: Grove, 1966.]

Théâtre I: Les Eaux et forêts; Le Square; La Musica. Plays. Gallimard, 1965.

Le Vice-consul. Novel. Gallimard, 1965. [*The Vice-Consul.* Trans. Eileen Ellenbogen. London: Hamish Hamilton, 1967.]

La Musica. Film (with Paul Seban). 1966.

L'Amante anglaise. Novel. Gallimard, 1967. [*L'Amante Anglaise.* Trans. Barbara Bray. New York: Grove, 1968.]

L'Amante anglaise. Play. Cahiers du Théâtre national populaire, 1968.

Théâtre II: Suzanna Andler; Des Journées entières dans les arbres; "Yes," peut-être; Le Shaga; Un Homme est venu me voir. Plays. Gallimard, 1968.

Détruire, dit-elle. Novel. Minuit, 1969. [*Destroy, She Said.* Trans. Barbara Bray. New York: Grove, 1970.]

Détruire, dit-elle. Film. 1969.

Abahn, Sabana, David. Novel. Gallimard, 1970.

L'Amour. Novel. Gallimard, 1971.

Jaune le soleil. Film. 1971.

Nathalie Granger. Film. 1972.

India Song. Screenplay. Gallimard, 1973. [*India Song.* Trans. Barbara Bray. New York: Grove, 1967.]

La Femme du Gange. Film. 1973.

Nathalie Granger [and] *La Femme du Gange*. Screenplays. Gallimard, 1973.

Les Parleuses. Interviews with Xavière Gauthier. Minuit, 1974. [*Woman to Woman*. Trans. Katherine A. Jensen. Lincoln: University of Nebraska Press, 1987.]

India Song. Film. 1975.

Baxter, Vera Baxter. Film. 1976.

Son nom de Venise dans Calcutta désert. Film. 1976.

Des Journées entières dans les arbres. Film. 1976.

Le Camion. Film. 1977.

Le Camion [and] *Entretien avec Michelle Porte*. Screenplay and interview. Minuit, 1977.

Les Lieux de Marguerite Duras. Interviews with Michelle Porte. Minuit, 1977. ["The Places of Marguerite Duras." Trans. Edith Cohen. *Enclitic* 7.1 (1984): 54-61, and 7.2 (1984): 55-62.]

L'Eden Cinéma. Play. Mercure de France, 1977. [*The Eden Cinema*. Trans. Barbara Bray. In *L'Eden Cinéma*, version scénique. Actes Sud-Papiers, 1988.]

Le Navire-Night. Film. 1978.

Le Navire-Night et autres textes. Screenplays. Mercure de France, 1979.

Césarée. Film. 1979.

Les Mains négatives. Film. 1979.

Aurélia Steiner: Melbourne. Film. 1979.

Aurélia Steiner: Vancouver. Film. 1979.

Vera Baxter ou les plages de l'Atlantique. Screenplay. Albatros, 1980.

L'Homme assis dans le couloir. Novella. Minuit, 1980. [*The Man Sitting in the Corridor*. Trans. Barbara Bray. New York: Blue Moon, 1991.

L'Eté 80. Journalism. Minuit, 1980.

Les Yeux verts. Essays. Cahiers du cinéma, 1980. [*Green Eyes*. Trans. Carol Barko. New York: Columbia University Press, 1990.]

Agatha. Play. Minuit, 1981. [*Agatha and Savannah Bay*. Trans. Howard Limolli. Sausalito, CA: Post-Apollo Press, 1992.]

Agatha et les lectures illimitées. Film. 1981.

Outside: Papiers d'un jour. Journalism. Albin Michel, 1981; P.O.L., 1984. [*Outside: Selected Writings*. Trans. Arthur Goldhammer. Boston: Beacon, 1986.]

La Jeune fille et l'enfant. Cassette (adapted from *L'Eté 80* by Yann

Andréa, read by M.D.). Des Femmes, 1981.

Dialogue de Rome. Film. 1982.

L'Homme atlantique. Film. 1982.

L'Homme atlantique. Novella. Minuit, 1982. [*The Atlantic Man*. Trans. Alberto Manguel. In *Two by Duras*. Toronto: Coach House, 1993.]

Savannah Bay. Play. Minuit, 1982; augmented ed., 1983. [In *Agatha and Savannah Bay*.]

La Maladie de la mort. Novel. Minuit, 1982. [*The Malady of Death*. Trans. Barbara Bray. New York: Grove, 1986.]

Théâtre III: La Bête dans la jungle (adapted with James Lord from Henry James); *Les Papiers d'Aspern* (adapted with Robert Antelme from Henry James); *La Danse de mort* (adapted from August Strindberg). Gallimard, 1984.

L'Amant. Novel. Minuit, 1984. [*The Lover*. Trans. Barbara Bray. New York: Pantheon, 1985.]

La Douleur. Memoirs. P.O.L., 1985. [*The War: A Memoir*. Trans. Barbar Bray. New York: Pantheon, 1986.]

La Musica deuxième. Play. Miunuit, 1985.

La Mouette de Tchékhov. Play. Gallimard, 1985.

Les Enfants. Film, with Jean Mascolo and Jean-Marc Turine. 1985.

Les Yeux bleus cheveux noirs. Novel. Gallimard, 1986. [*Blue Eyes, Black Hair*. Trans. Barbara Bray. New York: Pantheon, 1987.

La Pute de la côte normande. Essay. Minuit, 1986. [*The Slut of the Normandy Coast*. Trans. Alberto Manguel. In *Two by Duras*.]

La Vie matérielle. Essays. P.O.L., 1987. [*Practicalities*. Trans. Barbara Bray. New York: Grove Weidenfeld, 1990.]

Emily L. Novel. Minuit, 1987. [*Emily L.* Trans. Barbara Bray. New York: Pantheon, 1989.]

La Pluie d'été. Novel. P.O.L., 1990. [*Summer Rain*. Trans. Barbara Bray. New York: Scribner's, 1992.]

L'Amant de la Chine du nord. Novel. Gallimard, 1991. [*The North China Lover*. Trans. Leigh Hafrey. New York: New Press, 1992.]

Yann Andréa Steiner. Memoir. P.O.L., 1992. [*Yann Andrea Steiner*. Trans. Barbara Bray. New York: Scribner's, 1993.]

Ecrire. Essays. Gallimard, 1993.

Le Monde extérieur: Outside 2. Journalism. P.O.L., 1993.

2. Principal Works Devoted to Marguerite Duras

Alleins, Madeleine. *Marguerite Duras, médium du réel.* L'Age d'homme, 1984.

Andréa, Yann. *M.D.* Minuit, 1983.

Armel, Aliette. *Marguerite Duras et l'autobiographie.* Castor astral, 1990.

Bajomée, Danièle. *Duras ou la Douleur.* Éditions universitaires, 1990.

Bessière, Jean. *Moderato cantabile.* [Critical edition.] Bordas, 1972.

Borgomano, Madeleine. *L'Écriture filmique de Marguerite Duras.* Albatros, 1985.

———. *Une lecture des fantasmes.* Éditions du Cistre, Petit-Roeulx, Belgium, 1985.

Calle-Gruber, Mireille. "Pourquoi n'a-t-on plus peur de Marguerite Duras?" *Littérature* 63 (October 1986).

Fernandès, Marie-Pierre. *Travailler avec Duras: La Musica deuxième.* Gallimard, 1986.

Lise-Bernheim, Nicole. *Marguerite Duras tourne un film.* Albatros, 1981.

Marini, Marcelle. *Territoires du féminin.* Minuit, 1978.

Mertens, Pierre. *L'Agent double.* Complexe, 1989.

Micciollo, Henri. *Moderato cantibile de Marguerite Duras.* Hachette, 1978.

Seylaz, Jean-Luc. *Les Romans de Marguerite Duras. Essai sur une thématique de la durée.* Minard, 1963.

Tison-Braun, Micheline. *Marguerite Duras.* Rodopi, 1985.

Vircondelet, Alain. *Marguerite Duras ou le temps de détruire.* Seghers, 1972.

3. Festschrifts, Special Issues, Important Broadcasts

Tu n'as rien vu à Hiroshima. Éditions de l'institut de sociologie de l'université de Bruxelles, 1962.

Cahiers Renaud-Barrault 52 (December 1965).

L'Archibras 2, le surréalisme (October 1967).

Ça/Cinéma. Albatros, 1975.

Cahiers Renaud-Barrault 89 (October 1975).

Cahiers Renaud-Barrault 91 (May 1976).

"Les Lieux de Marguerite Duras." Michelle Porte, I.N.A. (May 1976).

Marguerite Duras. Albatros, 1979. [*Duras by Duras.* Trans. Nancy J. Peters and Amy Scholder, et al. San Francisco: City Lights, 1987.]

Le Magazine littéraire 158 (March 1980).

Marguerite Duras à Montréal. Montreal: Spirale, 1981.

Oeuvres cinématographiques. Éditions Vidéocritique, ministère des Relations extérieurex, 1983.

Cahiers Renaud-Barrault 106 (September 1983).

"Savannah Bay, c'est toi." Michelle Porte, I.N.A. (1984).

Apostrophes. Berbard Pivot, Antenne 2 (28 September 1984).

L'Arc 98 (1985).

Ecrire, dit-elle. Imaginaires de Marguerite Duras. Université de Bruxelles, 1985.

Revue des sciences humaines 202 (1986).

Entretiens de Marguerite Duras avec François Mitterand. In *L'Autre journal* 1, 2, 3, 4, 11.

Les Nuits magnétiques. Alain Veinstein, France-Culture (1987).

"Duras/Godard." J.-D. Verhaeghe, Océaniques-FR3 (1987).

"Marguerite Duras." Luce Perrot, TF1 (26 June-17 July 1988).

Les Nuits magnétiques. Alain Veinstein, France-Culture (1989).

Le Magazine littéraire 278 (June 1990).

Les Nuits magnétiques. Alain Veinstein, France-Culture, 1990.

Caractères. Bernard Rapp, Antenne 2 (5 July 1991).

Le Cercle de Minuit. Michel Fields, France 2 (1993).

4. General Works

Antelme, Robert. *L'Espèce humaine.* La Cité Universelle, 1947. [*The Human Race.* Trans. Jeffrey Haight and Annie Mahler. Marlboro, VT: Marlboro Press, 1992.]

Arban, Dominique. *Je me retournerai souvent.* Flammarion, 1991.

Blanchot, Maurice. *Le Livre à venir.* Gallimard, 1943.

———. *L'Espace littéraire.* Gallimard, 1955. [*The Space of Literature.* Trans. Ann Smock. Lincoln: Univ. of Nebraska Press, 1982.]

———. *L'Entretien infini.* Gallimard, 1969. [*The Infinite Conversation.* Trans. Susan Hanson. Minneapolis: Univ. of Minnesota

Press, 1992.]

———. *La Communauté inavouable*. Minuit, 1983. [*The Unavowable Community*. Trans. Pierre Joris. Barrytown, NY: Station Hill, 1988.]

Daix, Pierre. *J'ai cru au matin*. Laffont, 1976.

Dalloz, Jacques. *La Guerre d'Indochine 1945-1954*. Le Seuil, 1987. [*The War in Indo-China 1945-54*. Trans. Josephine Bacon. Dublin: Gill and Macmillan, 1990.]

Dumayet, Pierre. *Vu et entendu*. Stock, 1964.

Giesbert, Franz-Olivier. *François Mitterand ou la tentation de l'histoire*. Le Seuil, 1977.

Hamon, Hervé, and Patrick Rotman. *Les Porteurs de valises*. Albin Michel, 1979.

———. *Génération*, vols. 1 and 2. Le Seuil, 1987.

Knibiehler, Yvonne, and Régine Goutalier. *La Femme au temps des colonies*. Stock, 1990.

Lottman, Herbert. *La Rive gauche*. Le Seuil, 1981. [*The Left Bank*. Boston: Houghton Mifflin, 1982.]

Manceaux, Michèle. *Brèves*. Le Seuil, 1984.

Mascolo, Dionys. *Le Communisme, révolution et communication ou la dialectique des valeurs et des besoins*. Gallimard, 1953.

———. *Lettre polonaise sur la misère intellectuelle en France*. Minuit, 1957.

———. *Autour d'un effort de mémoire*. Maurice Nadeau, 1987.

Morin, Edgar. *Autocritique*. Julliard, 1959.

Nadeau, Maurice. *Grâces leur soient rendues*. Albin Michel, 1990.

Roques, Philippe, and Marguerite Donnadieu. *L'Empire français*. Gallimard, 1940.

Roy, Claude. *Nous*. Gallimard, 1972.

Le 14 juillet, 1958-1959. Séguier, coll. Lignes, 1990.

Sorcières 4 and 12.

Index

Fernández, Betty, 83, 86-87
Fernández, Ramón, 65, 83, 86
Ferré, Léo, 257-58
Ferreri, Marco, 258
Ferry, Jules, 2, 8
Flaubert, Gustave, 190
Flon, Suzanne, 227, 291
Forêts, Louis-René des, 171, 181
Foucault, Michel, 328-29
Fougeron, André, 131
François-Poncet, André, 210
Franju, Georges, 227
Frey, Sami, 215, 229, 239-40,
  258, 260, 263, 309, 334

Galey, Matthieu, 226
Gallieni, Joseph, 67
Galtier-Boissière, Jean, 97
Garance, 101
Garaudy, Roger, 131
Garcia-Ville, Luce, 254
Garcin, Henri, 254
Gascar, Pierre, 201
Gauthier, Xavière, 101, 265,
  272-73, 275, 287
Gautier, Jean-Jacques, 166, 226,
  235, 236, 255, 335
Gaxotte, Pierre, 210
Geismar, Alain, 257
Gélin, Daniel, 338
Genet, Jean, 166, 257
Génon-Catalot, Dr., 104, 111
Giacometti, Alberto, 110, 181
Gibson, William, 216
Gide, André, 71, 82, 144
Gir, 221
Girardot, Annie, 227
Giraudoux, Jean, 60
Giraudoux, Jean-Pierre, 201
Giscard d'Estaing, Valéry, 260
Glucksmann, André, 258
Godard, Colette, 264
Godard, Jean-Luc, 195, 258, 342
Gorbachev, Mikhail, 337
Goya, Francisco de, 194, 269
Gréco, Juliette, 113
Green, Julien, 329
Grévisse, Maurice, 293

Guattari, Félix, 258
Guevara, Che, 237
Guilleminault, Gilbert, 235,
  237, 238
Guitry, Sacha, 60

Hadj, Messali, 178
Haedens, Kléber, 149
Hahn, Reynaldo, 221
Halimi, Gisèle, 177, 258
Hallyday, Johnny, 344
Handke, Peter, 315
Heller, Gerhard, 83
Hemingway, Ernest, 60, 69, 128,
  139, 141, 173, 331
Heurgon, Jacques, 210
Hiss, Nicole, 254
Hölderlin, Friedrich, 192, 241
Horer, Suzanne, 274
Hours, Joseph, 211
Hugo, Victor, 7

Ibsen, Henrik, 60
Ionesco, Eugène, 226, 227, 338

Jacquemont, Maurice, 227
Jacquot, Benoît, 298
James, Henry, 317
Jarlot, Gérard, 201, 207-8, 215-
  16
Joan of Arc, 176
Joffre, Joseph, 67
Joly, Gustave, 166
Joplin, Janis, 263
Joyce, James, 87, 128
Joyeux, Odette, 124
July, Serge, 302, 336

Kafka, Franz, 71
Kanapa, Jean, 126, 150
Kanters, Robert, 226
Karmitz, Marin, 227
Keller, Helen, 216
Kipling, Rudyard, 20
Krivine, Alain, 244
Kubrick, Stanley, 258

Lacan, Jacques, 42, 89, 168, 225